The Culture of the Teutons

VILHELM GRØNBECH

THE
CULTURE
OF THE
TEUTONS

VOLUME I

Translated by William Worster

ANTELOPE HILL PUBLISHING

First edition, first printing 2023.

Originally published in Danish as *Vor Folkeæt i Oldtiden* in 1909.
Translated into English by William Worster, M. A.,
and afterward revised, in part rewritten, by the author, 1931.

Unless otherwise specified, all footnotes are provided by the editors of this edition,
including citations, as the original translation provided few. The wording of quotations is
given by the translator, unless another translation is specified in a footnote. Note that this
is an edited version of the existing translation by William Worster, not a new translation.

Cover art by Swifty.
Edited by Sebastian Durant and Tom Simpson.
Glossary by Sebastian Durant.
Index by Tom Simpson.
Layout by Margaret Bauer.

Antelope Hill Publishing | www.antelopehillpublishing.com

Paperback ISBN-13: 978-1-956887-90-7
EPUB ISBN-13: 978-1-956887-93-8

To the Memory of Vilhelm Thomsen

CONTENTS

By Matt Flavel, Alsherjargothi of the Asatru Folk Assembly

Before beginning the foreword of this essential work, I want to express my gratitude for being asked to contribute in this way. On a Tuesday night in 2010, while working the door at a popular local bar in Anchorage, Alaska, I opened *The Culture of the Teutons* for the very first time. Being it was an uneventful Tuesday evening, I had plenty of time to read. I have always had a deep interest in history and a profound commitment to understanding the soul of my folk and ancestors. *The Culture of the Teutons* is the single most impactful book I have yet read to further those pursuits. I found myself having to set the work aside every few pages and let myself digest and absorb what I was reading. The author was able to take complex ideas and stories from such diverse source material and crystallize the core values of our ancestors in an unprecedented and profound way.

Before understanding the culture of a people, we must first understand who the people themselves are. As sons and daughters of Europe, as Aryans, our roots run deep. We are the bearers of a torch that was lit in the distant past and a soul that is shaped by a noble ethos (Aryan means noble). The nobility that defines us and that has built civilization is derived from the ancient warrior values expressed so well in this book.

Many of us are reading this work out of a love of history. Some are reading *The Culture of the Teutons* from an interest in ancient sociology. In either case, understanding how our ancestors lived is fascinating, and understanding why they lived that way is essential for our identity. To really learn and absorb culture, we must not only know what a person or people did, but we must also understand why a person or a people acted in a certain way. *The Culture of the Teutons* breaks down the fundamental question of "why" in a profound way that is of immediate and enduring value. The "why" is essential if we wish to learn the lessons of the past and, in doing so, build a future for our children and our Folk.

In my position as a gothi (a priest of the Asatru religion), I am often asked for study or book recommendations. While we have numerous sagas, eddas, archaeological studies, works of mythic lore, epic poetry, and endless historical writings and studies, *The Culture of the Teutons* has always been the one book I recommend above all others. Religiosity aside, *The Culture of the Teutons* is an excellent resource to research and reconnect with the traditional values of our ancestors. Better than anyone else, Vilhelm Grønbech is able to distil the core values and principles that have defined the culture of our European people in a way that truly connects the dots between all the varied source material. *The Culture of the Teutons* ties together all the texts, stories, songs, and histories of our ancestors in a comprehensive way that shines a light upon the core values that shaped our race, that shaped our common Folk Soul.

Even while we may not all share the worship of the same gods as our ancestors, we all can find that spark of our Folk Soul. It is the inherent knowledge of ethics; of what is right and what is wrong; a fundamental agreement of proper and improper; a culturally accepted set of standards and virtues that noble men and women of old laid before us and that we can still recognize in our own behaviors and conduct today. Within the Folk Soul lies the recognition of the elements of those ancient songs, sagas, and poems. We can feel the truth of them in our very bones, the reality of these truths, deep within our soul. It is a message carried through our very bloodline. It is our inheritance.

Regardless of the faith of the reader, the importance of community has always been fundamental to our people. Devotion, Frith, Luck, and Honor are not new concepts. One meaningful concept that this book helped me comprehend more fully is that of honor, how our ancestors approached the meaning of honor and how that has evolved in the modern age. Honor to our noble forebearers was not an internal code as it is in our isolated and fragmented society of today. Honor was a matrix of reputation and deeds that defined your worth and place in society. This focus on reputation and accomplishment is more important now than ever before. The reality that deeds equal reputation comes through loud and clear in this book.

Another equally important lesson that is taught in *The Culture of the Teutons* is the importance and the true meaning of Frith. In this book, for the first time, we find examples of "proactive frith," a reciprocal exchange and relationship that does not merely exist to avoid conflict but rather is actively enforced in a shared web of responsibility forming the bonds that create a strong and functional community. By building those bonds, by uniting our families, and by tying our Folk together in one beautiful tapestry of strength, we build something much greater than that of the single thread of individuality. Standing strong and standing together for the honor of the whole community rather than the ego of the self and the individual is what we desperately lack today, especially in our traditionally-minded White community.

This work was originally published in 1909. Reading books from this period is such a treat because the works, while scholastically objective, are written with genuine enthusiasm for the subject and are unencumbered by the modern obsession with "political correctness." This work presents the subject on its own terms and judged by its own standards. Therein lies yet another value of this book. *The Culture of the Teutons* is immersive and goes a long way towards inculcating an understanding of the thinking and feeling of European culture prior to the coming of Christianity.

Often, in the modern times, we are told that as White people, we do not have a "culture," or we are asked to forsake our history and the accomplishments of our ancestors to make room for others. This book lays the foundation of the beautiful culture of our ancestors in poignant terms and in bold colors. Understanding and internalizing the values in these pages in not only something we should do, it is something we owe our ancestors, but more than that, it is something we owe our descendants.

VOLUME 1

INTRODUCTION

The term "Germanic" is ordinarily used to denote the racial stem of which the Scandinavians, the modern Germans, and the English are ramifications. The name itself is probably of extraneous origin, given to us by strangers.

We do not know what it means. Presumably, it was first intended to denote but a small fraction of these peoples: the fringe adjoining the Celts. Over time, however, it came to be accepted as a general designation for the whole. The Romans, having learned to distinguish between the inhabitants of Gaul and their eastern neighbors, called the latter Germani, thus rightly emphasizing the close friendship that from the earliest times united the northern and southern inhabitants of the Baltic regions and the riparian and forest-dwelling peoples of Northern Germany. This kinship was evident, not only in language, but fully as much in culture, even to its innermost corners.

The Teutons make their entry suddenly upon the stage of history. Their appearance falls at the time when Rome was working out the result of its long and active life, crystallizing the striving and achievements of the classical world into the form in which the culture of antiquity was to be handed down to posterity. Into this light they come, and it must be admitted that its brilliance shows them poor and coarse by comparison.

There is little splendor to be found here, it would seem.

We see them first from the outside, with Roman eyes, looking in upon them as into a strange country. And the eye's first impression is of a foaming flood of men—a wave of warriors—pouring in with the elemental fury of the sea over eastern Gaul, to break upon the front of Caesar's legions, and be smoothed away in a mighty backwash of recoil. Thus, roughly, Caesar's first encounter with these barbarians appears in the description by the great Roman himself.

And beyond this flood, we look into a dark, barren, and forbidding land, bristling with unfriendly forests and spread with marshes. In it, we are shown groups of men who, in the intervals of their wars and forays, lie idling on couches of skins or sit carousing noisily by daylight, and, for sheer lack of occupation, gamble away their few possessions: horses and women, even their very lives and freedom, down to the pelt upon their back.

And between the groups go tall, sturdy women with ungentle eyes and scornful mien. Among all these shouting and raving sounds here and there a voice of mystery: an old crone making prophecy to an awed stillness round—a vague suggestion that these riotous men at moments give themselves up in breathless silence to the worship of their gods. But what are they busied with in the gloom of their sacred groves? Some slaughtering of men,[1] no doubt, along with horrible sacrifice and drinking, for shouting and screaming can be heard far off.

To the peoples of the South, these dwellers in the northern wastes were simply barbarians. The Romans and the Greeks regarded their existence as the mere negation of civilized life. They lay stress upon the unpretentious character of Germanic life. The little needs of these poor people were easily satisfied.

A covering of skins for the body, perhaps a touch of paint about the face, some sort of weapon in the hand, and the external apparition is practically complete. They look magnificent, it must be granted, in their semi-nakedness. What human art neglects is here provided for by nature, which has given them beautiful muscles and splendid red or blond hair that would not shame the loveliest lady in Rome.[2] The German is a piece of nature's work, and his place is in a natural environment, among the forests of the mountain slopes. There he *lives*, whether in the excitement of the chase or in some fierce, warlike raid.

At home, he spends his time in a somnolent state of idleness and intoxication; he lies amid the dirt and soot and smoke in a place that he may call his house, but which is really nothing better than a shed, a stable where man and beast are equally at home. The need to shape his surroundings according to a personality of his own—which might well be called the instinct of nobility in civilization—is something he has clearly never felt.

He lives in the wilds. A house, for him, is merely a shelter from the violence of wind and weather, a refuge easily built, and as easily dismantled for removal to another place.

---

[1] Some historians believe that the Romans embellished these accounts of human sacrifice, in a way typical of a colonizing or inimical force, to vilify the barbarians.

[2] Interestingly, the height and muscularity of the Germanic peoples as reported by the Romans may have been due to their diet, which was higher in protein and fat, as compared to the more grain-based diet of the Roman soldiers. Jean Marco comments on the effects of diet in *Ancestral Journeys*. Jean Marco, *Ancestral Journeys* (London: Thames & Hudson Ltd, 2015). 195. Tacitus and Caesar mention the size and muscularity of the Germanic tribesman as well. Tacitus, *Germania*, Chapter 4. Caesar, *The Gallic War*, 1.39, 2.30, 4.1.

Living thus in a state of nature, and existing on what nature provides, he has in himself the wildness of that nature. True, he was credited by the fastidious onlookers of the South also with a certain greatness. He is capable of great devotion; he will risk his life for the sake of a chance guest whose only claim upon him is the fact that he came last evening to the dwelling of his host, and spent the night upon his couch. The women often exhibit an instinctive horror of anything that could in any way degrade them. But in reality, the barbarian knows absolutely nothing of such qualities as faithfulness and keeping to a given word. The power of distinction, which is the mark of true humanity, is something he entirely lacks. It never occurs to him that anything could be good by eternal law. He has no laws, and when he does what is good, his action is dictated solely by natural instinct.

These Germanic peoples live and move in hordes, or tribes, or whatever we may call them. They have kings of some sorts and something in the nature of a general assembly, which all men capable of bearing arms attend. But we should be cautious of supposing anything properly answering to a state institution as understood among civilized people. The king has no real authority; the warriors obey him today, and turn their back on him defiantly tomorrow. One day, their kings may lead them forth on any reckless enterprise; the next, they may be scattering, despite his orders, and in defiance of all political prudence, to their separate homes. And in their assembly, the method of procedure is simply that he who can use the most persuasive words wins over all the rest. The warriors clash their weapons, and the matter is decided. They are like children in regard to coaxing and gifts, but fickle and ungovernable in regard to anything like obligation, indisposed to recognize any definite rule and order.

Briefly, in the view of the Roman citizen, these Germanic tribes are a people of strongly marked light and shade in character—for such words as virtue and vice, good and evil, cannot be used to describe them by anyone with a linguistic conscience. The Roman may speak of their natural pride, their stubborn defiance, proof even against the chains of their conqueror's triumph, but such words as majesty or nobility he will unconsciously reserve for himself and his equals.

Here and there, among the highest types of classical culture, we may find a half-aesthetic, half-humane sympathy for these children of the wild. Even this is in its origin identical with the layman's mingled fear and hatred, inasmuch as it regards its object as a piece of wild nature itself. In the midst of their civilization, men could feel a spasm of wistful admiration in the face of nature, for the primeval force of life, the power that rushes on without knowing whither. Man at the pinnacle of his splendor might ponder in melancholy upon the happy lot of nature's children playing in the mire far below—a state which he himself, for better or worse, could never reach.

Tacitus, the romantic, voiced the praises of the simple life in the personal style of the decadent period: with original twists and turns of phrase, and a vocabulary of the very rarest words that he could find. He does not beautify his savage artificially and makes no attempt to show him as wiser or better clad than he is. On the contrary, he is at pains to point out how few and simple are the needs of savage life. His enthusiasm is expressed in the most delicate phrases. Among the Germani, he declares, good customs are of more avail than are good laws elsewhere: "interest and usury are unknown to them, and thus they eschew the vice more fervently than if it were forbidden."

In their customs, these savages find a naive and simple form of expression for dumb, primitive feelings:

> It is not the wife who brings a dowry here, but the husband who comes with gifts to his bride . . . and these gifts do not consist in women's fripperies . . . no; cattle, a saddled horse, a shield, a sword—these are the bridal gifts. And she in return brings weapons for her husband's use. This they consider the strongest of bonds: the sacredness of the home, and the gods of wedded life. To the end that a woman shall not feel herself apart from manly thoughts and the changing circumstance of war, she is reminded in the marriage ceremony itself that she there enters upon a sharing of her husband's work and peril. . . .[3]

And as between friends: "They rejoice in one another's gifts, giving and receiving freely, without thought of gain; friendly goodwill it is that unites them." In other words, no sickly cast of thought, but pure spontaneous feeling.

Tacitus is concerned to show particularly how all "virtue" and "vice" is a natural growth among the people he describes.

He depicts them with so affectionate a hand, and at the same time with unvarnished truth in detail, because he views his object as a piece of unspoiled nature. So thoroughly is he filled with the sense of contrast between himself and his barbarians that he fails to mark how every fact he brings forward infallibly tears the frail theory in which he tries to weave it.

The thing that fills civilized man with horror and loathing of the barbarian is the feeling of being face to face with a creature incalculable, a man devoid of law. Heedlessly, unthinkingly the savage keeps his oath and will as heedlessly break oaths and promises. He can be brave and generous in his unruly fashion, and in that same unruly fashion brutal and bestial. Any act of cruelty, any breach of faith, is far more repulsive when it stands without relation to anything else

---

[3] Tacitus, *Germania*, Chapter 18.

than when it appears as the infringement of an accepted moral law, a lapse from grace.

The barbarian has no character—that is the essence of the Roman verdict. When a civilized man does wrong, he does so at worst because it is wrong. Thus, the villain's consciousness of being wicked marks him as a human being with whom one can associate. But to receive a barbarian among one's circle of acquaintance is equivalent to building one's house in the immediate vicinity of a volcano. What if the barbarians do build some sort of houses, and till the soil? Heaven knows their agriculture is but primitive at best, the way they scratch at the surface of the earth and raise a miserable crop, only to seek fresh fields the following year. What if they do keep cattle, make war, and dispense some kind of justice among themselves? Or grant them even some degree of skill in forging weapons? They are not a civilized people for all that.

It was about the beginning of our era that the Germanic people first appeared in history. A thousand years later, the world saw the last glimpse of them. For a short period, the Northmen held the scene of Europe, working out their racial character and ideals with feverish haste, before they were transformed and merged in the mass of European civilization. Their going marks the disappearance of the Germanic culture as an independent type.

The Northmen, too, have been portrayed by strangers from the outside, and the picture has marked points of similarity to that image of them left by their anterior kinsmen in the records of the Roman historians: wild, bloodthirsty, little amenable to human reason, gifted with splendid vices, and overall devils. Thus runs the character given to them by medieval chroniclers. The civilized men who now judged them were Christians who saw the world not as divided in degrees of culture, but as divided between the powers of light and darkness; whence the incalculable must necessarily be ascribed to some origin in the infernal regions. The barbarians of classical times answer to the demons of medieval Christianity.

This time, however, the picture does not stand alone without a foil. Here in the North, a people of Germanic race have set up their own monument to later times, showing themselves as they wished to be seen in history, revealing themselves, not with any thought of being seen by strangers, but yet urged by an impulse toward self-revelation.

To outsiders, the Northmen seem to have something of the same elemental, unreflecting violence, the same uneasy restlessness that led the cultured world to stamp their Southern kinsmen as barbarians: they were reckless and impulsive—not to say obstinate—in their self-assertion, acting on the spur of the moment, shifting from one plan to another. The cool political mind might find considerable resemblance between the German brigands and the pirates of the North. But our more intimate knowledge enables us to discern the presence of a controlling and uniting will beneath the restless exterior—what at the first glance appears but aimless flickering shows, on closer inspection, as a steadier light. In reality, these Vikings have but little of that aimlessness which can be characterized as natural. There is more of calculating economy in them than of mere spendthrift force. The men are clear in their minds both as to end and means, will and power. While they may seem to be drifting toward no definite goal, they have yet within themselves an aim undeviating as the compass, unaltering however they may turn.

The old idea of the Vikings as sweeping like a storm across the lands they touched, destroying the wealth they found and leaving themselves as poor as ever, has, in our time, had to give way to a breathless wonder at their craving for enrichment.

The gold they found has disappeared. But we have learned now that there was gathered together in the North a treasury of knowledge and thought, poetry and dreams, that must have been brought home from abroad, despite the fact that such spiritual values are far more difficult to find, steal, and carry safely home than precious stones or metals. The Northmen seem to have been insatiable in the matter of such spiritual treasures. They have even, in the present day, been accused of having annexed the entire sum of pagan and Christian knowledge possessed by the Middle Ages. Looking at the Norse literature of the Viking Age, we find some difficulty in refuting this charge, though it may seem too sweeping as it is urged by Bugge and his disciples.[4] Others, again, ask scornfully if we are really expected to believe that our Northmen sat over their lessons like schoolboys in the Irish monasteries, studying classical authors and medieval encyclopedias. This would no doubt be the most natural explanation for modern minds who suck all their nourishment from books and lectures; we must probably assume that they gained their learning in some less formal fashion. On the other hand, if they had not the advantage of a systematic education, it is all the more incomprehensible that they should in such a degree have gained access to the art and science of their age. They had not only a passionate craving to convert the elements of foreign culture to their own enrichment, but they had also a mysterious power of stirring up culture and forcing it to yield what lay beneath its surface.

Even this thirst for knowledge, however, is not the most surprising thing about them. That they did learn and copy to a great extent is plain to see, but even now we may speculate without result, or hope of any result, upon what it was they learned and how much they may have added thereto of their own. There exists no magic formula whereby the culture of Viking times, as a whole, can be

---

[4] Sophus Bugge, a mid-nineteenth-century Norwegian philologist and linguist at Christiania University, which is now the University of Oslo. He's most well-known for his critical work on the Eddas, in which he posits that the Eddic poems are largely founded on Christian and Latin traditions imported to Scandinavia through England.

resolved into its original component parts. So thoroughly have they refashioned what they took, until its thought and spirit are their own.

The two sides must be seen together throughout. The Northman has not only a powerful tendency to extend and enrich his mental sphere, but this craving for expansion is counterpoised by a spiritual self-assertion no less marked, that holds him stubbornly faithful to the half-unconscious ideal that constitutes his character.

He does not face the world with open arms; far from it, he is all suspicion and reserve toward strange gods and ways and values, that he feels incongruous with his own self-estimation. All that is alien he holds aloof until he has probed its secret, or wrung from it a secret satisfying to him. All that cannot be dealt with as such, he shuts out and away from him; in fact, he is hardly aware of it. But wherever he can, by adapting himself at first to an alien atmosphere, extract its essence for his own particular use—there he will draw in greedily all he can, and let it work in him.

He has that firmness that depends upon a structure in the soul, and that elasticity which comes from the structure's perfect harmony with its surroundings, enabling him spiritually to conform to the need of his environment. He is master of the world about him, by virtue of a self-control more deeply rooted even than the will, identical with the soul-structure itself.

In his innermost being, there is a central will passing judgment upon all that penetrates from outside, a purpose that seizes upon every new acquisition, which seals and enslaves it to one particular service, forcing it to work in the spirit of its new master and stamping it with his image. Where this cannot be done, the alien matter is rejected and ignored. All that it takes to itself is transmuted into power—all power subjected to discipline—and flung out as a collective force. Thus, violence here is not a mere extravagance of power. The central will gives to each action such an impetus that it overshoots the mark in every case, setting a new one beyond. Thus, man's whole life is lived at such a pressure of power that he himself is ever being urged on toward ever further goals. But the scale and measure of his doing is a thing outside himself. The ultimate standards whereby his life is judged are the verdict of his fellows and the verdict of posterity: standards unqualified and absolute.

The violence is organized from the depths of the soul. It is energy that keeps the spiritual life awake and athirst, and thus creates the single-minded, firmly set personality of the Northman. These men are not each but an inspired moment, fading vaguely away into past and future; they are present, future, and past in one. A man fixes himself in the past by firm attachment to past generations.

Such an attachment is found more or less among all peoples, but the Northman makes the past a living and guiding force by constant historic remembrance, and historic speculation in which he traces out his connection with former generations and his dependence on their deeds. His future is linked up with the present by aim and honor and the judgment of posterity. And he fixes himself in the present by reproducing himself in an ideal type, such a type for instance as that of the chieftain: generous, brave, fearless, quick-witted, stern toward his enemies, faithful to his friends, and frank with all. The type is built up out of life and poetry together: first lived, and then transfused into poetry.

This firmness of spiritual organization which characterizes the Northman as a personality is no less evident in his social life. Wherever he goes, he carries within himself a social structure that manifests itself in definite political forms as soon as he is thrown together with a crowd of others speaking the same tongue. He is not of that inarticulate type which forms kaleidoscopic tribal communities. However small his people may be, and however slight the degree of cohesion between its component molecules, the social consciousness is always present and active. He is a people in himself, and has no need to build up an artificial whole by the massing of numbers together. As soon as he has settled in a place—for a little while or for a length of time—a *thing* shoots up out of the ground,[5] and about it grows a community. Whether his sense of social order finds scope to form a kingdom, or is constrained within narrower bounds, it is a tendency deep-rooted, part and parcel of his character itself.

Culture, in the truest sense of the word, means an elastic harmony between man's inner self and his surroundings, so that he is able not only to make his environment serve his material ends, but also to transfigure the impulses of the surrounding world into spiritual ideals and aspirations. The cultured man possesses an instinctive dignity, which springs from fearlessness and self-reliance, and manifests itself in sureness of aims and means alike in matters of formal behavior and in undertakings of far-reaching consequence. In this sense, these Vikings are men of character; they possess themselves and their world in lordly right of determination. Their harmony may be poor in the measure of its actual content, but it is nonetheless powerful and deep.

What a difference between these two pictures—the portrait that Southern pens have drawn of their Germanic contemporaries, and that which the last of the Germanic race have themselves imprinted into history. Yet for all that, we group them together under one name, and we do so fully conscious of what it implies. It was early realized that the two are so closely related as not merely to justify, but to necessitate our treating them together.

Such indications as we have of the primeval Germanic customs, laws, and ethical values prove that those earliest forbears of the race were one with their

---

[5] *Thing* is actually a Germanic word for "assembly," specifically a regular legislative meeting consisting of the free people of the community presided over by a lawspeaker.

younger kinsmen in mode of thought, and in that which unites thoughts and feelings and makes them the bearers of personality.

In this light from the North, we can see then that the Suebi and the Marcomanni and whatever they were called,[6] were not mere creatures of the moment, devoid of character, as the Romans fondly imagined. With the aid of the Northmen, we can interpret all—or nearly all—the scattered notes that have been handed down, and find something human in what our authorities found meaningless. We can dimly perceive, for instance, that the alternating fealty and infidelity of the Germanic tribes, which so often led the Romans to harsh measures, had in reality its foundation in an ethical system. And we can plainly see that behind their actions, with such vices and such virtues, stood a character widely different from the Roman, but neither more natural nor unnatural. In principle, the Germanic character was just as consistent, just as rational, and no less bound by the consideration of preserving a certain unity in the personality. And a political genius like Caesar recognized that if his plans concerning these barbarians were to be of any firmness in themselves, it was not enough that he thought them out in Latin. His eagerness to penetrate beneath the thought of these Germani, down to the habit of mind which determined their form of utterance, is in itself a testimony to the fact that these barbarians bore the stamp of culture and the mark of character.

We are better off than the Romans in that we have been guided to a view of the Germanic life from within. The Romans had excellent opportunities of observation and were often keen observers; the great majority of what the Romans and the Greeks wrote about the Germanic people is right in its way.

But every single remark, great or small, reveals its derivation from a sweeping glance across the frontier. We can always notice that the narrator himself stood far outside; he has seen what these people did, but he has not understood why they did so. In his account, we see their actions without perspective and without proportion, and the more precise his details are, the stranger the whole account seems. Such descriptions leave us with, at best, the same grotesque impression one would have after watching from a distance men talking and gesticulating, but without any idea of what affected them.

There is a great difference between making the acquaintance of a people from outside as the Romans did, following it home to gain a glance at its daily life, and on the other hand, being received into the midst of that people, seeing its men at home preparing for a campaign, and being there again to meet them on their return.

---

[6] The Suebi (alt. spelling, Suevi) were primarily a Roman classification of a large conglomeration of Germanic peoples originally from the Elbe River. The Marcomanni are one of the tribal subgroups of the Suebi.

We are more fortunately situated than the Southern writers in this respect, but are we much wiser? There may be some danger of arriving too easily at our understanding. The inability of the Romans to recognize the actions of the Germani as human may warn us against letting our own interpretation pass over what was really strange in our forefathers, erroneously attributing to them motives of our own.

The Northmen are a cultured people in the full sense of the word. We must recognize them as our equals. They lived as energetically as we do, found no less satisfaction in life, and felt themselves masters of life—masters who determined their aim and inflexibly had their way. But the recognition of this fact in itself emphasizes the distance between us, because it brings out more pointedly the difference between ancient and modern modes of conquering and enjoying life.

The difference is evident the moment we compare the Teutons with the other Northern European race of ancient times: the Celts.

For all our Germanic descent, we are more nearly related to the Celts.[7] They are a more modern type of people, we might say.

It needs not long acquaintance with them before one comes to intimacy. Here comes a man in whose face the whole world—of nature and of man—is reflected. The beauty of nature, the beauty of mankind, man's heroism, woman's love—these things thrill him, and lead him into ecstasy. He feels and feels until his soul is ready to burst—and then pours forth a lyric flood, plaintive and jubilant, wistfully pondering, and earnestly exalting all that delights the eye. A religious ecstasy comes over him. He gives himself up to the invisible, grasping and surrendering himself at once, living the invisible as a reality with real joys and real sorrows. He flings himself over into the full experience of mysticism, yet without losing hold of the visible reality—on the contrary, his inner sense takes its fill of the beauty of nature, of delight in the animal life of earth and air.

The violence of life meets an answering passion within him; he must go with it and must feel his pulses beating in the same hurrying rhythm as that which he feels without and about him. He can never make his pictures vivid enough or rich enough in color. Beauty overwhelms him, and in his feverish eagerness to let nothing be lost, he loads one picture on another. The terror and grandeur of life excite him till he paints his giants with innumerable heads and every imaginable attribute of dread; his heroes are of supernatural dimensions, with hair of gold or silver, and more than godlike powers.

Little wonder that the Celt often frightens and repels us by his formless exaggeration. He fills us at times with aversion, but only to attract us anew. Exaggeration is a natural consequence of passionate feeling that derives its strength

---

[7] "We" referring to the Danes.

and its character from the sensitivity of the soul to everything about it, down to the faintest motions in the life of nature and man.

Such a breadth of soul life is unknown among the Norsemen, not even to be found as an exception.

Compared with the Celt, the Northman is heavy, reserved, a child of earth, yet seemingly half-awakened. He cannot say what he feels, save by vague indication in a long, roundabout fashion. He is deeply attached to the country that surrounds him; its meadows and rivers fill him with a latent tenderness, but his sense of home has not emancipated itself into love. The feeling for nature rings in muffled tones through his speech and through his myths, but he does not burst into song of the loveliness of the world. Of his relations with women, he feels no need to speak, save when there is something of a practical nature to be stated; only when it becomes tragic does the subject enter into his poetry. In other words, his feelings are never revealed until they have brought about an event; they tell us nothing of themselves save by the weight and bitterness they give to the conflicts that arise. Uneventfulness does not throw him back upon his inner resources, and it never opens up a flood of musings or lyricism—it merely dulls him. The Celt meets life with open arms: ready for every impression, he is loath to let anything fall dead before him. The Teuton is not lacking in passionate feeling, but he cannot and will not help himself so lavishly to life.

He has but one view of man: man asserting himself, maintaining his honor, as he calls it. All that moves within a man must be twisted around until it becomes associated with honor, before he can grasp it. All his passion is thrust back and held until it finds its way out in that one direction. His friendship of man and love of woman never find expression for the sake of the feeling itself; they are only felt consciously as a heightening of the lover's self-esteem, and consequently as an increase of responsibility. This simplicity of character shows in his poetry, which is at heart nothing but lays and tales of great avengers, because revenge is the supreme act that concentrates his inner life and forces it out in the light. His poems of vengeance are always intensely human, because revenge to him is not an empty repetition of a wrong done, but a spiritual self-assertion, a manifestation of strength and value. Thus, the anguish of an affront or the triumph of victory is able to open up the sealed depths of his mind and suffuse his words with passion and tenderness. But the limitation that creates the beauty and strength of Teuton poetry is revealed in the fact that only those feelings and thoughts which make man an avenger and furthers the attainment of revenge are expressed; all else is overshadowed. Woman finds a place in poetry only as a valkyrie, or as inciting to strife; for the rest, she is included among the ordinary inventory of life. Friendship, the highest thing on earth among the Teutons, is only mentioned when friend joins hands with friend in the strife for honor and restitution.

There is abundance of passion in the poetry of the Northmen, but it appears only as a geyser, up and down, never bursting out and flowing forth in lyrical streams. Impressive, but gray; powerful, but sober. His epics are marked by a trustworthy simplicity and restraint of imagination keeping well within the bounds drawn by the grand reality of a warlike existence. His heroes are of a size generally comparable to the heroic figures of everyday life, and their powers are but the least possible in advance of ordinary standards. In life, there is none of that fever-pulse so characteristic of the Celts that comes of over-susceptibility, of the tendency to live every moment at the same pace as one's surroundings, or inability to resist the rhythm of one's environment. The Northman's response to impressions from outside is so long in coming that it seems as if his movements were dictated solely from within. An impulse from the world without does not fall deadly on his soul, but its force is arrested, laid in bonds, on impact with his massive personality.

And there is but one passion that can let loose this accumulated force: his passion for honor. For the Northman to be affected by this or that in what he meets depends on something that has happened—something past, and something ahead, an event which has happened to himself or his ancestors, and an event which must be brought to pass for the betterment of himself and his descendants. He does not live in the moment; he uses the moment to reckon out how can it serve him to the attainment of his end. He does not hate a thing for its own sake, or on his own account, for if he can purchase a chance of revenge by giving up his dislike, he tears his hate away. Where he can gain a chance by enmity, the hate wells up again in undisguised power. This does not mean that the Northman is temporarily beside himself when he is seeking redress for his wrongs.

Surely an avenger is all the time a son, husband, father, and member of a legal community; it is not a question of laying aside his humanity. On the contrary, this wholesale humanity of his puts on the armor of vengeance and comports itself accordingly.

In these very moments of ruthless self-assertion, the Teuton rises to moral grandeur—herein lies to us the test of understanding. There is something in the Northman's attitude toward life which chills away our familiarity at first sight— and if the chill is not felt very acutely nowadays, our complacency is largely due to the romantic literature of the nineteenth century.

By a love too ready and too undiscerning, the poets and historians have smoothed away the strong and wayward features of the saga men and toned down these bitter figures into recognized heroes and lovers. The old characters have been imperceptibly modernized with a view to making them more acceptable. The hardness and implacability of the Northmen have been pushed into the shade of their heroism and generosity and tacitly condoned as limitations, while the fact is that these qualities are based on the very constitution of their culture. If we are brought up suddenly against their everyday life, we are liable to brand them as narrow and even inhuman, and we do not immediately recognize that what we call poverty and inhumanity means nothing more and nothing less than strength and compactness of character. The ancients are just, pious, merciful, and of a moral consistency throughout, but on a foundation such as could not suffice to bear a human life in our own day.

The humanity of the Teuton is not the humanity of the modern European, hence our aloofness that no romantic revival has been able to overcome. In the North, the European hovers about with the gratification and lurking uneasiness of a guest; in Hellas he feels at home.[8] The heroes of Homer are as friends and intimates compared with the Vikings; these battling and boasting, suffering and weeping heroes and heroines are more of our own flesh and blood than the purposeful men and women of the sagas. We call them natural and human because they take life bit by bit, finding time to live in the moment, giving themselves up to pleasure and pain and expressing their feelings in words. In Greece, we find men whose patriotism and self-seeking egoism and affection take a course sufficiently near our own for both to join and flow together. Even their gods are not so very far from what we in our best moments, and in our worst, ascribe to the higher powers. There is hardly need of any adaptation on our part; the gods and men of ancient Greece can of themselves enter into us and be transformed. In Hellas, we soon learn to recognize, under the alien forms, the aims of our own time. Thus, in the words of Greek poets and philosophers, we constantly catch hints that sound as a still, small voice in times of crisis.

The reason is not hard to find: our intimacy with Hellas is the familiarity of kinship. The main stream of our thoughts and ideals flows from the South. However far we have drifted from classic standards in many respects, our intellectual and religious history—and no less the development of economic and social Europe—have kept our course in the channel of Hellenism and Hellenistic Rome. For this reason, we regard the problems and interpretations of greed as being eminently human and vital.

We are repelled by the Teutons, because their thoughts will not minister to our private needs. This instinctive recoil at the same time explains a furtive attraction which was not exhausted by the Romantic revival of the eighteenth and nineteenth centuries. The concentration of the Teutons exposes a narrowness of another kind in ourselves: every time we are confronted with a people of another type, a stone in the foundation of our complacency is loosened. We are surprised by an uneasy feeling that our civilization does not exhaust the possibilities of life; we are led to suspect that our problems derive their poignancy from the fact that, at times, we mistake our own reasoning about reality for reality itself. We become

---

[8] Greece.

dimly aware that the world stretches beyond our horizon, and as this apprehension takes shape, there grows upon us a suspicion that some of the problems that baffle us are problems of our own contrivance. Our questionings often lead us into barren fastness instead of releasing us into the length and breadth of eternity. The reason may be that we are trying to make a whole of fragments and not, as we thought, attempting to grasp what is a living whole in itself. And at last, when we learn to gaze at the world from a new point of view, revealing prospects that have been concealed from our eyes, we may perhaps find that Hellas also contains more things, riches as well as mysteries, than are dreamt of in our philosophy. After all, we have perhaps been no less romantic in our understanding of Greece than in our misunderstanding of the Teutons, and other primitive peoples.

To appreciate the strength and the beauty of the culture of the ancient Teutons, we must realize that their harmony is fundamentally unlike all that we possess or strive for, and consequently that all our immediate praising and blaming are futile. All things considered, we have little grounds for counting ourselves better judges than the classical onlookers. In our sentimental moments, we lose ourselves in admiration of the heroism and splendid passion of our forefathers, but in our moments of historical analysis we pride ourselves on styling them barbarians. This vacillation is in itself sufficient to show that in our appreciation, we have not reached the center whence the Teutons' thoughts and actions drew their life and strength. If we would enter into the minds of other peoples, we must consent to discard our preconceived ideas as to what the world and man ought to be. It is not enough to admit a set of ideas as possible or even plausible; we must strive to reach a point of view from which these strange thoughts become natural. We must put off our own humanity as far as it is possible and put on another humanity for the time. We need to begin quietly and modestly from the foundation, as if knowing nothing at all, if we would understand what it was that held the souls of these men together and made them personalities.

I. FRITH

The historians of the seventeenth and eighteenth centuries had one great advantage: they felt themselves as citizens of the world. They were never strangers to their subject matter, and knew nothing of that shyness which the stranger always feels. They felt themselves at home throughout the inhabited world so long as they remained in their own country or the lands immediately adjacent, in a bodily sense, and made all further journeys in the spirit alone. They did not sit fumbling over their material, but went straight to the persons concerned, whether men of the immediate past or those of earliest ages—whether Romans or Greeks, French, English, Hindus, Chinese, or Indians. The historian stepped forward without formality and took his hero cordially by the hand, spoke to him as friend to friend, or, let us say, as one man of the world to another. There was never any fear in those days that differences of language, or of circumstances in a different age, might place obstacles in the way of a proper understanding. Men were inspired with faith in a common humanity, and by the certainty that if once the human element could be grasped, all the rest would work out of itself. All mankind was agreed as to what God was, what good and evil were; all were agreed in patriotism and citizenship, in love of parents and of children—in a word, agreed in all realities.

If ever this straightforward simplicity that sought its rallying point in things of common human interest were justified in any case, it would be in regard to the Germanic peoples.

We find here a community based upon general unity, mutual self-sacrifice and self-denial, and the social spirit: a society in which every individual from birth to death was bound by consideration for his neighbor. The individuals in this community show in all their doings that they are inspired by one passion: the welfare and honor of their kin; and none of the temptations of the world can move them even for a moment to glance aside. They say themselves, that this passion is love. What more natural then, than that we, who from our own lives know love and its power, should begin with what we have in common with these people we are considering? Given this agreement on the essential point, all that appears strange must surely become simple and comprehensible.

Bergthora, wife of Njál (Thorgeirsson), was a true woman of the old school: strict on the point of honor, inflexible, and unforgiving. The key to her character, we might say, is given in the famous words: "Young was I given to Njál, and this I have promised him, that one fate shall come upon us both." There is something of common humanity in the words, something we can appreciate at its true value. On the male side, we have an even more old-fashioned figure to set up as a model: Egil Skallagrímsson,[9] the most typical representative in Viking times of love of kin. See him, as he rides with the body of his drowned son before him on the saddle,[10] carrying it himself to its last resting place, his breast heaving with sobs until his tunic bursts. It is all so direct in its appeal, so obvious and natural, that one feels involuntarily as if one could read Egil's whole soul in this one episode. Life standards, customs of society, morals, and self-judgment derived from such elementary emotion surely cannot be hard to understand?

We can easily put it to the test.

In the history of the Faroe Islands, we find two women occupying prominent places: Thurid [Torkilsdóttir] and Thora, wife and daughter of Sigmundur Brestisson. Both are strong, resolute characters like Bergthora, and both are guided in all their actions by love of Sigmund and his race. Sigmund was an ideal chieftain of the Christian Viking period: strict on the point of honor, never relinquishing a shred of his right, and always able to gain his cause. Frank, brave and skillful—altogether a man to admire and remember. After a life of ceaseless fighting for the supreme power in the Faroes, he is murdered, having barely escaped from a night surprise. Time passes, and one day, Thrond of Gata makes his appearance in Thurid's house, asking Thora in marriage for his foster son Leif. Thrond was a man of different stamp, one of those who is ready enough to strike, when first they have their victim safely enmeshed by intrigue: one of those who can plot and plan with all the craft of evil, and always find others to bear the danger and disgrace of carrying out their schemes; a Christian by compulsion, and an apostate, not only practicing the rites of the old faith in his daily life, but even dabbling in black magic. Thrond had been Sigmund's bitterest opponent; it was he who had arranged the killing of Sigmund's father, and the surprise attack

---

[9] The eponymous character of *Egil's saga*, one of the most renowned poems of the Icelandic Sagas. *Egil's saga* covers a roughly 150-year period, detailing Egil's family tree over that time.
[10] Within *Egil's saga* is a twenty-five-stanza skaldic poem called "Sonatorrek" ("The Loss of Sons") in which Egil laments his sons Gunnar and Bodvar dying of fever and drowning, respectively.

which ended in Sigmund's death was led by him. Yet Thora holds out to her suitor the prospect that she will accept his offer, if he and his foster father give her an opportunity to avenge her father. And she keeps her promise: she marries Leif, and has her reward in seeing three men killed in honor of her father.

Once more these two women appear in the history of the Faroe nobles. It happens that a son of Sigmund's cousin has been slain while staying in the house of Sigurd Thorlakson, a kinsman of Thrond's. Sigurd had at once struck down the slayer, and these three being the only ones present at the fateful moment, some shadow of suspicion attaches to the host. The mere possibility that one of Sigmund's kinsmen lies slain and unavenged is enough to keep Thurid and Thora in a state of unrest day and night. Poor Leif, who will not or cannot take any steps in the matter, hears nothing but scornful words about the house. When then Sigurd Thorlakson, in his blindness, asks on behalf of his brother for Thurid's hand, her daughter wisely counsels her as follows: "If I should advise, this must not be refused, for if you are minded to vengeance, there could be no surer bait." And she adds: "No need for me to set words in my mother's mouth." The plan proceeds. Sigurd is invited to speak with Thurid. She meets him outside the homestead and leads him to a seat on a tree trunk. He makes as if to sit facing the house, but she seats herself resolutely the other way, with her back to the house, and her face toward the chapel. Sigurd asks if Leif is at home—no, he is not. If Thurid's sons are at home—yes, they are at home. In a little while, both they and Leif appear, and Sigurd goes off mortally wounded.

These two were Thurid, "the great widow," and Thora, "whom all held to be the noblest of women." Their greatness lay not so much in the fact of their loving truly and faithfully, as in their understanding of what that love demanded, but their fulfilling its demands in spite of all. The question asked of us here is not what we think of these two, but if we are able to accept the appreciative judgment of their love as it stands, without reserve.

On a closer scrutiny of Egil's love and sorrow, we find, too, some characteristic features that are likely to trouble our serene faith in a common humanity. It is related that, having made provision for his son in the hereafter by setting him in a burial mound that might content him, the old champion himself was minded to die. However, his quick-witted daughter, Thorgerd, artfully brought back his interest in life by reminding him that nobody else would be able to honor the youth with a laudatory poem, thus enticing him to make a lay of his loss.

And fortunately for us, this poem in which Egil laid down the burden of his sorrow has been preserved. There is a depth of meaning in the fact that the most beautiful poem remaining to us from ancient times is a poem of kinship and love of kin, and that it should be Egil himself, the oldest-fashioned of all the saga heroes, who made it.

Unfortunately, our understanding and enjoyment of this confession are hampered in a very high degree by the difficulties of its form. Egil was not only a man of considerable character, he was also what we should call a poet, whose soul found direct expression in verse. The kennings, or metaphors, which were part and parcel of ancient poetry, fell from Egil's lips as images revealing the individual moods and passions of the poet. But so strange to our ears are the poetic figures of the ancient skalds, that it needs a great deal of work on our part before we can approach him from such a position that his picture-phrases appear with life and significance. Given the patience, however, to acquire familiarity with the artificial metaphors of the skald—enough to realize what it is that forces itself through the poet's mind in this cumbersome form—we can feel the sorrow of this bereaved father dropping heavily, sullenly from verse to verse.

He complains that sorrow binds his tongue: "Little chance is here to reach forth Odin's stolen goods; heavy they are to drag from their hiding of sorrow—thus it is for one who mourns." Egil applies the parallel of Odin, who with great pains brought the poet's cup—the mead of inspiration—from the giant's cave to himself in his struggle to force a way to expression through the walls of his own sorrow.

The sea roars down there before the door where my kinsman's Hel-ship is laid. My race bends to its fall, as the storm-lashed trees of the forested. . . .

Cruel was the hole the waves tore in my father's kin-fence; unfilled, I know, and open stands the son-breach torn in me by the sea.

Much hath Ran [the queen of the sea] stolen from me. I stand poor in love-friends. The sea hath sundered the bonds of my race, torn a close-twisted string out of myself.

I say to you: could I pursue my cause with the sword, there should be an end of the ale-maker [Ægir, the king of the sea]. If I could I would give battle to that loose wench of Ægir's [the wave]. But I felt that I had no power to take action against my son's bane. All the world sees emptiness behind the old man where he strides along.

Much the sea hath stolen from me—bitter it is to count up the fall of kinsmen—since he that stood, a shield among the race, turned aside from life on the soul-ways.

I know it myself, in my son grew no ill promise of a man. . . .

Ever he maintained that which his father had said, ay, though all the people thought otherwise. He held me upright in the home, and mightily increased my strength. My brotherless plight is often in my mind. When the battle grows, I take thought, peer about and think what other man stands by my side with courage for a daring deed, such as I need often enough. . . .

I am grown cautious of flight now that friends are fewer.

These are words that, with their great simplicity, can be repeated in all times—at least as long as life is still a struggle. It would be hard to find higher praise for such a poem.

From what we can understand of them, the following verses consist of variations on these fundamental thoughts:

> No one can be relied on, for men nowadays lower themselves and are glad to accept payment instead of revenge for the blood of brothers. He who has lost a son must beget another—none else can replace the lost scion. My head is drooping, since he, the second of my sons, fell beneath the brand of sickness, he whose fame was unsmirched. I trusted in the god, but he was false to his friendship with me, and I have little heart now to worship him.

In spite of his bitterness, however, he cannot but remember that he has himself the art of the poet, and a mind able to reveal the plans of enemies, and he cannot forget that this mastery of words, the comfort of many ills, is a gift from the god who has betrayed him.

> Darkly he looks toward the future: I am strongly beset, death stands on the cape, but blithely, unruffled by fear I will wait for Hel.

The first part of the poem is properly independent of time: the reader has no need to look into a distant age and a distant culture in order to understand it. It is the form, and that only, which binds it to Egil and skaldic poetry, and the exegesis of the learned. Even Egil's passionate outburst against the high powers that have usurped the mastery of the world hardly appears to us as strange. On the contrary, we might perhaps approve the words as thoroughly human, and even award them honorable mention as being "modern" in spirit.

Our weakness for all that savors of titanic defiance, however, must not blind us to the peculiar form of expression in which it is voiced by Egil. His verses do not express instinctive defiance of fate, but an earnest longing for vengeance and restitution. He is lamenting that he is unable to pursue his cause, or in other words, uphold his right. Is it really to be understood that Egil only relinquishes plans of revenge because he stands alone in the world, without followers or kin? We must ask: if one lacks the courage to take arms against a god, can it mend matters greatly to march up with a few staunch friends and kinsmen at one's back? In the asking of this question, our sympathy gives place to a vague poetic feeling that is equivalent to giving up all attempts at understanding.

Sorrow can always drive a man to such extremes of his being that his words run into apparent contradictions, but the inconsistency of passion never sets meaning at defiance. It has its explanation in the fact that the opposites have their point of intersection somewhere in the soul. At times, the feelings are exalted to such a degree that they appear irreconcilable, but the sympathetic listener feels he has no right of criticism until he has followed the lines to their meeting point. In Egil, the cohesion between the apparent contradictions is no doubt very firm. There is an inner contact between defiance of the gods and the outburst of help-lessness at the sight of one's solitary plight. We can ponder and speculate as much as we please.

A true understanding of Egil's thought here—that he would feel himself master of death if he had a strong circle of kinsmen about him—is not to be won by mere study of these lines. We cannot get at it unless Egil himself and the men of his time give us the real solution. Egil appears to regard life in the light of a process of law, where the man with a strong circle of kinsmen wins his case because he is backed by a crowd of men ready to swear on his side, and whose oaths carry weight enough to crush his opponent.

Let us imagine that this idea of his is not merely a piece of poetic imagery, but that life itself, with all its tasks, appeared as a lawsuit, where a man with many and powerful kinsmen could further his aims and fortunes—materially and spiritually—gaining power over his surroundings, not only by battle, but by oath, in virtue of that power of race which he possessed. Let us further imagine that this faith in the power of kinship is great enough to reach out beyond life and embrace death itself within its scope, believing itself capable of summoning and outswearing the gods, ay, shaking heaven and earth. Egil's words have then a new significance and lose nothing of their weight, but they become anything but "modern." The titanic defiance disappears—or almost disappears—and in its place we have the despairing cry of a suffering human soul. The paradox then lies not where we at first discerned it, but in quite another direction.

And reading now from these words backward and forward, the other verses that at first flowed so glibly from our tongue will have gained a strange power and violence—both where he speaks of a string torn out of him, a breach, and also where he calls to mind his son's help, and reveals his own discouragement when he looks about him in the fight for one to aid him. It would be strange if we did not now feel, in place of the confident enjoyment of the words, a sense of uncertainty that makes us hesitate at every line. The words have become vague, because we have lost our own ground and failed to get a new foothold. Torn out! Our fancy flutters doubtfully away from the metaphorical meaning—which at first appeared the only one the words could have—and hovers about the idea of an actual bleeding to death, but without finding anything to hold by.

And our uncertainty cannot but increase when we discover that Egil's image of the family is a fence of death, built up stake by stake, as a breach in the family and those left. That these images are common, everyday illustrations, one is tempted to say, is part of the technical stock-in-trade. We cannot give ourselves up to the mighty feeling of the poem until we have grasped exactly what it is this breach, this wound, consists of, what precise meaning lies in the word "help." We begin to perceive that we must learn the meaning of every word anew.

Here our trust in primeval, common feeling as a means of communication between men of different cultures breaks down for good. We cannot force our way into understanding through mere sympathy or intuition; there is no other way but to turn around and proceed from the external inward to the generally human.

We must begin with the kin, the race or family, a gathering of individuals so joined up into one unit that they appear incapable of independent action. As to the feeling which so unites them, this we must leave until later. The point here is that the individual cannot act without all acting with and through him; no single individual can suffer without affecting the whole circle. So absolute is the connection that the individual simply cannot exist by himself: a slight loosening of the bond, and he slips down, the most helpless of all creatures.

We cannot gain speech of the individual human being. Here lies the difference between Hellenic and Germanic culture. The Hellene is nearer to us, for we can go straight to him, speak to him as man to man about the life of man, let him introduce us into the strange world—as it seems to us—in which he lives, and let him show us the aims that determine his daily thoughts and actions. His utterance and expression form an idea as to how he reacts in the face of what he meets. The barbarian does not move. He stands stiffly and uninvitingly. If he speaks, his words convey no meaning to us. He has killed a man.

"Why did you kill that man?" we ask.

"I killed him in revenge."

"How had he offended you?"

"His father had spoken ill words to my father's brother; therefore, I craved honor as due from him to us."

"Why did you not take the life of the offender himself?"

"This was a better man."

The more we ask and pry, the more incomprehensible he becomes. He appears to us as a machine, driven by principles.

The Hellene exists as an individual, a separate person within a community. The Germanic individual exists only as the representative, nay, as the personification of a whole. One might imagine that a supreme convulsion of the soul must tear the individual out from that whole to let him feel and speak as for himself. But actually, it is the opposite that takes place: the more the soul is moved, the more the individual personality is lost in the kin. At the very moment when man most passionately and unreservedly gives way to his own feelings, the clan takes possession of the individual fully and completely. Egil's lament is not the lament of a father for his son; it is the kin that utters its lament through the person of the father. From this breadth of passion springs the overpowering pathos of the poem.

If we want a real understanding of such men as Egil, we are driven to ask: what is the hidden force that makes kinsmen inseparable? First, we learn that they call each other "friend" (*frændi* in Icelandic, *freond* in Anglo-Saxon), and a linguistic analysis of this word will teach us that it means those who love (each other). But this brings us no farther, for etymology tells us nothing of what it is to love. We can perhaps get a little nearer by noting the etymological connection between the word "friend" and two others that play a great part in the social life of those days: "free" and *frith*.

In frith (i.e., peace), we have the old kinsmen's own definition of the fundamental idea in their interrelationship. By frith, they mean something in themselves: a power that makes them "friends" one toward another, and "free men" toward the rest of the world. Even here, of course, we cannot take the direct meaning of the word for granted, for that little word has not passed the centuries unscathed. Words such as "horse" and "cart" and "house" and "kettle" may remain more or less unaltered throughout all vicissitudes of culture, but terms used to designate spiritual values necessarily undergo a radical change in the course of such spiritual transformations, as have taken place in the souls of men in the North during the past thousand years. And the nearer such a word lies in its origin to the central part of the soul, the more sweeping changes it will undergo.

If ever word bore the mark of the transforming influence of Christianity and humanism, it is this word frith. If we look closely into the older significance of the word, we shall find something sterner: a firmness that has now given place to weakness. The frith of earlier days was less passive than now, with less of submissiveness and more of will. It held also an element of passion which has now been submerged in quietism. But the word tells us indisputably that the love which knit these kinsmen together is not to be taken in a modern, sentimental sense; the dominant note of kinship is safety and security.

Frith is the state of things which exists between friends, and it means, first and foremost, reciprocal inviolability. However individual wills may clash in a conflict of kin against kin, and however stubbornly individual heads may seek their own way according to their quota of wisdom, there can never be question of conflict, save in the sense of thoughts and feelings working their way toward an equipoise in unity. We need have no doubt but that good kinsmen could disagree with fervor. However, the matter might stand, there could, should, must, *inevitably* be but one ending to it all: a settlement peaceable and making for peace—frith.

A quarrel had no lethal point. Two kinsmen could not lift a hand one against the other. The moment a man scented kinship, he lowered his arms. The ending of *The Saga of Björn, Champion of the Hitardal People* has a touch of something heroic and comic about it,[11] stemming from this very fact. Bjorn fell after a brave fight by the hand of Thordr Kolbeinsson and his companions. The grounds of enmity between the two were numerous and various, but we may safely say that Bjorn had done all in his power to interfere with Thord's domestic bliss.

Among the opponents, Thord's young son, Kolli, takes a prominent part. The moment he was beaten to his knee and at bay, Bjorn says, "You strike hard today, Kolli."

"I do not know whom I should spare here," answers the youth.

"True enough, for your mother has surely urged you not to spare me. But it seems to me that you are not wisest in the matter of knowing your kin."

Kolli answers, "It is late in the day you tell me of it, if we two are not free to fight." And with these words, he withdraws from all further participation in the battle.

Even in the Icelandic sagas from the period of dissolution, we find very few instances of men entering into combinations which might lead to family conflicts. The by no means lovable Faroe chieftain Thrond of Gata is offered money to take sides against his cousins; before accepting, however, he pays tribute to the sense of what is right by saying to the tempter: "You cannot mean this in earnest." On another occasion, when we read that a certain man must have been sorely blind to take part in a fight where his own sons were on the other side, there rings through the words a mixture of wonder and repugnance. This speaks louder than the sharpest condemnation, for this wonder springs from the thought: how *can* he do such a thing?

It is hard to get at a true impression of the fundamental laws in human life that provide the very essence of a conscience—harder still to render such an impression living to others. They are not to be illustrated by noteworthy examples. In books of great deeds, a quality such as frith will never be represented in proportion to its importance; it goes too deep. It does not find direct expression in the laws; it underlies all accepted customs, but never appears in the light itself.

If we would seriously realize what is strongest in men, we must feel through their daily life, with all its inhibitions and restraints in little things. But once our eyes are opened to the unbroken chain of self-restraint and self-control that constitute the inner connection in the life of working human beings, we may find ourselves almost in fear of the power that sits innermost in ourselves and drives us according to its will. When one has worked through the spiritual remains of our forefathers, one must infallibly emerge with a constraining veneration for this frith. The Northmen are ever telling of war and strife, quarrels and bickering—dispute now over a kingdom, now an ox, now some piece of arrogance on the part of an individual, now a merciless combination of accidents by the hand

---

[11] *The Saga of Björn, Champion of the Hitardal People*, or *Bjarnar saga Hítdœlakappa*.

of fate, leading men into a chaos of strife. But we notice that even in the most violent turmoil of passion, all alike are ever amenable to one consideration: every single happening stands in some relation to frith.

And behind every law decree, there is a perceptible fear—a sacred dread— of interfering with one particular thing: the ties of kinship. We feel that all law paragraphs are based upon an underlying presumption that kinsmen will not and cannot act one against another, but must support one another.

When the Church began to exercise its supervision in matters of legislation, it noticed first of all an essential failing in the ancient code: namely, that it knew no provision for cases of killing between kinsmen. This crime therefore came within the clerical jurisdiction; the Church determined its penal code, just as it provided terms for the crime by adaptation of words from the Latin vocabulary.

When the lawgivers of the Middle Ages gradually found courage to come to grips with this ancient frith, in order to make room for modern principles of law, the attacks had first to be made in the form of indulgences: it was permitted to regard a kinsman's suit as irrelevant to oneself. It was declared lawful to refuse a contribution toward the fine imposed on any of one's kin. It took centuries of work to eradicate the tacit understanding of this ubiquitous frith principle from the law, and establish humanity openly as the foundation of equity.

Strangely enough, in the very period of transition when frith was being ousted from its supremacy as conscience itself, it finds definite expression in laws, namely in the statutes of the medieval guilds. These guilds were a contin- uation, not precisely of the clan, but of what was identical with clanship: that is to say, the old free societies of frith, or communities of mutual support. The guild laws provide that members of the guild must have no quarrels between them- selves. In the regrettable event of such quarrel arising between two of the same guild, the parties are forbidden, under pain of exclusion in disgrace, to summon each other before any tribunal but that of the guild itself. Not even in a foreign country may any member of a guild bring suit against a fellow member before a magistrate or court.

The Frisian peasant laws of the Middle Ages also found it necessary to lay down hard and fast rules for the obligations of kin toward kin, and decree that persons within the closer degrees of relationship (such as father, son, brother, uncle, aunt, etc.) may not bring suit one against another before the court. They must not sue or swear against one another, but in cases where they cannot agree in a matter of property or the like, one of their nearest of kin shall be appointed judge.

The guild statutes are as near to the unwritten law of kinship as any lifeless, extraneous provision can be to the conscience that has life in itself. And they give us, indeed, the absolute character of frith and its freedom from all reservation. But they cannot give the very soul of it, for then, instead of insisting that no quarrel shall be suffered to arise between one brother and another, they would simply acknowledge that no such quarrel ever could by any possibility arise. In other words, instead of a prohibition, we should have the recognition of an impossibility. The characters in the Icelandic sagas are still in this position, though we may feel that the cohesion of the clan is at the point of weakening. They have still, more or less unimpaired, the involuntary respect for all such interests as may affect the clan as a whole, an extreme of caution and foresight in regard to all such enterprise as cannot with certainty be regarded as not affecting the interest of all its members.

Even the most reckless characters are wary of making promises or alliances if they see any possibility of prejudicing a kinsman's interest. They go in dreading such conflicts. The power of frith is apparent in the fact that it does not count as a virtue, something in excess of what is demanded, but as an everyday necessity, the most obvious of all alike for high and low, heroic and unheroic characters. And the exceptions, therefore, show as something abhorrent and uncanny.

Clanship was not the only form of relationship between individuals, and however wisely and cautiously a man might order his goings, he could never be sure of avoiding every painful dilemma. He may find himself in a position where, apparently, the power of frith within him is put to the test.

For instance, with Gudrun. Her husband, Sigurd, has been slain by her own brothers, Gunther and Hogni. She voices her resentment in stirring words. In the *Lay of Gudrun,* we find it thus: "In bed and at board I lack my friend to speak with—this wrought Gjúki's sons. Gjúki's sons have brought me to this misery, brought about their sister's bitter weeping." The poems of the North also make her utter words of ill-omen; it sounds like a curse when she says, "Your heart, Hogni, should be torn by ravens in the wild places, where you should cry in vain for aid of man." But there is no place in the saga for even the least act on Gudrun's part to the prejudice of her brothers. She seeks by act and word to hinder Atli's plans for vengeance against Gunther and Hogni, and when all her warnings are in vain, she makes Atli pay dearly for the deed. The Northern poets, while laying stress on her sorrow, keep it throughout inactive—they do not even attempt to soften the contrast by any kind of inner conflict in her soul. There is no hesitation, no weighing this way or that. Frith was the one absolute thing to them. The poet lets Hogni answer Gudrun's passionate outburst with these deeply significant words: "If the ravens tore my heart, your sorrow would be the deeper."

The Sigurd poems are fashioned by Northern hands dealing with ancient themes; they give us Germanic thoughts as lived again in Norse or Icelandic minds. Altogether Icelandic, both in theme and word, is the tragedy which leads to Gisli Surson's unhappy outlawry. The two brothers, Gisli and Thorkel, are depicted by the writer of the saga as widely deferent in character, and in their sympathies, they take different sides. Thorkel is a close friend of Thorgrim

(Thorsteinsson the Godi), their sister's husband; Gisli is warmly attached to Vestein, brother to his own wife, Aud. Relations between the two half-brothers-in-law have evidently long been strained, and at last Vestein is slain by Thorgrim. Gisli takes vengeance secretly by entering Thorgrim's house at night and stabbing him as he lies in bed.

Thorgrim's avengers, led by a natural suspicion, pay a visit to Gisli before he is up; Thorkel, who lives with his brother-in-law and is of the party, manages to enter first. Once he sees Gisli's shoes on the floor full of snow, he thrusts them hurriedly under the bed. The party is obliged to go off again without having accomplished anything. Later, however, Gisli, in reckless verse, declares himself the culprit, and a party rides off to summon him to account. Thorkel is with them as before, but once more he manages to warn his brother. On the road, the party comes to a homestead where he suddenly remembers there is money owed to him, and takes the opportunity to dun his debtor. But while his horse stands saddled outside the house and his companions imagine him counting the money inside it, he is riding on a borrowed mount up into the woods where his brother has hidden. And when at last he has settled his various money affairs and taken to the road again, he is overtaken by little accidents on the way, sufficient to delay the progress of the party considerably.

Gisli's blow was a serious matter for Thorkel. He says himself to Gisli: "You have done me no little wrong, I should say, in slaying Thorgrim, my brother-in-law and partner and close friend." The great obligations which are customarily laid upon friends are evidence of the seriousness with which such intimacy was regarded, and how deeply the parties engaged themselves and their will in the relationship. Thorkel's position is therefore bitterer than immediately appears. But friendship must give way to frith; it is not a matter of choice on Thorkel's part. Here again we have the same contrast as in the Gudrun poems. Thorkel's bitterness and his frith can have no dealings with one another; they cannot come within reach of each other so as to give rise to any conflict, for they belong to different strata of the soul. To us, perhaps, it may seem as if there was a link missing from the sober statement of the story, but the words as they stand are good Icelandic psychology.

This frith is something that underlies all else, deeper than all inclination. It is not a matter of will, in the sense that those who share it time and again choose to set their kinship before all other feelings. It is rather the will itself. It is identical with the actual feeling of kinship, and not a thing deriving from that source.

Thorkel has his sorrow, as Gudrun has hers, but the possibility which should make that sorrow double-edged is out of the question, as is the mere thought that one could take sides here. Thus, there can never be room for any problem. The fact of kin siding against kin is known to poetry only as a mystery or a horror, as the outcome of madness, or as something dark and incomprehensible—something that is not even fate.

From early times, men's thoughts have hovered about the fact that a man could come to slay his kinsman. The sad possibility of father and son, each unknown to the other, meeting in battle and shedding each other's blood has even been treated poetically. A magnificent albeit small fragment of these poems is found in the German *Hildebrand Lay*, where the father, returning home after long absence in foreign lands, meets his son, who forces him to engage in single combat against his will. We find the pair again portrayed by Saxo as two brothers,[12] Halfdan and Hildiger. In the *Hildebrand Lay*, it is the skepticism of the son in regard to the father's declaration of kinship that brings about the disaster; the father *must* accept the challenge, or stand dishonored. In Saxo, the inner force of the conflict is weakened by the fact that Hildiger, for no reason, keeps his knowledge of their kinship to himself until he lies mortally wounded. Saxo's story, however, is evidently derived from the same situation as that preserved in the German lay.

Hildiger tries a crafty trick to escape from fate, declaring in lordly fashion that he cannot think of engaging in single combat with an unproven warrior. But when Halfdan, undismayed, repeats his challenge and strikes down one set of antagonists after the other, Hildiger, who sees his own fame thus threatened by Halfdan's prowess, cannot endure any longer to refuse this challenge.

An Icelandic version, preserved in the *Ásmundar saga kappabana*, mirrors Saxo's account so closely that we are forced to presume a close relationship between the two. One of the brothers here has still the old name, Hildebrand, and the other has been assimilated with Asmund, the hero of the saga. The difference between the more natural presentment in the *Hildebrand Lay*, and the dramatic artifice in the Northern variants, is mainly due to the saga writers' anxiety to preserve as much effect as possible for the final plaint.

The story of the fatal meeting between two kinsmen is, as an epic theme, not specifically Germanic. We can follow it westward, among the Celts, and southward—even as far east as Asia. As a matter of literary history, it likely has its origin in the south, but it is more important to note how the theme has been reborn again and again, among one clannish people after another: proof that the same thoughts were everywhere as a weight upon so many people's minds. Men pondered and speculated over this mystery in the ordering of life, that a man could be driven against his will to harm his kin. In the Germanic tradition, the case is clearly and simply stated: frith was inviolable, but honor, too, had its own

---

[12] Saxo Grammaticus, preeminent Danish historian and author of the *Gesta Danorum,* the first historical work on the history of Denmark. The *Gesta Danorum* includes the legend of Amleth, which later inspired Shakespeare's *Hamlet.*

absolute validity, so that the two could collide with such force as to destroy both on impact, and the man with them.

The close of the *Hildebrand Lay* is unfortunately lost: the very part that must have shown us the united plaint of the two combatants over what had passed. The loss of the poem's ending is all the more serious, since this was the dominant point of the whole poem. Saxo's reproduction, and still more the modernized elegy of the Icelandic saga, gives but a faint echo. But even in these later, imitative works, we seem to find pathos of an altogether different nature from the usual: not the merciless seriousness of death, but a wonder rising to horror. Not a confident appeal to fate with a sense of comfort in the conviction that there is reparation for everything—and that reparation will be made for this as well, if those that remain are of any worth—but only helplessness and hopelessness.

The same note is struck elsewhere, as in *The Saga of Hervor and Heidrek*, where Angantyr, upon finding his brother's body on the field of battle, says, "A curse is upon us, that I should be your bane. This thing will be ever remembered. Ill is the doom of the Norns."[13] The words express his sense of being a monster; so desperately meaningless is his fate that it will force the thoughts of posterity to hover about it, that he will be a "song for coming generations." The close of Hildebrand's complaint runs, in Saxo's paraphrase, approximately as follows:

> An evil fate, loading years of misfortune on the happy, buries smile in sorrow and bruises fate. For it is a pitiful misery to drag on a life in suffering, to breathe under the pressure of sorrow-burdened days, and go in fear of the warning [omen]. But all that is knit fast by the prophetic decree of the Parcae,[14] all that is planned in the council of high providence, all that has once by fore vision been fixed in the chain of fates, is not to be torn from its place by any changing of worldly things.

There is nothing corresponding to these lines in the saga. The first part of the poem expresses the same as Saxo's paraphrase:

> None knows beforehand what manner of death shall be his. You were born of Drot in Denmark, I in Sweden. My shield lies sundered at my head; there is the tale of my killings; there [presumably on the shield] lies the son I begot and unwilling slew.

What this refers to we do not rightly know. And then the poem closes with a prayer imploring the survivor to do "what few slayers have any mind to." Namely, to wrap the dead man in his own garments: a termination which sounds

---

[13] The Norse goddesses of fate.
[14] A trio of goddesses thought to control fate.

altogether foreign in its romantic sentimentality to the Northern spirit. Saxo here has undoubtedly worked from another version, nearer the original. His portrayal of the evil days people lived through in fear fits more or less accurately to the old thought. Such a deed buries all hope for the future and spreads among the survivors an everlasting dread. It is futile to guess how the words originally stood in the Northern version, but Saxo's *omen* in particular seems to hold a true Northern idea: that such a deed forms an ill-boding warning. For the rest, fate rules. What is to come will come, but here is a thing breaking out beyond fate. One can say that the fate of the kinsmen was burst asunder.

The same hopeless keynote rings through *Beowulf's* description of the old father's sorrow when one of his sons has by chance slain his brother. The poet compares him to an old man who sees his beloved young son dangling in the gallows—a desperate illustration for a Germanic poet to use:

> Then he lifts up his voice in a song of anguish, as his son hangs at the ravens' pleasure, and he cannot help him; old and burdened with days, cannot save him. Always he remembers, morning after morning, his son's passing; an heir in his stead he cares not to wait in the castle. . . . Sorrowing he sees his wine-hall waste, the chamber wind-swept, empty of joy, in his son's house. The gallows rider sleeps, the hero in his grave. No sound of harp, no pleasure now in the homestead, as there was once.
>
> He takes his way to the couch, sings a sad chant, lonely over the lonely one; everywhere, in the fields as in the home, there is too wide a space. So raged sorrow in the prince of the Weders, sorrow for his son Herebeald; in no way could he gain payment for that killing through the life of the slayer, nor by rewarding the young hero with bitter doings toward him, though he had no love for him. Misery held him fast, from the day that the wound was dealt him, until he passed out from the joyous world of men.

But frith demands more than that kinsmen should merely spare each other. Thorkel Surson was a weak character. He was content to place himself in an equivocal position when he kept his place among his brother-in-law's avengers. He says to Gisli: "I will warn you if I come by news of any plans against you, but I will not render you any such help as might bring me into difficulties." Gisli evidently regards such caution as a dishonest compromise with conscience.

"Such an answer as you have given me here, I could never give to you, and I could never act in such a way," he retorts.

A man will not ride in company with his kinsman's adversaries. A man will not lie idle while his kinsman's suit is in progress, and the fact that this same kinsman has nailed his brother-in-law fast to his bed by night is plainly of no weight in Gisli's judgment. A man does not sneak around by a back way to offer his kinsman a trifle of help—no, when the latter is finally outlawed, he must at least be able to count on support. This seems in all seriousness to be Gisli's idea.

And Gisli is in the right. Frith is something active, not merely leading kinsmen to spare each other, but forcing them to support one another's cause, help and stand sponsor for one another, and trust one another. Our words are too dependent for their strength on sentimental associations to bear out the full import of clan feeling; the responsibility is absolute, because kinsmen are literally the doers of one another's deeds.

The guild statutes provided as follows:

> Should it so happen that any brother kills any man who is not a brother of the Guild of St. Canute [i.e., of our guild] then the brethren shall help him in his peril of life as best they can. If he be by the water, they shall help him with a boat, oars, dipper, tinder box and axe. . . . Should he need a horse, they are to provide him with a horse. . . . Any brother able to help, and not helping . . . he shall go out of this guild as a nithing. . . .[15] Every brother shall help his brother in all lawsuits.

That is to say, if one brother has a lawsuit, twelve brethren of the guild shall be chosen to go with him to its hearing and support him. The brethren are also to form an armed guard about him, and escort him to and from the place where the court is held, if need be. And when a brother has to bring oath before the court, twelve members of the guild shall be chosen by lot to swear on his side, and those so chosen are to aid him in manly way. A man failing to support his brother by oath—or worse, bearing testimony against him—is subject to heavy fines.

There are two kinds of cases, involving two kinds of killing: one, a guild-brother kills a stranger, or, two, a stranger kills a guild-brother. In the former case, the brethren of the guild see that the slayer gets away in safety on horseback or by ship. In the latter case, the rule runs as follows: no brother eats or drinks or has intercourse with his brother's slayer, whether on land or on ship. The guild brethren shall aid the dead man's heirs to vengeance or restitution.

It is perhaps difficult to realize that this double-valuation had its place in a community of citizens and not in some freebooters' camp. It stands valid as the supreme law for decent, conservative, enlightened men—men, who in those days represented, so to speak, progress in historic continuity. This partisan solidarity in frith is their strong attachment to the past, and the cultural worth of this partisan spirit is revealed by the fact that it lies behind the reform movements of the Middle Ages as their driving force. As the brethren here in the guilds, so kinsmen also were filled to such a degree with "love," so eager to help that they could not

---

[15] An Old Norse term meaning a person without honor; a scoundrel, a coward, or a wretch.

well find any energy left for judging right and wrong. They were not by nature and principle unjust nor partisan. Faith and the sense of justice can well thrive together, but they belong—to use a phrase already used before—to different strata of the soul and thus miss contact with each other.

The uncompromising character of frith is strikingly illustrated by the last appearance of grand old Egil at the moot place. It happened one day, when Egil was grown old and somewhat set aside, that a quarrel arose between his son, Thorstein, and Onund Sjoni's son, Steinar, over a piece of land. Steinar defiantly sent his herd to graze there; Thorstein faithfully cut down his herdsmen. Steinar summoned Thorstein, and now the parties were at the law-*thing*. Then the assembly perceives a party riding up, led by a man in full amor: it is old Egil with a following of eighty men. He dismounts calmly by the booths, makes the needful arrangements, then goes up to the mound where the court is held and calls to his old friend Onund: "Is it your doing that my son is summoned for breaking the peace?"

"No, indeed," says Onund, "it was not by my will. I am more careful of our ancient friendship than to do so. It was well you came. . . ."

"Well, let us see now if you mean anything by what you say. Let us two rather take the matter in hand than that those two fighting cocks should suffer themselves to be egged on against each other by their own youth and the counsels of other."

And when then the matter is submitted to Egil's arbitration, he calmly decides that Steinar shall receive no indemnity for the slaves killed. His homestead is confiscated, and he himself shall leave the district before flitting day.

There is a touch of nobility about Egil's last public appearance, the nobility of a greatly simple character. He accepts the office of arbitrator and decides the case—as we can see against all reasonable and justified expectation—as if only his own side existed. He does so with a cool superiority, which leaves no doubt that he acts with the full approval of his conscience. Here again Egil stands as a monumental expression of a dying age.

The same naivete is seen directly in another old-fashioned character: Hallfreðr Óttarsson, called the Wayward Skald. On one occasion, when his father with rare impartiality has judged against him, he says, "Whom can I trust, when my father fails me?"

The straightforward simplicity when taking one view as a matter of course places Hallfreðr, as it does Egil, outside all comparison with great or small examples of selfishness or injustice, and makes them *types*. More than types of their age, they are types of a form of culture itself. Not the exceptions, the marked individualities, and not the men who were somewhat apart from the common, but men generally. The idea of frith is set so deeply beneath all personal marks of character and all individual inclination that it affects them only from below, not as one inclination or one feeling may affect another. The characters may be widely different, but the breach in character does not reach down to this prime center of the soul. Egil was a stiff-necked man who was hard to deal with at home and abroad. He would be master in his house, and a treaty of peace in which he did not himself dictate the terms he would not be disposed to recognize. Another man might be more easygoing, peaceable, ready to find a settlement, quick to avoid collision, and eager to remove causes of conflict. But he could never be so, except on the basis of frith and kinship.

Askel, the right-minded, peace-making chieftain of the Reykdale, is perhaps rather too modern a character to go well in company with Egil. But his story, as we find it in the saga of the Reykdale men, gives us a graphic picture of the principles of reconciliation. Askel is so unfortunate as to have a nephew whose character is such that strife seems necessary to him, and Askel's task in life is to follow on the heels of this Vemund and put matters right again after him. He carries out his task faithfully to effect reconciliation, and make good the damage done by his kinsman.

Vemund's achievements in the greater style begin with his joining company with a wealthy but bad man, Hanef of Othveginstunga, whom he knits closer to himself by accepting an offer of fostering a child. Hanef naturally makes use of these good connections to carry on his rascally tricks to a greater extent than before. He steals cattle. In spite of earnest representations from Askel, Vemund takes up his friend's cause, and even craftily exploits his uncle's respected name to gather men on his side. The result is a battle in which Hanef and two good men fall on one side, and on the other, a free man and a slave. Askel comes up and makes peace between the parties, judging Hanef and the slave as equals—likewise man for man of the others slain—leaving the opponents to pay a fine for the remaining one. Thus judges the most impartial man in Iceland when it is a question of making good what his kinsman has done ill.

Vemund's next noteworthy achievement is cheating a Norwegian skipper by selling him a shipload of wood which had already been sold to Steingrim of Eyja Fjord.[16] Steingrim retaliates by having Vemund's slaves killed, and Vemund's part of the wood brought home to him. Askel has to go out and settle matters again, and when Vemund finds that this intervention has not procured him reparation for the slaves, Askel offers him full payment for them out of his own purse. Vemund refuses to accept this, tacitly reserving to himself the right to settle accounts in his own fashion when opportunity offers. He tries in vain to balance matters by stealing a couple of oxen Steingrim has bought. His disinterestedness in the affair is shown by his offering them to Askel as a gift, but he gets no real result out of this either, only a couple of killings and a settlement—the last of

---

[16] A fjord in northern Iceland, commonly known as Eyjafjörður, or "Island Fjord."

which is, of course, Askel's work. The only objection Vemund has to this settlement is that Askel has once again not considered the killing of the slaves in the earlier affair.

He now tries another way, hiring a wretch to insult Steingrim in a peculiarly obnoxious fashion; this time Askel's attempt at peacemaking fails, owing to the bitter resentment of the other party. Not until an attempt at vengeance has led to the killing of Vemund's brother, Herjolf, does the right-minded chieftain succeed in effecting a settlement whereby Herjolf is to be paid, and two of Steingrim's companions are to be exiled forever, and two others for two years. Thus, the game goes on with acts of aggression on Vemund's part, always as mischievous as ever. Intervention on the part of Askel is always in full agreement with the principles of frith, until at last the measure is full. When Steingrim and his followers place themselves in the way of Askel and Vemund and their men, Askel accepts the combat without enthusiasm, but also without demur. And that was the end of Askel and Steingrim.

Smartness and diplomacy were not forbidden qualities according to the old usage. Any man was free to edge and elbow his way through the world, even in matters directly concerning his relationship to brothers and kin. He could take little liberties with the frith as long as he was careful not to affect any actual breach, however slight, but he must always be prepared to find it rising inflexibly before him. It was quite permissible to let one's kinsmen know that one personally preferred another way of life than the one they had chosen to follow, and that one would be happier to see them adopt one's own principles. This at least could be done in Iceland at the period of the sagas, and I do not think this freedom was then of recent date, but frith stood firm as ever. As for disowning the action of one's kinsmen and taking up a personal, neutral standpoint, such a thing was out of the question.

A man is brought home lifeless. The question of what he has done, of his antecedents generally, fades away into the dimmest background. There remains only the fact that he is our kinsman. The investigation seeks to answer whether he was slain by the hand of man, or by something else. Has he sustained wounds? If so, of what sort? Who was the slayer? And thereupon the kinsmen choose their leader, or gather around the born avenger and promise him all assistance in prosecuting the case—whether by force of arms, or by law. The kinsmen of the slayer are well aware of what needs to be done now. They know that vengeance is on their heels: so simple and straightforward is the idea of frith. It reckons with facts alone, taking no count of personal considerations and causes which led to this violent conclusion.

Throughout the whole of the old Nordic literature, with its countless killings—justified or not—there is not a single instance of men willingly refraining from attempts at vengeance on account of the character of their slain kinsman.

They may be forced to let him lie as he lies, they may realize the hopelessness of any endeavor to obtain reparation, but in every case, we can apply the utterance occasionally found: "I would spare nothing could I be sure that vengeance was to be gained." It is certainly saying a great deal to assert that there is not a single instance. There might have been—and there probably were—cases of homicide, the further course of which we do not know. The positive testimony lies in the fact that the saga writer rarely fails to emphasize the bitterness of despair which fell to the lot of men forced to relinquish their revenge. The bitterness of this enforced self-denial is also apparent in the prohibitions, which occasionally had to be issued in both the southern and northern parts of Teutonic territory, against taking vengeance for an offender lawfully judged and lawfully hanged.

On the other hand, the slayer comes home and states, simply and briefly, that so-and-so has been killed and "his kinsmen will hardly judge me free of all blame in the matter." The immediate effect of these words is that his kinsmen prepare for defense, to safeguard themselves and their man. If in the course of their preparations they let fall a word about the undesirability of acting as he has just done, it is merely an aside, an utterance apart from the action, and without any tendency to affect it. It serves only to enhance the effect of determination.

An Icelander greets his kinsman in the doorway with the earnest wish that he would either turn over a new leaf and live decently, or else find some other place to stay. Once said, the two go indoors and discuss what measures are now to be taken in regard to the visitor's latest killing. Or the offender may answer, as Thorvald Krok—who was guilty of simple murder—answers the reproach of his kinsman Thorarin: "It is little use to bewail what is now done; you will only bring further trouble on yourself if you refuse to help us. If you take up the matter, it will not be hard to find others who will aid."

And Thorarin replies, "It is my counsel that you move hither with all of yours, and that we gather others to us."

A crude, but not altogether unique instance of the compelling power of frith is found in the story of Hrolleif of the *Vatsdoela*. This ne'er-do-well ships to Iceland with his witch of a mother. He makes his appearance at the farm of his uncle Saemund and claims to be received there in accordance with the bond of kinship between them. Saemund shrewdly observes that he seems regrettably nearer in character to his mother than to his father's stock, but Hrolleif brushes the reproach away with the simple answer: "I cannot live on ill foretellings."

When life with Hrolleif in the homestead becomes unendurable, after Saemund's son Geirmund complains of him as intolerable, Hrolleif opines that it is shameful thus to rail over trifles and discredit one's kin. He is given a holding and kills a man, for which killing Saemund has to pay the fine. When at last he has crowned his record by killing Ingimund, Saemund's foster brother who on the strength of their friendship had given Hrolleif land of his own, he rides straight to Geirmund and forces the latter to protect him, by the words: "Here I will suffer myself to be slain, to your disgrace."

We find it hardly remarkable that Saemund, when a neighbor calls with well-founded complaints against his nephew's doings in the district, should give vent to a sigh: "It were but good if such men were put out of the world."

And what does the neighbor say but this: "You would very surely think otherwise if any should attempt it in earnest."

Here lies the great difficulty: Saemund is obliged to hold by Hrolleif as far as ever possible; not merely to cover him, but further, to maintain his cause in face of his opponents.

Here is a scene from *Vallaljots saga*, where Ljot's words are particularly characteristic. There have been killings and other matters between Ljot and his kinsmen on the one hand—and the two sons of Sigmund, Hrolf and Halli, on the other. All dissension has now been buried by a fair reconciliation, thanks to the right-minded intervention of Gudmund the Mighty.

Bodvar, a third son of Sigmund, has been abroad during these doings; he now returns and is forced to seek shelter during a storm in the house of Thorgrim, Ljot's brother. Against Thorgrim's will, and in spite of his endeavors to prevent any of the household from leaving the place while the guests are there, one man, Sigmund, slips away and hurries off to make trouble. Ljot will not kill a non-offending man and break the peace agreed on, nor will he raise hand against his brother's guests. But there are others who still bear a grudge, and Bodvar is killed as he goes on his way from Thorgrim's house. What can the eager avengers do now but come to Ljot, the best man of the family?

"It may cost a few hard words, but we shall be safe with him," one of them suggests.

"It was he who counseled against vengeance," another points out, but he is met with the retort:

"The more we are in need of him, the more stoutly he will help."

They then inform Ljot that they have taken vengeance for their kinsman, and the saga goes on.

"It is ill to have evil kinsmen who only lead one into trouble. What is now to be done?" asks Ljot.

They set out to find Thorgrim, and of course the saga has no need to state that Ljot is one of the party.

Ljot asks, "Why did you house our enemies, Thorgrim?"

He answers, "What else could I do? I did my best, though it did not avail. Sigmund did his best, and when all is said and done, it fell out otherwise than I had wished."

Ljot responds, "Better had it been if your plans had been followed, but...now it is best that we do not stay apart.... It can hardly be otherwise now than that I should help, and I will take the lead. I have little wish for great undertakings, but I will not lose what is mine for any man."

Thorgrim asks what is to become of Eyjolf, who of his own will had taken an eager part in the act of vengeance: Ljot will undertake to protect him, and get him away out of the country.

"But Bjorn," says Ljot, "is to stay with me, and his fate shall be mine."

Bjorn was Ljot's sister's son, and had been the leader of the party who had killed Bodvar.

There is a sounding echo of the active character of this frith in the old German's paraphrase of the Sermon on the Mount. In Germanizing Christ's command as to unreserved self-denial: "If thine eye offend thee, thy hand send thee, cast them from thee," he says, "Go not with the kinsman who leads to sin, to wrong, though he be never so closely thy kinsman; better to cast him aside, to abhor him, and lay waste love in the heart, that one may rise alone to the high Heaven."

Again, personal sympathies and antipathies can, of course, never stand up against the authority of frith. Relations between Thorstein and his father had never been very cordial. To Egil's mind, this son of his was ever too soft, too easygoing a man. Egil could not thrive in his house, but went in his old age to live with a step-daughter. His personal feelings toward his son could not make him stop a single moment to consider whether or not he should interfere.

The *Bandamanna saga* has a little story based on this theme, of a father and son who never could get along together but are drawn together by their common feeling against all outsiders. The son is Odd, a wealthy man; Usvif, his father, is poor. Odd gets entangled in a lawsuit, which his ill-wishers take advantage of to squeeze him thoroughly. They have sworn together not to let him go free until they have stripped him. Then artful old Usvif comes along, and under cover of his notorious ill will toward his son, goes about among the conspirators, opening the eyes of a few of them to the hazardous nature of their undertaking:

> As purely as my son has money in his chest, so surely also has he wit in his head to find a way when that is needed. . . . Do you properly know how much of the booty there will fall to each, when there are eight of you to share. . . ? For you need not think my son will sit waiting at home for you; he has a ship, as you know, and save for homestead and land, a man's wealth will float on water, that much I know. . . . Nay, but what a man has gotten, that he has.

And here the old man is near letting fall a fat purse hidden beneath his cloak, the price he had demanded of his son beforehand for his help. Thus, he went unhesitatingly about the work of frith as he understood it, and took a hearty pride in his and his son's success in settling the matter.

All must give way to frith: all obligations, all considerations of self, everything down to the regard for one's own personal dignity—if such a thing could be imagined as existing apart from the feeling of kinship.

The great heroic example of daughterly and sisterly fidelity is Signy. The *Völsunga saga* tells, presumably based throughout on older poems, how a disagreement between Volsung and his son-in-law, Siggeir, Signy's husband, leads to the slaying of the former. Volsung's only surviving son, Sigmund, has to take to the woods, and there he ponders on revenge for his father. Signy sends one after another of her sons out to aid him, and sacrifices them mercilessly when they show themselves craven and useless. At last, she herself goes out, disguised and unrecognizable, to Sigmund's hiding place, and bears her own brother a son: an avenger of the true type, instinct with the feeling of clanship. "The war-skilled youth closed me in his arms; there was joy in his embrace, and yet it was hateful to me also," runs the stirring Old English monologue. And when at last the long-awaited vengeance comes, and the fire blazes up about King Siggeir, she throws herself into the flames with the words:

> I have done all that King Siggeir might be brought to his death; so much have I done to bring about vengeance that I will not in any way live longer.
> I will die now with Siggeir as willingly as I lived unwillingly with him.

To such a length is she driven by frith. She cannot stop at any point, in face of any horror, so long as her sisterly love is still unsatisfied. She is carried irresistibly through motherly feeling and the dread of incest, for there is not the slightest suggestion in the saga that Signy is to be taken as one of those stern characters in whom one passion stifles all others from the root.

One is tempted to regard this episode as a study, as a piece of problem writing, and as a conscious attempt to work out the power of frith upon the character. I think the suggestion has something to justify it, because the story as it stands has its idea. Consciously or unconsciously, the poet and his hearers were concerned to bring it about that the frith on one side and that on the other (a woman's relationship to her husband is also a sort of frith) were so forced one against the other that the two showed their power by crushing human beings between them. Signy *must* take vengeance on her husband for her father's death, despite humanity itself, and she *must* take vengeance on herself for her own act. Her words say as much: "So much have I done to bring about vengeance that I will not in any way live longer." This does not come as an empty phrase; rather, these words ring out as the theme of the poem. Gudrun may sorrow for her husband, but she cannot take action against her brothers. Signy must aid in furthering vengeance

for her father, even though it cost her her husband, and her children, and something over.

The frith of the guild statutes is no exaggeration; it requires the brethren to
take up one another's cause, to consider only the person and not the matter itself.
And the frith of kinship has one thing about it that can never find expression in a
paragraph of laws. That is to say, spontaneity, necessity, and the unreflecting
attitude that says, "We cannot do otherwise."

And whence comes this "We cannot do otherwise," but from depths that lie
beneath all self-determination and self-comprehension? We can follow the idea
of frith from its manifestation in man's self-consciousness, down through all his
dispositions, until it disappears in the root of will. We dimly perceive that it is
not he that wills frith, but frith that wills him. It lies at the bottom of his soul as
the great fundamental element, with the blindness and the strength of nature.

Frith constitutes what we call the base of the soul. It is not a mighty feeling
among other feelings in these people, but the very core of the soul, that gives
birth to all thoughts and feelings, and provides them with the energy of life—or
it is that center in the self where thoughts and feelings receive the stamp of their
humanity, and are inspired with will and direction. It answers to what we in ourselves call the human. Humanity in them bears always the mark of kinship. In
our culture, a revolting misdeed is branded as inhuman, and conversely, we express our appreciation of noble behavior by calling it genuinely human. By the
Teutons, the former is condemned as destroying a man's kin-life, the latter
praised for strengthening the sense of frith. Therefore, the slaying of a kinsman
is the supreme horror, shame, and ill-fortune in one, whereas an ordinary killing
is merely an act that may or may not be objectionable according to circumstances.

Down at this level of spontaneity, there is no difference between me and
thee, as far as kinship reaches. If frith constitutes the base of the soul, it is a base
which all kinsmen have in common. There they adjoin one another, without any
will or reflection between them as a buffer. Kinsmen strengthen one another;
they are not as two or more individuals who add their respective strengths together, but they act in concert, because deep down in them all there is a thing in
common which knows and thinks for them. Nay, more: they are so united that
one can draw strength to himself from another.

This peculiarity of man is well-known by the bear, according to a saying
current in the north of Sweden: "Better to fight twelve men than two brothers,"
runs a proverb ascribed to the wise animal. Among twelve men, a bear can pick
off one at a time in rational fashion, but the two cannot be taken one by one. And
if the one falls, his strength is passed on to his brother.

This solidarity—as exemplified in the laws of revenge—rests on the natural
fact of psychological unity. Through the channel of the soul, the action and the
suffering of the individual flow on, spreading out to all who belong to the same

stock, so that in the truest sense they are the doers of one another's acts. When they follow their man to the seat of justice and support him to the utmost of their power, they are not acting as if his deed were theirs, but because it is. As long as the matter is still unsettled, all the kinsmen concerned are in a state of permanent challenge.

The slayer is not the only one who stands in danger of perishing by the sword he has drawn. Vengeance can equally well be attained by the killing of one of his kin, if the offended parties find one easier to reach than the slayer himself, or judge him more "worthy" as an object of vengeance. Steingrim's words have a most natural ring when he comes to Eyjolf Valgerdson and tells him that he has been out in search of Vemund, but, having been prevented from doing so, instead took Vemund's brother Herjolf: "Eyjolf was not well pleased that it had not been Vemund or Hals [another brother of Vemund's]," Steingrim said, "though we had rather seen it had been him."

And Eyjolf likewise had no objection to this, despite the fact that Herjolf does not appear to have had any share in Vemund's doings. The ring of the words—the passionless, practical, matter-of-fact tone in which the speeches are uttered—tells us much better than a roundabout explanation that we have to deal with a matter of experience here, and not a reflection or an arbitrary rule.

In another saga, a man named Gudbrand has to pay with his life for the amorous escapades of his brother Ingolf, who had caused offense to Ottar's daughter with his persistent visits to her home. Her father vindicated the honor of his daughter by having Gudbrand killed. Ingolf himself was too wary to give the girl's protectors a chance upon his life, and so they had no choice but to strike at him through the body of his kinsman.

Similarly, all those united by one bond of kinship share any scathes suffered by one of their clan members: all feel the pain of the wound, and all are equally apt to seek vengeance. If a fine is decreed, all will have their share.

Thus, the kinsmen proclaim their oneness of soul and body. This reciprocal identity is the foundation on which society and the laws of society mast be based. In all relations between man and man, it is frith that is taken into account, not individuals. What a single man has done binds all who live in the same circle of frith. The kinsmen of a slain man appear *in pleno* as accusers. It is the clan of the slayer that promises indemnity (i.e., the clan that pays damages for the slaying). And it is the clan of the slain man that receives the fine, and the sum is again shared in such a manner as to reach every member of the group. The two families promise each other, as one corporation to another, peace and security in the future.

When a matter of blood or injury is brought before the tribunal of the law-*thing*, the decree must follow the line of demarcation drawn by kinship. The

circle of frith amounts to an individual, which cannot be divided save by amputation, and its right constitutes a whole that no judgment can dissect.

Germanic jurisprudence knows no such valuation of an act as allows of dis-
tributive justice: it can only hold one party entirely in the right, and the other
entirely in the wrong. If a man has been slain, and his friends waive their immediate right of vengeance and bring their grievance before the law court instead,
the community must either judicially award the complainants their right of frith
and reparation, or doom them from their frith and declare them unworthy of seeking redress. In the first case, the community adds its authority to the aggrieved
party's proceedings, thereby denying the accused all right to maintain their kinship, or to defend and aid the slayer. In the latter case, when the killing was done
in self-defense or on provocation, the law-*thing* says to the complainants: "Your
frith is worsted; you have no right to vengeance."

We have been taught from childhood to regard the story of the bundle of
sticks as an illustration of the importance of unity. The Germanic attitude of mind
starts from a different side altogether. Here, unity is not regarded as originating
in addition to something; unity is first in existence. The thought of mutual support
plays no leading part among these men; they do not see it in the light of one man
after another coming with his strength and the whole then added together, but
rather as if the force lay in that which unites them. For them, then, the entire
community is broken—and the strength of its men therewith—as soon as even
one of the individual parties to it is torn up. And thus, they compare the group of
kinsmen to a fence, stave set by stave, enclosing a sacred ground. When one is
struck down, there is a breach in the clan, and the ground lies open to be trampled
on.

Such then is the frith which in ancient days united kinsmen one with another,
a love which can only be characterized as a feeling of identity. So deeply rooted
is it that neither sympathy nor antipathy, nor any humor or mood, can make it
ebb or flow. No happening can be so powerful as to reach down and disturb this
depth. Not even the strongest feelings and obligations toward non-kinsmen can
penetrate so as to give rise to any inner tragedy, any conflict of the soul.

Signy, to use her as an example, was driven to do what she would rather
have left undone. The thrilling words, "there was joy in it, but it was hateful to
me also," are undoubtedly applicable to her state after the consummation of her
revenge. So closely can the Northmen approach tragedy that they depict a human
being who suffers by taking action. But there is no question of any inner conflict
in the sense of her considering, in fear, what course she is to choose. The tragic
element comes from the outside. She acts naturally and without hesitation, and
her action whirls her to destruction. When disagreement between kinsfolk is first
consciously exploited as a poetic subject—as in the *Laxdoela* account of the two

cousins driven to feud for a woman's sake—we find ourselves on the threshold of a new world.

The *Laxdoela* portrays the tragic conflict in a man's mind when he is whirled into enmity with his cousin by the vengeful ambition of a woman. The strong-minded Gudrun (Osvifrsdottir) is never able to forget that once she loved Kjartan and was jilted by him. When she marries Kjartan's cousin Bolli, she makes him a tool of her revenge. At last, the day of reckoning has arrived: Kjartan is reported to be on a solitary ride past Bolli's homestead. Gudrun was up at dawn, says the saga, and woke her brothers:

> Such mettle as you are, you should have been daughters of so-and-so the peasant—of the sort that serve neither for good nor ill. After all the shame Kjartan has put upon you, you sleep never the worse for that he rides past the place with a man or so. . . .

The brothers dress and arm themselves. Gudrun bids Bolli go with them. He hesitates, alleging the question of kinship, but she answers, "Maybe, but you are not so lucky as to be able to please all in a matter. We will part, then, if you do not go with them."

Thus urged, Bolli takes up his arms and goes out. The party placed themselves in ambush in the defile of Hafragil. Bolli was silent that day, and lay up at the edge of the ravine. But his brothers-in-law were not pleased to have him lying there keeping lookout; jestingly, they caught him by the legs and dragged him down. When Kjartan came through the ravine, the fight began. Bolli stood idly by, his sword, Foot-Bite, in his hand.

"Well, kinsman, and what did you set out for today, since you stand there idly looking on?" teased Kjartan.

Bolli made as though he had not heard Kjartan's words. At length the others wake him to action, and he places himself in Kjartan's way.

Then said Kjartan, "Now you have made up your mind, it seems, to this cowardly work. But I had rather take my death from you than give you yours."

With this, he threw down his weapon, and Bolli, without a word, dealt him his death blow. He sat down at once, supporting Kjartan, who died in his arms.

Bolli's indecisiveness lies altogether outside the sphere of frith. In these chapters, there is a touch of the medieval interest in mental problems, but the old, heartsick, and ignoble melancholy still rings through.

There is less of tragedy than of moral despair in Bolli's words to Gudrun when she congratulates him on his return home: "This ill fortune will be long in my mind, even though you do not remind me of it."

Frith, then, is nothing but the feeling of kinship itself; it is given, once and for all, at birth. The sympathy we regard as the result of an endeavor to attune ourselves to our neighbors was a natural premise and a feature of character.

Compared with the love of our day, the old family feeling has a stamp of almost sober steadfastness. There is none of that high-pressure feeling which modern human beings seem to find vitally necessary to love, and none of that pain of tenderness which seems to be the dominant note in our heartfelt sympathy—between man and man as well as between man and woman. The Christian hero of love is consumed by his ardor; he is in danger of being sundered himself by his own need to give out and draw up in himself. The people of older times grew strong and healthy in the security of their friendships; frith is altogether balance and sobriety.

It is natural then that security should form the center of meaning in the words that the Germanic people are most inclined to use of themselves: words such as *sib* and frith. Security—but with a distinct note of something active, something willing and acting, or something at least which is ever on the point of action. A word such as the Latin *pax* suggests, first and foremost, a laying down of arms, a state of equipoise due to the absence of disturbing elements. Frith, on the other hand, indicates something armed, protection, defense—or else a power for peace which keeps men amicably inclined. Even when we find mention in the Germanic writings of "making peace," the fundamental idea is not that of removing disturbing elements and letting things settle down, but that of introducing a peace-power among the disputants.

The translator of Anglo-Saxon poetry is faced with innumerable difficulties, because no modern words will exhaust the meaning of terms like *freoðu* and *sib*, indicating "frith." If the translator contents himself with repeating "peace" again and again in every context, he will thereby wipe out the very meaning which gives sense to the line. If he attempts to vary by different interpretations, he can only give the upper end of the meaning; he pulls off a little tuft of the word, but he does not get the root. The energy of the word, its vital force, is lost. When in one place enemies or evildoers beg for frith, the word means fully an acceptance in a pardoning will, admission to inviolability. When God promises the patriarch in Genesis frith, it bears the full meaning of grace: the earnest intention to be with him and protect him, fight for him, and if need be, commit a wrong for his advantage. And it is not only men, but also, for instance, places or strongholds which can furnish those in need of frith.

And frith is the mutual will, the unanimity, gentleness, and loyalty in which men live within their circle. According to the writer of the Anglo-Saxon Genesis, the state in which the angels lived with their Lord before they sinned has frith; it was this frith that Cain broke by his fratricide "forfeiting love and frith." So also

Mary says to Joseph, when he thinks of leaving her: "You will rend asunder our frith and forsake my love."

When Beowulf has killed both Grendel and his mother, the Danish King in grateful affection says, "I will give you my frith as we had before agreed." And he can give nothing higher than this. But there is the same entire sense of affection and obligation when the two arch-enemies Finn and Hengest, after a desperate fight, enter into a firm alliance in frith—even though the will gives way soon after.

But the sense of the words is not exhausted yet. They denote not only the honest, resolute will to find loyalty; implicit trust forms the core, but about it lies a wealth of tones of feeling, joy, delight, affection, and love. A great part of the passages quoted above, if not all, are only half-understood unless that tone is suffered to sound as well. In the Anglo-Saxon, *sib* (or peace) ranges from the meaning of relief, comfort—as in the saying: *sib* comes after sorrow—to love. When the Northmen speak of woman's frith or love, the word glows with passion.

We need not doubt but that the feeling of frith included love, and that kinsmen loved one another deeply and sincerely. It is love between one and another that has drawn the little Old Scandinavian word *sváss* (Anglo-Saxon *svæs*) away from its original meaning. It probably means, primarily, approximately "one's own, closely related," but in Anglo-Saxon poetry it shows a tendency to attach itself to designations for kinsmen. At the same time its content has become more and more intense—intimate, dear, beloved, joyous. In the Scandinavian, it has concentrated entirely about this sense and is there, moreover, a very strong word for expressing dearness. From all we can see, the relation between brothers—and also between brothers and sisters—was one of close intimacy among the Germanic people, as it was generally with all peoples of related culture. The brotherly and sisterly relationship has a power unlike any other to intensify will, thoughts, and feelings. The kinship has possessed both depth and richness.

Besides love, there is in frith a strong note of joy. The Anglo-Saxon word *liss* has a characteristic synthesis of tenderness and firmness that is due to its application to the feelings of kinship. It denotes the gentleness and consideration that friends feel for one another, and it indicates the king's favor toward his retainers. In the mouths of Christian poets, it lends itself readily to express God's grace. But then *liss* is also joy, delight, and happiness: just that pleasure one feels in one's home, among one's faithful friends. These two notes—which were of course really one—rang through the words of *Beowulf*: "All my *liss* is in thee, but few friends have I without thee." Thus he greets his uncle Hygelac, as if to explain the offering of his trophies to his kinsman: "All frith is ruined by the fall of fearless Tryggvason." These simple words disclose the boundless grief which Hallfreðr felt at the death of his beloved king.

Gladness was a characteristic feature in a man, nothing less than the mark of freedom. "Glad-man"—a man of happy mind—a man must be called, if the judgment were to be altogether laudatory. The verse in *Hávamál*, "Glad shall a man be at home, generous to the guest, and gentle," indicates what is expected of a man, and this agrees with the spirit of the following verse from *Beowulf*: "Be glad toward the Geats, and forget not gifts for them," as the queen adjures the king of the Geats. In fact, just as bold or well-armed are standing epithets of the man, "glad" must be added to indicate that nothing is wanted in his full humanity. So when *Beowulf* tells us that Freawaru "was betrothed to Froda's glad son," the poet does not intend to explain the disposition of the prince, but simply describe him as the perfect knight.

Gladness was an essential feature in humanity, and thus a quality of frith. The connection between joy and friendly feeling is so intimate that the two cannot be found apart. All joy is bound up with frith; outside it, there is not and cannot be anything answering to that name. When the poet of Genesis lets the rebellious angels fall away from joy and frith and gladness, he gives, in this combination of words, not a parallel reckoning up of the two or three most important values lost to them by their revolt, but the expression in a formula of life itself seen from its two sides.

Our forefathers were very sociable in their gladness. Intercourse and well-being were synonymous with them. When they sit about the board, or around the hearth—whatever it may be—they grow boisterous and quick to laughter, and they feel pleasure. Pleasure, of course, is a word of wide scope of meaning in their mode of speech, extending far beyond the pleasures of the table and of conversation; pleasure is properly society. In other words, it is the feeling of community that forms the basis of their happiness. *Mandream*, delight in man's society, is the Anglo-Saxon expression for life and existence, and to go hence is called to "give up joy," the joy in mankind, joy of life, and joy of the hall. It is to forsake delight in kinsmen, in honor, in the earth, in one's inheritance, and in the joyful site of home.

Now we are in a position to understand that gladness or joy is not a pleasure derived from social intercourse; it draws its exhilarating strength from being identical with frith. The contents of joy are a family privilege, an heirloom. The Anglo-Saxon word *feasceaft* means literally "he who has no part or lot with others," or "the outlaw who has no kin," but the word implies the meaning of "unhappy" or "joyless," but not, as we might believe, because one so driven out must come to lead a miserable existence; rather, because he turned his back upon gladness when he went away. "Gladness" must be taken in an individualizing sense, as of a sum of gladness pertaining to the house, and which the man must leave behind him in the house when he goes out into the void. There is no joy lying about loose in the wilds. He who is cast out from gladness of his own and those about him has lost all possibility of feeling the well-being of fullness in himself. He is empty.

Kinship is an indispensable condition to the living of life as a human being. It is this which makes the suffering occasioned by any breach in a man's frith so terrible and without parallel in all experience, so intolerable and brutal, devoid of all lofty ideal elements. To us, a conflict such as that which arises in Gudrun when she sees her "speech-friend" slain, and her brothers as the slayers, might seem to present the highest degree of bitterness: a thing to rend the soul asunder. But the Germanic mind knew that which was worse than tearing asunder, which is to say, dissolution. A breach of frith gives rise to a suffering beneath all passion; it is kinship itself—a man's very humanity—which is stifled, and from that place follows the dying out of all human qualities. What the wretch suffers and what he enjoys can no longer produce any real feeling in him. His very power of joy is dead. The power of action is killed. Energy is replaced by that state which the Northmen feared most of all, and most of all despised: *redelessness*.[17]

"Bootless struggle, an overarching sin, falling like darkness over Hrethel's soul" says *Beowulf* about the fratricide; in these words is summed up the helpless, powerless fear that follows on the breaking of frith.

This places a new task before us. Joy is a thing essential to humanity. It is inseparably attached to frith; it is a sum and an inheritance. But this joy, then, contained something in itself.

In *Beowulf*, the hero's return from strife and toil is sung as follows: "Thence he sought his way to his dear home, loved by his people, home to the fair frith-hall, where he had his battle-fellows, his castle, his treasures." What did these lines mean to the original listeners? What feelings did the words "dear," "loved," and "fair" call forth in them? What we have seen up to now teaches us approximately but the strength of these words—and what we are *not* to understand thereby.

What were the ideas attached to this joy?

The answer is contained in the old word "honor."

---

[17] Or the inability to find the way.

II. HONOR

Frith and honor: these are the sum of life, the essence of what a man needs to live fully and happily.

"Be fruitful and multiply, and replenish the earth," says God in Genesis to Noah on his leaving the Ark. The Anglo-Saxon poet of Genesis gives it as follows: "Be fruitful and increase; live in honor and in frith with pleasure."

Once upon a time, there lived in Iceland, in Ísafjörður, an old man by the name of Havard. He had been a bold man in his day, but he was not rich and did not have great influence. His only son, Olaf, was envied for his prowess and popularity by the local chieftain residing at Laugabol, the powerful and intractable Thorbjorn. Thorbjorn sought to be more than the first man of note in that place: he would be the *only* man of note, and he killed Olaf to attain that end. When the news was brought to Havard, he sank down with a deep groan and kept in his bed a whole year.

Indeed, there was no one who really believed that a solitary old man would be able to exact reparation from the domineering men of Laugabol. Havard's grave wife kept the homestead going by fishing with the manservant by day and doing the rest of her work by night. At the end of the year, she persuaded the old man to pull himself together and set off to demand payment of a fine. He was met with great scorn. His demand was not even refused; he was told to look outside the enclosure, where he would find a creature just as old and lame and halt as himself: an old horse. The horse had lain kicking for a long while past, but now, after some scrapings, might perhaps manage to get on its legs again. Havard was told he was welcome to keep this poor beast if he wanted consolation for the death of his son.

Havard staggers home and goes to bed for another year.

Once again. he humors his wife and makes the attempt; he is loath to go, but says, "If I knew there should be vengeance for my son Olaf, I would never care how dearly I might have to buy it." So he rides to the law-*thing*.

Thorbjorn, when he first sees the old man enter the booth, cannot at once recollect why Havard might have come there.

"This," says Havard, "the slaying of my son Olaf is ever in my mind as if it were but newly done. Therefore, it is my errand now to crave payment from you." He gains nothing for his pains but new bloody scorn. So downcast is he now as he leaves the booth that he scarcely notices when two men with some standing pass him a kindly word. And his third year in bed is rendered heavier to bear because of his aching joints. His wife Bjargny still manages the work of the place, and finds time between tasks to persuade her kinsfolk to render aid, and to gain knowledge of Thorbjorn's journeys and the way he goes.

Then one day she comes to his bedside again, when the third summer had come: "Now you have slept long enough! Tonight, your son Olaf is to be avenged. If you wait any longer, it will be too late." This was something different from the comfortless task of riding out to ask for reparation. Havard sprang from his bed, secured his revenge before daybreak, and came the next morning to Steinthor Thorlaksson of Eyri to report his killing of four men. He reminded Steinthor of his words at the last law-*thing*: "For methinks you said then, that if I should need a trifle of help, I might as well come to you as to other chieftains."

"Help you shall have," answered Steinthor, "but I should like to know what you would reckon a great help, if this you now crave is but a trifle."

And thereupon Havard seated himself squarely and at ease in the second high seat at Eyri, where he laughed at the future with its troubles, and jested with all he met, "for now there was an end to all fretting and misery."

Havard had suffered a shame and a loss of honor. It shakes him in every limb. The evil grips him, aged man as he is, so that he sinks down in palsy. And there he lies, while a single thought gnaws so insistently at his mind that he thinks he has not slept all those three years. At the law-*thing* he walks, as an onlooker describes him, "a man unlike others, large of growth and something stricken in years; he drags himself along, and yet he looks manly enough. He seems filled with sorrow and unrest."

But when at last reparation comes, honor flows once more through his veins, honor newly born and giving new birth again. His limbs are straightened and his lungs are filled. With a sigh of awakening, Havard feels life once more pour through and from him. His strength wells up. His mind grows young, so young that it must learn anew the meaning of danger and of difficulty. It is filled with restive joy of life: the true rejoicing in life that cares nothing for death.

Paulus Diaconus tells of an aged Lombard,[18] Sigvalde, who, like Havard, was sorely tried, and also like Havard, reaped joy in many folds for his sorrow. He had lost two sons in battle against the invading Slavs. In two battles he avenged them with great eagerness, and when a third battle was about to take place, he insisted on going out to fight, in spite of all protestations: "for," he declared, "I have now gained full restitution for my sons. Now I can meet death gladly if need be." And so, he went to his death out of sheer abundance of vitality.

Honor at once brings up the thought of vengeance. It must be so that he who thinks of honor must say vengeance, not only because the two are always found together in the stories, but more because it is only through vengeance that we can see the depth and breadth of honor. Vengeance contains the illumination and the explanation of life; life as it is seen in the avenger is life at its truest and most beautiful—life in its innermost nature.

Life is known by its ecstasy. There is a sort of delight in which men go beyond themselves and forget themselves, to sink down into the infinite and the timeless. But then, too, there is an ecstasy wherein men go beyond themselves without losing their foothold in time, a delight in which they live through the highest and deepest—*their* highest and deepest—as in a feeling of power, so that they stand a while in enjoyment of the growth of their strength, and then storm on, stronger and bolder.

It is by this life-filled delight that life must be known. In it, culture reveals its essence and its value. In order to attain to a just estimate of a strange age, we must ourselves participate in its ecstasy. Living through that one moment gives more than many years' experience, because a culture's whole complement of thought and feeling lies close-packed there in its highest power. In this great moment of experience, the refracted rays of daily life must be made clear. The joy of life, its sorrow, its beauty, its truth, and its right reveal to us here their innermost being. What is the substance of a people's joy and of its sorrow? The answer to this question forces us far into the culture of that people. But it is equally important to measure the degree of strength in joy. What is the measure of height for these people: jubilation, delight, refreshment of the soul, shouts of laughter, smiles, or what? And what is sorrow to them? A thing they can enjoy, if only in the ennobling form of poetry, or a pestilence, a thing terrible and despicable in itself?

In the days when Christianity constituted a culture, a spiritual atmosphere, and as life-giving and necessary to life, we feel what Christianity was by trying to sympathize with the experience of a father when he praises God, because his children have been found worthy to suffer for the sake of Jesus' name. The Jew reveals himself in the moment he places a newborn son on his knee, and by his

---

[18] Paul the Deacon, a Benedictine monk who authored historical works on the Lombards.

blessing consecrates him to be the upholder of his race. Hellas must be experienced through the aged Diagoras, as he sits on the shoulders of his sons after their victory at the games, surrounded by a jubilant throng, and "accounted happy in his children." The Germanic ecstasy is reached in the moment of vengeance.

Havard and Sigvalde tread holy ground. However far we may be from understanding their motives and reasoning, their presence inspires us with awe. It is not their manhood, their violence, their humor, or their quickness of wit that arouses our interest; we feel dimly that vengeance is the supreme expression of their humanity, and we are urged on by the need to convert our veneration into a sympathetic understanding of the ideals guiding their acts.

Vengeance makes them great, because it develops every possibility in them, not merely a few bloodthirsty attributes. It strains their power of achievement, almost beyond its reach, and makes them feel stronger and bolder. But it teaches them, also, to wait and bear in mind, and to calculate. Year after year a man can wait and watch, arranging all his plans and actions so as to grasp the most fleeting opportunity of satisfying his honor; ay, even to his daily work about the homestead, looking to his hay and his cattle, it is so disposed that he can watch the roads and see at any moment if the wanted man should ride that way.

Vengeance teaches him to reckon time and space as trifles. One may come through time by remembering, and one can be driven over sea and land, when one has an object in view. A boy of six, seeing his father slain before his eyes, can at once find the right word: "Not weep, but remember the better."

Vengeance raises him up and transfigures him. It does not merely raise him, but holds him suspended and thrusts him into a higher plane. And this can happen because the desire of redress is not only the loftiest of all sentiments, but also the most ordinary and most generally human. Whatever differences there might be between human beings otherwise, there is one point they meet: they should and cannot help but seek restitution when wronged.

What, then, was vengeance?

It was *not* the outcome of a sense of justice. There are peoples who see in justice the vital principle of existence, whereby the world is held together and kept going. For them, there is a kind of direct relationship between the behavior of human beings and the motion of the planets, so that a crime unpunished hangs brooding like a peril over mankind. In order to avoid famine, defeat, or disturbances of the order of the world generally, one must, in case of need, execute the sons for the crimes of their fathers, and *vice versa*. The Germanic people are not of this sort. Justice demands an altogether different type of conscience from that with which our forefathers were equipped.

Neither did these barbarians understand the symmetrical morality which restores the balance by striking out an eye for an eye. The Germanic mind had as little conception of the word "retaliation" as of the word "punishment."

If the thirst for vengeance is understood as meaning the wish to see one's desire upon one's enemies, then the word does not accord with the Germanic idea. Vengeance was planned with every care, and carried out in the most cold-blooded fashion, one is tempted to say with a businesslike *sangfroid*. The avenger plants his axe in his opponent's head, wipes off the blood in the grass, covers the body according to custom, and rides on his way. He has no lust for further deal-ings with the fallen man; mutilation of the dead is, in the history of the Northmen, a thing so unique as to mark the doer of such a deed as an exception—that is to say, as an inferior man. Ugly memories can, on rare occasions, lead a man to forget himself. Havard dealt Thorbjorn a further wound across the face after he had given him his death blow, because Thorbjorn had once struck him in the face with a pouch in which Olaf Havardson's teeth had been kept since the day they were loosened by the blow that killed him. But Havard's deed at once calls forth the question from his companion: "Why do you deal so by a dead man?" Even if the man were not dead, it was considered unmanly to strike him once he lay mortally wounded. The act would be that of a nithing.

There is little of exultation over the fallen, and even when it occurs, it is plainly only a casual attendant circumstance, not the main point in the feeling of satisfaction. Behind the outward calmness of vengeance, the mind is in a turmoil of rejoicing and pride. The accomplishment of the deed serves better than any-thing else to call forth enthusiastic words in praise of the act, in praise of him who wrought it, of him for whose sake it was done, and of the race to which both parties belonged. But these outbursts come from the depths; they are the outcome of life's ecstasy.

For the punisher, as for the man of vindictive nature, all thoughts circle about that other one, what is to be done with him, whether he can be properly and feel-ingly struck. The avenger has the center of his thoughts in himself. All depends on what he does, not on what the other suffers. The avenger procures something: he *takes* vengeance.

Two things are requisite for right vengeance: that the offender should fall by stroke of a weapon, and that the weapon should be wielded by the one offended. If the slayer, before the matter could be settled, perished in some other manner—either died a natural death, or was killed by accident—then the offended parties had nonetheless their vengeance due to them. They must then look to the of-fender's kin, just as in case of his escaping alive out of their hands (e.g., by choosing that season to travel and see the world, and learn good customs of the kings in other lands). Nor would the injured family regard it as any restitution that the offender should fall by the hand of a third party unconcerned in the affair; their vengeance was yet to come, for they had not yet "gotten honor over their kinsman."

But then also, the other party must necessarily have an honor, if the injury was to be wiped out. The most unfortunate death a man could die was to be killed by slaves, and more particularly when these slaves were acting on their own behalf, without any man of distinction as instigator, for there was no vengeance to be gained from bondmen. One of the earliest settlers in Iceland, Hjorleif, was set upon and slain by his slaves. When his foster brother Ingolf found the body later, he cried out in distress: "This was a wretched fate for a brave man, that thralls should be his bane." Havard, when taking vengeance for the killing of his son, suffered the slaves to go free; the deed would not be "more avenged" by his taking their worthless lives as well. Almost as wretched as death by the hand of slaves was his lot who died by the hand of a vagabond: a man having no companions in honor, and no foster brother or comrades-in-arms in the world. Not only was there the risk of vengeance being lost, since it vested in a single individual, but the honor to be gained from taking vengeance against such a man was in itself but slight.

Even among true kinsmen, however, there might be degrees of value in revenge. If the family felt the injury very deeply, either because the member slain was one of their best men, or because his kinsmen generally set a high price upon their honor, then they might prefer to aim immediately at a better man among the offender's kin. This tendency to take vengeance on a kinsman of the offender who was counted "worthier" as an object of revenge dies late in the North.

In the introduction to the Norwegian law book of the Frostathing,[19] we find "Haakon the King, son of King Haakon, son's son of King Sverri" still mournfully bewailing "the ill mis-custom, which long hath been in the land, that where a man hath been put to death, his kinsmen will take such of the slayer's kin as is counted best, even though the killing were done without his knowledge, will, or nearness to the deed, and will not take vengeance upon the slayer, even though it might be easily come by," whence evil men flourish, and the good have no reward of their peaceable life, "and we see ourselves robbed of our best subjects in the land," sighs this father of his country.

The bitterness of tone is in itself a token that comfort is yet far off. True, the peasant freeholders would gladly live in safety in the country, and if the king could help them to such peace, then an edict or so were welcome enough. But sure as it was that peace might be furthered by refraining from killing of men, it was no less sure that man could not live by not being killed. And when a man now suffered need, what could the king do for him? The surplus of healing for a wounded honor that the king's good subjects gained for themselves in ancient ways was not to be replaced by anything the king had to offer in new ways of law. And as long as honor stood as a fundamental factor in the moral self-

---

[19] An early Norwegian court and one of the major *things* in medieval Norway.

estimation of the people—stood, indeed, as the very aim of justice—there could be no lopping an end off by a sharp rescript. Prohibitions and law reforms from above are at best only the precursors, heralds of a change of mind that takes centuries to take effect. As long as "law" and "right" had not found one another in a new unity, so long would the "abuse" among the people—their misunderstanding of their own good—be stronger than both kingly power and prudence.

"No man in all the land had such brave vengeance taken for him as this one; for no other man were so many taken in payment." This was, and continued to be, the best proof that the fallen man had been among the greatest of his time. Vengeance, then, consists in taking something from the other party. One procures honor from him. One will have one's honor back.

An inflicted injury occasions a loss to the sufferer. He has been bereft of some part of his honor. And this honor is something he cannot do without in case of need—not a thing he requires only for luxury, and which the frugal mind can manage without. He cannot even console himself with the part that remains, for the injury he has suffered may be likened to a wound which will never close itself up, but bleed unceasingly until his life runs out. If he cannot fill the empty space, he will never be himself again. The emptiness may be called shame; it is a suffering, a painful state of sickness.

Njál, peaceable, peace-making Njál, has not many words about the matter, but the human feelings are as unspoiled in him as in the valiant warrior Egil. He looked at his aged body and said, "I cannot avenge my sons, and in shame I will not live," and thereupon laid himself down on his bed in the midst of the flames. In a character such as Kveldulf, the suffering displayed itself in violent convulsions. His son Thorolf had fallen in something approaching open feud with no less a man than King Harald himself; it seemed hopeless for a simple yeoman to crave honorable amends from the mighty king of Norway. He himself was old and past his time, but the hunger for honor turned into a stimulant in his body, calling up the last remains of strength to strike down a man or so "whom Harald will count it ill to lose." Different as the two men are by nature—representing, one might say, the two opposite poles of Icelandic culture—they yet think and feel alike, and act on the same principle: that honor is a thing indispensable, and vengeance inevitable. As long as men still lived the old life, irrespective of whether the outward forms were pagan or Christian, a man could not, under any circumstances, let his vengeance lie; there was no ignoring the claims of honor, for this was a thing that came from within, manifesting itself as a painful sense of fear.

There was once an Icelander who did a great thing, all but superhuman. After the general battle at the law-*thing* in the year 1012 when the prospects of reconciliation were dark, and everything pointed to a fatal breaking up of the free state itself, the great chieftain Hall of Sida stood up and said:

All men know what sorrow has stricken me in that my son Ljot is fallen. One or another of you may perhaps think that he would be among the dearest of those fallen here [i.e., one of those whose death would cost most in reparation]. But this I will do, that men may be agreed again; I will let my son lie unavenged, and yet give my enemies full peace and accord. Therefore I ask of you, Snorri Godi,[20] and with you the best of those here, that you bring about peace between us.

Thereupon Hall sat down. And as his words rose, a loud murmur of approval, all greatly praising his goodwill:

> And of this, that Hall was willing to leave his son unavenged, and did so much to bring about peace, it is now to be said that all those present at the law-*thing* laid money together for payment to him. And the count of it all together was not less than eight hundred in silver; but that was four times the fine for killing of one man.

But blood need not be shed to endanger life. Honor might ooze out as fatally from the wound made by a blow from a stick, or by a sharp word, or even by a scornful neglect. And the medicine is in all cases the same.

When a man sits talking among others, and emphasizes his words with a stick in such fashion that he chances to strike his neighbor's nose, the neighbor ought perhaps to take into consideration the fact that the striker was short-sighted, and had talked himself into a state of excitement. Nor can it be called quite good manners to jump up on the instant and endeavor to drive one's axe into the nose of the other, but should the eager and short-sighted speaker chance to be found dead in his bed a few months after, it would be understood that someone had been there "to avenge that blow from a stick." No one would on principle deny the name of vengeance to the deed. And if the man so struck were a man of honor, no outsider would deny his right to act as he had done; on the contrary, they would immediately realize that the blow to his nose might prove as fatal to him as the loss of an arm or a leg. Unless honor was taken for the injury, the little sore would, so to speak, lead to blood poisoning.

It happened thus with the Icelander Thorleif Kimbi. While voyaging abroad on a Norwegian ship, he had the misfortune to act in a somewhat hotheaded fashion toward his countryman Arnbjorn, while they were preparing a meal. Arnbjorn started up and dealt Thorleif a blow on the neck with his hot spoon. Thorleif swallowed the insult: "Nay, the Norsemen shall not make game of us two

---

[20] A notable Western Icelandic chieftain mentioned in many sagas, such as *The Saga of the People of Eyri*, *Njal's saga*, and the *Laxdoela saga*.

Icelanders, and haul us apart like a couple of curs, but I will remember this when we meet in Iceland." Thorleif's memory, however, seems to have been weak.

When one day he sets out to ask the hand of a girl in marriage, her brother answers him as follows: "I will tell you my mind: before I give you my sister in marriage, you must find healing for those gruel scars on your neck that you got three years ago in Norway." And that blow of a spoon and the refusal based on the scars brought two whole districts into feud, and led to deep and lasting dissension between the families concerned. From the point of view of the age, there is nothing disproportionate in the cause and its effects.

If a man were called thief or coward when he was not, or beardless—which perhaps the fact forbade him to deny—he would in any case have to win full and complete indemnity for the assertion, if he wished to retain his dignity.

Njál had the disability that no hair grew on his face. Gunnar Hámundarson's wife, Hallgerd, saw it and was not silent about the matter:

> So wise a man who knows a way for everything that he should not have hit upon the plan of carting manure where it was most needed; he shall be called the beardless old man, and his sons be named Muckbeards. And you, Sigmund, you ought to put that into verse. Come, let us have some gain of your art.

Sigmund does all in his power to win fair Hallgerd's admiration and her applause: "You are a pearl, to pleasure me so." The insults have power, not only over the young, hot-blooded sons, but equally so over Njál himself.

The verses come to Bergthora's ears. And when they were sitting at meet, she said, "You have been honored with gifts—you, father, and your sons. There will be little fame for you if you give nothing in return."

"What gifts are these?" asked Skarphedin.[21]

"You, boys, have one gift to share between you: you have been called Muckbeards, and the master here is called the beardless old man."

"We are not womanly-minded, to be angered at everything," said Skarphedin.

"Then Gunnar was angered on your behalf, and if you do not seek your right here, you will never avenge any shame."

"The old woman takes pleasure, it seems, in baiting us," said Skarphedin, and smiled. But the sweat stood out on his forehead, and red spots showed in his cheeks, and this was an unusual thing. Grim was silent, and bit his lip, and Helgi

---

[21] Skarphedin Njalsson, a renowned warrior in *Njal's saga*.

showed no sign. Hoskuld followed Bergthora when she went out.[22] She came in again, foaming with rage.

Njál says, "There, there, wife, it can be managed well enough, even though one takes one's time. And it is thus with many matters, however trying they may be, that even though vengeance be taken, it is not sure that all mouths can be made to say alike."

But in the evening, Njál heard an axe rattle against the wall. "Who has taken down our shields?"

"Your sons went out with them," said Bergtora.

Njál thrust his feet into a pair of shoes, and went out around the house. There he saw them on their way up over the slope.

"Where did they go?"

"After sheep," answered Skarphedin.

"You need no weapons for them; it would seem you were going on some other errand."

"Then we will fish for salmon, father, if we do not come across the sheep."

"If that is so, it is to be hoped that you do not miss your catch."

When he came in to bed, he said to Bergthora, "All your sons have gone out armed. It would seem that your sharp words have given them something to go out for."

"I will give them my best thanks if they come and tell me of Sigmund's fall."

They come home with the good news and tell Njál. And he answers, "Well done!"

For everything there is but one form of vengeance: vengeance in blood. If it were only a question of retribution or self-assertion, payment could no doubt be made in the same coin. When men have such faith in the power of scornful words over honor,[23] one might think they would also regard their own taunts as of some effect. But to give ill words for ill words did not win honor back; the sting of the other's words remained, and one might lose one's revenge. A man would hardly dare to take his enemy prisoner and put him to scorn, instead of putting him to death at once. There was the fear of bringing degradation on oneself instead of restitution, and thus it was reckoned unmanly to humiliate an enemy instead of killing him. Vengeance was too costly a matter to jest with.

Honor was a thing that forced men to take vengeance, not merely something that enabled them to do so. The guilds lived, like the old circles of kinsmen, in frith and honor, and in their statutes the principles underlying ancient society are reduced to paragraphs. A man is thrust out of the guild and pronounced a nithing

---

[22] Hoskuld Dala-Kollsson, an early Icelandic chieftain and a main character in the *Laxdoela* saga. He is also the father of Olaf the Peacock.

[23] A similar belief can be seen in early Irish literature. Satire or clever insults directed against public figures was so effective that it was seen to be a sort of magic, and was taken very seriously.

if he breaks peace with his brother in any dispute arising between them, wherever they may meet, whether in the guild hall, in the streets of their town, or out in the world. He incurs the same sentence, if he fails to take up the cause of his brother, when he is in need of assistance in dealings with people outside the brotherhood. But no less does a brother sin, if he suffers dishonor without calling in the aid of his brethren. And if he does not thereafter avenge the wrong with the aid of his guild brethren, he is cast out from the brotherhood as a nithing.

Though frith is not directly expressed in the codes of law, it was nevertheless manifest. Its authority is so obvious that the lawyers do not become conscious of it until they begin to find themselves in opposition. Honor, on the other hand, is amply recognized in the codices of the lawmakers.

For partners in frith, vengeance is a *duty*; the law sanctions this duty as a *right*. The laws of Iceland allow for killing on the spot in return for an attack or for a blow, even though they may leave no mark on the skin. In the case of more serious blows and wounds, and of insults of a graver character, the offender may be freely struck down when and where he is found before the next assembly of the *Althing*.[24] Thus far, vengeance is valid.

But if a man goes home with the little insult still upon him, or lets autumn, winter, or spring go by without settling accounts for the greater offense, then he has forfeited his right to settle by his own hand, and can only bring suit against his opponent in law. Thus runs a law divided against itself. The line of development tends toward a restriction of the right to vengeance, but so long as the necessity of vengeance is admitted in principle, the limits are drawn in a purely external fashion. No wonder then that these loosely-built barriers prove too weak to hold back the pursuer.

In the laws of Norway, the process of restriction is carried a step further. Vengeance is for the most part only recognized in cases of the very gravest injury. Authority must necessarily sanction the vengeance taken by a man for the killing of his kinsman or the dishonoring of his womenfolk; to include such vengeance under the head of crime, though it were of the mildest order, was out of the question even in the early Middle Ages. But here also, the laws of the Norwegian kings would seek to draw the limit for personal action. There is some hesitation, perhaps, in regard to abuse of the very worst kind. Can one deny a man's right to answer with the axe when addressed in such words as: "You old woman, you bitch, a jade like you, a slave that you are!"? But a wound or a blow, a nudge, a jeer: a man should be able to carry those to court.

Nevertheless, a stronger substratum shows clearly through. Haakon Haakonson, in his great novel from the middle of the thirteenth century which serves

---

[24] The supreme parliament of Iceland, founded in 930. It is one of the longest-running parliamentary bodies in the world.

as an introduction to the Frostathing's Law, cannot say otherwise than that vengeance for wounds and genuine insults must stand valid, when it is taken before the opposite party has offered to pay a fine. The vague arbitrariness of the addition: "save where the king and other men of judgment deem otherwise" is characteristic of all helpless reformatory movement from above; it is giving the old regime one's blessing, and tacking on an empty phrase to stand in the name of reform. And if the offender, trusting to his wealth and power, or to influential kinsmen, repeated his insolence, then the offended party had the right to choose whether he would accept settlement or not.

Half-humorous is an improvement that at one time seems to have been regarded with great hopes: that a man taking vengeance shall be held guilty of no crime as long as his vengeance does not exceed in magnitude the wrong for which it is taken. Any surplus is to be duly assessed at its proper value on settlement and indemnity paid accordingly: a well-intentioned idea, if only it were possible to agree as to what punishment fitted the crime, and what the surplus, if any, might be worth. The thought looks better in the form of a gentle exhortation, as put forward to guide the conscience of the king's retainers: "Do not take vengeance too suddenly, and let not the vengeance taken be disproportionate." Thus run the words in King Magnus VI of Norway's court's law of 1274.

All these interferences bear the stamp of weakness and lukewarmness. The improvements themselves show us how clearly and simply the old regime is imprinted on the mind: that injury, whether of this sort or that, demands its cure, and that the cure is certainly to be found in vengeance. True, new ideas are beginning to germinate, but for the present, the reformers have nothing wherewith to lay a new foundation, and are thus obliged to build upon the old, basing their edicts against vengeance upon the fact that vengeance is a thing no man can do without.

Surely enough, a contrast may be noted between law and life. The man of law appears to have had a keen eye for shades and degrees of offense, which practical men never recognized, or recognized only while in company with the jurists. These Norsemen, good souls, sat at the law-*thing* and listened with interest when those versed in law expatiated on the distinction between a wound laying bare the bone but closing entirely on proper treatment, and the legally graver case where a piece of flesh of such and such a size was shorn away and fell to the ground. The hearers would make a mental note of how much was to be paid for the first sort, and how much for the second. Or they would be given a classification of the various terms of abuse. "Full fine shall be paid, firstly, when a man reviles another as having lain in childbed; secondly, if he declares that the other is possessed of unnatural lusts; thirdly, if he compares him with a mare, or a troll, or a harlot." Likewise, there is a full fine if he be called slave, or whore, or witch; for the rest, there are only words of abuse for which a minor fine can be claimed, or which can be avenged by saying, "you are another."

Then the assembly dispersed, and the good men went back to their homes, and took vengeance in blood as well for great injuries as for small insults, as if no such scale had ever been. Or the Icelanders, those hard-bitten champions who quarreled and fought and took their revenge in all the simplicity of honor, went to their *Althing* and heard the lawman recite the chapter on killing, in all its artificial complexity, with conditions, possibilities and circumstances endlessly tangled and woven in and out. Never a man laughed; on the contrary, all listened with the deepest interest.

This picture has a magnificent humor of its own. If we did not know better, we might be led to imagine a schism in the community. But no. In Iceland, at any rate, there is no trace of any distinction between a law-giving caste and a lawless mob. The same headstrong yeomen who fought with one another in their own districts were jurists to a degree, with a fondness and a gift for the intricacies of law. It is these peasants, indeed, who have made Icelandic law the fine-patterned web of casuistry it is. Law, in the saga isle, has its own particular stamp of almost refined systematism that we find in Iceland and nowhere else, built up by constant lawsuits and constant legislation. Something similar applies in the case of Norway. Even though there were men learned in law everywhere, in the narrower sense, to be found beside the unlearned, the distinction is only valid as a matter of actual knowledge, and does not apply to the interest displayed.

Another and more likely explanation may be advanced. Men do not remain always at the same stage; they move only with part of their soul at a time. The same individual contains a progressive self, which asserts itself triumphantly when the man appears in some public function or in co-operation with other kindred soul-halves. And an old-fashioned, conservative self takes the lead at home in daily life, and manages altogether to take advantage of any disturbance of balance in the soul—to surprise and depose its rival. The laws of Norway and of Iceland do not represent any primeval law; on the contrary, both are phenomena of progress. It is the progressive self that speaks through them. And strangely enough, while the Norsemen have a scale of values for wounds, according to whether they penetrate to a cavity (which costs one-half mark) or do not go beyond the skin (price one ounce), according as the breach heals without a scar (price one ounce) or with a scar (six ounces), the Icelanders, on the other hand, have plainly not advanced beyond the stage of calling a wound a wound. If we could follow the course of the laws back century by century, we should see how the forms became increasingly simple, see them more and more nearly approaching the simplicity of everyday thought.

This, however, does not by any means imply that the forefathers of those Norsemen and Icelanders had no idea of distinction. A valuation of the injury inflicted lies, after all, so deeply in the character of the law that it must be thought to have its roots in the attitudes of mind among the people. Even though we find, in the Icelandic law book, the *Grágás*,[25] the limit for right to vengeance set very far down, so that a simple blow is included; the mere presence of such a limit still denotes that certain injuries were counted too slight to be paid for in blood. Undoubtedly our forefathers must, at an early stage of their existence, have made the discovery that a man might sometimes do another harm on purpose, and sometimes by accident. Or they have been led to observe that certain epithets in their vocabulary were stronger than others. The difference was recognized in their everyday affairs.

The interest in shades of difference was strong and deep, and undoubtedly of ancient date; men knew and recognized well enough the possibility of a difference between small injuries and great. There is no reason to doubt but that men were from the first more inclined to come to a peaceable settlement in the case of slight wounds than in the case of wounds more serious. Whether it was possible would depend on the individual character of the case: what had led up to the injury, how it had been dealt, and not least, who the offender was. And whether he and his kin were of such standing that a peaceable settlement with them meant honor. But one thing was certain: the will to reconciliation was not based on any inclination to let the insignificant blow pass unheeded. If the culprit would not or could not make good the damaged honor, then vengeance must be taken, no less than in matters of life and death.

On this point, law was as stiff and uncompromising as any private feeling enjoining unconditional restitution. That the offender is not in a condition to pay, or that he no longer exists, does not dispose of the fact that the other party stands there in need of payment. The slightness of an offense does not diminish the necessity of its being made good. And in face of this basic principle, all attempts at progress come to a standstill. The law reformers of Norway thrust vengeance as far as possible into the background. They urge that the courts are ready for those who need them. In addition, there will now be royal officials whose task in life will be to give men the restitution they previously had to get for themselves as best they could. But they cannot refrain from adding, that if the opponent will not give way, and the will of the official is not enough, then the man who takes vengeance himself for his dishonor shall be regarded with all possible consideration; ay, if the vengeance taken does not exceed the initial offense, he shall be held not guilty:

---

[25] The Icelandic name for what is known in English as the Gray Goose Laws, a collection of laws from the Icelandic Commonwealth period (930–1262).

If payment of the fine for killing a man be not made, then the dead man's kinsmen may take vengeance, and they are to be in no way hindered by the fact that the king hath given the slayer peace and leave to be in the country.

These are the very words of King Haakon's great reform edict, which prefaces the Frostathing's Law.

In this ideal of justice, the apparent conflict between the theories of law and the practice of everyday life is accounted for. The Teutons had a strong inclination for peaceable settlement of disputes, but mediation stood outside trying to effect reconciliation by mutual agreement, without in the least prejudicing the right of frith. Later law reflects an original Teutonic sense of justice insofar as it works two separate tendencies into one system. The lawyers of the transition age tried to make mediation an integral part of the judicial proceedings and thus tend toward a legal system built up on the weighing and valuation of the offense at the same time as they worked for the abolishing of the ancient right of private revenge. By this harmonizing process, Teutonic jurisprudence was gradually led into correspondence with Roman law, but it was slow in abandoning the idea of absolute reparation as the paramount condition of right and justice.

The demand for personal restitution, indeed, is not a thing that life and society merely acknowledge; it is the very innermost secret, the sustaining power itself, in the legislation of the North. When the Gulathing's Law breaks out with this:[26] "Then it is well that vengeance be taken," or when it says, "None can demand payment for injury more than three times without taking vengeance between them," then it is not defiance of law, mischievously putting on the legal wig and uttering cynicisms with comic seriousness. These sentences are nothing but the direct expression of that law-craving energy which has built up and maintained the entire network of ordinances from which they emerge.

The spirit of the law may be characterized as a juridical sympathy with the offended party and his sufferings. The law-*thing* is the place where he comes to seek healing. In other words, any attack is regarded from the point of view of personal wrong. It matters not whether a man comes bearing the body of his slain kinsman, or leading in a thief caught in the act and bound, or with the odium of a scornful word to be wiped out, the cry is the same: "Give me restitution; give me back my honor."

A deed can never be a crime in itself; it only becomes a crime—if we will use the word—by its effect upon a person. If it falls upon a man sound and whole, it is equivalent to damage done, and he must have it made good. The fine society takes upon itself to procure for him, if he appeals to it, is, according to ancient terminology, his "right"—which means, approximately, his value. And if there

---

[26] One of Norway's first *things*, or legislative assemblies.

is "no right in him [i.e., if he is a man without honor]," then there can be no crime.

The law-maintaining energy that goes out to the complainant from the seat of justice is by no means less compared to elsewhere where the judge sits to punish and protect. On the contrary, it is the stronger, inasmuch as it is inspired by the fundamental idea that restitution must and shall be made, since the well-being of the complainant stands in jeopardy. He is marked a fallen man if we cannot procure him "honor." If the culprit is out of reach, his kinsmen must come forward. It is not a question of finding any offender, but of finding someone to make restitution.

Among the southern tribes of Teutonic stock, the right to vengeance is everywhere on the decline during historical times. The extreme standpoint is represented by the Burgundians' law, which decrees capital punishment for killing, and thus aims at abolishing altogether the taking of the law into one's own hands. But the good Burgundians were not yet farther on the road to perfection than that the lawgiver finds it necessary in the same breath to point out that no other than the guilty person is to be prosecuted. The remaining peoples had evidently not advanced beyond the stage of restrictions when they began to write down their ordinances. Unfortunately, owing to the casual nature of the laws, we are only able to follow the movement by occasional glimpses here and there.

The law of the Alemanni seems inclined to distinguish between satisfaction of the impulse to revenge arising at the moment, and vengeance planned and carried out in cold blood. A man who, with such helpers as may be at hand, sets off immediately in pursuit of a slayer and strikes him down in his own house is fined the simple price of a man's life. However, if he procures assistance first, the fine is raised to nine times that sum.

Among the Franks, it is the Carolingians who first set about reforms in earnest. In the earlier periods, vengeance is still fully recognized at any rate for more serious injuries. The Salic Law mentions punishment for anyone independently taking down the severed head on a pole set up by an avenger to advertise his deed. We happen to learn of a good man, Gundhartus, who was obliged to remain at home by reason of his threatening vengeance. In his need, he has applied to Eginhard, who now (presumably about the year 830) writes a feeling letter to Hraban, urging this servant of Christ to release the man from his military service, as his coming to the army would infallibly throw him into the power of his enemies. The kings' attempts at reform amount, for the most part, to earnest and cordial exhortations to the parties concerned in order to compel people to be reconciled and give up taking vengeance.

Most instructive are the limitations to which vengeance is subjected in the law of the Saxons. In the first place, it is banned in every case where damage has been done by a domestic animal, or by an implement slipping from the hand of

the person using it; the owner shall pay a fine, but shall be secure against vengeance. Furthermore, a man innocent himself is not to be held responsible for acts
of his people. If the deed is of his secret devising, then of course, he must be
fined or suffer vengeance, but if the person actually guilty has acted on his own
initiative, it is permissible to disown him, and let him, with seven of his nearest
kinsmen, bear the blame—to serve as the objects of vengeance, that is. Finally,
in the case of murder, the family is, in its wider sense, entitled to purchase immunity from vengeance by payment of the third part of the simple fine for killing.
The entire remainder of the enormous indemnity (nine times the fine simple) falls
upon the murderer and his sons, and they alone are open to vengeance if payment
is not made.

In the brief Frisian law, we find the following: He who incites another to
homicide—here again the relation of master and servant is probably in mind—
can only escape vengeance if the offender has fled; he then pays a third part of
the fine. If the slayer remains in the country, then it must be left to the judgment
of the offended parties whether they will relinquish their vengeance on the instigator and accept a settlement. And where a man can swear himself free of all
participation in his servant's act, he also escapes vengeance, but he must pay the
fine all the same.

The Lombard legislators are greatly occupied with the question of vengeance, and are much concerned about the problem of how to force it back within
somewhat narrower bounds. The decrees accordingly provide an interesting picture of the position of vengeance—in law proper, and where the injured parties
take the law into their own hands; in cases of accidental homicide, mishaps in
the course of work where several are together, etc. As is also in cases of damage
caused by cattle or other animals not under control, vengeance is barred. According to the edict of Rothari, personal vengeance must not be taken for an insult or
a blow: a fine must here suffice. In return, the king puts up the price:

> For which reason we have for every kind of wound and blow set payment
> higher than our forefathers knew, to the end that the fine may thrust aside
> vengeance, and all suits be made amenable to complete reconciliation.

There is a passage in King Liutprand's edict which gives us an accidental glimpse
into the life of the Lombards: it shows how vengeance once let loose is flung
backward and forward between the parties. The king has recently learned of a
distressing episode: a man had taken and hidden the clothes of a woman bathing.
Liutprand hastens to decree a very heavy fine for such misdemeanor; the culprit
in such a case should be rightly fined in a sum equal to that paid for a killing.
Liutprand explains:

If the woman's father, brother, husband, or other kinsman were to come by, then there would have been a fight. Is it not better then that the sinner should pay the price of a man's life and live, than that vengeance should arise over his body between the families, and greater fines thence arise?

The Lombard lawgivers appeal, for the rest, to the good sense of their subjects. It is a question of smuggling a higher standard of morality into the old-fashioned minds, and gradually expelling vengeance from the sphere of what is legal and fitting. The Lombard maids appear to have grown beyond the good old custom of remaining virtuously content with the husband chosen for them by their family. There are constant instances of a betrothed maiden running off with her chosen swain, and the elopement naturally gives rise to regular vengeance and feud. Liutprand now tries whether the prospect of losing all her dowry might not induce a maiden to respect her betrothal. She is to lose her lot, and go naked and empty-handed from her home. He sternly forbids father or brother to give way to leniency here "that strife may cease, and vengeance be done away with."

Among the peoples to the north, the Danes—and the Anglo-Saxons—stand more or less worthily beside the Burgundians. Nominally, all vengeance is disowned. But the lawgivers cannot make their own language conform to the new ideas. When they endeavor to give reasons for the inability of women and churchmen to take or pay fines, the matter falls of itself into the old words: "for they take vengeance upon no man, and no man upon them." Or an expression such as this slips in: "If the person wounded choose not to declare the deed, but to take vengeance. . . ." In the edict of Valdemar II regarding homicide, there is also the most remarkable contrast between subject and language.

The purpose of the edict is to free kinsmen from liability to pay a share of the fine: "While the slayer is in the country, no vengeance shall be taken upon any other man." If he takes to flight—when the injured parties, of course, stand empty-handed—then his kinsmen shall offer payment. If they do not, and one of them should be killed by the avenger, then they have only themselves to thank for not offering to pay. Naturally, however, the avenger is not exempt from paying for his kill; he has, so to speak, to pay for his right, just as the Burgundian who commits his act of homicide when "driven by pain and anger" to retaliate on the spot. The old regime is thus nominally broken off at the root.

The Swedes were hardly as far advanced as their southern neighbors. The Swedish laws lay particular stress on the point that vengeance is only to be taken on the actual offender, not on his kin. A breach of this principle comes under the heading of "unrightful vengeance," an idea also known in Denmark. This can be seen, for instance, where Valdemar II's ordinance abolishing the ordeal by fire distinguishes between the killing of an innocent man and killing "in rightful vengeance."

In Gotland, where the progress of development was in no respect behind the times (but in many respects followed a peculiar course), they had their own fashion of avoiding vengeance. The precepts of the law of Gotland as to what is to be done in cases where "the Devil hath wrought that a man should take a man's life" are doubly interesting, emphasizing on the one hand the difficulties in the way of abolishing vengeance, and on the other, offering a solution by making use of old-fashioned means. It is laid down that the slayer shall flee with his father, son, and brother, or, if these do not exist, then with his nearest kinsmen. He shall then remain forty nights in one of the three church sanctuaries of the island. From there, they shall proceed to find themselves a dwelling place away from their home; they are free to choose an area of three villages and the surrounding forest, as far as halfway to the nearest inhabited district—provided that there is no law-*thing*, market town, nor more than one church in the district. There they remain, and for three successive years, they are to offer payment to the offended party. If the offended party accepts the fine on its first offering, no blame shall attach to the offender. If the offended party refuses the fine on its third offering, then the people are to dispose of the money, and the offender shall go free.

Vengeance is in the process of restriction everywhere. First of all, it was made conditional upon the intent to harm, then it was limited to the case of more serious injuries only, such as homicide and adultery. Finally, it is reduced to a sort of retaliation upon the culprit himself, his family being free from all liability to share the blame. These very subtractions open up perspectives to a time when the necessity of restitution threw all consideration of premeditated malice completely into the shade—for instance, when every wound had to be traced back to someone responsible, even in cases where the weapon itself had acted against the will of its owner. But the chosen palliatives suggest a time when the sufferer stood more in need of spiritual than of bodily healing, and a time when vengeance was the universal medicine.

But there is more than this in these remains of kingly and clerical efforts to suppress individual vengeance. It is openly recognized that revenge was a necessity, for which the reformers must provide some substitute. Restrictions are made solely on the condition that restitution is secured by other means, and under the supposition that in case the new and lawful way should lead to nothing, then the kinsmen are to have the right of seeking their honor rather than risk its loss. This, as we have seen, was the final note in Valdemar's edict against kinsmen's help; they have only themselves to thank for having brought down vengeance upon themselves by neglecting to offer indemnity. Even the Anglo-Saxons are forced, no less than the Lombards and the Norsemen, to leave the right to vengeance open as a last resource, when the offender will not or cannot make restitution in any other way.

In some entirely isolated instance, we may find the conception of law as existing for the purpose of punishment as a warning to evildoers and a protection for the good, such as in the preface to the Law of Jutland, in the Burgundian Law, and here and there in some royal rescript. It stands there as a lesson learned and repeated, altogether isolated, without any effect upon the laws themselves; set there, as it were, to show how incommensurable is the principle with all Germanic thought. As long as the reformers cannot demolish the fact that injury poisons a man, they are forced now and again to contradict themselves. They were too much men of their world to fancy that suffering could be abolished by abolishing the principal means of curing it.

In Denmark, the fine for homicide was divided into three parts: one falling to the dead man's heir, one to his kinsmen on the father's side, and one to those on the mother's. But even where there are no kin on the mother's side, says Erik's Law, and even though:

> [H]is descendant are slave-born, and thus not capable of inheriting, or out of the kingdom, so that it is not known where his kin are, then the kinsmen on the father's side—even though they have already taken both first and second parts—shall also take the third, for their kinsman shall not be slain without his death being paid for. If a free man, full payment shall be made.

So firmly is the ancient principle still rooted in these comparatively progressive men of law. Honor is the central thing in a man's being. Restitution is a share of honor that the offended party shall and must have for his life's sake. And it is this healing of the soul which courts of justice are to procure for the complainant.

In the law of Gotland, we find reference to a man in holy orders who has an injury to avenge, but is refused payment for it. He is to appear at the law-*thing* before all the people, and make his complaint, saying, "I am a learned man, and ordained into the service of God; I must not fight or strike a blow. I would accept payment if it were offered, but shame I am loath to bear."

We have here a picture in brief of the essence of Germanic sense of right: shame we are loath to bear.[27] And from the seat of justice comes a ringing answer to the cry, for the law is in reality something more than a recognition of the necessity of vengeance to a man's welfare. The court must take up the cause of the

---

[27] Germanic pagans operated in a shame culture. Of course, the person referenced above is a Christian, but he was probably not very far removed from his pagan ancestors in terms of his worldview. Pagans operated in a system in which bad behavior brought shame, and the cure for it was redemption (or restoration of honor) by their deeds. Christian society instead held that bad behavior caused guilt, and forgiveness was the cure. See George Fenwick Jones, "Heathen Shame Culture" and "Christian Guilt Culture" in *Honor in German Literature*, 5:10–58. University of North Carolina Press, 1959. http://www.jstor.org/stable/10.5149/9781469657608_jones.5.

injured party and throw in its weight and authority on his side, because it would place him outside the pale of society if the court disallows his claim to restitution.

Law is based upon the principle that an individual who suffers shame no longer counts among men; he cannot in the future claim the protection of the law. If a man is called craven, and fails to clear himself by challenge and victory, then he *is* craven, and devoid of right—thus runs the sentence, both in the South and in the North. It is true enough that the injury is a private matter, inasmuch as it is a private distress for which a man must himself seek healing; the community takes no initiative in respect of pursuing the offender. But no less true is it that public opinion would place the sufferer beyond the pale if he did not rehabilitate himself. And the sufferer can, in a way, transfer his distress to the community by making complaint: he makes the people participators in the shame and its consequences.

The law-*thing* must procure him restitution, as far as can be done with the means at its disposal. It must declare itself at one with the injured person, and renounce his opponent, unless reconciliation can be affected. If the people cannot do this, then the people will perhaps be infected by his feebleness. The complainant has, so to speak, power over the people and its conscience, but not in virtue of a common justice and not in virtue of a constitutional principle that says, "you must not," and demands punishment not in virtue of anything but this: "If nothing is done, I must perish, and I can drag you with me." A man who fails to avenge an insult is a nithing, and is deprived of the protection of the law.

The cry for honor comes so piercingly from the lips of kinsmen because it is forced out by fear. It was no doubt largely a matter of form, when in Friesland, one of the slain man's kin took his sword and struck three blows on the grave, calling out in presence of the whole family: "Vengeance, vengeance, vengeance!" A matter of form, too, is the ritual whereby the complainants draw their swords and utter the first cry, carry the body up to the law-*thing*, and after two more cries, sheathe their swords again. But the forms are not more violent than feeling justifies. There was tension enough in the men to let the cry ring out far and wide.

The law knows no such unrestrained violence. It speaks advisedly, weighing its words, but earnestly, as one who sees a human being in peril of life. When all is said and done, the law's insistence on the indispensability of honor is just as emphatic as the cries of the kinsmen. The distinct and form-bound utterance of the man of law does not permit the demand to leap out upon us as in the wild cry of the relatives: "vengeance, vengeance." And yet perhaps, if our ears are properly opened to what it is the man of law sets forth in his brief, rhymed sentences, we may by that indirect testimony itself gain the most overwhelming impression of honor's energy—an impression the more powerful from the fact that we here see the energy transmuted into a supporting power of society.

The process of Germanic law rests on the principle that an accusation (brought forward in due form, of course) is enough to compel a man to defend himself via the law process. Anyone must be ready to nullify the mere unfounded charge by his own oath and that of his compurgators.[28] If not, he succumbs to the accusation. According to the old mode of thought, the matter is as fully decided as if he had publicly declared himself guilty. It is not known how widespread the fear was of an innocent man being sentenced by this method, because silence was really not regarded as a mute confession; rather, the charge itself was considered as a way of introducing guilt into a man. He who fails to fling back the charge lets it sink into him and mark him. The accused does not prove himself clean; he cleanses himself.

This is the dominant principle in the Germanic law process, the bond that holds the people united in a community of law. In everyday life also, it seems as if one man had power over another by virtue of his mere word. One can egg on a man to show his strength, his courage, and his foolhardiness in the way one suggests. One can force him, by expressing a doubt of his manhood. The North-men have a special term for such compelling words: *frýjuorð* they are called, words whereby one indicates one's belief in another man's lack of manly quali-ties.

For instance, there was a man called Már, whom certain people desired be gotten rid of for good. Accordingly, one day a suspicious-looking person comes up to his homestead, and tells him that one of his oxen is lying out in the bog. Már knows very well where his oxen are, but when the suspicious visitor insin-uates it is strange that a man should be afraid to go look for his cattle, the yeoman feels compelled go out into the bog, and there he meets his death.

The words "you dare not" are enough to make a man stake his life. Gregorius Dagson lost his case and his life because he could not resist the power of a taunt. When he and Haakon met, there was a stream between them. The ice was dubious to cross safely: Haakon had had holes cut in it and covered up with snow. Gre-gorius did not like the look of the ice—better, he thought, to go around by the bridge. But the peasants could not understand that he should be afraid of going against so small a party on good ice. Gregorius answered:

> I have not often needed that any should taunt me with lack of courage, and
> it shall not be needed now. See only that you follow when I go on ahead; it
> is you who have wished to make trial of bad ice. I have no great wish my-
> self, but I will not bear with your gibes. Forward the banner!

---

[28] That is, someone who vouches under oath for the character of an accused person. The practice of compurgation is largely obsolete today, but was commonplace in medieval England, Scandinavia, and France. It even found place in pre-Islamic Arabia, and into early Islamic jurisprudence.

Altogether a score of men followed him, the rest turned back as soon as they felt the ice underfoot. There Gregorius fell underneath the ice. This was as late as the year 1161.

A man has power over his neighbor by the use of *frýjuorð*, because the taunting words place the honor of his opponent in danger. If honor fails to rise and show its strength in response, paralysis steals over it. The man sinks down to a nithing. When an Icelander or a Norseman shouts at his opponent, "Be you every man's nithing if you will not fight with me," his words act as the strongest magic formula, for if the other will not take up the challenge, he becomes in fact a nithing all his days. In the *Hildebrand Lay*, the father utters his anguished cry of woe to fate: "Now must mine own child strike me with the sword! Give me my death with his axe, or I must be his bane." But what is to be done? "He shall be most craven of all the Easterlings, who would now refuse you battle, since you are so eager for it. . . ." So irresistible is the power of the taunt that it can force upon a man the deadliest of all misfortunes: the killing of his kinsman.

An insult or an accusation, no less than the blow or stroke of a weapon, bends something within the man: something that is called honor; something which constitutes the very backbone of his humanity. In this respect, a man could make his fellow an inferior in law and right. The Uppland Law gives us a fragment of an old legal form from pagan times in regard to an accusation of cowardice.

The one party says, "You are not a man, you have no courage!"

The other says, "I am as good a man as you!"

Then they are to meet with weapons at a crossroads; he who fails to appear is a nithing and devoid of right. Or as the Lombards said: if one calls another craven, then he must be able to maintain his assertion in trial by combat. If he succumbs, then he should rightly pay for his falseness. If any call a woman a witch or a whore, her kin must clear her by combat at law, or she must bear the punishment for witchcraft or whoredom. Here, the insulting party infuses cowardice or whoredom into the other by his assertion. Similarly, the complainant puts robbery or other mischief into his opponent before the law, and forces him to cleanse himself.

The honor that has been bent within the accused party must be raised up again, and given back its power to rule the man. The insult can be regarded as a kind of poison that must be cast out and flung back upon the sender. And thereafter, the sufferer must get back honor again from the offender for the full and complete strengthening of his humanity. Mere self-preservation forces one to seek restitution for any injury, for a man cannot carry on life in shame. It is of this feeling that the constitution of society is born, a fundamental law hard enough to hold hard natures together in an ordered community under the guardianship of law.

If a man were slack in revenging an injury, his friends would step in, saying, "We will amend it if you dare not, for there is shame for us all in this." But even when reparation had been exacted from the enemy, the matter was not wholly mended. The bitterest part of the shame stuck, because one of the kinsmen had suffered an insult to lie upon him instead of shaking it off at once, and thus drawn the shame down over himself and his kin. This wound was not healed by the shedding of blood, and what was worse, there was no restitution possible.

The insult—the injury—might come from within by virtue of a kinsman showing cowardice or slackness in letting slip an opportunity to show himself and accentuate his existence in honor. Or he stamped himself as a son of dishonor by committing an act that could not be defended: let us say, by "murdering" a man. Finally, the family could be stricken by a bloody stroke that was in itself irreparable: when the slayer was one of its own members.

Then the kinsmen may utter such words as these: "Better gone than craven; better an empty place in the clan where he stands." We know something of what it must have cost to say such a thing. To utter these words, a man must do violence to his feeling of frith. He must be filled with a dread that overshadows his natural fear of seeing the number of his kinsmen diminished and the prospect of a rich coming generation narrowed down. He must be driven so far as to forget what pain it meant to each one personally in the circle, when a string—a close-twisted string—was torn out of it. If we have realized what frith meant—the very joy of living, and the assurance of life in the future—and if we can transmute this understanding into sympathy, we cannot help but tremble at the words, "better a breach where he stands."

When shame comes from within in such a way as to preclude all restitution, it produces paralyzing despair. In the *Gylfaginning*,[29] we read of Baldr's death as follows:

> When Baldr was fallen, speech failed the gods, and their hands had no power to grasp him. One looked at another; all had but one mind toward him who had done the deed, but none could avenge it. The peace of the place was too strong. But when the gods found speech again, then burst forth their weeping at first, so that none could say any word to the others of his sorrow. But Odin felt the ill fortune heaviest, for he best knew how great a loss the gods suffered in Baldr's going.
>
> But when the gods came to themselves, then Frigg asked if there were any among the gods who would gain all her love by riding out along the Hel-road, to see if he might find Baldr and offer ransom to Hel for suffering him to return home to Asgard.

---

[29] English: *The Beguiling of Gylfi*. It is the second part of four of the *Prose Edda*, following the prologue.

The reader can hardly doubt that the author has drawn this vivid description from actual experience. The myth itself was undoubtedly handed down from earlier times. Whatever it may have held in its popular form, whatever its center may have been before it gained its final shape, it must have touched and released a fear in the poet himself that lay awaiting the opportunity to burst forth. With the weight of an inner experience, the single moment is made a fatal turning point. The gods are standing, young and happy, rejoicing in their strength and well-being, and then, suddenly as a hasty shiver comes, gray autumn is upon them. They have no power to determine, no strength to act. And while we watch, the shadows draw out, longer and longer, until they fuse, at the farthest point into unavoidable darkness. By its inner pathos, the scene announces itself as a turning point in the history of gods and men; we are made to feel that the killing of Baldr ushers in the decline of the gods and the end of the world.

A man might actually come to live through a catastrophe that brought irreparable ruin upon a whole circle. From some such experience—of the feeling of frith in the moment before its dissolution—the myth has drawn all its life. I am not in any way presupposing that the poet should himself have seen such a disaster in his own family; the overwhelming force of the deepest, most elementary feelings can so easily transform itself into a premonition of what the loss would mean, that an apparently very slight impulse may raise them in tragic form. Out of this collision between subject and experience—this inspiration, as we call it— rose the generally recognizable picture of frith violating itself. Thus, the kinsmen stand in their need. Their hands sink down, they look timidly at one another, fearing to look straight before them, and yet afraid to meet one another's glance. None can utter a word. In a moment, all vital force is broken.

No one knows anything. All sway from side to side between two possibilities, as *Beowulf* aptly paints it in the line about King Hrethel: "He could not let the doer of that deed hear ill words, and yet he could not love him." In place of the old determination, which never paused to consider anything but the means, we have blind fumbling. The gods can find no other way but to send a messenger to Hel; they even go on a beggar's errand afterwards, imploring all living and all dead things to raise Baldr from the realm of death by their crying. This is no exaggeration transposed to human conditions. The kinsmen who bear the shame between themselves have no power for vengeance or defense. Insult from outside is too strong for them. They bow their heads involuntarily, where they would otherwise stand firm. They fight without hope, with the despairing consciousness that the disaster will not cease. This misery is properly speaking what the ancients called redelessness, the inability to find a way.

And with this, the downfall of the family is certain. When Beowulf's retainers had forsaken their king in his fight with the dragon, the consequences of their cowardice are depicted in the following words:

None of your kin shall ever now reach gladly for gold, see sword out-stretched in gift; waste is the dwelling of the fathers, waste is life. Every man of your race shall go empty-handed away, and leave his land of herit-age behind, as soon as brave men far and wide hear of your flight, your craven deed. Better is death than life in shame.

This passage in the Old English poem leads us, first and foremost, to think of the disaster as a civic death. We can imagine the family driven into exile by a weight of sentence openly expressed or mutely understood. We are right to some degree, but the sentence is not the primary fact: it is only the outcome of deeper causes, for the trouble lies not merely in the scorn of men. Shame does not merely render the kinsmen unworthy of participating in human existence, but also, and most strictly, incapable of so doing. There is something wrong within. If it were not that the cowardice of individuals infected their companions and rendered them incapable of showing manhood, the race would not to such a degree become like a rotten bush that could be torn up at a grasp and flung out into the field. Lack of frith is in its innermost essence a sickness, and identical with lack of honor. The Northmen call such a condition "nithing-hood": the state of being a nithing, or a person without honor, whereby they understand dissolution of that inner quality which makes the individual at once a man and a kinsman.

We encounter the word "nithing" now at every step. In it lies the whole fear of a loss of honor not made good. And at every encounter, the word has a deeper and more ill-boding ring. To be a nithing means that a man has lost his humanity. He is no longer reckoned as a human being, and the reason is that he has in fact ceased to be so.

The state in which Hrethel and his fellow sufferers find themselves forms a diametrical opposite to Havard's fullness of life. In men without honor, a disso-lution of all human qualities takes place. First and foremost, the frith of kinship is destroyed. The strong coherence that alone enables the members of a family, not only to act unanimously, but to act at all, fades away. The lack of honor eats through the frith, so that the kinsmen wither and rush all different ways, as a mob of solitary units—that is to say, a mob of nithings.

In the house where a kinsman lies unavenged, there is no full and true frith. The family lives in a state of interregnum: a miserable and dangerous pause in which all life lies as it were prostrate, waiting its renewal. The high seat is empty; none may sit there until honor is restored. The men shun their neighbors and do not go to any meetings of men. Their avoidance of others is due to the fact that they have no place to sit where people are gathered together. Wherever they go, they must submit to be regarded as shadows. Nithing-hood is in a process of growth, encroaching over a new stratum of the soul for every opportunity of vengeance suffered to go by. There is no joy. What is told of an Icelander—that he did not laugh from the day his brother was slain till the day he was avenged—applies in a wider sense, inasmuch as the power of joy itself was frozen.

The intermediate state is dangerous, for if restitution is delayed too long, it may end with loss of the power to take revenge. Then anticipation and determination give place to helplessness, despair, and self-effacement.

The course of events is alike in all matters of honor. Whether the injury is a killing, a slander, or anything else, it brings about an emptiness in those who suffer it. If they do not gain their right before the seat of justice, either by laying the offender low, or by clearing themselves of the charge and obtaining restitution, then they must perish. And it is immaterial whether the defeat is due to lack of will or of power, or merely lack of good fortune. The great terror lies in the fact that certain acts exclude beforehand the possibility of any restitution, so that the sufferer was cut off from all hope of acquiring new strength and means to rid themselves of the feeling of emptiness. In a case of kin slaying kin, the helplessness is increased, for here something is to be done which cannot be done. The kinsman's arms fall down if they move to touch the one responsible. And even if the slayer's kinsmen could bring themselves to attack him, there is no restitution for them in shedding his blood. It cannot be used to sprinkle their honor and give it new life.

We should probably feel this helplessness in ourselves as a strife of the soul, in which the will itself is consumed in an inner conflict. Thus, we can undoubtedly come to experience something of the dread our forefathers felt for nithinghood, but the question is if we can penetrate into the center of suffering by doing so. The thing that weighed most heavily upon them was their powerlessness; the issue in their soul was between the will to act and the inability to act. The symptoms of nithing-hood thus consist at once of fear and dullness. For the soul torn by inner strife, helplessness can be a relief, but for the Germanic character, the culmination of despair was reached when action was impossible because it had no aim. It was impossible to take vengeance on a kinsman. But what difference did it make if the slayer were kinsman or stranger, when the latter, for instance, was a slave without honor, or a vagabond without kin? When one could not reach beyond the slave to a master, or beyond the beast to its owner, or beyond the solitary individual to a group of warriors, one was left to bear the wound, and the wound meant emptiness in any case.

Any breach in the frith raised the same feeling of dread. In effect, there was no such thing as a "natural" death. However the breach was made, it was felt as a peril, a horror, and an offense. Egil's despairing cry against the "ale-maker" sounds modern to a certain extent—it is man asserting his right in front of everyone as though it is a god. In point of form, his challenge also seems rather to belong to a transitional age when gods and men had somewhat lost touch with one another. But Egil's challenge really contains a highly primitive element.

Beneath the late form lies an old feeling of death, primeval fear and primeval defiance. Death was an anomaly, a thing unnatural and incomprehensible; one peers around to find who has brought it about, and if no slayer is to be found in the light, one seeks him in the darkness. One seeks, perhaps, the worker of this "witchcraft." The oppression of natural death has, in the Germanic mind, been lost out of concern for the future of the dead, but again and again the old despair can rise up again in a feeling of injury to frith.

Egil here shows himself as the most original and the most ancient of the Northern characters. His exclamation, "If I could pursue my cause..." has in it quite as much of hopelessness and helplessness as of defiance. It is a sense of nithing-hood lying in wait that gives his words their bitterness. But Egil is strong enough to conquer helplessness; he rises, through the feeling of solitude, up to the defiance of resignation. The downfall of frith forces his spiritual individuality forward in self-defense. He boasts of what his poetry and his will can achieve over men, even though they may be powerless to move the gods. He will now sit and wait until Hel comes, unshakably the same as he has always been. In this assertion of his personality, Egil reaches far ahead of the culture in which he is spiritually set. As long as frith was the indispensable foundation for all human life, such trials could never lift a man up. Then, sorrow was merely a poison that ate its way through frith, sundered the family, and set nithing-hood in place of humanity.

From the moment kinsmen declared themselves unable to find anyone to serve as the object of their vengeance, they sealed their death warrant spiritually as well as socially.

If the shame is due to spiritual suicide, then there is no restitution to be found in all the universe. The loss remains irreparable. Only one possibility remains as the only way of saving the family: the extirpation of the evildoer. The dishonor can be burned away before it poisons the whole body, but it needs a terrible effort to break through the frith and lay violent hands upon oneself.

The Baldr poem gives us here once more a poetic expression of the feelings at issue among the kinsmen. Or here we should perhaps say *one* of the Baldr poems, because from all appearances, there were two. On the one hand, we have the version followed by the author of the *Gylfaginning*, where the slaying of Baldr is linked up with the sending of Hermod to the underworld. The other form seems to have connected Baldr's death with the myth of Odin's and Rind's son, Vali. Unfortunately, we never get the connection in full, but are forced to make do with our own conclusions, drawn from scattered hints in ancient literature. The poet of the *Voluspa*, in his allusive manner, compresses the entire episode into the following lines:

Of that tree which seemed so slender came a fateful arrow of sorrow; Hod loosed it from the bow. Baldr's brother was born in haste, he, that son of Odin, wrought night-old his slaying. He washed not his hands, combed not his head, ere he bore to the flames him who had shot at Baldr.

And in another Eddic poem, *Baldr's Dreams*, the avenging of *Baldr* is prophesied as follows:

Rind gives birth to Váli in the Western Halls. That son of Odin wreaks night-old his slaying; washes not hand, combs not head, ere he bears to flames the shooter of Baldr.

Saxo has heard the story in this form. He lets Odin, who "like all imperfect deities often needs aid of men," learn from a Laplander that in order to provide an avenger for Baldr, he must beget a son with Rind, a Ruthenian princess. He gives us a detailed description of Odin's difficulties as a suitor in the Western Halls, where he tried his luck as a hero, then as a goldsmith. When neither heroic deeds nor golden rings made any impression on the maiden, he tried again as a leech, who both produced and cured the sickness. But whether these calamities properly belong here, where the question is only of an avenger for Baldr's death, we do not know.

Unfortunately, we are left without any indication as to how and where this myth was fused into the legend of Baldr, but it certainly looks as if the poet who worked up the story was playing upon primitive notions. He felt the need of an avenger who was a kinsman, and yet not a kinsman. The young hero carries out the deed before he has washed or combed himself (i.e., before he has become a human being). In any case, even though we cannot arrive at any certainty regarding the feeling of the Viking Age in connecting the two items, we may take the story as a symbol of the helplessness of kinsmen when their honor has been injured by one of their own. We experience their feeling of helplessness in themselves, and understand their sense that the trouble must be gotten rid of.

There is one thing we can say for certain: when it was a question of wiping out the shame—of extirpating the author of the shame—the kinsmen would rarely have called in human help. They have opened the way out into annihilation, or the way to the forest. They have not, properly speaking, cut him off from themselves, but rather indirectly forced him to cut himself off, and not until the evildoer had torn himself away from the family did they lift their hands and declare him solemnly as outside the pale of frith and humanity, and his place empty.

As long as there was the slightest possibility of preserving the vitality of the family without violence to its organism, the painful amputation would probably be postponed. In the case of members who, by cowardice and inactivity, were gradually bringing dishonor upon their kin, the others would probably first make trial of all goading and inciting words. This was the women's great task, and from all we know, they proved themselves equal to it. We have illustrations enough to make plain the influence of Germanic women over their husbands, brothers, and fathers. They could etch in the details of an injury, stroke by stroke, as when Gudrun says to her sons, "Your sister [Svanhild]—Ermanaric had her trodden underfoot by horses, white horses and black, along the road of war, gray horses, broken to the rein, horses of the Goths." They could use living illustrations more striking than those of any Jewish prophet.

In the same vein, the fiery Icelandic widow Thurid set a joint of beef on the table, carved into only three pieces, and let the sons interpret for themselves that their brother was hacked to larger pieces. After the meat, she served a stone to follow as dessert—this was to mean that they were as fit to be in the world as stones on the table for food, "since you have not dared to avenge your brother Hall, such a man as he was; ye are fallen far from the men of your race." Sigrid, sister of Erling Skjalgson, accompanied her brother-in-law Thorir Hund to his ship after showing him the body of her son Asbjorn (Selsbane), who had perished in open revolt against King Olaf II. Before Thorir went aboard, she spoke her mind:

> Ay, Thorir, so my son Asbjorn followed your kindly counsel. He did not live long enough to repay you after your deserts, but if I cannot do so as well as he would have done, it shall not be for lack of will. I have a gift here I would give you, and glad should I be if it might be of use to you. Here is the spear that went in and out of his body; the blood is on it still. It fits the wound Asbjorn bore, you can surely see. . . .

Thorgerd, wife of Olaf the Peacock, was a daughter of Egil and had her father's pride of race. One day she bade her sons go with her on a journey westward. When the party arrived outside the homestead of Tunga, she turned her horse and asked, "What is the name of that place?" The sons answer, "That you surely know. It is called Tunga." "Who lives there?" "Do you not know that, Mother?" Thorgerd answers with a deep breath:

> Ay, I know it full well. There lives he who was your brother's bane. You are little like your brave kinsmen, you who will not avenge such a brother as Kjartan. Egil, your mother's father, would not have acted thus. It is ill to have deedless sons—ay, such as you are, you should have been your father's daughters and given in marriage. So says the proverb, Halldor: there is a dullard in every family. One misfortune Olaf had, it is not to be denied,

is that his sons turned out badly. And now we can turn back. It was my errand to remind you of this, if you did not remember.

Halldor is right when he says, "We shall not hold it any fault of yours, Mother, if it passes from our mind."

Nor were the women afraid of using eloquent and easily interpreted gestures. Procopius relates how the Goth women,[30] upon seeing what little fellows their husbands had surrendered to, spat in their husbands' faces and pointed with scorn at the triumphant enemies.

These examples form a mighty responsory to all the foregoing, explained by it and explanatory of it. Through the words and actions of these women, there speaks a feeling of the enormous tension that the life of honor produced in men. Therefore, the words have a meaning beyond the individual situation to which they are applied in the saga. They give us the certainty that such honor's need could drive men to their utmost. There is in them an indirect suggestion of what might happen if the incitement failed of its effect.

In one case, we know for certain that the concerned party speedily proceeded to forcible amputation, and wiped the shame off the earth. When a woman had been dishonored, her kinsmen's endeavors were directed first and foremost toward obtaining honor from the offender. But this was not as a rule the end of the matter. The dishonored woman was considered a shame to her kin; she was a burden upon the race, and brought its honor into the same danger as did a craven among the men. Even after a woman was married, her kinsmen were responsible for her. The husband would lay the dishonor upon them, and bid them cleanse themselves and her.

Gregory of Tours gives an instance of how such a matter was dealt with in those days, an example typical in all essentials of Germanic thought and action. A woman was said to have deceived her husband, so his kinsmen went to the woman's father and said, "You must cleanse your daughter, or she must die, lest her fault should smirch our race." The father declared himself convinced of her innocence, and in order to stop the accusation, offered to clear her by oath.

If the kinsmen cannot clear themselves, then they must bear the shame with her; they must let themselves be made nithings or else put her out of the way. There was a family, says Gregory, who learned that one of their womenfolk had been seduced by a priest; all the men hurried to avenge the blot upon their race by capturing the priest and burning the girl alive.

The family undertook this uprooting for its own welfare, from the instinct of self-preservation. The necessity for the deed has left its mark in the laws, and we even find traces indicating that the right was once a duty. Rothari's edict to the

---

[30] A Greek historian of late antiquity; the chief historian of the sixth century.

effect that the authorities shall intervene if kinsmen do not avail themselves of their right to take action against a kinswoman who has misconducted herself with a man, is doubtless an emphasizing of an ancient sense of right. Swedish laws refer to the right of parents to drive their daughter away.

If a woman has dishonored her father's or her husband's house, she is whipped from house to house, or forced to take her own life—thus Boniface describes the domestic rule of the Saxons in pagan times.[31] The latter alternative points back from the judgment of society to what we have called racial amputation; the shame is wiped out, without any direct violation of frith on the part of the kinsmen.

The reason why the family took such extremely harsh measures against their womenfolk was not that the Germanic standard regarded woman's frith and inviolability as inferior. On the contrary, since woman occupied the very innermost place in the family's frith, the danger arising from a decay of her honor was the greater. Therefore, the misfortune caused by a wife or a girl must be checked at once and effectively. But we have sufficient indications to show that men with fatal shortcomings, too, were cut off with the same rude hand, but also with the same wariness, lest any guilt of blood should attach to the survivors.

---

[31] An English Benedictine monk and missionary to the Germanic parts of the Kingdom of the Franks during the eighth century. He was canonized as a saint, and became patron saint of Germania known as the "Apostle to the Germans."

III. HONOR THE SOUL OF THE CLAN

Without honor, life is impossible. Not only is it worthless, but it is impossible to maintain. A man cannot live with shame, which in the old sense means far more than now—the "cannot" is equal to "is not able to." As the life is in the blood, so actually the life is in honor. If the wound is left open, and honor suffered to be constantly oozing out, then follows a pining away—a discomfort rising to despair that is nothing but the beginning of the death struggle itself.

Humanity itself is dependent on the pulsing in the veins of a frith-honor. Without it, human nature fades away, and in the void there grows a beast nature, which at last takes possession of the whole body. The nithing is a wolf-man.

There was no difference. All human life (human life, of course, did not include slaves and suchlike creatures) was subject to the same necessity. All agreed that shame must be wiped out, and honor upheld. And yet, on coming to the question of what constituted shame, what was the honor that it was kinsmen's duty to maintain? There would at once be differences manifest between men. An injury was an injury, and produced the same effect in peasant and in chieftain. But men of high birth were more tender on the point and more sensitive than common folk, as for instance in regard to being indirectly slighted. And the people respected their right, or rather their duty to feel so. The difference lay not so much in the fact that they regarded certain things as constituting insult, where baser natures might ignore them, but rather in that their natures were finer and their skin more delicate; they felt an insult where the coarser breed would feel nothing. Still more sharply, perhaps, is the dissimilarity apparent on the positive side of honor. Men of standing were expected to have a keener sense of what was fitting. Those of inferior degree might edge their way through life with little lapses here and there, and be none the worse for that. But to formulate the difference correctly, we must enter on a close examination of the nature and contents of honor.

The first part of *Egil's saga* is built up over the contrast between Thorolf Kveldulfsson, the chieftain at Torgar, and the sons of Hilderid, wealthy yeomen from Leka of unremarkable standing. In Thorolf, the saga writer has drawn the Northern ideal of a well-to-do freeman: active, courageous, fond of magnificence, affectionate in friendship, true and frank toward those to whom he has promised loyalty, but stiff with those toward whom he feels no obligation. In the face of intrigues and calumny, he is almost blind; that is to say, he sees little, and he does not care to see what little he does see. If the king will not be persuaded of his open dealing, he exhibits a nonchalant defiance and obstinacy. When his fiefs are taken from him by the king, he manages to live his life as a man of position by trading voyages and Viking expeditions. He answers the king's confiscations by harrying along the shores and holding on his course undeviatingly, all the way into combat with the king of Norway.

Hilderid's sons are named after their mother, and this gives an indication of their story. Their mother, the beautiful but lowborn Hilderid, once found favor in the eyes of the old Bjorgulf; he married her, but the wedding took place in such careless fashion that the family found pretext therein to deprive the late arrivals of their birthright. In vain the young men endeavor to obtain recognition and claim their inheritance from Bard, grandson of Bjorgulf and their coeval kinsman. After Bard's death, Thorolf, having married his widow, becomes the representative of Bjorgulf's inheritance. He, too, scornfully dismisses the "bastards," offspring of a "ravished woman." Then they decide to make their way at court; they arouse Harald's suspicions in regard to the splendor of Thorolf's household, and cunningly obtain a transfer of Thorolf's fiefs to themselves under the pretext that the lands can be made to yield more revenue to the king's coffers. They lay the blame on Thorolf when their fine promises fail, and finally bring about the fall of the rebel himself. But the miserable wretches have no time to enjoy their hard-won victory before retribution is upon them. Thorolf's friends take a very thorough vengeance.

Calmly and objectively the saga writer tells these happenings, but through his sober words judgment is passed with surety upon these men. Thorolf could not act otherwise, for he was of high birth. He could serve the king as long as his service brought him nothing but honor, but he could not allow anyone, even a king, to dictate to him how he should spend his honor, how many housecarls he might have about him, or how splendidly he might equip himself and his retainers. He could not bow so low as to stand on a level with an accusation or a calumny, and offer his defense; he could see no better than that the king's interference with his affairs was an insult that justified him in taking his own measures accordingly. The king has seized his trading vessel—well and good: "We cannot lack for anything now, since we share goods with King Harald," and he promptly falls to harrying the coast of Norway. The craftiness of Hilderid's sons, their lies and calumnies, their time-serving and power of accommodation were natural and inevitable traits of character in men descended, on their mother's side, from the sly, wealthy, lowborn Hogni of Leka, who had "raised himself by his own wits."

The contest between Thorolf and his lowborn brothers-in-law discovers a fundamental principle in Teutonic psychology: high birth and nobility of character mean one and the same thing. But though these words are a fair translation of Teutonic wisdom; the sentence has lost its precise import by being transferred into modern surroundings. The play of color and shade in the words is changed, because our modern culture sees them in a different light.

When the story is rendered into our tongue, it treats of a hero who stumbles over his own nobility, whom fate, so to speak, masters by his own virtues. His noble frankness is changed to blinkers that blind him to calumny, his fondness for the straight road becomes a bit in his mouth, his independence a rein he must answer, and thus fate drives him proudly straight on and straight down to his fall. On the other hand, we have two ignoble strugglers, who, when once the disaster has been sufficiently established, are trodden out on the ground as a sacrifice to justice. One is loath to find oneself giving way to this sort of aesthetic indulgence. But can the reading be otherwise? Our interest in these intriguing parvenus ends, in reality, with their part as villains of the piece.

We are here face to face with an essential difference between "ancient" epic and "modern" reproduction of the conflicts of human life in poetic form. Our epic is based on an arbitrary judgment disguised as morality, or as an idea, or an artistic principle; before ever any of the characters have entered the world, the author's ordering mind has twined their fate, predestined some to being glorified in the idea, and others to glorifying the idea by their downfall. So thoroughly has it become our nature to demand this sense of a poetic providence in, or rather over, the subject matter that we unconsciously arrange the old poetry accordingly for our enjoyment. We put all the interest on one side of the conflict, and thereby break off what was the point of the story for the original hearers.

The ancient poetry knows nothing of a higher point of view; an absolute, predetermined result only worked out in the story to prove it. The balance lies always much nearer the middle between the two parties than our aesthetic and moral sense will allow. The "moral" does not appear until the collision and reckoning between the two factors. It is often impossible to say on which side the poet's sympathy lies in a narrative of family feuds, because the interest of the story is not sifted into sympathies and antipathies. Anyone who has read Icelandic sagas with a fairly unprejudiced mind will again and again have noticed in himself an aftereffect of this equilibrium—perhaps with a certain surprise, or even dissatisfaction.

The Icelandic sagas are desperately poor in villains. *Njál's saga*, sentimen-
tally overdone as it is, may be left out of the question, because, as a whole, it
belongs to another world. But just because the epics gives a contest between men,
and not a mere exhibition with its end planned beforehand, the triumph comes
still more crushingly and brutally. It follows on a combat victory, where the right
of the one strikes down the right of the other and shatters it to fragments. However difficult it may be for us to understand, the old poetry was for its hearers a
piece of reality—of the same tangible reality as that which took place under their
personal participation.

The contrast, then, between Thorolf and Hilderid's sons becomes a real conflict. The character of the former is predetermined by his honor; his nobility sets
definite bounds to his freedom of action. He cannot lie, cannot choose a crooked
way, and cannot serve time. He would have fallen away from his nobility and
been subjected to the condemnation of honor had he done certain things—for
example, had he dismissed half of his retainers and let them go about telling that
Thorolf of Torgar no longer dared to maintain as many men as before. Or if he
had brought his disputes with men of lower rank before a court with the obligation to submit to its decision. Or further still, if he, trusting in the justice of his
cause, would face his petty accusers, humbly offering proofs of his honesty.

The character and behavior of the two brothers are equally a necessary consequence of their birth, whence it follows that they have the right to be as they
are. They are fighting for their—and their mother's—honor; their actions are dictated solely by a sense of human dignity. They have no other means of achieving
their righteous vengeance than the means they employ, and the saga writer cannot
deny them the share of appreciation they deserve in face of their highborn, high-
minded opponent, who from the constitution of his blood fights and must fight
with other weapons. Nevertheless, the saga describing their doings contains a
condemnation of the baseness they display. Necessity does not imply justification; on the contrary. They are in the right, but in and by the conflict to which
honor forces them, they become villains by their right.

We have here a dilemma that forces us to look far and wide when seeking to
estimate a people's honor and ethics. Our task is not accomplished until we have
reached so deep down that this contrast ceases to be a contradiction.

A highborn, high-minded man must show his nobility not only in the way
he deals with an injury, and in care for his behavior, but also by taking up the
affairs of others. A man facing difficulties would turn confidently for help to the
great man of his district. An Icelander who had lost his son and could not see his
way to take vengeance—or win his case at court by himself—went to the headman of his district and said, "I want your help to gain my right in this matter,"
and he gave grounds for his demands as follows: "It touches your honor also that
men of violence should not have their will in these parts."

The headman had then to take up the matter himself. If there was wizardry abroad, then the chieftain must "see to the matter," otherwise he could ill "hold his honor." Furthermore, apart from having to deal with living miscreants, a man who aspired to leadership might be called upon to exorcise a ghost, on the ground that here was a task his honor required him to undertake. The man would be obliged to meet any claim so made on him, without regard to his own well-being or woe. An applicant for aid could, if needed, threaten to let himself be cut down where he stood, with consequent dishonor to the man whose door was closed to him.

It touched the chieftain's personal honor as a man if he failed to devote all his energies to the fulfillment of such obligations as went with his position. He had not an official honor to spend first; if he failed to live up to his duties as a leader of men, his chieftainship sank at once to nithing-hood, without stopping on the way at the stage of ordinary respectability. A man born to chieftainship and looked up to as a chieftain must keep open house for all who sought protection. He had no right to inquire into the worthiness of the applicant and his cause; the fact that the man had sought refuge with him was enough to bind his honor in the eyes of the world. If the great man gave up the fugitive instead of undertaking the intricate and complicated business a guest of this sort often brought with him, his action would be stamped, not merely as weak, but as dishonorable.

This oneness throughout is a true characteristic of the old honor. It knows no shades of distinction, no more or less vulnerable points, and no circles each with its relatively independent life. It is itself throughout, from the very innermost core of manly feeling to the very outermost periphery of a man's social influence.

A man of high standing's fulfilling his obligations does not grant him further prestige beyond what his ordinary human dignity allows. He cannot, then, throw away his social prestige without perishing morally as well.

A nobleman's reputation is a great, well-grown honor. There lies in the appeal to a man's chieftainship nothing less than an appeal to "honor," rendered more poignant by the suggestion of a more-than-common sensitiveness in his particular honor. "Be you every man's nithing, if you will not take up my cause," says the applicant for help, with the same weight as when another says, "Go your way as a nithing, if you do not take vengeance."

The word "virtue" contains, in brief, a history of culture. It meant in ancient times as much as "to be good enough, to be what one should be." In Anglo-Saxon, *duguth*, "virtue," is a derivative of the verb *dugan*, "to avail, to be able to." Virtue in the modern sense presupposes liberation of moral forces for an aesthetic purpose. Against the background of an average morality, which any man can attain and any may find worth his while, the superior form unfolds its full magnificence. The barbarians know no virtues, because they have no minimum of morality. However high a man may rise above the common level, he never gets beyond his duty, for his duty grows with him.

In the Icelandic, we may read of a hospitable yeoman: "He was so gallant a man, such a *þegnskaparmaðr*, that he gave any free man food as long as he would eat." Curiously enough, the word here used in his praise, *þegnskapr* (thaneship) simply refers to that manly honor, or conscience, invoked by every man upon taking oath before a court of law. And just as naturally, without any symbolic extension of the word, the man who can afford to feed his fellows yet shuts his store against them is called a food-nithing—a nithing in regard to food. He was a nithing, fully as much as the man who committed perjury.

The king was generous, so men are loud in his praises. He flung the gold about him, as one could see from his men and women displaying their gold-gleaming arms and breasts. How splendid a king they had! Never was born such a king under the sun. But woe to the prince whom generosity forsook. Niggard-liness was a sign (among other signs) that he was nearing his downfall.

There is an ill-boding ring in *Beowulf*'s words about Heremod: "Blood-fierce thoughts grew in Heremod's soul. He gave not rings to his Danes, as was due. Joyless, he bided the time when he gathered the harvest of his deeds: long-lasting war in the land." A mysterious curse brooded over him, withering his will to give: nithing.

These barbarians can admire the extraordinary, as we see already here. Their words of praise leap high in the air. But the very passion of their acclaim has an oppressive effect on us. They raise a cheer for the king, as they would for the sword dancer who comes nearer and nearer to death the wilder and more skillful his dancing; a slip, and he will lie there under a mass of scorn and contempt. Through poems and sagas runs a murmur of applause, expressed or indicated in masterly ways, for the true hero's scorn of death. But anyone who is at all famil-iar with the spirit of these poems knows also that there is but one contrast to this praise, and feels instinctively what the verdict would have been if the hero had not laughed the pain to death.

The poet of the *Atlakvida*, describing Hogni's defiant scorn when his heart is cut out, places the hero's contempt of death in relief by letting the executioners first show his brother a slave's bloody heart as if it were Hogni's. But then said Gunther, king of men:

Here lies the heart of Hjalli the craven, unlike the heart of Hogni the brave;
it quivers here, lying on the platter, but half that it quivered in the breast. . . .
Here lies the heart of Hogni the brave, unlike the heart of Hjalli the craven;
little as it quivers now lying on the platter, it quivered less in Hogni's breast.

A modern reader is at first moved by the poignancy of the scene, but upon a second reading, his admiration is likely to give way to a musing wonder at the manner in which the poet points the intrepidity of the hero by contrasting it with the abject fear of a slave. So poor in shades of distinction is the old valuation of men and manhood.

The Germanic morality cannot be arranged in a hierarchy of good qualities. There is not the slightest approach among the Teutons to a system in which one virtue is vaulted above another like a series of heavens. Such an order of precedence presupposes centralization; all men must be united under the same condemnation before they can be classified. Neither has the Germanic mind any conception of a common moral Gehenna. Strictly speaking, evil, nithing-hood, has no reality at all, but must be interpreted as a negative, as a total lack of human qualities. Nithing-hood is the shadow every "honor" casts according to its nature. Therefore, the boundary line between admiration and contempt stands sharply, without transition stages or any neutral gray.

And therefore, the boundary lies differently for different people. What makes a man a nithing—a criminal and a wretch—depends on what made him a man of honor.

For the man of kingly birth, the limit was set very high. His honor consisted in having at his disposal as many men as his father had had (if not more), and to be called the greatest, the bravest, the quickest of wit, or the most generous within the horizon that had formed his family's sphere of power. Immediately outside that honor stood the death of a nithing. This is the secret thought that sets its mark on all Germanic chieftains, determines their fate, and predestines them to a certain way of life. It has found typical expression in the Icelandic saga's description of that famous family council at Westfold, when Olaf II (who later on was called the Saint) declared his intention of unifying Norway.

There are three persons present at the council. On one side of Olaf sits his stepfather, Sigurd Syr, the peasant king. He listens to the impetuous words of the young pretender, following in a long glance the bold plan as it rolls over Norway. He measures the breadth of the road, the hardness of obstacles the enterprise must meet, and asks where the hands to force it through the narrows are. Sigurd cannot help but feel that there is more youthful eagerness than foresight in the plan, but he sums up his considerations in these words:

> I can well understand that a yeoman king such as I am has his way, and that yours must be another, for when you were yet but half a child you were already full of emulation and would be foremost in all you could. . . . I know now that you are so set upon this that it will be fruitless to argue against it, and little wonder that such counsels should thrust aside all others in the

hearts of daring men, when they see Harald's race and kingdom about to fall.

On Olaf's other hand sits the king's mother, Asta. She is now the dutiful wife of the peasant king, but she cannot forget that she is the mother of a descendant of Harald Fairhair. For so many years she has been forced to curb her ambition; now, her son loosens all bonds, and her pride of race stiffens and straightens her. Standing midmost in that honor which Sigurd surveys from afar, she finds other words:

> It is thus with me, my son, that I am happy in you and would be happiest to see your power the greatest. To that end, I will spare nothing that I can do, but there is little help to be had from me here. Better to be king over all Norway a little while, as Olaf Tryggvason, than live life to its end in easy ways, as can the petty kings here about.

And from the innermost of the race come Olaf's words: "You will not be so far from rising up to avenge this shame upon our kin, but that you will do your utmost to strengthen him who takes the lead in raising it." Shame upon our kin: that is the salient point in Olaf's history, according to the saga writer. His race had been first in all Norway, and the honor of the family demands that he should maintain this position above all the clans of the country.

Having now considered the highest forms of honor, it is natural then to seek out the lowest degree. What was the scantiest amount of honor men could live on? In a way, the answer is given in the common denominator of what is human as expressed in the laws; we could calculate a man's value from the sum of those things he was declared justified in seeking reparation for; indirectly, we have done something of the sort. To arrive at the right proportion, however, we must make the active side of honor somewhat stronger than is directly made out in the formalities of legal paragraphs. The Norse laws, as we have seen, will here and there set a man outside the law for lack of manhood, whether the weakness display itself in his failing to accept a challenge, or in his coming out second best. They show that it is not a mere phrase of etiquette when a man holds it "better to die than be held a nithing for having given way without fight."

In such cases, pacifism eats as deeply into its man as does the dishonor he incurs by leaving his brother unavenged. But in ambitious races, or indeed in any healthy stock, honor could not content itself with standing still under cover of a shield; a man could not wait until the test was forced upon him, but must seek out an opportunity of showing himself off. There is a characteristic phrase in Old Norse for a young man who has shown himself a worthy descendant of worthy ancestors: he is said to have vindicated his kinship or, literally, "led himself into his kin."

When Glum the Icelander on his first voyage abroad came to the house of his grandfather Vigfus, and made toward the high seat where his kinsman sat "big and stout, playing with a gold-inlaid spear" to greet him and declare his kinship, he met with a very cool reception. The youth was given a seat at the far end of the lowest bench and had little attention paid to him. The young man waited patiently, until one day an opportunity arose to distinguish himself by killing a man. Then Vigfus suddenly thawed: "Now you have given proof that you are of our kin. I was but waiting until you should lead yourself into your kin by a show of manhood."

The same expression is used by Haakon Sigurdsson to Sigmundur Brestis-son, son of the Faroe chief, when, after the killing of his father, he seeks refuge among his father's friends in Norway. "I will not be sparing of food for you, but you must lead yourself into your kin by your own strength," by healing the mortal wound dealt to your frith and your honor. When Vigfus uses the word, there is thus something more behind it than the mere manifestation of ability; it means nothing less than entering into frith, the transition from the dangerous shadow-existence to life duly fortified in honor. And the saga is undoubtedly right in letting Vigfus express himself so solemnly.

The Icelanders have a characteristic term for a youth who has not shown that he feels his father's life as his spur and standard. They call him *averrfeðrungr* (i.e., one who is worse than his father). The famous explorer Leif commenced his career with the vow that he would not be *averrfeðrungr*. And in this lies a suggestion of the point of view for the bringing up of youth. The young man was drawn as early as possible into the common life of honor of the family, and led to feel himself as sharing in its responsibility. And the older members will hardly have lacked effective words wherewith to spur on a dullard.

The opening chapters of the *Vatsdoela* picture how old Ketil Raum went looking at his son, shaking his head in increasing disapproval, until one day he could no longer keep silent.[32] He began moralizing:

> Young men nowadays behave differently from what was their wont when I was young. Then, they were eager to do something for their own renown, either by going a-viking, or gaining goods and honor elsewhere in danger-ous undertakings. Now they care only to sit with their backs to the fire and cool themselves with ale, and there is little manliness or hardihood to be looked for that way. You have certainly nothing much either of strength or height, and the inner part answers no doubt to the outer, so you will hardly

---

[32] Norwegian Viking leader in the ninth century. Among his descendants are Ketil "Flatnose" Björns-son, who ruled over the Isle of Man and the Scottish Isle of Hebrides in the mid-800s.

come to tread in your father's footsteps. In olden time, it was the custom for folk of our sort to go out on warlike expeditions, gaining wealth and honor, and that wealth was not handed down from father to son. No, they took it with them to the burial mound, wherefore their sons must need find theirs by the same road.

And so on for a long while. Unfortunately, the saga writer here seems to have something of that hectic admiration for the good old days that generally indicates that the good old days are irrevocably past. This goes naturally enough with his showing of old Ketil as something more rhetorically gifted and more inclined to historical moralizing than was usual in the chieftains of the ninth century. In the good old days, such a waking up would have been delivered in words less learned, but a great deal sharper. Nor is it probably quite good history when the saga lets a thoroughly romantic robber lie hidden in the woods so near to Ketil's homestead that Thorstein (the Red), the son, can prepare a grand surprise for his father without giving himself away by lengthy and numerous preliminaries.

Later on in the *Vatsdoela*, there is an everyday scene showing how a youth actually claimed his right to recognition, in the days when life had no romantic robbers to offer, but only its own brutal prose. The Vatsdoela clan, represented first and foremost by Thorgrim of Karnsá, is in danger of losing the headmanship of the district, and with it the traditional supremacy of the family. At the assembly convened to elect the headman, Thorgrim sits in the high seat, and in front of him on the floor among the slave children, is the twelve-year-old Thorkel, his illegitimate son whom he has never been willing to acknowledge. Thorkel comes up and stands looking at him, and at the axe he carries in his hand. Thorgrim asks whether he finds the axe so much to his liking that he would care to strike a blow with it, as there was a man present in whose head it would fit nicely. Then he says, "I should reckon you had yourself won your place among us Vatsdoela folk." The boy loses no time in fitting the axe as suggested, and Thorgrim keeps his word, seeing that "the lad has led himself into his kin."

The compiler of the opening chapters of the *Vatsdoela* is far inferior, both in understanding of the past and in point of art, to the master spirit who reconstructed the family council at Westfold. Fortunately, tradition in Iceland was strong, and it shows willingly through in the tirades of the saga writer. This father, waiting and waiting for some manifestation of his son's true kinship with the old stock, is a genuine figure. He is historically right in demanding that the son shall win his place for himself. There came a time in the life of every young man when he placed himself among the older members. And the older ones waited, letting example serve. But when the proof failed to appear, the youngsters must be given to understand that there was danger in such an intermediate state as that of one who has not yet vindicated his kinship. And when the author lets his hero dwell on the obligation involved by the deeds and ways of one's forefathers, the authority of tradition speaks even through his flowery phrasing.

A curious point of etiquette among the Lombards, noted by Paulus Diaconus, seems also based upon the presumption that the young son of a princely house had to win his place by demonstrating ambition before he would be granted the privileges that were due to him by birth. We read that when the Lombard prince Album had distinguished himself in a battle against the Gepids,[33] the warriors earnestly entreated his father to honor him with a seat at the royal table. The king answered by referring them to the established custom which forbade a king's son to sit at his father's table before he had received arms from the prince of a foreign people.

The scenes in *Beowulf* appear almost as a pendant to this little story. There, the hero sets out to a foreign court, achieves great things, receives with delight the costly weapons and jewels as his reward, and returns with honor to his ancestral hall. There, he would recount his doings to his kinsman in the high seat, and lay gifts of honor at his feet. Despite the fact that Beowulf, according to the first part of the poem, was already a hero of renown when he made his expedition to the hall of the Danish king, the words that close the description of his youth sound indisputably as if this act of prowess formed a turning point in the hero's story:

> Long he bore with slighting. The youth of the Geats counted him not good, and thus the king of men would not himself account him worthy to a place on the ale-bench; they surely thought that he was without courage, a feeble atheling, but the distress of the brave one was turned about.

And then his kinsman takes the opportunity to make him grants of land:

> Seven thousand, hall and ruler's seat, both had right by birth to the land, seat and inheritance, but the one before the other. To him, the better man, fell the kingdom.

This can, to my mind, only be taken as indicating that there was in the poet's mind a marked association of ideas between achievements of youth, winning one's place in the family, and taking up one's inheritance.

It is perhaps not unlikely that the Germanic people, like so many others at a corresponding stage of civilization, demanded a proof of manhood in some sort or other before receiving their youths into the circle of the men. What applies to the sons of princes must also have applied to free men of lower rank.

---

[33] An east Germanic tribe who lived in modern-day Romania, Hungary, and Serbia.

Cassiodorus' epigram, "To the Goths, valor makes full age," has perhaps more of truth in it than one is predisposed to think of anything coming from the pen of such a deft phrasemaker.

The games of children reveal the manner in which adults regarded one another. Little Thorgils (Leifsson, son of Leif Erikson) had attained the age of five without having struck down any living thing. He had to steal a horse and redden his spear in its guts, because his companions had decided not to accept anyone who had not shed blood as their playfellow. The men took care that none should enter their company with virgin weapons. Naturally, the baptism of blood takes a prominent place in a community such as among the Germanics, where battle and war stand in the foreground as a man's proper trade. The deed of arms—the test of arms—is, by the forcefulness wherewith it reveals ambition in a flash, well suited to form a sacrament of initiation. Cognomens such as "Helgi Hunding's bane" or "Hygelac Ongentheow's bane" compress the whole epic into a name. In the old conception of blood as a powerful dew of life lies harsh materialism and heroic idealism naturally and inseparably interwoven.

Vengeance for a father slain—or vengeance for a kinsman in the wider sense—was often enough in those unruly times the means whereby youth showed their right to a seat in the home. However, to regard honor as solely and exclusively in the sign of slaughter leads to an overly restricted estimate of life. More was demanded of a well-born youth than merely to be a slayer of men. He claimed his place, and held his place in the family by his generosity, hospitality, helpfulness, or readiness to take up the cause of kinsmen and fugitives, by nobility of manner and magnificence. And eyes were watching from every side to see that he filled his place in every respect. The place he had to fill was the broad, spacious seat which his father had judged necessary for himself.

Ancestral ways and ancestral measures constitute the standard; on this point, Ketil Raum speaks as the man of experience. Olaf could find no better way of expressing his sense of duty than by saying, "Harald Fairhair's inheritance."[34] And men of lower rank could find no other way of determining what was good for them than by saying, "Thus our kinsmen of old would never do," or, "Thus our kinsmen of old were wont to do."

Family tradition constitutes the entire ethical standard. A fixed line of demarcation, separating evil from good, was not known. There was, of course, a broad average, as among all peoples. The Germanic people knew that certain acts, such as stealing, first and foremost, and murder, alongside others, brought dishonor upon a man, whoever the culprit might be. Just as they knew that killing was killing, they knew injury was injury, but that did not mean that anyone

---

[34] Olaf saw it as his calling to unite Norway into one kingdom, as Harald I Fairhair had largely succeeded in doing.

keeping himself free from such dishonest acts was to be regarded as an honorable man. His tradition told him what was evil for himself and what was good—this distinction served as a complete moral compass. To accept blood money, for instance, was for most people honorable and decent enough. But if one came from a stock that boasted of never having carried its kinsmen in a purse, or always having demanded double fine for a kinsman slain, a breach of such tradition was considered hypocrisy. The constitutional honor of the race could not bear such a departure.

The Icelandic *verr feðrungr* came gradually to mean a scoundrel or an immoral person; in other words, a nithing. This transition surely has its deep motives, or may have, at any rate. It stands in complete agreement with the spirit that inspires clan morality. The ethical standard is not based on what is generally applicable to all. Indisputable moral standards that all agree to call right or wrong are only a crude average formed by the individual "honors" in juxtaposition. Each circle has its own honor, an heirloom that must be preserved in the very state in which it is handed down, and it must be maintained according to its nature. Honor is the patch of land on which I and mine were born, which we own, and on which we depend. Such is our honor that it be broad and rich, well stocked with cattle and corn, or poor and sandy. Honor is a spiritual counterpart of earth and its possession, wherein all cows and sheep, all horses and weapons are represented—not as a number or a value, but in their individuality.

And as the individual items of the property each have their counterpart in honor, so, naturally, are the kinsmen themselves personally represented. Honor forms a mirror that retains the images of those it has reflected. There stand all the kinsmen, in their finest array and with their finest weapons, and the more costly their armor, the more precious is their honor. There are all the happenings within the family as far back as man's memory can reach—all great deeds, all costly entertainments, every magnificent piece of hospitality. They all stand there and demand their rights. There, too, everything degrading will appear, and woe to him who shall look therein without finding relief for the eye in mighty deeds of restitution.

"Woe," said the Swedish peasants, "to the race that sees one of its own buried without the churchyard wall." This was the greatest misfortune that could fall upon a house; even when the dead man lay buried outside in unhallowed soil on account of his sins, his kinsmen would not rest until they had bought him a place within the churchyard. And this not primarily, or even principally, out of regard to his future rest in peace, but in order not to hand down a shame to his posterity. Thus, the peasants of the North, even in late centuries, felt kin-shame as an intolerable burden, a thing that had to be lived through again, day after day.

Honor is so far from being something ideal and indeterminate that it can be actually counted and felt. Honor is the property and influence of the family; it is the history of the race, composed of actual traditions from the nearest generations and of legends of the forefathers. Honor is the cattle and the ancestors of the clan, because both live just as much in the kinsmen as outside them. Livestock, like weapons and jewels, exists in the kinsman's soul not merely as an item of this or that value. It does not hang on externally by a sense of proprietary interest, but lies embedded in feelings of a far more intense character.

Familial history is not sensed merely as a series of events following one on the heels of another; nay, the living are *filled* by their ancestors. All history lay unfolded in its breadth, so that all that had once happened was happening again and again. Every kinsman felt himself as living all that one of his kin had once lived into the world, and he did not merely feel himself as possessing the deeds of old: he actually renewed them in his own doings. Any interference with what had been acquired and handed down, even if acquired from raiding or robbery, had to be met with vengeance, because a field of the picture of honor was crushed by the blow. But an openly expressed doubt as to whether that old grandfather really had done what he was said to have done is just as fatal to life, because it tears something out of his living kin; the taunt touches not only the dead man of old, but still more him who now lives through the former's achievements. The insult is a cut into the man himself; it tears a piece out of his brain, making a hole which is gradually filled with ideas of madness.

An injury tears out a piece of the soul, with all the thoughts and feelings attached to it. The wound produces the same vertigo as a mother feels when robbed of a piece of her soul by the death of her child. A whole portion of her thoughts and feelings becomes superfluous, and her instinctive movements become useless. She reaches out at night into the dark, grasping at something, and her hands are filled with emptiness. The void in her soul produces a constant uncertainty, as one might imagine if one's natural adjustment were disturbed, so that the hand misses its mark every time it reaches out for an object. Such a void in the soul wakes fear in its wildest form. If the mother imagines to herself that someone has killed her child, or that she herself has taken its life, or if she fears that the world is about to crumble to pieces, we know that these feelings are only the food with which her head is trying to sate her fear. She must grasp at all sorts of dreadful imaginings to appease for a moment this craving of dread. There is, from a psychological point of view, no disproportion between her feeling and the thought of the world coming to an end. If the breach is not closed, the soul dies of that intolerable hunger, and her sorrow ends in madness.

This comparison between the clansmen's loss of honor and the mother's loss of her child is exactly to the point, because it illustrates an identical psychological state manifesting itself under different conditions. The bereaved mother is on the point of becoming a nithing in the old sense of the word; in fact, she would be a nithing in the old days, if she did not obtain restitution. And that which takes place in one whose honor is wounded is just such a displacement of the entire soul, a spiritual earthquake shattering a man's self-esteem and moral carriage, and rendering him not responsible for his actions, as we should say.

Only in the very extreme cases of our civilization can we find anything that covers the experiences of the ancients. For the innate depravity of shame lies in the fact that spiritual life was then dependent upon a certain number and a certain sort of ideas. Good breeding was a family treasure, possibly not differing greatly to our eyes as regards the different families, but in reality distinctively marked from earliest youth, stamped by traditions, determined by environment, and consequently not easily changed. Personality was far less mobile than now, and was far less capable of recuperation. If a kinsman lost an idea, he could not make good the loss by taking up ideas from the other side. As he is bound to the family circle in which he grew up, so he is dependent upon the soul-constituents fostered in him.

The traditions and reminiscences of his people, the enjoyment of ancient heirlooms and family property, the consciousness of purpose, the pride of authority, and good repute in the judgment of neighbors found in his circle make up his world, and there is no spiritual treasury outside on which he can draw for his intellectual and moral life. A man nowadays may be excluded from his family, whether this consists of father, mother, brothers and sisters, or a whole section of society. He need not perish on that account, because no family, however large, can absorb the entire contents of a reasonably well-equipped human being's soul. He has parts of himself placed about here and there—even nature is in spiritual correspondence with him. But man as a member of a clan has a void about him. It need not mean that his kinsmen lack all wider interest, and it does not mean that he is unable to feel himself as member of a larger political and religious community. However, these associations are, in the first place, disproportionately weak, so that they cannot assert themselves side by side with frith. Furthermore, they are only participated in through the medium of kinship or frith, so that they can have no independent existence of their own.

A man cast off from his kin cannot appeal to nature for comfort, for its dominant attribute is hostility, save in the form where it faces him as inspired by humankind, cultivated and inhabited. And in the broad, fair fields it is only the land of his inheritance that meets him fully and entirely with friendly feelings. It will also be found that in cases where a nithing is saved to the world by being received into a new circle—a family or a company of warriors—he does not then proceed by degrees from his former state over to the new; he leaps across a channel, and becomes a new man altogether.

Honor is identical with humanity. Without honor, one cannot be a living being; by losing honor, one loses the vital element that makes man a thinking and feeling creature. The nithing is empty, and haunted forever by the all-embracing dread that springs from emptiness. The despairing words of Cain have a bitterness of their own in the Anglo-Saxon, steeped as they are in the Teuton's horror of loneliness: "I dare not look for honor in the world, seeing I have forfeited thy favor, thy love, thy peace." He goes full of sorrow from his country, and from now onward there is no happiness for him, being without honor and goodwill (*árleas*). His emptiness means, in a modern phrase, that he has nothing to live for. The pains he is to suffer will cut deeper than before, seeing they are now all heaped up in himself alone, and they will produce more dangerous wounds, since there is no medicine to be found against them. Thus, it is literally true that no one can be a human being without being a kinsman, or that kinsman means the same as human being.

There is not a grain of metaphor in the words. Frith and honor together constitute the soul. Of these two constituents, frith seems to lie deeper. Frith is the base of the soul; honor is all the restless matter above it. But there is no separation between them. The force of honor is the feeling of kinship, and the contents of frith is honor. So it is natural that a wound to honor is felt on one hand as an inner decline, and on the other as a paralysis of love. By the import of honor, we learn to know the character of the gladness which kinsmen felt when they sat together by the fire warming themselves in frith.

This interpenetration of frith and honor makes itself apparent, for instance, in the use of the Anglo-Saxon word *ár*. When an exile comes to a king to sue for *ár*, the word may be translated as "favor" or "protection," but we must bear in mind that the acceptance by the king (i.e., the *ár* given to him by the king) procures for him peace and human dignity. In Christian language, God is the giver of *ár* (grace, making the lives of men prosper). *Ár* thus embraces luck, honor, and mutual goodwill, and the translator of Old English poetry is constantly brought to a standstill for want of a comprehensive term in his own language. Thus says Hrothgar's queen about her sons' cousin, Hrothulf:

> I know my Hrothulf the happy, know that he will hold the youths in honor
> [*ár*], if you, king of the Scyldings, go out of the world before him. I think
> he will return good to our sons, when he remembers how we gave him ár
> when he was small, to his joy and his exaltation.

When there was strife between Abraham's and Lot's men, the patriarch's love of peace is expressed by the Anglo-Saxon poet in the following words: "We two are kinsmen; there shall be no strife between us," and the Englishman adds further explanation: "*ár* dwelt in his mind."

Insight into the nature of honor opens a way to the understanding of the character of gladness. The sentences that have been quoted, referring to men's living in happiness and honor, when they sit in a circle around the fire with happy, fearless thoughts, have now obtained their full meaning which cannot be exhausted in modern words.

Honor implies vengeance in ancient society, but honor, as we have seen it up to this, does not elucidate what made the shedding of blood so powerful a medicine for spiritual suffering. Honor contains much that points out beyond the limits here drawn, and that can only find its explanation in a still wider view of the spiritual life of these men.

IV. LUCK

Besides honor, man needs something which in the ancient language is called luck. Our translation, however, draws the sense of chance into the foreground and fails altogether to indicate the true force of the word. The associations of the modern term, stressing the sense of chance or fortune, all run counter to the spirit of ancient culture, and there is no other way of reaching a full understanding than by patient and unprejudiced reconstruction of Teutonic psychology.

Whichever way we turn, we find the power of luck. It determines all progress. Where it fails, life worsens. It seems to be the strongest power in the world, its most vital principle indeed.

When a man's fields yielded rich harvest, when his lands were rarely visited by frost or drought, he was said to be *ársæll* (i.e., he possessed the luck of fertility). When his cattle throve and multiplied, always returning hale and undepleted from their summer grazing grounds, then he was *fésæll* (i.e., he had the luck of cattle).

The dweller on a barren strip of coast had little use for luck in the fields, but would on the other hand probably be lucky with his fishing, else he would be *byrsæll* (i.e., he would always have the wind in his favor). There was a famous family in Northern Norway, the men of Hrafnista, of whom it is said that as soon as they hoisted sail, a wind sprang up—even though it had been perfectly calm a moment before. According to Saxo, Hadingus, too, had a peculiar power to make best use of a wind. Even though his pursuers were running before the same wind and did not have fewer sails, they could not overtake him.

In the North, this trait is not a fairy tale motive, nor the invention of an imaginative saga writer. The Olafs of Norway likewise had the reputation of being favored by the weather, and this reputation undoubtedly was backed by many historical examples. Olaf I Tryggvason was so much more *byrsæll* than other men that he sailed in one day as much as others in three. In the list of the kings of Sweden, there is one Eric Weatherhat, so called from his supposedly having the wind in his hat: he could change it by turning his headgear about.

This particular form of luck was not lost when the coast-dwellers of the Northern Sea moved over to Iceland. It is told of an Icelander that he was so *byrsæll*, he could always determine in which harbor he would wind up. And it is said of another Icelander that he sailed in one day as much as others in three.

Other men, instead, had luck in battle as their dominant attribute. When professional warriors, like Arnijot Gellini, seek to express their faith in a few words, they can find nothing to say but that they trust in their strength and their *sigrsæli*, their gift of victory. Among the chieftains, this gift of victory shows in its full splendor. We find men of military genius who bring victory in their train wherever they go. All the Norwegian kings of Harald Fairhair's race had this great gift of victory. And when Haakon Sigurdsson was able for a time to fill the place as ruler over Norway, it was due not least to his luck in winning victories, in pursuing and killing. It kept the people on his side, for they held that no one could be like him in respect of this particular gift. A similar tone is apparent in the opening of the story in *Beowulf*, about Hrothgar's kingdom; unto him was given war-speed and battle-honor so that his kinsmen followed him until the younglings were waxen and gathered about him in their host.

"Winner of battles" the king is often called in Anglo-Saxon, and the name expresses what the Germanic people asked of, and trusted to, in a ruler—in the great leader of the land, the king himself, the minor leaders, and local princelings as well as freebooter kings without land. The presence of the chieftain was a guarantee to the people of victory in the fight. The Anglo-Saxons gathered boldly to oppose the foreign Vikings, if only they had a man of chieftain's rank to take the lead and call the local forces together. As long as he was standing, they would fight with scorn of death, for hearth and home. But when word went around to assemble in mutual aid, without the inspiration of a born leader, they would remain at home, or they would run off to the woods and leave the invaders to work their will in the village.

Once, when the East Anglians were attacked by Penda—the victorious and generally feared king of Mercia—they found no other resource in their need than to go to their old king, Sigeberht, who, out of love for the heavenly light, had renounced the throne and shut himself up in a monastery. They begged him and implored him to come out and lead the host, and though he thrust aside the weapons, with uplifted hands calling to witness his monk's vow to God in Heaven, they forced him into the battle. This picture of the king in monk's cowl, dragged into the fight with a willow stick in his hand and there slain, is the more touching for its deep historical significance.

"And when they saw that their leader was fallen, they fled every man"—this sentence occurs again and again in the sagas, and its truth is confirmed again and again by history. If the great man's war-luck failed, what could the lesser luck of lesser men avail? Gregory relates that Clovis I won the decisive battle against the Alemanni by vowing himself to Christ when things were at their worst; hardly had he turned his mind in the right direction when his enemies took to flight.

The opening of the narrative agrees, albeit poorly with the sequel: "And when they saw their king was fallen, they surrendered and begged for mercy." The fact is that the pious tendency of the historian has had its way at the first, and that required only Clovis I and Christ; in return, history has its way with the clerk in the after-sentence, and gives the king of the Alemanni his due. But even admitting that the myth of Christ as the giver of victory is but ill grafted, the pious author is intrinsically right in making Christ manifest his glory in displacing the power that had been strongest among the heathen: viz, the king's luck.

These little pictures from life transfer us at a stroke to another world. Luck is working before our eyes with all the power it had over men's minds, to strengthen and to strike with numbness. In its foremost representative, the king, luck's peculiar character is properly revealed. The king's war-luck can prevail against an army. When the king comes, surrounded by his little host, the peasants are scattered like lambs at the scent of a wolf. This happened constantly in an age when every man was a warrior from his youth up. It is not very likely that the king's retainers should be very far ahead of the well-to-do yeomen of the country in respect to courage and skill at arms. The king's bodyguard corps was in Norway, and—as was typical at the time among Germanic peoples—was primarily composed of young volunteers, each of whom served a number of years till he had attained such a degree of training and renown as he considered fitting for his position in society.

Throughout the first two centuries of Norwegian history (that is to say, the infancy of the kingdom of greater Norway), when the sovereignty was never undisputed for more than ten years, tradition records hardly a single battle wherein a peasant army succeeded in offering effective resistance to the king's bodyguards, led by the king himself. The victory at Stiklestad, where the yeomen won the day over the king's men, is a triumph almost unique in history: the victors fled from the field in panicked terror, and the conquered prince came out of the battle as a demigod. When Olaf II showed himself amid his array, the peasants' arms "fell down," their minds were confused in a moment, and they were on the verge of every man running away. Strenuous urging and incitement, with reminders of Olaf II's hated rule, were needed to keep them in their places. And if we may believe the saga's description of the fight, the courage of the peasants was rather a sort of desperate convulsion in which their fear found vent, because their legs refused to carry them from the field. Olaf II's fall let loose a panic in the peasants' army; the men scattered and ran to seek cover in their homes, and six months later, the king was adjudged a saint.

Whether the saga men are to be taken as recorders of fact or as imaginative poets, the value of their sketches as psychological documents remains unimpaired. In the minds of the Northmen, the Battle of Stiklestad and the days preceding it were clothed with a mystic spell, and the memories were condensed into a picture, at once soberly realistic in details and mythic as a whole. In Olaf II, the ancient king's luck was transfigured; in the strength of his luck, he was exalted to martyr's glory, and his sainthood bridges over the gap between the old faith and the new creed. The Christian poets praise the king saint for giving all men harvest and peace.

To get a comprehensive view of the king's luck, we have to ask: what was demanded, in the old days, to make a man a true king? War-speed, the power of victory, is but one of the distinguishing marks that place the leader in a class apart from everyday characters. His constitution is marked throughout by greater strength and hardihood. Life is more firmly seated in him, whether it be that he is proof against weapons, or that they seem, perhaps, to turn aside from the spot where he stands. The first time Olaf I Tryggvason misses his mark is when he aims his bow at Earl Eric. "Truly, this earl's luck is great," he exclaims.

In the ancient way, it is said of Harald Wartooth that Odin had granted him immunity from wounds, so that no cutting edge could scathe him. And even though perhaps such a degree of hardiness was only found among the very few particularly favored, we must presume that the king had this advantage over ordinary warriors, that his wounds healed more easily and more completely. At any rate, he possessed a healing power that could be communicated to others. The Germanic chief had here at least one qualification for saintly rank, and one that counted for much in the early Middle Ages, when Christianity justified itself to a great extent by its power over sickness. There is no doubt but that these germs of saintliness in the kingship were eagerly fostered, we may perhaps venture to say, with unconscious purpose. The miracles and legends of Southern Europe cling easily to Olaf II, and it came naturally for people to seek healing at the king's resting place.

At the time when Olaf II's brother Harald Hardrada and his son Magnus reigned jointly over Norway, a mother came with her son who had lost his memory to ask advice of King Harald. The king opined that the patient suffered from dreamlessness, and counseled her to let the boy drink of Magnus' washing water, and thereafter sleep on Magnus' couch. The effect was instantaneous: both kings appeared to him in a dream, and said the one, "Have health," and the other, "Have quickness and memory," and then the boy woke laughing, having recovered the power of remembering. The kings of the Franks had no less of this healing power: a mother cured her son with a decoction from the fringe of King

Gunntbram's cloak. In earlier times, it was presumably a common belief that the king had "hands of healing," as we find in the invocation of Sigdrifa: "Give us two athelings [herself and Sigurd] speech and wit and hands of healing while we live."

The most violent attacks of nature, too, fell scatheless upon the king's luck. "Kings never drown," said William Rufus when he put out into the channel in a boat during a gale, to quell a revolt in Normandy on its first outbreak. Olaf the Saint, on his crossing to Norway, was in great danger during a storm, but "the good men with him, and his own luck, brought him unscathed to land."

With equal right, Olaf might have said that kings were never weather-bound. At any rate, it was one of a chieftain's natural attributes that his luck always gave him a favoring wind. The waters, too, carried shoals of fish into the ruler's lands. It is said of Haakon Sigurdsson that in his time, fish came up into all the fords. Luck of fertility prevailed over his fields, giving close ears of corn and good weight in the ear. Lucky in seasons and in procuring peace are the titles given to the mythical kingly ideal of the Swedes, Fjolnir Yngvifreyson, and if we add *sigrsæll* (victorious), we have the triple chord that embraces all life. A king without wars might be an exception, but he must be *friðsæll* (mighty for peace) in the sense of keeping the war outside his own frontiers, or at least preventing it from harrying the fields. War is to throw up a flood of honor and renown about him, heap up jewels and spoils, but not fail destructively upon the lands swelling with corn and the cattle heavy with fat.

Old sayings sum up the hardness and the massiveness of the chieftain's gift: "It is hard to fight against the king's luck," and "Much avails the king's luck." The wisdom implied in these sayings amounts to such sage counsels as this: one must not set oneself athwart the great man's luck, but let oneself be borne on by it. When a man entered the king's ranks and let his own war-luck be inspired by the higher, he became, in the most literal sense, worth more himself. The king was so full of luck that he could radiate it out to all those near him and could even send it away to act at a distance. If one could get a chieftain to approve an enterprise by his words, "I will add my luck," then one had his war-luck in one's weapons and his weather-luck in one's sails. Of such a man it can simply be said, "He goes not alone, for king's luck goes with him." And a request to undertake a desperate enterprise on the king's behalf was often granted with the words, "I will attempt it with your luck."

A man in the king's favor (for instance, Hallfreðr, the Wayward Skald) lived all his life in the shadow of the king's luck. When on one occasion he was attacked from behind, he prayed to Christ for aid, and succeeded "with God's help and by Olaf's luck" in beating off the attack. His opponents knew him for a man protected by special favor, and were cautious in attacking him; his bitter foe, Gris, whom he had injured most bloodily by ravishing his wife, was glad he had the chance to avoid meeting him in single combat, and declared that he was "loath to fight against the king's luck."

The belief in the king's power to put his luck into others and their undertakings is worked up by the Icelanders into an amusing tale about the failing and success of a poor man, Roi.[35] Roi was a skillful smith and an enterprising merchant, brave and "born with wits," though somehow fortune declined to favor his plans. However, much gold he might amass, it sunk as soon as he put it to sea, and when he had forged his way up again using his skill at his trade, he lost all his savings in his business deals. Then he considered going to King Sweyn Forkbeard and proposing partnership. When he appeared before King Sweyn with his plans for trading, the king's men spoke strongly against the idea of entering into partnership with a man so notoriously unlucky in his dealings, but Roi retorted confidently, "The king's luck is more powerful than my ill fortune," and the king himself was too far-seeing not to give this argument more weight than all objections. From that day forward, wealth sought out Roi. On peaceable trading expeditions, he harried the coasts of the Baltic for gold, and never once lost cargo at sea; he shared his spoils with the king, thus turning his friendship into affection. And to crown it all, he won the princess. Though his bride was of no higher birth than the daughter of a Swedish grandee, she was at any rate as good as the average princess.

It is the criterion, in fact, of the king's luck that it overflows and fills others with its abundance. On the field of battle, the king's luck sweeps like a storm out over the enemy. It opens a road for those who follow after him, and whirls them on to victory, but beneath this stormy power there runs a quiet, unbroken stream of luck that can bear—and actually does bear—the people up, inspiring its work with blessing, and making it thrive. We chance upon a piece of information from the Burgundians, to the effect that they gave their kings the credit for good harvests in the land, and in return, made them suffer when the harvest failed.

The Northmen judged in precisely the same fashion. According to mythical history, the Swedes even went to the point of "sacrificing" their king, Domaldi, "for good harvest," a persistent famine having occurred during his reign. At the introduction to Norway's history stands Halfdan *ársæli*, the greatest harvest-giver the people had known, as a kind of prototype of Harald Fairhair's dynasty. For a long time, it looked as if the luck of the Halfdan family was broken. In the time of the sons of Eric, there were years of great dearth, and the longer they ruled over the country, the harder grew the general distress. We are expressly told that the people "laid the bad harvests to the charge of these kings." Then arose a new race of rulers, in whom the blessing was full and whole. During the reign of Haakon Sigurdsson, such a change took place in the harvests that not

---

[35] From *Hróa Þáttr Heimska* (*The Tale of Roi the Fool*), an Icelandic short story.

only "did the corn grow up wherever it had been sown, but the herring came up all around the land." But with the other branches of the old stock, Halfdan the Harvest-Giver rose up again, and in Olaf the Saint his heritage was canonized: "God's man gives all men harvest and peace"; thus sings the poet Thorarin Loftunga in honor of the sainted king.

We must not, however, rush to the conclusion that Teutonic kingship rested upon certain persons' magic power of styling themselves magicians. From a modern point of view, a king might seem sufficiently tasked in having to govern sun and moon and an element or so besides, and any demand beyond such meteorological aptitude would be thought excessive. Still, other qualities were needed to raise a man to chieftainship under the old conditions. To appreciate the genius of the Teuton king, we must walk around and look at him from the social point of view as well, and our understanding will depend on our ability to combine the knowledge gained on these two sides.

We need not seek far and wide to ascertain what the king looked like; both ideal pictures and actual portraits have been handed down to us. In Harald Fairhair's race, the type appears as follows: tall (taller than the most of men), strong, handsome (the handsomest of all men), forward in the fight, skillful above all others in the use of weapons, and an all-rounded athlete, archer, and swimmer. Among the kings of Norway, Olaf Tryggvason is the perfect realization of the ideal; he could strike equally well with both bands, throw two spears at once, and walk on the oars while the men were rowing—while juggling with three swords in the air.

Ambitious and ever watchful that none should in any respect outstep him. Never content with the honor gained as long as there was more to gain. Deep and far-seeing in his plans. Clever to use all means that could further the end in view. Eloquent and persuasive, so that men wished no other thing than what he proposed. Glad, cheerful, generous to his men, and winning, so that all young brave men were drawn to him. Rich in counsel and faithful. Stern toward his enemies and those of his friends. A perfect friend to him who was his friend. This is the Germanic type of king that inspires the innumerable encomiums in Teutonic literature. It is reflected in the description of Offa by the poet of *Beowulf*: "the spear-bold man, praised far and wide for gifts and war, wisely ruling the land of his heritage." It is elaborated over and over in the Nordic songs and sagas. Tall, handsome, brave, skillful, and generous: these words indicate the totality of virtues that no king could do without; lacking one quality, he would lack all.

The praises really indicate a demand, a formulation of what was required of the king. The king, who ruled over wide lands, was not the only one who must fulfill the requirements of the ideal. Even the chieftain, whose sphere was restricted to a small district, had to possess a certain, not insignificant portion of all these qualities. This comprehensive moral and physical perfection belonged to the nature of chieftainship. Even a petty village leader was expected to stand firmly by the rights of his friends, and see that none encroached on them; he must be so respected that outsiders were loath to interfere with them. Any man in the village had the right to bring an injury he was unable to repair himself to the door of the chief, and if it were left there unavenged, it brought down infallibly nithing-hood upon the chieftain's whole race. It needed strength to take up such a heritage. When disputes arose within the district itself, the chieftain was the proper person to put matters right, to solve the difficulty so that "all were content with his decision." When we call to mind that the king, in such a case, found himself placed between two "honors," both equally susceptible and equally in-dispensable, we may presume that he would need to be gifted with a very high degree of craft and ingenuity—and generosity withal, so that he was not afraid of sacrificing something of his own in order to heal a wounded honor.

We can provide a background for our supposition by considering how the Icelandic chieftain Thorkel Krafla behaved on one occasion, when a man had been killed at the law-*thing*. With a party ready for vengeance, he went to the booth where the slayer was. In the doorway, he was encountered by the man's mother, who had a claim on Thorkel after having once saved his life. She tried to make her influence felt, but he met her intervention with these words: "Matters stand differently now than when we last spoke together, so go you out, that you need not see your son stricken down." She immediately acted on the hint and dressed her son in her own clothes and sent him out with the women. When Thor-kel had seen him safely out, he placed himself in the doorway and talked sense: "It is not fitting that we should kill our own neighbors and *thing*-fellows; it is better at least to come to an agreement." This is an episode from the late saga times, but an episode of the sort that occurs frequently enough on the steppes and in the mountains, where the tribe still lives in ancient fashion under the rule of a chief.

It was no sinecure to inherit royal dignity. Kingship required genius and great gifts, but these qualities were included in the royal character. That the born leader could achieve such great things, could procure his subjects right and honor, and—what was still more difficult—maintain their honors in their proper relation one to another is due to the very depth and might of his luck. It was easier for him than for others to bring men to agreements, and get men to follow him. The young men looked up to him and wished naught but what he willed, and the older men brought their difficulties to him because he was *vinsæll* (i.e., had the luck or gift of friendship), because he had *mannheill* (i.e., the gift of dealing with men). It can also be said in explanation of his popularity that he gained affection early "by his beauty and his gentleness in speech" (*bliðlæti*). Of another king it is spoken that he won the love of his men for being mighty and wise and a great harvest-giver. The word translated as "wise" is a very expressive term denoting craft, quickness of wit (adroitness, in other words), and diplomacy. His friend-luck depended on various factors, not the least of which was due to his power of strewing gold about him; youth did not flock to the court of a niggardly king. But all these gifts enter into the king's luck: diplomacy as well as generosity, and beauty as well as eloquence. There is no separating the qualities that we should call natural from the gifts of healing and fertility.

It would be foolish to regard the superiority of the king's bodyguards over the peasant army as due to a superstitious panic for the king's person, and deny that the fatal significance of his fall to the outcome of the battle stood in natural relation to his importance as leader of the fight. And this was well-known: such words as "leader of the host" or "ranger of battles" were often used as epithets for a chieftain.

There is not the least reason to regard these honorable titles as of late origin, and accuse the other Germanic peoples of lacking insight as to the king's gen-eralship. Surely as the king could and should bring about victory—radiating strength and courage into those who came near him, and darkening the eyes of his enemies till they stumbled over their own plans—so surely was it also of great importance to him to possess a well-disciplined army, and be able himself to take advantage of tactical opportunities with a corps that in a way hung together of itself. All these things—the discipline of the army, the generalship of its leader, the force of his blow, his power of compelling victory—are part of the king's luck. Whether we say the king had luck in learning the use of weapons and the art of war in order to remain unwounded in the midst of the fight, or whether we credit him with a gift for the profession of arms (a gift which made lethal weap-ons fall harmlessly from him), it comes to the same thing. The king was the luck-iest, that is to say, *inter alia*: the bravest, most skillful, wisest, and most ingenious of warriors.

To sum up, luck, in the view of the Teutons, is not a thing that comes from outside, setting the seal upon abilities and enterprises.

Every day we encounter instances of the great differences between men's fortunes. Poor folk have "but one luck, and that a slender one"; they may strive and struggle as much as they will; they gain no more than the minimum reward for their pains. With others, "luck hangs about them like dirt," as the proverb runs in Jutland; they simply cannot get rid of it. But the Teuton did not draw the inference from this experience that will, result, ability, and luck come from dif-ferent sides of existence and play blindman's buff with one another. He did not lay down inefficiency as the prime principle in human life and appoint fate or gods to keep all the strength and bear all the blame for evil results.

A man's luck of harvest is the power that inspires him to watchfulness and restless work, letting his arms wield the pick with good effect, which sets pace and force in his actions. It leads his pick so that he does not strike vainly in a stubborn, defiant soil, but opens pores for fruitfulness. It sends the corn up out of the ground, sharpens the young shoot to pierce the earth above it, saves the naked, helpless plant from freezing to death, and the grown corn from standing unsusceptible to sun and rain and turning to nothing out of sheer helplessness. It follows the crops home, stays with them through threshing and crushing, and gives the bread or the gruel power of nourishment when the food is set on the board.

The luck of harvesting and sailing and conquering are equally two-sided according to our notions. A man is blessed in his cattle when the animals grow fat and heavy with what they eat, when their udders swell full with milk, when they multiply, when they go to their summer grazing without scathe of wolf or bear, and when they come home fully hale in the autumn. But his luck is equally apparent in his power to seek them out and find them, should they stray, in places where no other would think to look.

Sailing implies maneuvering, conquering implies valor and shrewdness, and luck in wisdom implies skill "in making plans when needed." The sons of Ingimund were men of great luck: "It is hard to stand against the luck of the sons of Ingimund." Men feared Jokul's courage and berserker violence, but not less the "wit and luck" of his elder brother, Thorstein.[36] This luck displays itself in his always knowing or guessing beforehand what his opponents had in mind; he saw through every artifice of war, even when wrought by witchcraft, so that it was never possible to take him and his brothers by surprise. Their luck shows itself in the fact that they could wait, let time go on, make preparations, or strike on the instant without hesitation; the blow always fell at the right moment for them. When their father had been killed in their absence, and the slayer, Hrolleif, had got away safely to his kin, Thorstein restrains his brother by saying, "We must seek him out by craft, and not rush wildly on." He then pays a visit to the man who had concealed Hrolleif, and by dexterous handling gets him to give up the unlucky one and send him away from the homestead.

Thorstein quietly argues:

> It matters nothing what you may say; he is undoubtedly here. It is more to your good that he should be rendered harmless, such ill as he does against your will. It is not only for my father's sake that I am after him; he has wrought too much mischief that we can sit still now. We can take him outside your boundaries, so that no shame falls to you in the matter. Only tell him yourself that he is not safe here, and a hundred in silver I can well spare.

And as calmly as Thorstein has argued his case here, so too he stays on as a guest till the following day. On the way back from the homestead, he informs his

---

[36] Referencing Jokul and Thorstein of *The Saga of Thorstein, Viking's Son*.

brothers that Hrolleif must surely have gone home to his mother, the witch-wife, and must be taken there before she has time to work her arts over him. With hard riding, they were able to surprise the party in the midst of their preparations for the black magic by which the old hag intended to make her son hard against perils. They managed things so cleverly that she did not acquire power over them by catching sight of them before they had seen her. They saw through all dazzlement, and recognized the old woman herself in spite of all her tricks, and she was indeed right when she said, "I was near to having revenged my son, but these sons of Ingimund are men of great luck."

Thus it fell out with all who had matters outstanding with Thorstein—however they might set their plans, whether they had recourse to witchcraft or simple cunning, they always found him ready for them. He saw through everything from a distance, and when he arrived on the spot, no optical illusions "could avail, for he saw all things as they were": in their true nature, as another saga has it.

Naturally, a chieftain could not be suspicious and always go about scenting danger, for such a craven caution would be an infallible sign that he had not the luck of wisdom, but fumbled ever in the dark. The king simply saw through the shell of things, and knew what lay hidden behind pretended friendliness, and could therefore sit calm and secure where all was well, without letting his comfort be encroached upon by forebodings. When Harald Fairhair had been to Thorolf's splendid feast at Torgar, the two sons of Hilderid came up and wished him joy of his lucky journey, adding:

> It fell out as was to be thought. You were, after all, the wisest and luckiest [hamingjumestr], for you saw at once that all was not so fairly meant as it seemed, and we can also tell you now that it was planned that you should be slain there, but the peasants felt a catch in their breasts when they saw you.

It must be admitted that the pair of them knew how to flatter a king.

And if we would see an instance of what lack of luck (*gæfuleysi*) is, we find an illustration in the saga which treats of the dealings between Hrafnkel and his antagonist Sam. By a stroke of courage and a great deal of friendly assistance, Sam got the upper hand over the powerful and overbearing chieftain Hrafnkel. But when he had gotten his enemy underfoot, he contented himself, despite all well-meaning advice, merely with humbling him and forcing him to leave his homestead and the district. Hrafnkel raised a new farm and quietly worked his way up again.

When six years had passed, he was strong enough to begin thinking of bygone things. One day, he learned that Sam's brother had come home from an illustrious career abroad, so Hrafnkel lays wait for him on his very first ride from the landing place and slays him. Sam seeks out his old friends and helpers, but they meet him with cold words:

> We once made all things ready for you so that you could easily be upper-most. But it fell out as we knew it would, when you gave Hrafnkel his life, that you would come to mourn it bitterly. We counseled you to kill him, but you would have your way. No need to look closely to see the difference in wisdom between you two, Hrafnkel and you. He left you in peace and used his strength first to make away with the man he deemed of most account. We will not let your want of luck bring us to our downfall.

The Norwegian pretender Olaf Ugaefa—the Unlucky—gained his name from the half-heartedness of his plans when a night attack on Erling Skakki failed. Erling had fewer men, was taken by surprise, and suffered great loss, but the darkness covered him. Under shelter of a fence, he slipped away down to his ships. And his men said that Olaf and his followers had shown but little luck in the fight, so surely as Erling's party were given into their hands, had they acted with more wisdom.

There is all the difference of luck between rede—good, prudent and success-ful plans—and unrede, bad plans that may look sound enough, but are wanting in foundation. A wise man prepares his enterprises according to the time and circumstances they are to fit in with. He is capable of looking about him and interpreting what he sees. He does not let himself be confused by possibilities, but with strict logic discerns the actual state of things. When Thorstein judged that the time had come to avenge his father's death, he rode straight to the very homestead where the slayer lay concealed and called upon his protector to deliver up the wretch.

Upon the yeoman's making a show of innocence, he only said, "You, Geirmund, are Hrolleif's only kinsman of note, therefore he is with you and no-where else," and his conclusion had all the surety of a man of luck. It was not a result of suspicion, supposition, or probability, but of knowledge and of insight. But the wise man can do more than this: he judges men beforehand, and thus is not led astray by ill-fated connections with men whose counsels are barren. From sure signs in face and ways and manner he deduces what is hidden in the stranger, whether he is a man of luck (*hamingjusamligr*), one who will be an acquisition, or one whom it were best to avoid.

The very wise man knows also the world outside human life, and can guess the connection between manifestations and actions. He knows the weather and understands the speech of animals, or at least knows what they *would* say. He has a store of "ancient knowledge" in regard to things and events of the past—a knowledge that not only gives him dignity and esteem, but also security in his judgment of things now happening, and insight into the nature of things. He sees the past spread out about him in the same way as the present; the two penetrate and interpret each other. But his wisdom was poor if he did not also have (apart from the mastery of past and present) some familiarity with the yet unborn. "Keen-sighted" and "foreseeing" are identical terms among the ancients.

The unknown came to the man of luck in many ways. He was a great dreamer who was aware of things before they arrived, and saw beforehand men moving on their contemplated ways. Hrafnkel Freysgodi's father, Hallfreðr, even moved his entire homestead because a man came to him in a dream and said, "You are unwary lying there, Hallfreðr. Move your farm westward across Lagarfljot. All your luck is there." The same day as he had brought all his goods into safety, his old home was buried under a landslide. Thorstein Ingimundson, also, avoids the machinations of a witch-wife through a vision in a dream. And when she finds she is unable to draw him into the trap, she may well say, "It is hard to stand against the luck of these sons of Ingimund." But the direct knowledge must be added to dreams and clairvoyance, which may be expressed in these words: "few things come to him who is unaware, so surprise him," or in the simple form: "my mind tells me."

Therefore, the "wise" man can follow his plan through time beforehand, test it and adapt it before it is dispatched, or he can hold it back until the way is ready. But if wisdom could go no further, then his rede or counsel would, after all, be only as useful as a boat thrust out on the waters without a crew, entrusted only to favorable current and favorable wind. The wise and strong man's luck followed his plan, steering, pushing on, and keeping it toward the goal. The thought goes forward, doing with force and effect what it was sent to do. It is as if it had eyes to see with and sense to speak for itself. At any rate, it can force its way into folks' minds and turn them as it will. All that it meets on its way through the world it takes to itself and uses as its implement.

The success of a plan depends wholly on what it has in it from its first out-going, for it has its origin in a conception that gave it life and inspired it with luck. The projects coming from the greatest minds are at one and the same time the boldest and the safest of execution. The king's luck takes form as mighty thoughts of conquest—as when Harald had the luck to make all Norway one—and as inventions of genius, as for instance when a war-king conceives the idea of the wedge-shaped phalanx, which is mythically expressed as a device suggested by a god.

If a man should not have enough luck in himself to foster such a "counsel" as he needs, he goes, presumably, to a man of might and begs him to put something of his own virtue into the undertaking already planned. And naturally, if one went to a man about some difficult business and asked his advice, one expected to be given good (i.e., lucky) counsel (*hell ráð*) and not empty words that one had to fill oneself with progress and blessing. Empty, luckless folk might come to grief with spiritual values because they did not understand how to use them. If properly handled, the counsel must return with fruit. Naturally, the ancient word rede, or counsel, comprises several meanings which are sharply differentiated in our dualistic culture: plan and resolution on the one hand, and advice on the other. Rede is nothing but luck applied to one's own or to other people's affairs.

If a plan really has life in it, then it can only be checked by a greater luck killing it. A thought from some greater wisdom can go out and offer battle. The higher wisdom need not wait until the counsel has been dispatched; it can lay itself like a nightmare upon a poorer man's luck and make it barren and confused. To cite a real-world example, take what happened to the wise Thorleif of the Upplands. When Olaf Tryggvason, for very Christian reasons, sought the life of the obstinate heathen chief, he sent his faithful servant, Hallfreðr, the Wayward Skald, to carry out his design. When the poet hero turned up in disguise at Thorleif's homestead, the old man asked what news he brought—more specifically, if he knew anything of a certain Hallfreðr:

> [Hallfreðr] has often appeared to me in dreams. Not that it should be strange for me to dream, but there will come king's men to this place before long, and as to this Hallfreðr, I can never properly make him out from what folk say, and my luck is at an end in the matter of what is to come.

In other words: I may dream of him, but I see nothing in my dreams but a veil over the future.

When a man brought forth speech out of his store of words, the hearers could discern whether he was a man of luck. The Northmen (and probably the Germanic peoples generally) expressed a great admiration for art in their words. Encomiums of fine oratory are frequent in their literature, and their delicate wording, together with keen judgment of effects, almost makes us sharers in the complacency with which the listeners settled down when a man stood up among them who had luck to send his words safely into what harbor he pleased. The lucky man's speech would fall in those short, sharp images that the Northmen loved: the well-formed sentences leading one another forward instead of stumbling one over another, just as the separate movements, stroke and guard, fitted together when executed by a lucky body.

The words of luck found an outlet in such proverbial concentrations of speech that struck at the very center of a difficulty, and they cut with one sharp blow the question in dispute. Luck inspired a man at the moment of his fall to utter words so poignant as to be held in memory of his honor. But words, if uttered by a man of great luck, had likewise the double-edged peculiarity as the

LUCK ♦ 113

weapons of victorious fighters: they struck down among men, loosed the spell of lukewarmness and lack of courage, or made open foes of secret haters—as Egil thanks the gods that he could do. There was a great difference between what a king said and what a peasant said, even though they meant more or less the same thing. When Olaf Tryggvason stood up at the law-*thing*, where men crafty in words were gathered to oppose him, all were cowed out of opposition by the utterances of the king.

Words were dangerous. They could bite through luck and affix themselves in a man. They were not to be likened to sharp arrows that wounded, but might then be pulled out and flung to the ground. Because they had life in them, they would creep about inside the victim, hollowing him out until there was no strength left in him, or they would change him and mold him according to their own nature.

It was often a good plan to belabor one's enemies with words before attacking with weapons; one could in this way weaken the opponent's watchfulness, blunt his courage and adroitness, and dilute his invulnerability. In Saxo's narrative of Fridleif's fight with the giant, the king commences the combat by uttering taunts. According to the medieval monk, the giant was easier to cope with when he had first been irritated by scornful verses:

You three-bodied giant, almost knocking your head against the sky, why do you let that foolish sword dangle at your side. . . ? Why cover that strong breast with a frail sword? You forget how big you are, and trust in that little dagger. I will soon make your onslaughts vain, when you strike with that blunt edge.

Now there is danger that the sword may prove too light and its edge unable to cut through.

Seeing you are such a timid beast . . . you shall fall flat on your face, for in that proud body you bear a craven and fearful heart, and your courage is not equal to your limbs. . . . Therefore, you shall fall without fame, having no place among the bold, but set in the ranks of those whom no man knows.

Now it is best for the giant to look to his courage and his honor, and strike before the words have taken effect. He will be robbed of his courage if the power from Fridleif's mouth is not flung back as quickly as possible.

Once, when the Britons were attacked by the king of the Northumbrians, they had taken a small army of monks with them, and placed them in a safe spot to pray during the fight. King Ethelfrid, with practical sense, first sent his men to cut down the monks, and then proceeded to deal with the warriors. "If they call on their god to help them against us," he said, "then they are fighting against us, even though they use no weapon, since they oppose us with their prayers." Granted, such prayers were actually addressed to God, but Ethelfrid knew that even though the strong words made a slight detour, they would certainly end in the men for whom they were intended.

The power of words is such that they can transform a man when they enter him, and make a craven or a nithing of a brave man. The insinuation does not merely depreciate him in his neighbors' eyes—nay, the reverse: the contempt of the world is a result of the taunting gibe having entered the man, attacked his manhood, and in the truest sense rendered him a poorer creature. It eats its way in through honor and frith, and will not rest until his humanity is bitten through at the root. The greater the tension in the sender's luck and honor, the stronger the word, and the more dangerous the wound. The utterances of petty folk, with little mind beyond their needs to lay in their words, might perhaps be taken lightly; certain great men, indeed, might ignore them altogether. But if there were luck behind the words, it was wisest to lose no time in rendering them harmless by getting one's honor back through vengeance. The counsel offered by Norwegian and Icelandic laws for cases of milder, everyday misuse of the vocabulary (viz, to answer back word for word) is only valid to a very limited extent, and it must be received with the greatest caution. One must never forget that answering back does not give reparation, and it is wise then to consider whether one can afford to forego a strengthening of one's honor.

But words can, of course, equally well carry a blessing with them. A good word at parting is a gift of strength to the traveler. When the king said, "Good luck go with you, my friend," the man set out carrying a piece of the king's power in him. "Luck on your way to your journey's end, and then I will take my luck again," is a saying still current among the Danish peasantry. A good word given upon coming to a new place meant a real addition to one's luck. When Olaf the Peacock moved into his new homestead, old Hoskuld, his father, stood outside uttering words of good luck. He bade Olaf welcome with luck, and added significantly: "This my mind tells me surely: that his name shall live long." Orðheill, word-luck, is the Icelandic term for a wish thus charged with power, either for good or evil, according as the speaker put his goodwill into his words and made them a blessing, or inspired them with his hate, so that they acted as a curse. There was man's life in words, just as well as in plans, in counsel. Thoughts and words are simply detached portions of the human soul and thus in full earnest to be regarded as living things.

The ancient word rede (Anglo-Saxon ræd, Icelandic ráð) is a perfect illustration of Teutonic psychology. When given to others, it means counsel; when applied to the luck working within the mind, it means wisdom, or a good plan. From an ethical point of view, it means just and honest thoughts. But the word

naturally includes the idea of success, which accompanies wise and upright devising, and on the other hand, power and authority, which are the working of a
sound will. Men setting about to discuss difficult matters stand in need of rede
and quickness of mind, says an Old English writer.

According to the Anglo-Saxon poet, the lost angels fell because they would
no longer keep to their rede, but turned away from God's love; they did that
which was sinful, and at the same time ill-advised, and thereby brought about
their own undoing. Satan complains that Christ has diminished his rede under
Heaven, rendering him powerless. A redeless man is weakened by lack of will,
lack of power, and lack of self-assertion. The poet of the Anglo-Saxon Christ
uses this expression in order to depict the abjectness of the damned when they
stand on the left side at the Judgment Day, and hear the Lord's command: Go
hence, accursed ones: "They cannot withstand the bidding of the King of Heaven,
bereft of rede." Not until we have mastered the whole content can we realize the
depth of Satan's exclamation: "Why should I serve? I can raise myself a higher
seat than God's. Strong companions, famed heroes of unbending courage, that
will not fail me in the fight have chosen me as their lord, with such one can find
rede."

To feel the force in the ancient thoughts, we must take care that our dynamic
theories are not allowed to slip in. Rede is not energy residing in words, but the
words themselves as well as the soul. Luck stretches in one unbroken continuity
from the core of man's mind to the horizon of his social existence. This, too, is
indicated in the meaning of rede, which comprises the state or position of a man,
his influence, and his competence.

The inner state of a man in luck is described in Icelandic as a whole mind,
heill hugr, which of course comprises wisdom as well as goodwill and affection.
The man of whole mind is true to his kin and his friends, stern to his enemies,
and easy to get on with when lesser men come seeking aid. His redes are really
good gifts to the receiver—whole redes (Icelandic, *heil ráð*).

Outwardly, luck is dependent on the mutual love of kinsmen. With the flour-
ishing of frith go luck and well-being. And in the opposite case, when men cannot
agree, all life sickens and fades until everything is laid waste. This rule applies
to all frith communities—not only the family, but also temporary connections in
the sign of frith (and under any other sign, no alliance was possible). When men
united in any undertaking (such as fishing, or other occupations), the result would
depend upon the power of the individuals to maintain friendly and sincere relations with one another. In the *Laxdoela* saga, we chance upon this piece of information: "Wise men held it of great weight that men should well agree when on
the fishing grounds, for it was said that men had less luck with their catch if they
came to quarrelling, and most therefore observed caution."

The state of honor likewise determines the rise and fall of the family. The man who gains renown wins not only the advantages that go with the esteem of his fellows, he augments the blessing: the power of growth and fertility, both in his cattle and in his fields. He lays the foundation for new kinsmen in the family: the women will bear more easily and more often, and the children will be more hopeful and forward. Even in late centuries, the reciprocal responsibility of honor and luck were so rooted in Norwegian popular beliefs that men could say, "No man has luck to gain and keep wealth until he has slain two men and paid for the deed to the heirs and to the king." And the same association of ideas underlies the faith of Norwegian peasants in the luck and healing power of families descended from stern and murderous men, whose honor could be proved by numerous killings.

If frith and honor become sick, the result is a decline in all that appertains to the family—decline, and finally downfall. As we have seen, *Beowulf* has already given a description of the effects of villainy: the dying out of one's stock and the wasting of its goods. These verses wherein the wages of cravenness are so depicted no doubt allude primarily to the sufferings originating from men's contempt for those lacking honor; the picture can be applied word for word to an earlier and more original view, according to which the social consequences of shame were only correlative to its directly destructive effect: "Never more shall any of that race grasp gladly the gold."

The Northern description of the aforementioned phenomena is only an enlarged form of this curse. Men grow poorer and poorer; their power of action, their courage, confidence, mutual feeling, and feeling of frith are scorched away: "Brothers fight and kill each other, cousins tear the frith asunder, whoredom great in the world…. No man spares another." However near of kin they may be, the heat of the sun declines, and the earth grows cold and bare. Early frost and late frost bite off the young shoots. Summers grow weaker and weaker, and winters more and more stern.

The poet of the *Voluspa* is certainly inspired by his contact with Christendom for his eschatological vision, but there are only insignificant traces of direct impulse from Christian ideas. The inspiration caught from the West has worked so deeply in the poet that the ancient legends and images rise up and take on a new significance. His faith in the old ideals and his anguish at seeing them crumbling in the turmoil of the Viking Age impregnate one another. With the touch of Christianity, this interpenetration of ethics and experience produces a coherent view of history on the strength of a leading idea. The poet's vision molds the traditional legends to his purpose without in any perceptible way changing their contents, and connects a mass of disparate materials into one unified vision. This vision is the accumulation of guilt that drives the gods through one disastrous deed after another into their doom. And to the poet, guilt is tantamount to a breach of frith and honor. The force of his idea reveals itself in the fact that he has placed the myth of Baldr's death in an intimate connection with the tenet of doomsday. The picture of the gods killing one of their brothers is given a central place, so that it gathers up the force of the events going before, and ushers in the twilight of the gods and of the world.

It was a maxim borne out by experience that luck and progress are dependent on frith and honor, but the sentence could with equal truth be read conversely: luck is the condition that determines frith and honor.

When frith is broken so that kinsmen forget themselves toward one another, the fault lies in luck: either it has in some way suffered scathe, or it is by nature inadequate, leaving men helpless and without bearing. A good woman by the name of Saldis rejoiced in her daughters' two sons; they were both promising lads. Moreover, they loved one another tenderly. One day, Oddbjorg, a woman who could read the future, walked into the homestead. Saldis presented her grandchildren to the guest with pride and bade her prophesy, adding, "See to it, that your words turn out happily."

"Ay, promising are these two lads," Oddbjorg admitted, "if only their luck will last, but that I do not see clearly." No wonder that Saidis spoke harshly to her; but Oddbjorg only answered, "I have not said too much. I do not think their love will last long." On being pressed further, she blurts out, "They will come to seek each other's lives." And so it happened.

When Sverri delivered the funeral oration over King Magnus V, his kinsman and opponent, he began thus:

The man by whose bier we now stand was a brave man, gracious to his men, but we kinsmen had not the luck to agree well together with many fair words, such as he knew how to turn the way he would.

It is instructive to see how Sverri, a highly accomplished and reflective speaker, always has recourse in the old ideas during his calculated endeavors to speak in a popular tone. He himself is modern throughout, and he purposely joins his cause with Christianity and the strong element that has a future before it. But to get a grip on men's minds, he knows it is necessary to speak in a popular form, and he understands how to do it.

To form a happy couple, the bride and bridegroom need luck. Hrut—an Icelander of unusual qualities and high extraction,[37] and also a man of great insight—was late in marrying. One day, his friends proposed a match with a lady of good family named Unn. Hrut hesitantly agreed to the match, saying, "I do not know whether we two will have luck together." Hrut did not know at the time

---

[37] Hrut Herjolfsson, an Icelandic chieftain who visited Norway.

that he would fall under the spell of an imperious woman, but on a visit to Norway, he found favor with the Queen Mother,[38] and their intimacy embittered the subsequent conjugal life of Hrut and Unn and finally wrecked their marriage.

Villainy—the act and state of the nithing—is identical with so-called "unluck." After Gudrun congratulates him on having killed his cousin Kjartin, Bolli retorts, "Late will that unluck pass from my mind." In the *Völsunga saga*, Sinfjotli is taunted with his violent career in these words: "All unluck came upon you, you who killed your brothers." Strikingly effective is the outburst of feeling in Kálfr Árnason's words after the Battle of Stiklestad. Kálfr and his brother Finn had fought on opposite sides in the battle—Finn being a staunch supporter of King Olaf II, whereas Kálfr occupied a prominent place among those who worked for his downfall.

When the fight was over, Kálfr searched the field and offered help to his brother, who lay severely wounded. But Finn aimed a blow at him, calling him a faithless villain and a traitor to his king. The blow failed, and Kálfr gratefully exclaimed, "Now the king is watching over you, not wishing you unluck, but knowing that I needed care." Kálfr, who had been Olaf II's bitterest opponent, now extols the fallen king's luck as being strong enough to prevent the unbounded sorrow and anger of a king's man from turning to villainy.

In *Gisli's saga*, there is an exchange of words where "unluck" and "villainy" are used alternately with equal force. After Gisli had killed his sister's husband, he was hunted from one hiding place to another; however, the incessant pursuit by his enemies was for a long time successfully thwarted by the exertions of his wife, Aud. On one occasion, when the leader of the avenging party, Eyjolf, tries to drive Aud into giving up her husband, she pours out her scorn and insults him so cuttingly that he shouts, "Kill the dog, even though it is a bitch." Thanks to another brave man of the party, Havard, Eyjolf was saved from the ignominy of laying hand on a woman. Upon seeing Eyjolf forget himself, Havard exclaimed, "Our doing here is shameful enough, without wreaking such villainy as this; up, and do not let him get at her." Eyjolf now turned his wrath toward his friend, saying, "It is a true word: choose your company badly at home, and you will rue it on the road." But the saga proceeds, "Havard was much liked, and many were willing to follow him; also, they would gladly save Eyjolf from that unluck."

When villainy is called unluck, the latter term is not to be taken as an excuse; on the contrary, the word conveys a strong condemnation of the man who is denounced as being unlucky. When King Haakon (in the previously mentioned condemnation of taking vengeance on the wrong man) calls such an act "unluck," he is choosing the very sharpest term he can find in his vocabulary: the word that

---

[38] Gunnhild, Mother of Kings, queen of Eric Bloodaxe. In *Njal's saga*, Gunnhild had a scandalous love affair with Hrut. Eventually, she cursed him with priapism (a disorder in which the penis remains erect for long periods) and ruined his marriage to Unn.

comes nearest to the idea of deadly sin. Unluck is mischief, and an "unlucky" man is the same as a nithing, or in certain cases, a potential nithing.

The bluntest way of refusing a man who appeals for friendship is by saying: "You do not look to be a lucky man [úgæfusamligr], and it is wisest to have no dealings with you." These words simply imply moral as well as prudential misgivings. To draw out the full import of the sentence, we must give two parallel renderings. First, you have no luck in your doings, and you cannot bring those about you anything but ill-fortune. Second, you are not to be trusted, and a man may expect anything of you. And even when Njál says of his sons that they are not men of luck, the sentence had probably at that time a bitterer undertone than we now perceive. It implies that the young men want wit and forethought, and that they are lacking in self-control and moral restraint.

The uncanny symptoms of villainy lie in the fact that luck and honor are identical. Luck is the combination of frith and honor seen from another side, and unluck, in the old sense, is simply the reverse of that feeling of kinship we have now learned to understand.

It is luck that enables men to maintain their frith and their friendship, to keep their promises, and to refrain from dishonorable acts. But luck is more. It gives men the will to act morally; rather, it is moral will itself. When Hrut utters his misgivings, "I do not know whether we two will have luck together," he is thinking of their power to have and keep mutual love, and their ability to create frith in their home, as much as of their power to enjoy each other and have offspring.

In the Germanic idea, the moral estimate is always ready to rise to the surface; in fact, for the expression of goodness, piety, and uprightness, the Teutons have no better words than lucky (Anglo-Saxon sælig, Gothic séls, and similar terms), which embrace the idea of wealth and health, happiness and wisdom. In later linguistic periods, the ethical side of the idea often becomes dominant, and determines the use of the word in Christian writings. Thus, the Gothic séls—and its opposite, unséls—are for the translator of the Bible the best equivalent for the "good" and "evil" of the New Testament.

V. Luck Is the Life of the Clan

Luck is the ultimate and deepest expression of man's being, and that which reaches farthest. We cannot get behind it. However far we may go into the human soul, we can never get sight of luck from behind. First and foremost, the feeling of kinship is an outcome of luck, and when ill will and villainy break forth, these disorders prove that the heart of that family is ruined. We can then with absolute surety foretell that the one villainy will be followed by others, and the work of that race will be barren. Thus, naturally, the people argued in the case of Sigurd Slembe,[39] when, after having killed his brother, he claimed the title of king: "If you are truly a son of King Magnus, then your birth was unlucky [and *iflboding*, *úgiptusamligr*], and thus, too, it has fallen out if you have murdered your brother."

The unluck is by no means a consequence that comes halting along in the wake of misdeeds or dishonor. The Germanic mind actually counts on the fact that unluck sooner or later will arise in the place where dishonor has manifested its appearance, for the very reason that the concatenation of events was not dependent on God's keeping a strict balance. Fault and retribution are not connected by an intermediate link that may perhaps be sundered.

Luck, then, is the power that inspires a man and emanates from his person, filling his words and his deeds; it comprises all the requirements of the family, its powers and possibilities, its accomplishments and its hope, its genius and character. Luck contains the very existence of the clan. The family is called

---

[39] Alternatively spelled Slembi. He claimed to be the illegitimate son of King Magnus III (Olafsson or Barefoot). During the civil war era in Norway (approximately 1130–1240), Sigurd was one of many who laid claim to the throne. He raised an army to try to take the throne alongside his nephew, but was captured and tortured to death.

kynsæll, lucky in kinship, when kinsmen are numerous, and new members are constantly being born to fill the places falling vacant. In Anglo-Saxon, the same idea is expressed by *tuddorspéd*, which means luck in offspring and power of cohesion. In luck there lies, moreover, existence from the social point of view, the outward esteem in which the family is held. Prosperous kinsmen are said to possess man-luck (*mannheill*) (i.e., the luck to have the friendship and affection of others) and luck of fame (*orðheill*), so that people speak well, both in goodwill and with respect of them. In the Anglo-Saxon Genesis, God promises Abraham's son *freondspéd* (luck in friends, or, as we might equally well translate it, a wealth of friends). Finally, luck involves honor, both that which shines out in the splendor of renown, and that which lies compressed to a power of tension in the human soul.

Luck sets its stamp upon a man outwardly. From where had the Northmen gotten their keenness of vision, which enabled them to apprize a man at a glance? At the first meeting, they would say either that he is a man promising luck and honor (*sæmligir* and *hamingjusamligr*), one luck is to be expected of (*giptuvænligr*), or that he bears the mark of unluck (*úgiptubragð*). Partly on the strength of intuition, as we say; or, as the ancients put it, because the mind of the beholder told him what to think of the stranger, albeit partly on external criteria. Luck manifested itself openly in the newcomer's mien, gait, behavior, bearing, and not least in his well-nourished appearance, his health, his dress, and his weapons. Only a family of wealth and speed is able to send its youngling out in many-colored clothes and with a splendid axe, an "heirloom" of a weapon.

When Njál's sons, along with their friends, made their famous round of the booths at the *Althing* to gather supporters for the decisive suit, Skarphedin managed to stifle the dawning goodwill of one great man after another, because he could not repress his ironic smile and bitter words of scorn. The keen-sighted chieftain Snorri Godi discovered the secret of Skarphedin's failure when he said, "Doughty you look, Skarphedin, but your luck is near its end, and I should think you have but little of life remaining." At earlier times, when the words still retained their original force, a man's doom was contained in the single sentence: Luck forsook him.

This luck—or in another word, *hamingja*—comprises all that made up a man's humanity, both his body and his soul. To gather the full value of the term, we must bear in mind that this *hamingja* constitutes a whole, which is homogeneous throughout. Even though it may manifest itself in different forms—according as it makes its way out through eyes, hands, head, and through cattle or weapons—it is one and indissoluble. Behind the visible man, or more correctly, behind the visible circle of kinsmen, there is a spiritual sum of force of which the kinsmen are representatives. In a trial of strength, the whole *hamingja* is at stake; in the result, it emerges either stronger and more handsome in all its limbs, or palsied throughout.

It is this compact strength which makes king's luck so invincible to ordinary men. "You have not luck to measure yourself against the king," one may say; and this means, you have not kinsmen enough, not wit, courage, war-speed enough; your power to victory is too slight, your gift of fertility too weak. While you sleep, the king's *hamingja* will take yours by surprise, blind it and confuse it; his *hamingja* will pit itself against yours in other men's minds and cripple it, and before you come to face each other in open fight, you will be a paralyzed man. The Northmen have an expression: *etja hamingju*, literally, to urge luck with a man just as one might urge a horse with him, to let one's war stallion bite and try its strength against his. Indeed, every trial of strength between men was a strife between two powers of luck, a spiritual conflict. The result of the fight depended to a great extent upon the man's quickness and agility, just as the luck of a horse depended on its owner's ability to support it and urge it on. But there was still something stronger that filled the scene; the struggle between the combatants was only part of a contest fought in a larger field of battle by powers that never slept.

"You have not luck to measure yourself against the king," said Kveldulf to his son Thorolf, when the relations between the king and the young chieftain drew nearer and nearer to open conflict. But long before that time, the old man had warned his sons against having anything whatsoever to do with Harald: "My mind tells me that we kinsmen will not have luck with this king, and I will not go to meeting with him."

The saga lets Thorolf's brother make use of the same expression in his explanation to the king, when the latter is half-forcing him into his service: "Thorolf was a far more notable man than I, and he had not luck to serve you. I will not serve you, for I know that I have not luck to yield you such service as I should wish, and as might rightly be expected." The fact was that these big yeomen had not the aptitude for such a position, or they had not the will to adapt themselves to it, which is essentially the same thing.

And here we come to a deep-rooted peculiarity in the psychology of the ancient character. The idea is that if one earnestly wills something, then the power will come. Conversely, the idea that the power perhaps may be there does not manifest for lack of will had no validity for the Northman. All his peculiarities were due to the nature of his luck: obstinacy as well as courage, pride as well as inclination to serve the greater man, violence and intractability as well as fearlessness. Luck is the nature of the mind, the character, and the will. With our ideas as to the reciprocal effects of desire and will, we must again and again in these old sagas find ourselves face to face with insoluble riddles. It often seems as if men would gladly relinquish destructive undertakings, as if they would

gladly clear away misunderstandings and enmity, but something invisible leads
their endeavors to miss the mark. We may say that they cannot because they will
not, or they will not because they are not able, for both sentences are equally true.
When we, in such cases, call in the idea of trust in fate and servitude to fate, it is
easy to lose sight of the true reason why these men cannot resist fate, or in other
words, that they will their own fate. It is the will in them that forces them up
against desire and calculation and brings their most serious plans to naught, because the will has its nature, and cannot act beyond the limits drawn for it by its
own character. The luck of Kveldulf's sons was once and for all of such a character that it could not fit in with the king's. Therefore, it was best to keep them
apart. It was not so much the difference in strength that determined the relations
of men one with another in the world, but quite as much the dissimilarity in character between them.

The luck of the chieftain was of a far different volume from that of the peasant. "You are rich in luck [literally, 'your luck goes a long way'] and all turns
out well in your hand," says Saemund characteristically to the old Vatsdoela
magnate Ingimund, when he himself can no longer manage his headstrong kinsman Hrolleif, and begs Ingimund to receive him. The secret of the chieftain's
power to achieve the impossible lies, however, not in the bulk of his luck, but in
its distinctive character.

This peculiarity of luck constitutes the natural foundation of a Germanic
king's authority and influence. He has very little formal power, or hardly any;
whether men will obey his commands or not depends on their inclination at the
moment.

The Southerners observed the anarchy that displayed itself in the Germanic
hosts, and gave up all attempt to find any common sense in the Teutons' monarchical principles. According to the classical writers, these barbarians show no
respect to their prince, and they do not salute him. If the king's decision dis-
pleases them, then they surround his tent and force him with loud cries to alter
his plans. They bring matters to war where he wishes peace, and peace when he
desires war. It may happen that in a fit of dissatisfaction with him, they simply
drive him out.

Behind the words of the Romans, we seem to catch an ironic question: what
on earth do such creatures want with a king at all? We have no reason to discredit
the observations of our authorities; they are, for the most part, made with the
intelligence that comes with a cultured mind, and with the cultured mind's watchful interest in barbarians pressing ever closer on the frontiers of civilization. It is
another matter that the observer only saw the outward movements, and by his
very culture was prevented from perceiving the nervous system that produced
them. These statements must stand in some relation or other to the no less unde-
niable fact that the Germanic royal families possessed a remarkable toughness.

We find tribes drifting vagabond-fashion about over the greater part of Europe, now fighting for their lives, now sitting comfortably at ease in conquered territory, but always, century after century, under the same race of kings.

Procopius gives a priceless narrative of the Herules' fidgety experiments in kingship, wherein both the front and the reverse of barbarian loyalty are portrayed with the keenness of caricature. The Herules,[40] he says, one day hit upon the idea of trying what it was like to live without a king; accordingly, they took their only royal personage and slew him. No sooner had they tasted the sweetness of freedom, however, than they discovered that it did not agree with them. Regretting what they had done, and feeling that they must get back the old state of things at any cost, they sent an embassy from the Mediterranean countries up to the North to fetch them a king of the old stock. The ambassadors go traipsing through Europe and find a prince in Scandinavia; unfortunately, he dies between their fingers on the way.

Undismayed, they turn back for a new specimen, which they manage to bring safely through to the South. Meanwhile, the others at home, having plenty of time to reflect, took it into their heads that in a matter of such importance it would be wrong not to consult Justinian. Surely enough, the emperor happened to know a native Herule living at the court of Byzantium, whom he could therefore highly recommend. But just as everything is going well, a message comes to the effect that the Scandinavian prince previously requisitioned is on the way. The Herules, having put Justinian and his good men to such inconvenience, can do no less than show themselves worthy of the confidence shown in them. They follow their ruler with enthusiasm into the field, ready to put the latecomer to the right-about. Unfortunately, they have a quiet night to think matters over, which they utilize to go over to the side of the traveler from afar, leaving the imperial candidate to find his own way home to Byzantium.

A most curious history this is, but one bearing the stamp of verisimilitude. Such kaleidoscopic characters are only to be equaled in the accounts given by Europeans of what they themselves have seen among savage and barbarous peoples. The analogy with the researches of modern ethnologists increases the likelihood that Procopius is merely relating simple notorious facts, but this comparison also suggests the possibility that Procopius has missed some hidden principle guiding the acts of the barbarians. The explanation lies partly in the political relations between the Herules and the emperor of Byzantium, partly, and chiefly,

---

[40] The Herules (aka the Heruli) were an early Germanic people who harried the Romans in the Balkans and Aegean Sea, and were described by Roman authors as one of the tribes of the Scythians. They were later absorbed into the Hunnic confederation under Attila. They also participated in conquest of the Italian peninsula alongside Theodoric the Great of the Ostrogoths and Justinian of the Byzantines. The Herules were largely destroyed by the Lombards in the early sixth century, and its scattered population were later absorbed into the Eastern Roman Empire and ceased to be a distinct group.

in the people's spiritual dependence upon the right king: king by the grace of God, as we might say, or by the grace of luck, as the Herules might have said. Jordanes has formulated the monarchical principle in his simple, medieval manner: the Goths regarded their noble families as more than human, as demigods, "those in whose luck they, as it were, conquered."

In Sweden, the king, Olaf, and his people lived an open and honest life together, without any illusions. The fundamental paragraph in the part of the Westgöta law treating the king's rights and duties runs thusly: the Upper Swedes are to take the king and drive him out. And if we compare this poignant maxim with the description given by the historian Snorri of the *thing*-meeting at Uppsala, we may find here a powerful historical illustration of the rule. On this occasion, Thorgny the Lawspeaker addresses the angry king as follows:

> Now we yeomen will that you agree with Olaf II and marry your daughter [Ingegerd Olofsdotter] to him. But if you will not have it as we say, then we will all go against you and kill you, and not suffer you to disturb the law and the peace of the land. Thus, our forefathers did aforetime; they cast down five kings into a well because they were swollen with overweening pride, as you are now to us. Choose then at once what terms you will.

There is nothing very splendid about a royalty whose representative must suffer such a form of address. But when the lawman gives historical precedent for such obedience on the part of the king, he is unwittingly presenting the relation between king and people from another side. Thorgny asks King Olof Skötkonung to understand what sort of people his ancestors were: men who every summer went out on forays and subjugated the eastern lands. The earthen strongholds they raised over in Finland, Estonia, and Courland are still to be seen. These heroes, he goes on, were not too proud to listen to the advice of other men. Thorgny is perfectly right. But if the miserable Olof had taken after his ancestors, he could safely have asked for advice from other men, without fear of being forced into a peace that went against his will.

Unfortunately, we know hardly more about these forefathers of Olof's than Thorgny here tells us. This much, however, is fairly certain: it was not the peasants who planned those forays and ravagings outside the country. It was the king. Eric the Victorious, Bjorn, and these conquering rulers of Sweden by whichever name they were called gained both honor and advantage from the wars. The peasants no doubt got their share of honor—and possibly also their share of the booty—but the advantages of territorial acquisitions can never be so fully exploited in the work of a farm as they can at the king's court. The king neglected nothing of his work at home by being away on expeditions, but the peasants might well have work enough of their own to keep them busy during the summer.

It might be, then, that other men listened well enough and willingly enough to what those kings said.

This trial of strength between the peasants' spokesman and the Uppsala king rises to the position of a symbol of the Germanic kingship, in which its peculiar strength and its peculiar weakness are each sharply defined. Here, as everywhere among the peoples of the North, it is the king's initiative that furnishes undertakings for the people. He stands (and not to the eye of the alien chronicler alone) as the conqueror, from whom plans emanate, and those plans emanate in the form of commands. He commands, but he has nothing beyond what we should call his personality to rely upon for the enforcement of his commands. There are no statutes and no royal prerogatives to support him when he begins to show himself redeless. All his power lies in the firm grip of superior luck. If that should fail but a moment, then the people come forward with their grievances, saying such things as, "we will not suffer injustice at your hands." There is little then that the king can do that will not naturally be included under the heading of injustice. But as long as the king's plans are put forward with the effectiveness of luck, men will follow his call, carry out his plans, and submit without audible protest to arbitrary acts and interference with their liberties. Then there is little that cannot be included under the heading of "law" or justice.

At a hasty glance, it might seem as if the kingly power was something floating loosely over the life of the people. And yet, the truth is that kingship is an institution that no revolutions, let alone momentary fancies, can shake. He who sits in the king's seat has it in his power to make himself the state; on the other hand, he can make himself a powerless shadow of the state, but he cannot efface himself. While rights may wax and wane, the chieftainship stands fast, because the one family represented by the king or the chieftain possesses a luck of altogether egregious character, not only stronger and more manifold, but in its essence fundamentally different from that of all others.

When the people sweep the king aside, then the reason is that they feel the decline of his "speed" (i.e., his power to victory). However, the luck itself—that family luck from which his personal influence wells up—is a thing they cannot do without. They know there is danger in thrusting him out: he has something peculiar in him that is not to be found anywhere else in the land. He has a luck in which they trust, with a faith rooted deep down in the lower strata where not only vital courage but vital fear lies. The individual holder of the title may degenerate, but the people of the land will keep to his stock nevertheless. They must have a representative of the superlative *hamingja* with them in the fight, or all their courage will be in vain. A child could accomplish more than a host of courageous and skillful warriors. Little King Ingi, poor child, was at the age of two wrapped in a fold of Thjostolf Mason's cloak, and carried under the banner in the forefront of that battle that was to decide his right to Norway. Luck was evidently with him, for the men carrying him in their midst won the day. But it was too frail to stand all the hard knocks, for his legs and back were never sound thereafter.

In the same way, the Frankish queen Fredegunde used her little son Chlotar as a shield against misfortune. She had had her husband Chilperic killed in order to set her son in his stead. Now the avenger comes upon her, in the person of Chilperic's nephew, aided by numerous allies. Fredegunde staked all on a single throw, ventured an attack at dawn, and gained the victory; indeed, she had herself carried little Chlotar on her arm in the midst of the army throughout the battle.

By emphasizing the peculiar position of the king's luck, we modern people, whose thoughts always group themselves in categories, invariably lump the Teuton kings together as a species, and register the king's luck as an item in Germanic culture. Thus, we lose sight of the true secret that every king's luck was a thing apart from all else, and it owed its influence to individual powers of its own.

The history of the Norwegian kingship—its centuries of conflict with the old chieftainship, as represented by the Hersirs,[41] or petty kings—may serve as a grand illustration of the individuality of king's luck. The kings of Norway were famed for their power and authority. Olaf Tryggvason ruled, apparently, as a self-constituted despot: he "forced Norway to Christianity"; those who would not as he willed, he mutilated, killed, or sent headlong out of the country. He could set out upon the strange expedition against the Vends followed by the chieftains of Norway and their fleets.[42] But in the sagas, Olaf by no means always appears as triumphing over the will of the people and their leaders.

As soon as the king ventures into countries not in the strictest sense his by inheritance, the local chiefs come out against him as his equals and offer terms. When Olaf Tryggvason appears in the Gulathing with his proposal for conversion, he is given this answer by Olmod the Old:

> If it is your mind to force us, and encroach upon our law [i.e., the state of law we live in] and make us subject to you, then we will resist with all our might, and let victory decide. But if you will make it worthwhile for us kinsmen, then you might gain our services.

They price their loyalty at nothing less than a matrimonial alliance with the house of Norway, and demand the king's sister for their kinsman Erling Skjalgson. And the king at once sees the honor of such a proposal. Olaf then holds another meeting with the peasants to discuss the question of religion. When Olmod and Erling

---

[41] A Viking military commander of an administrative division, usually of a hundred men, that owed loyalty to the king.
[42] A Balto-Finnic people residing in modern-day north-central Latvia.

Skjalgson (Olaf's new brother-in-law), with all the circle of their kin, support the king's proposal, "no man dared to speak against it, and all the people were made Christians." It was on this occasion that Erling Skjalgson declined the offer of an earldom with the famous words: "My kinsmen have been Hersirs." Later, Olaf the Saint was similarly obliged to come to an agreement with Erling, and what this agreement meant appears as plainly as could be desired on a later occasion: when Erling actually raises an army and comes at the head of a couple of thousand men to claim his rights.

What we see here is the trial of strength between the old petty kingships and the new sovereignty of the country as a whole. And the minor princes are, where they stand on their own ground, the stronger party. The people followed them seemingly blindly, "wishing no other thing than they said," setting their shoulders firmly to the demands put forward by the chieftain, and often actually maintaining them. The men did what they did in full confidence in the luck that inspired their chief. The yeomen trusted in his luck, because they had felt its force in themselves. These princes belonged to a race that had for generations formed the center of the life of their district.

The family had had luck and wealth enough to take up solitary adventurers and give them a place at its board, and to inspire them with strength to fight its battles. It had had power enough to radiate luck over those who tilled the soil and herded cattle on their own account. Fertility and ripening oozed from its fields to those of the others. In the wake of these kinsmen, others could sail with a full wind in the strength of these highborn men they conquered—in their luck and wisdom, they were agreed.

The Hersir was no more a despotic ruler than was the king of the country, perhaps even less so; he had little power to command. In actuality, he was more powerful than a despot. The luck of his race was interwoven with the most commonplace actions of the other families, both in their peaceful occupations and in their internal bickering. He judged between them, and he could do so because the traditional word of the law and its spirit were a living force within him. He was the personification of the social spirit, as we might say. But we feel now distinctly that this modern formula is too authoritative to embrace the whole of his influence; it must be replaced by the old saying: he had law-speed in him. He was the object of dependence so deep that it lay rooted in the self-reliance of his dependents.

Harald Fairhair had made Norway one kingdom, and conquered the local princes. But to crush them was more than he or his successors could do; the luck of the usurpers did not even succeed in piercing through that of the Hersirs, so as to find root in the people itself. The old relationship between the villagers and their chieftains was a thing the successors of Harald had to leave untouched. In reality, as far as regarded a great part of Norway, they ruled only indirectly. For a long while, Norway continued to be an assembly of lands, and the "peoples" retained the old intercourse with their chiefs; only through them did they come into contact with the sovereign. Again and again, we find a touch of something foreign, even of indifference, in their attitude toward the "outland" king. What was he to the peasants? They could not feel his luck moving the ground beneath them, whereas the luck of their Hersir manifested itself in their harvests.

It is not easy to exaggerate the feeling of independence in the lands and the peoples under Harald and his dynasty, right down to the period of the great struggles for the throne. But the more we emphasize it, the keener the light we throw thereby on the power of a king like Olaf Tryggvason. His victorious march through Norway and his expedition to Vendland to secure the dowry of his queen appear in their true magnificence against such a background. Differently, but no less conspicuously, the puissance of the monarch reveals itself in the Battle of Stiklestad, in which the sovereignty, despite the fall of the king and despite the victory of the peasants, celebrates its apotheosis.

Comparing this meeting between chieftains and king with that other scene between Olaf Tryggvason and Erling at the Gulathing, we can see that the political status of Norway is changing. The great event is not to be understood without regard to the growth of the royal power under the influence of European history. But Olaf's superiority is of far greater weight than any generation can build up, even though, with the haste of a period of transition, it may heap revolution upon revolution. To be firmly established, the historical interpretation of these years must be based on a sympathetic understanding of the people's instinctive veneration for the luck of the sovereign, and the sovereign's unreflecting confidence in his own luck.

Through the interaction between these tendencies and religious and political ideas coming from abroad, Norway grows from a Teutonic kingdom into a medieval Christian state. The death of Olaf constitutes a turning point in Norwegian history, because all the current issues of the time (national as well as cosmopolitical) find their confluence in Olaf and lift him into royal sainthood.

Snorri Sturluson's description of the conflict between Olaf and the peasants is a worthy counterpart to his picture of the scene at Westfold. The words and the events of those memorable days have a weight that reaches far out beyond the moment, as if the great powers that carry history onward were here finding expression through men and masses of men. The description combines inner truth, such as could only be prompted by spiritual intimacy, with correctness in external facts, such as only a faithful report can preserve. The first thing that strikes us is the complete helplessness of the peasants and their leaders; the men run hither and thither, questioning, fumbling. None of the chieftains dare take the lead; one thrusts the responsibility upon the other. Olaf's party, on the other hand, bears throughout the stamp of calm, confident waiting; they maintain order and a sense of unity. Olaf possesses that unifying inspiration that carries the whole army in an elastic grip; the opposing chieftains are lacking in assurance, and feel their weakness acutely. In the peasants' army, the flow of luck threatens to come to an end at every moment. Individually, each of the petty chiefs might be stronger than the king, but together, they cannot prevail against him. At home in their districts they are equal to anything, but they count for very little outside.

Here the secret of Olaf's descent comes to light: the luck of the sovereign had such an extensive character that it could radiate out over the whole of Norway, and could be distributed among a whole army without ebbing. The luck of Olaf was not dependent on a certain soil or an individual body of men, but could be victorious wherever the king showed himself.

It seems contradictory that the king's luck should embrace the whole of Norway, but suddenly lose its force when applied to a limited district. The contradiction exists only for us, however. We judge the two lucks according to strength and do not see that the decisive difference lies in their character. The luck of the local chieftain was absolute, but could only answer to the soul of the valley: the district and the people. It might, of course, also extend to the fishing grounds outside the village territory, or seafaring expeditions undertaken by the villagers themselves, but in order to cover other lands and other communities, it had first to undergo a transformation by drawing up the alien power into itself and assimilating it.

Every luck is of its own sort. To go out fishing with a cattle breeder's particular luck would give the same result as if one tried to catch cod with a plowshare. To rule and give fertility in the East with a luck that pertained to the West was no less topsy-turvy; to defend or conquer Norway called for the luck of a Harald. When Harald's dynasty was on the wane at the end of the tenth century, Haakon Sigurdsson (a ruler of powerful stock residing at Lade, near Trondheim) had succeeded in usurping the kingship of Norway. He used his power with a great deal of insolence and overbearing, which exasperated his people. His grip on Norway was insecure, because it depended on his personal shrewdness and force of character. Despite all inclination to revolt, the Norwegians were nevertheless practically forced to wait the hour when Olaf Tryggvason set up his luck as a worthy opponent to that of the Earls of Lade.

The saga says that when Olaf came to Norway, he was received by the peasants with these words:

> We thought, after the fight with the Jomsborg Vikings, that no chieftain could compare with Haakon Sigurdsson in war-speed and many other qualities he had to make him a chief, but . . . all are now grown so weary of his insolence that he shall lose both kingdom and life as soon as we find him. We believe that this will come about with your help and luck, such a man

of luck as you are who got a hold of his son Erlend at the first attempt. Therefore, we pray you be leader for this host.

In the sentence, "we believe that this will come about with your help and luck," we can all read the explanation of a century or so of Norway's history. And if we are to determine more precisely what constitutes the luck of Harald's house, we have nothing to say but this: the *hamingja* of a Norwegian king consists in being king of Norway, able to sit now at Viken (now at Trondheim), able to gain the victory with an army of Trondheim warriors as well as with an army of Viken warriors, and able to march over Norway from one law-*thing* to another on a kind of peaceful conquest—as his ancestor once did in full warlike earnest when he broke the petty kings to his will. And the only explanation of this luck is the history telling how Harald created it and how his sons maintained it.

This faith in the individual luck as something that is at once a will and an impulse—a necessity and a talent—appears with peculiar splendor in the last great representative of that dynasty. Sverri, the unknown priest from the Faroes, had a double fight to wage when he landed in Norway to claim the crown on his unsubstantiated pretension that he was descended through his father, Sigurd Mund, from Harald Fairhair. The submissive faith that went out to every pretender if he could only declare himself a descendant of Harald had, in this case, to be built up among the people by the usurper himself. Through his victories, he had to create, layer by layer, a conviction in the minds of the hesitant that the luck that upheld him must be the most decisive one: Olaf's. His genius is shown in the fact that he, by every means of eloquence, artifice, and guile—nay, deceit—manages to force the testimony of facts as far over to his own side as possible, and hammer it firmly into the minds of the people. And this spiritual fight is the more impressive, insofar that it never clearly comes to the consciousness, but is waged between instinctive feelings in the king as well as in the people.

Whether Sverri himself believed in the traditional luck, or only worked upon the potential belief that he knew was dormant in the people, is an idle question. In the history of every faith there comes a time when it can be used as a weapon by strong characters, such as are keen-sighted enough themselves not to be fettered down by its limitations. The secret of their influence lies in the fact that they are able to rise above their fellow men in their reasoning, and at the same time draw strength from a belief that is as instinctive and positive in its way as the blind confidence of the mass. Sverri was such a man.

Sverri is the most interesting character in the history of Norway, because he translates the old idea of the king's luck into modern theories of the rights and nature of kingship. His character as the spokesman of an age of transition reveals itself in the contrast between his explicit reasoning and their underlying logic. As soon as he sets out to justify his claims, he drifts into an interpretation of the

Psalms of David as prophetic foretelling of his own fate; he calls himself the messenger of God, sent out to strike down the insolents who have seated themselves on the throne without being kingly born. It is only in the theory of the king's eternal predestination in God's counsel—his call and his obligation to answer the call, his prospect of having some day to account to God for the talent entrusted to him—that he finds sound foothold for himself.

Beneath this theorizing, there is the conviction that every possessor of king's luck has not merely the right, but the duty to demand his share of the kingship, and that all right and law in the land must give way to the king-borne's need to rule. "Olaf's law" is the symbol of his kingly pretensions. In other words, Sverri's life still centers about the presumption that there is in every descendant of Harald or Olaf a power that forces him to be king of Norway or die. Kingly birth is not a will *or* a duty, nor is it a will *and* a duty, but at once a duty with the elasticity of will in it, and a will with the mercilessness of a duty. Kingly birth is a nature as essentially urgent as that which forces a plant to fix its roots in the earth, save that the plant can fulfill its destiny in many sorts of soil, whereas luck knows but one place to live. The kingly will, according to Sverri, cannot be imagined save as the outcome of a power that strews kingly actions about it, actions of sovereign dimensions, that cannot be carried out by any but the one: the descendant of Harald.

The priest from the Faroes forced the people to say, "Sverri is quick of wit; Sverri is a conqueror," and in return the opposing party could not say, "many are quick of wit; many are conquerors." They had to fall back on a denunciation of his religion, saying, "It is by power of the Devil that he lays his plans and fights his battles."

Harald's kingship shows us the essence of luck and its qualities, emphasized in the light of history. Its absolute individuality cannot be explained or characterized otherwise than by inheritance: that which we have derived from our kinsmen of old, and that which they had power to be and to do. The difference between rich and poor consisted, not in the fact that the latter had been given only a small sum of luck, but that their luck was poor and inelastic, with but few possibilities, and those limited and weak. The luck of a well-to-do yeoman *was* like himself: broad and safe, rich in cattle and crops, shining with splendid clothes and weapons. That of the chieftain added hereto the greater authority: love of magnificence and the power of conquest. But this does not give us the essential point: namely, that the luck of every yeoman and every chieftain was a character with its peculiarities, its strength and weakness, its eccentricities, and linked throughout to a certain property. Again, we have to dismiss the singular form, with its tacit assumption of community in things human, and instead of luck, use the plural form lucks, in order to emphasize the fact that these characters are not emanations of any primeval principle.

Or, we can, in place of the word inheritance, use the word "honor." In honor, we have distinctly that which luck can and must be able to affect in order to maintain itself. The family has derived its renown from its ancestors. From them it has its ideals, the standard of all behavior: how bold, active, firm, noble, irreconcilable, generous; how lucky in cattle, in crops, in sailing the kinsmen are to be. From them also, the family has inherited that part of luck that is called friendship and enmity. Honor, and thereupon luck, constitutes, as we have said, an image of the world of the family. In the quality of esteem and social position, it contains symbols of the family's surroundings, seen as personifications of the kinsmen's friendship and hate, their condescension and dependence. But these personifications are not characterless types; they resemble to the last degree the enemies and friends of the family. The luck reproduces the sharply defined features of its environment.

The saying that kinship is identical with humanity, which at first sight seemed a helpful metaphor, has now revealed itself as nothing but the literal truth. All that we find in a human being bears the stamp of kinship. Seen from outside, a man can find no place in the world save as a kinsman, as member of some family—only the nithings are free and solitary beings. And the very innermost core of a man—his conscience, his moral judgment, as well as his wisdom and prudence, his talents and will—have a certain family stamp. As soon as the man steps out of the frith and dissociates himself from the circle into which he was born, he has no morality, neither any consciousness of right, nor any guidance for his thoughts. Outside the family, or in the intervals between families, all is empty. Luck, or as we perhaps might say, vitality, is not a form of energy evenly distributed; it is associated with certain centers, and fills existence as emanations from these vital points, the families.

The power to live comes from within, pouring out from a central spring in the little circle, and from there absorbing the world. In order to fill his place as a man, the Germanic individual must first of all be a kinsman. The morality, sense of right, and sense of law that holds him in his place as member of a state community (as one of a band of warriors, or of a religious society) is dependent upon his feelings as a kinsman; the greater his clannishness, the firmer his feeling of community will be, for his loyalty cannot be other than the sense of frith applied to a wider circle.

A comparison at this point between ancient culture and the civilization of our time will bring out the nature of luck, making for expansion as well as for concentration. We, on our part, must always be human beings before we can be kinsmen. Our happiness in the narrowest circle depends on a wider life outside, and we have to go out into the world to find food for our home life. We cannot get on in the world at all. We can neither pursue our occupation, nor cultivate our egoism or our family prejudices, so as not to come into conflict with the rest of mankind—not unless we assimilate ourselves to a certain extent with what we call humanity. Among us, a life of kinship is only possible when the individual drags home the riches of humanity and sets the family stamp upon them. It is the mark of an egotistical nature to collect thoughts and ideals in the larger field of society, and to hurry home to transform them into family blessings. In our culture, the one-sided family life involves a limitation and a consistent lowering of every spiritual value; it can only lead to poverty of ideas and dullness in all feelings. Thus, family egoism is a vice for the simple reason that it is impossible in itself; it can only lead a parasitic existence. Its doom lies within itself, for a logical carrying out of its principles leads to suicide in the same way as a state of Amazons or a state of chaste men would annihilate itself.[43]

For the ancient clansman, the course lies in an opposite direction. It is frith that shapes his character, and an intensifying of frith means a deepening of his character. A strengthening of the personal maintenance of honor and family involves a greater depth and greater tension in moral feelings and moral will, because it means an enrichment of the conscience. The more self-centered and *sui generis* a kinsman is, the stronger his personality and the greater his worth as a man.

Clan-feeling is the base of all spiritual life, and the sole means of getting into touch with a larger world. The same power that makes the Germanic individual a kinsman prevents him from becoming a limited family being and nothing more. The strength and depth of frith and honor mold the clans together in alliances, and call larger communities into existence. The nature of luck necessitates two particular institutions: the community comprising the *thing*, which judges and mediates, and the kingdom or state, which performs common undertakings. He who has felt the strength and depth of these men's frith and honor will not be in danger of misjudging the family in his historical view. But then again, he will not be tempted to set it up as the unit in existence, as the secret that explains everything in the society and the life of our forefathers.

---

[43] In Greek mythology, a female-only group of hunters and warriors who would kill or give away their sons and only raise daughters.

VI. THE WORLD

After long and attentive observation of an object, one begins to feel the need to view it against its proper background. The formal measurements of the thing itself must be expressed in relative dimensions to make it part of the reality of the world.

One who with unprejudiced mind reexperiences vengeance as it was reexperiences honor as a motivating power among men, brutal and sublime as it really was. To him, our forefathers will appear with new life. They will begin to live and move, awakening in the observer a sympathy far removed from the idealism wherewith a modern age ennobles its poetic or political *idées fixes*. If we could attain to see these men as a part of the world—men whose life in honor and luck we have learned to know—and to regard luck as part and parcel of men's ideas of life in general, the reality of men and their luck would be enhanced.

Midgard (Anglo-Saxon *Middan-geard*, Old Icelandic *Miðgarðr*) was the name given to the world men live in, and it extends far out on every side. Farthest out, where the heavens merge into one with the earth men tread, or the sea they fish in, there are the boundaries of this world of men. The way there is a longer one than the stay-at-home generally believes. One may walk or sail day after day—five days, or perhaps even more—before reaching the mountains that shut men in, or the deep hole where the waters pour down.

Out there, at the boundary of Midgard, is the meeting place of ways from below and from above. One of them bends steeply back, but where it leads we can never rightly learn. It would seem that no one has ever passed that way, for the rainbow bridge (now called Bifrost, or Bilrost) is impassable to all save those who can move unscathed through fire. The rainbow stands all aflame, and its colors may be seen glowing from afar. But we take it that it leads to some higher land, above the heads of men dwelling in Midgard.

On the other side, a way leads down into the third world that extends both outward from and in under Midgard. The road lies through deep, dark valleys, filled with the roar of icy, foaming torrents. It is clammy and resounding in the depths, but the ground is firm. The path will bear mortal as well as dead men, and is so often traveled that there is no need to be ignorant as to where it leads, and what is to be found at the journey's end.

This third world is, as far as we know, of endless extent. There is nothing to hinder a bold adventurer from forcing his way ahead in the land that spreads out from Midgard and down into the frosty depth—as long as he trusts his own courage to face the unknown, and trusts his own strength and wit to clear a way through perils, difficulties, and temptations all unlike those known on earth. He will need to be a strong man, for strength here is measured by a far higher standard—and besides, however great his strength, it will only avail him in lesser things. The rest he must win through by craft and mother wit. Even here, however, the normal human quota of wit will not suffice, for all that he sees is of alien nature now. He needs to be a great guesser.

They are hardly many who venture so far afield, and some of those adventurers whom nothing affrights will doubtless never return. But there were always enough of those who did to give an eyewitness description of Utgard (or Out-earth, as this world is called in the North).

These eyewitnesses told that when the boundary of Midgard was passed, the light that shines upon the earth disappeared. Daylight gives place to twilight, with errant gleams of light that dazzle and confuse without banishing the darkness. The road leads over damp, rimy hills, where icy winds come sweeping down, through rivers turbulent with venom and with swords. In this place sit monsters and creatures, neither man nor beast, with glaring eyes. Their glance darts forth an uncanny light like a flame; their jaws emit dense clouds of acrid breath, fierce enough to singe the hair of a man's head and blind his eyes. Their claws are fleshed in carrion where they sit.

Farthest out is the haunt of the giant eagle Hraesvelgr, the devourer of the dead (or so it is said, for none would seem to have reached so far). When he rises from one corpse to swoop upon another, his pinions raise so violent a storm as to sweep in upon earth itself.

All is horrible, ill-boding, and uncanny—teeming with deception for eyes accustomed only to human dimensions. The quasi-human forms that move there in the mist and gloom are so immense as to be hardly recognized as living until it is too late. What seems perhaps a ravine may prove to be the entrance of a house, with a giant's legs bestriding the valley midway. Inside the cave, his womenfolk sit tending a fire, gray, lank-haired, in a pose that reveals the ugliness of every limb. The streams a wanderer has to pass are of another character than the waters of Midgard. Stepping out into them, he finds them rising about him, things living and hostile of mind. And so it is with everything there, all is instinct with an alien will. Nothing is what it seems. All is dazzlement and illusion.

Things seeming dead turn living at a touch.

Only a genius of luck—able not only to edge and wind its way, but also to discern the hidden qualities of what it meets and face it with a cunning of its own unearthly way—can avail to bring one safely through.

Such is the Northmen's account of their Utgard. Farther south, in Denmark and Sweden, where the hills and the mountains gave place to broad fields and all but impenetrable woods, the world must have had a different guise. I can imagine that in some places, it might be compared to a vast clearing, with darkness rising all about in trunk and branch, interwoven to a dense wall.

Beyond is the place where outlaws prowl about with the wolves for company. There, too, is mist and gloom. And there are paths that are no roads, being otherwise than those trodden by the feet of men. Great marsh waters are there, under forests of enchantment and unease. Storms rise from the lakes, when the wind lifts the waters and flings them as boding clouds over the earth, darkening the day. In Jarnvidr, the forest of iron, dwell the misshapen she-giants with their spawn: creatures with nose and claw as sharp as swords, and as keen to rend human flesh. Brood on brood the creatures bear, wolves and ogres together. In the marshy gloom, where every branch is an iron claw that snaps at him who passes, a man may stumble blindly till he finds his end as food for some foul beast. Cattle straying there return with the marks of having been breathed upon, and are fit for nothing thereafter.

One might guess at a third conception of Midgard prevailing, perhaps, on the broad plains whose boundaries were formed by earth and sky closing directly in. The story of Hadingus and his visit to the underworld, as retold by Saxo, may perhaps have come from a land where the walls of the world were formed by the horizon. A man would then go—as many have gone at other times—through the verge of the heavens as through a dense, dark cloud, a solid mass of blackness, and emerge into a land of wide-spreading plains, where all was good and pleasant to the eye. But if nothing here showed fearsome and ill-omened, it was only that the peril was more deeply hid.

Common to all things of the underworld is this quality of the incalculable, confusing eye and ear. A branch turns to a serpent as one grasps it, and strikes one dead. There are creatures that can twist the neck of a stranger by a mere glance. Fruits and fluids have power to maze a man's wits. There is no knowing the nature of things so as to avert ill consequences by countermeasures.

Sharply contrasted with the dread of this outland world is the delight in Middle-Earth. Here, men look out over the fields with gladness in their eyes. We read in *Beowulf* of the world of men:

> One who knew of far-off things happening in the early times of men, he said, that the Almighty had made the earth, the beauteous fields, encircled by waters; the victorious God had set sun and moon for a light to lighten the people of the land, and decked the lap of earth with branches and leaves.

This stands in contrast to the domain of monsters and the haunt of trolls, where steep cliffs leave little room between for a single man to pick his way, and where unknown roads lead down over sheer precipices. A joyless forest growth hangs over the gray rock. Strange serpents move in the waters, and trolls lie stretched upon the headlands.

These pictures in *Beowulf* illustrate the Germanic contrast between land and unland. In this connection, it matters little that the poet characterizes the "land" in alien words, and glorifies its mildness by describing it as founded in the will of a god beyond its bounds, beautified by the reflection of his creative will. We are here only concerned with the categorical distinction: the one place is waste, the home of evil and unluck, the other the dwelling of the host of the people, living in luck, in frith, and in honor.

In place of the Anglo-Saxon poet's "fair fields and bright" we may use, quite simply, the Northmen's soberer term *fjölnýt fold*, "the much-useful earth." Of that other region, we read that even the stag pursued by hounds in the forest yields up its life rather than venture out into that water, for the place was not *heore*. We may as well leave the old word as it stands, for whatever modern substitute we choose would need a load of explanation to give its proper weight. The word *heore* (modern German *geheuer*, Old Icelandic *hýrr*) means that which is mild, gentle, pleasant, or safe. The opposite *unheore*, *úhýrr* is not merely something harsh and unpleasant, but the uncanny or ill-boding: a place, a state, an atmosphere lacking in all that human beings need in order to live. It is the luckless air that stifles them. *Heore*, in other words, is "lucky" in the old sense. What more need be said? Yonder place is *unheore*; this place, the dwelling of men, is the joyful site of their home. The forest that hangs over the marsh is called joyless, void of that delight that is the distinguishing mark of human life.

Strangely enough, it might seem, for there was no lack of things uncanny here in Midgard. Witch-folk and witchcraft made themselves felt often enough. In the midst of the fair earth, in its most joyous life, the greatest and fairest of all kingly halls, where rejoicing rang loudest, among the bravest of men, the greatest lovers of life and scorners of death—here, one day, is thrust in the *unheore* in the shape of Grendel. Here is witchery, devilment, and all that brave men fear before all else: death in dishonor, in craven terror, in loathsomeness. That is to say, without fight or burial.

The ancients are right in their way when they declare that the world is great, that a man must travel night and day to reach the boundary of death and enchantment itself, but they know, too, that these frontier powers are well able to reach over into this world itself at times. Most peoples have their Hell-farers: those who ventured so far as to be swallowed up in the land of the giants, returning after to their own as from a strange land. The Northmen were hardly the only Germanic people to relate such journeys of adventure. But the stories derive their interest and their reality from everyday experience. A man might learn the quality of yonder "unland" only a league or so from his home; the very fact that every listener must have had some experience of uncanny powers enabled him to appreciate the verisimilitude of the explorer's sober narrative.

It needs more than simple imagination to place oneself in the ancient world and feel at home there, with its Midgard as the center of the universe. We cannot reconstruct a picture from the facts at our disposal, as the numerous abortive attempts to chart the Northmen's cosmos prove. True, the giants lived beyond the horizon, but how are we to make this agree with their stealing about at nights outside men's doors? Midgard is properly only the world of day; once the sun has set and men have withdrawn into their houses, the earth is given over to things harsh and wild. In reality, earth is not the same by night as by day any more than is a man of unluck who goes about in the daytime with a human countenance seemingly like his fellows, but steals forth at night adorned in a wolf's pelt and runs ravening abroad. All the *unheore* that by day is held fettered and bound by the light, rises up as the sun grows faint, to stride forth in its giant power: "All dead ones of ill will grow stronger by night than in the light of day." We may perhaps try to clear the tangle and uphold the system by holding on to the idea of the world as stratified.

Utgard—I use this late Icelandic name for want of a better, since words such as "desert," "wilderness," or "realm of death" each denote but one side of the unknown. Utgard extends, as we know, under the earth and can shoot up into it through innumerable openings at any time. Here and there in the middle of the fair fields are gateways leading down into the home of monsters. It was perhaps through one such way of entry that this or that bold explorer penetrated into the innermost region of the realm of death. One could at least get as far that way as by the long way around through the horizon. But this home of giants under our feet is not a province of the main land out beyond the horizon. Can one go down into the earth and then home around by the frontiers of earth? Who can say? No one denies it, for no one has declared it to be so. If the question were put forth, it would certainly be answered in the affirmative, but that affirmative is borne of the thoughts the problem calls forth, not given of itself beforehand. The cave in the earth is Utgard itself, identical with the place beyond the horizon. And the lair of monsters does not owe its existence to any subterranean communication with a world below. The ancient view of the world will not fit in with our geographical maps, in which the different countries lie neatly side by side with linear frontiers, because the ancient world was not measured with the eyes solely as a mere external plane without depth.

It needs something more than imagination and something more than constructive power to place Midgard and Utgard in their due relation to one another. Reexperience is needed. We have to build up the world anew, without regard to all we have learned, irrespective of atlas and topography. With us, the world is formed by setting observations in their place according to measuring tape and compass, but if we are to build up Midgard and Utgard as well, then we must take experiences as a weight—and bear in mind, however, that no scales and standard weights can here avail; all must be weighed in the hand. Experiences are too many and too various to be expressed in numbers and measurements at all. They consist not only of the impressions produced by the external eye, but have also an inner reality.

When we learn that the ancients imagined the limit of the world as situated close outside their village, we are apt to conceive their horizon as narrowed accordingly; however, the decisive point in their view of the world lies rather in the fact that the contents of their horizon were far deeper than we think. How large is the village? The answer must come from meeting the question in words of our own, but as near as possible to the thoughts of the ancients themselves. The village houses us; it is filled with honor, with luck, and with fruitfulness. This is equal to saying that it is the world. Yes, the village is Midgard itself. How large, we may also ask, is the sacred tree that stands in the center of the village, the tutelary tree of the clan? In virtue of its sacred character and power of blessing, it bears up the world with its roots and shades the world with its branches. And so, it is the world-tree, and what matter if the eye can take in its visible shadow at a glance?

The discussion of luck and honor has given us the experiences of the ancient Teutons; we need only to let them act upon us in their full weight. On the one hand, we have human beings and human life, as deep as it goes in its intensity; on the other, the giants, the luckless nithings, and the luckless land. That part nearest to us, the playground of men, is impregnated throughout with luck and with *heore*, while yonder *unheore* increases in density and ill favor the farther we move from the homes of men. Farthest out, it fills all there is until it becomes personified in material shapes of mocking mimicry, such as one may find at nights or in the forest. Who is there but knows the boundary of his land, there where his luck ends? Who but knows the boundary of the land of men, where all luck ends? Do we not stand, at every moment, in the midst of our luck, looking out to every side where the *unheore* rises as a barrier against our honor and our will?

Such experiences—gauging by depth and constitution as well as by dimensions, feeling night as a boundary of such kind as that formed by a mountain range—could not be at ease in a geography determined by measurements of superficial area. Topographical reality is not set arbitrarily aside to give place to an imaginary landscape, but to give a true likeness of the Teutonic universe. It must be adapted to include also the spiritual reality—if we can use such a word as "adapt" without necessarily supposing a conscious rearrangement of observations. In the question as to the relative position of the two realms and the nature of their boundaries, all accidents of place must give way before the overwhelming influence of difference in character. The land of luck is a whole, which is not and cannot be broken by enclaves of unluck, *unheore*. And all that is *unheore* has its place as a whole outside, something only to be reached by passing beyond the landmarks of Midgard. Far from needing any subterranean connection between the cave under the earth and the land beyond the horizon, the fact is that in the conception of the Teutons, they are one and the same place, including in the geographical sense. To go out into the night is traveling in demon-land.

Despite all the power of demons and of Utgard, this truth still holds well: that Midgard belongs to men, and belongs to them because they are the strongest, the conquerors. When witchcraft ventures forth into the domain of the sun, it comes but to be crushed, and in its downfall glorify the light. *Beowulf* was not written with an intention to numb poor victims for the sacrifice by filling them beforehand with a surplus of horror and dread. In the Germanic stories and songs, men make short work of witchcraft: they carve it into small pieces, burn it, and bury it under solid cairns of stone, then rejoice at the fame accrued from doing so.

There is a momentous difference between the realm of the sun and the frosty dark. In the former, men stand as those fighting on their own ground, with a host of allies about them; trees and stones, animals and weapons, and the land itself is on their side. They know all they see, know that all is what it seems, know there is order in which they can trust. They have the secret of the things about them, and can thus force nature to furnish aid. If by some carelessness they stumble, they can rise to their feet again. They can find counsel and make good damage done to them, and obtain restitution if they need. But out yonder, the slightest false step places them at the mercy of unknown powers. The tree trunk against which they stumble holds them fast and throws them to the stone, the stone again to its neighbor, and this again casts them at the feet of some vampire, where they end as bloodless carrion, sucked dry. Out there, they move among a horde of wild beasts, never daring for a moment to lower their glance, not knowing what dangers threaten them. Here, nature bids them welcome at every step and puts itself at their disposal.

They know the nature of everything and possess its secret, or more: they hold its soul in their hand. They know their world right in to its innermost corners, are intimate with all creeping and walking things that live in its many dwellings. If a beast leaps across the path, they know with a fair degree of certainty from where it comes and to where it is bound, and why it took that road. Their knowledge is more a sort of personal familiarity than any lore of nature.

There are, of course, a host of things that a man must see and know as long as he stands face to face with nature, himself exacting tribute and taking what he needs. He must know, and does know, where to find the plants and animals that provide him with food and implements; he must be able to follow on the heels of the higher animals and outwit them by craft. And he must have a sure knowledge of nature's ways and whims, so as to take his measures accordingly. A dearth of food is not uncommon among the poorest and everymen—the earliest gods gave man, among a wealth of other gracious gifts, the belt that could be drawn tight to assuage the pangs of a hungry belly. Had these strivers not been able to adapt themselves to nature, exploit its most secret sources of supply, and reckon out the rhythmical march of the seasons, their saga would soon have ended. Game laws and protective measures, for instance, owe their origin undoubtedly to those same gods who gave the wonderful belt.

Naturally, however, they notice much more than is strictly needed for self-preservation. They are not content with superficial observation of the fact that certain insects have spotted wings, for example, so they count the spots in the manner of simple folk in the North, and note the difference in number as between different individuals, taking measures for the time to come according to the hint conveyed in the number of spots. The natural science that lives in these men knows no lacuna, for their observations are not gathered haphazardly, but guided from the very beginning by tradition.

The senses of youth are not only trained and attuned to yield their utmost, but are set to work in unity. Young men are taught not merely to lie in wait, but to go raiding themselves and capture the swiftest, rarest creatures in flight. Naturally, the observer's knowledge of nature extends only so far as his eye and ear can reach; where observation ceases, there his knowledge ends abruptly. When the birds of passage fly away before the winter, and creeping things seek refuge underground, then only guesswork can help natural observation over the gap. Then man puts forward his hypothesis—and forfeits all the prestige that his observations have gained with modern scientists. We come prepared by the ignorance of the town-dweller to admire the man who knows the nature that surrounds him, but also with a brain alert, from both the fruits of hand and textbook study, to pass judgment on the results of any knowledge, and so we are apt to misjudge the wisdom of primitive man. But though we may grant the truth that the hypotheses of the primitive observer of nature cannot compete with empirical science, yet it is no less true that his guesswork bears the mark of his familiarity with nature. The more we emancipate ourselves from the authority of our age, venturing to regard its wisdom as relative and not as the standard whereby all else must be judged, the easier we find it to respect the simple myths and the relative, forward-pointing character they often show. Properly viewed, they hide within themselves a depth of knowledge and insight.

It must be so. Primitive men—in the sense of people at grips with nature daily, not in the mythical sense accorded to the word in modern science—primitive men must know their surroundings thoroughly. Such people are not to be judged solely by their literary expressions of natural science. No doubt their familiarity with nature is clearly indicated by their stories and explanatory myths—as to what place the various birds have their particular cries, why one sort of creature brings forth a whole brood of young at a birth or lays a nest full of eggs while another struts about with its one ugly offspring. Or in their riddles, as for instance that of the Northmen about the spider: a marvel with eight feet, four eyes, and knees higher than its belly; or of the ptarmigan: play-sisters that sweep across the land, white shield in winter time, but black in summer.

But such myths and riddles float, after all, but on the surface of men's knowledge, and only exceptionally give any indication of the depth at the bottom. They hint here and there at what was seen, but give no clear showing of how men saw it. The hunting implements and hunting methods of a people, their sense of locality, and their protective measures for game are evidence of their intimacy with the most secret ways of nature. Perhaps, too, are their games. If we would realize the infinite sensitiveness of the "wild man's" brain, and how faithfully it can hold this medley of memory pictures clear and alive, the best way is to see him at play, giving mimic exhibitions of his surroundings. The gestures of bird and beast, or their gait, their fear, their prudence, their parental cares—these he can reproduce with the highest art, or the highest degree of naturalness.

It is a cause of wonder to European observers that the intimacy of primitive man with nature's ways seldom, if ever, embodies itself in impressionistic description or representation. It seems as if the art of realistic narrative is rather an exception among the unlettered peoples of the earth whose songs and stories have been gathered up by the missionaries and ethnologists of modern times. And our supposition that man has been slow in acquiring the skill of painting things as they are seen is confirmed by the epic poetry of races who, like the Greeks and the Teutons, have been able to turn their folk-poetry into literature before their thoughts were drawn into philosophical or theological channels. Judging from

Homer, *Beowulf*, and the *Edda*,[44] we can, apparently, with perfect right declare our forefathers lacking in realistic spontaneity.

In folk-poetry, we find no reflection of the changing and many-shaded life without; here, all is art and style. Earth may be called perhaps the broad or the far-pathed, and these epithets are then repeated with wearying zeal as often as earth is mentioned in the verse. Day invariably dawns with the dawn-red spreading its rosy fingers out from the horizon. When our forefathers set about to describe their battles, they can find nothing better to say than that the wolf stood howling in anticipation toward the approaching warrior, the feaster of the gray beast; the raven fluttered in the air and screamed down to his gray brother, and at last came the hour when the bird of carrion swooped down upon its prey and the gray beast ran splashing about in blood. This schematic description is used without regard to the character or outcome of the fight. Wolf and raven stand for battle and slaughter, whether we have armies in collision and whether their leaders fill the beasts with food, or whether only a couple of men descending upon a third, "giving him to the wolves."

The poet announces the murder of Sigurd by his brothers-in-law thusly: "There you can hear the ravens croak; eagles croak gladly in their food. Hear you the wolves howling over your husband." Folk-poetry exists upon regular formulas (as it was coined) for the various actions of life: hunting, battle, feasting, and going to bed. Persons, animals, and things are distinguished by standing epithets bearing the stamp of their qualities once and for all.

Oxen invariably come "dragging their feet," whether the spectators have or have not any occasion to notice their gait—nay, they must drag their feet, even when they appear in a situation where it is impossible for them to move their legs. Did not the suitors of Penelope waste the property of her husband by daily slaughtering his sheep and his foot-dragging cows? When a man rises in an assembly to speak, he stands there as the swift-footed or the chariot-guiding hero. A man's ship is swift-sailing, seafaring, as well as curved, straight-built, and many-thwarted. And he can, indeed, when he has drawn up his vessel on land, sit down beside the moorings of the sea-cleaving craft, and here receive the strangers who come walking down to his swift-sailing ship. It is as natural for Beowulf to fit out his sea-traversing ship as in Icelandic poetry for the horses of the rollers or props to gallop over the sea. The vessel that carried Scyld's dead body out to sea is called ice-clad, but if a modern reader should from there infer

---

[44] Grønbech often uses shorthand to refer to both the *Prose Edda* and/or the *Poetic Edda*. The *Prose Edda* is a thirteenth-century Icelandic textbook from which we derive most of our modern knowledge of Norse mythology, thought to be largely written or compiled by Snorri Sturluson. The *Poetic Edda* is the modern name for a collection of Old Norse poems, including the *Voluspa*, *Hávamál*, various heroic lays, etc.

that this event occurred during wintry weather, he would pretend to have more knowledge than the poet of *Beowulf* possessed.

An Old English poem gives a picturesque description of warriors hurrying to battle as follows:

> The warriors hastened forward. The high-minded ones, they bore banners, the shields clanged. The slender wolf in the forest rejoiced, and the black raven, greedy for slaughter. Both knew that the fighting men had in mind to bid them to a feast of those doomed to death. At their heels flew, greedy for food was the dew-feathered, dirt-colored eagle.

On closer examination, we find convention apparent in every single connection. In no other circumstances is a poet required to describe the setting out of an army. The anticipations of bird and beast set forth, at such length does not indicate that the battle is to be fiercer, or the number of the slain greater than in other battles— no, wolf and eagle are always looking forward to the coming feast. The eagle here is not "dew-feathered" because this particular battle opens in the early morning; it comes sweeping on dewy wings in the hottest noon. Dew forms part of the picture where an eagle is concerned.

In the Icelandic, the "pine-perched watcher" (that is to say, an eagle) can, despite his lofty situation, still tear the bodies of the slain if need be. Shaker of branches—or branch-scather—is the epithet aptly given to the wind in Gudrun's plaint over her loneliness when she says, "Lonely I am left as an aspen in the grove, bereft of kin as fir of twigs, stripped of joy as the tree of leaves when the scather of branches comes on a sun-warm day." But in the old days, there was nothing incongruous in referring to the wind by that same name of branch-scather when it came tearing over the waters and raising the waves.

Among the Germanic people, the king is called ring-breaker, strewer of treasure, furtherer of battle, or feeder of wolves. The men are ale-drinkers and receivers of rings or wearers of armor—and they are mail-clad whether they happen to be wearing armor at the time or not. Thus, we may find the "war-famous, treasure-giving king listening with delight" to Beowulf's offer to fight with Grendel, and another time we watch the "battle-urging lord" go to bed.

As the valkyrie says to Helgi, "Methinks I have other work to do than drink ale with buckle-breaking prince," so Helgi cries to his brother: "It ill behooves the ring-breaking princes to quarrel in words, even though they are at feud." After the slaying of Fafnir,[45] the titmice in the bushes make remarks about Sigurd and Regin, and one says, "If he were wise, the clasp-wasting king, he would eat the

---

[45] In the *Völsunga saga* (or *Saga of the Völsungs*), Fafnir is the son of king Hreidmar. He transformed himself into a dragon in order to guard his hoard of gold obtained through patricide. Fafnir is later slain by Sigurd.

serpent's heart." Gudrun, after the dreadful deed that she has wrought upon her sons, addresses the ill-fated Atli thusly: "Thou, sword-giving king, hast chewed the bloody hearts of thy sons in honey. . . . Never more shalt thou see them, the gold-giving princes, setting shafts to their spears, clipping the manes of their horses and bounding away." And the same poet who makes Gudrun utter these words, praises the coolness of Gunther in the serpents' den when he refuses to disclose the hiding place of the Nibelung treasure,[46] for "thus should a ring-spreading chieftain keep firm hold of his gold."

No wonder readers of the present day glance around ironically with lifted brows and say, "Where is the much-lauded simplicity? The natural innocence we heard about, after which folk-poetry was named in contrast to the poetry of art? If there is anything of nature at all in these poems, then the qualities by which we generally recognize natural innocence must have been sadly crushed out of it."

Style (or rather, convention) is the proper word for these poets and their technique. How, indeed, should one translate into any modern tongue the description in *Beowulf* of the warriors returning to the king's hall? "They went thither, where they learned that the guardian of heroes—Ongentheow's bane, the young, the good warrior-chief—meted out rings in the midst of the borough." The reader must not draw from these words the coldly logical conclusion that an Anglo-Saxon chieftain sat all day in his high seat like a sower, in such a manner that a stranger might find his way in by listening for the ceaseless tinkle of gold. Nor can the passage serve as basis for the hypothesis that Hygelac had recently returned from an expedition and was now distributing orders of merit, or that it was payday. On the other hand, the lines contain more than a poetic indication of the place where he was wont to exercise his generosity; they do actually imply that Hygelac is at the moment seated in his high seat in the hall. The sentence cannot be rendered in any other tongue than that in which it was written. The king is he who metes out rings, and the hall is the place where he binds men to him by gifts and hospitality.

And yet, taking a long look at the convention in this old poetic speech, we cannot but perceive that there is something astir beneath it. Closer acquaintance gives one a strong impression that behind this conventional art lies a rich experience fraught with life. These poems cannot be classed with the work of epigone schools living on a tongue in which literary acceptance takes the place of sense and force. We feel that the men who wrote these poems thus had their eyes full of pictures from memory. They possessed a wealth of imagination, but an imagination rooted in the senses. Their vocabulary shows signs that the users of the

---

[46] In the Eddic poem *Atlakvida* (or *The Lay of Atli*), Atli, king of the Huns based on Attila the Hun, invites the Burgundian king Gunther to his court. Upon arrival, the Huns attack him and his brother. Gunther refuses to disclose the location of his gold, and is thus thrown into a pit of serpents, where he dies playing the harp.

words lived their lives first hand in experience. But neither do these men speak as artists, choosing and rejecting with conscious delicacy of taste from among the expressions of the language. They choose without knowing, being themselves in the power of their images of memory.

Anyone coming to Homer from Xenophon, the *Edda*, or from the sagas will probably always remember his first feeling of wonder—unless indeed he had the misfortune to make the transition upon a rather low school seat, where all Greek seems very much the same. That is, as an arbitrary pattern of vocabulary words—whether the lines run out full length and are called prose, or break off short and become poetry. The moment he closed one book and opened the other, he crossed a mysterious boundary line, entering into a world altogether differently lit. The sagas and the works of the historians deal with kings and peasants and warriors, and they tell of these personages with just that familiarity and just that degree of strangeness we should expect from the length of time that lies between them and ourselves.

But the others? Where shall we find the key that unites these scattered notes into a tonic system? It is not the contents that we find difficult, as the soul of Homer is familiar enough to us. But the words have often something strange, almost mystical about them, as if they belonged to another age. Does not the novice feel that these rare words—some of unknown meaning—are merely the wreckage of a sunken tongue? He will hardly be aware that what leaves him at a loss is a feeling of heterogeneity: these archaic words call for an altogether different environment than that of the common and general Hellenic or Scandinavian out of which they rise. They point back to a time when they did not stand alone in an alien world, but had about them a circle of known and knowing kin, all bearing the stamp of that same ancient dignity and power. The youthful reader goes about for a while with a feeling of internal schism, until habit eases the mind, and relieves him of his painful craving for an interpretation that should go beyond the ordinary limits of exegesis.

The young student did not know what his unrest meant; he could not translate it into questions, less still into thoughts. But nonetheless he was right when he felt the presence of spirits where his teacher apparently saw and heard nothing. Many of the words that checked him in wonder are actually relics of an age when speech was coined after another method than now. With all respect for the majesty of accidental circumstance, we may safely assert, for instance, that the Anglo-Saxons would not have hit upon such an army of words for "sea" if they had not needed them. There is something imposing in such a series as: *brim, egor, flod, flot, geofon, häf, härn, holm, lago, mere, stream, sund, sæ*. Often enough, the poets are accused of creating a meretricious wealth by half-illegal means, a craving for variety leading them to take words of poor content and make them stand for more than they properly mean. We may try to thin out the impressive phalanx by taking, let us say, *stream*, and saying this is really a current, and only in a looser sense applied to sea. Or we may say of *brim*, that it means, strictly speaking, breakers, and is only applicable as a last resource to sea. But such comfort is false.

Each of the words had undoubtedly a meaning of its own, but only in the sense that it served to indicate a whole by emphasizing some particular quality therein, or the whole viewed in the light of one such quality. The poets are not always as guilty as we make them, for their method can (even though it may degenerate into arbitrary aesthetic trick-work) yet claim the support of ancient tradition, and justification in the original character of the language. The old words invariably had a deep background. What we understand as the meaning proper has arisen by specialization, a certain quality or side of a thing being torn away from the original whole and set up as an abstract idea in itself. Roughly expressed in our differently attuned manner of speech, we may say that *stream*, for instance, did not stand for a current, but for the sea as moved by a current. The abstract idea of motion without a thing moved would not occur to the minds of the ancients.

This wealth of expression is evidence, *inter alia*, of the fact that in the old days, men had clear and precise ideas of the world and things therein, and could not speak of them save in sharply definitive words. Similarly, the characterizing epithets in Homer bear witness to a definite and dominant mental imagery. He calls the oxen "foot-dragging" or rather, "the oxen, they who in walking press one leg in against the other"; such an expression would hardly be used unless one were forced to use it, unless by the pressure of an idea within which shapes the words of itself. Like realism can be traced in the poetic vocabulary of the Northmen, and indeed of the Germanic peoples generally. Here in the North, there is a preference for substantive expressions, where the Southerners are lavish in adjectives.

In the North, we find mention of "the branch-scather, the ring-breaker, the battle-wager," whereas in the South, the prince would be referred to by name, and the quality given in an adjective. However significant this difference may possibly be as indicating the character of the language—and thus indirectly of the people concerned—it reveals at any rate no great dissimilarity in the mode of thought. In the foregoing, I translated purposely with adjectives, in order to call up something of that sensitiveness to the value of combinations which has been dulled by over-literal reshaping of Old Icelandic poems. Ring-breaker and ranger of hosts, for instance, are not titles, as we are led to believe.

These words, like all the rest, degenerated under the abuse to which they were subjected by the skalds, but there is no reason to suppose that they stand in the *Edda*—or indeed in the works of the earlier court poets—without force of meaning. The variations themselves contradict such an idea. When we find, for instance, "ring-breaker" (now *hringbroti*) or "he who scatters rings abroad" (now *hringdrifi*), among other combinations, we have no right to accuse the poet of having an eye for prosody. And in any case, the words must once have had suggestive power.

With regard to the Germanic writers' poetic vocabulary, we can gather but an approximate idea. Its original wealth and force, and its character generally, do not appear fully in the somewhat late secondhand versions, which now stand as sole representatives of the great poetic culture of Northern Europe. Here in the North, we have often to search for the old word-pictures among a host of half-misunderstood and altogether not comprehended terms which have been included in some skaldic handbook or other, when the poems in which the words were living things have disappeared. Many an epical expression was only saved from oblivion by cleaving as a name to some mythical being.

In Snorri's manual for courtly poets we find, for instance, the abrupt hint that the mode of referring to a buck may be varied by calling the animal *hornumskvali* (i.e., "the one that clashes its horns" or "the one with backward-curving horns"). In the same way, a bear may be hinted at as *iugtanni*, which must imply some quality or other in the brute's teeth, or "blue-toothed." Another of his names is "step-widener," which must be designed to indicate his characteristic gait, or his footmarks, in somewhat similar fashion as when he is spoken of as "wide-way." We find the raven called "dew-feathered" and "early-flyer," and the hawk "weather-bleacher"—bleacher taken passively (or rather in a neutral sense), as with "step-widener" above. The same suggestive power is inherent in the name *duneyrr* applied to deer, meaning probably "the one who scuttles over pebbles with rattling hoofs."

The keenness of characterization which lay in these old epithets is something we can only partially appreciate nowadays. The terms of our dictionary are always too wide in scope of meaning, compared with the verbs and substantives which our forefathers had at their disposal. We have no word precise enough to fit that *skvali* which was used to denote a collision of horns, and this one instance may serve to show how loosely all our translations cover the original form of speech. Etymology is too clumsy and expedient to render any help as soon as the quest is extended beyond the dead terms into the living thought and feeling that once inspired the language and filled the words with subtle associations. We may lay down by analysis that the word *slithherde*, when applied to boar in Anglo-Saxon, can be rendered "ferocious," but the etymologist knows as much and as little of its real life as the man who merely hears the word pronounced. Our examples, then, cannot be more than vague indications of a world rich in things seen and heard and tasted, which is now closed forever.

Homer is not folk poetry. The *Iliad* and the *Odyssey* bear sufficiently evident marks of having passed through a complex civilization. The *Edda* and *Beowulf* are by no means primeval Germanic poetry; we find in them both over-refine-ment and decadence. Undoubtedly, there is in the former as in the latter a certain, not inconsiderable conventionality discernible, a necessary consequence of the fact that the form belongs to an earlier age than the contents. The style of the skalds, whether Anglo-Saxon or Icelandic, cannot be acquitted of mannerism, but their stiffness is nothing but the ancient poetic language carried to its utmost consequences, and thus exhibiting in high relief the natural tendencies of primi-tive thought. The rigor of style is an inheritance from earliest times, and the inner heterogeneity that we feel in Homer—and to a lesser degree in *Beowulf* and some of the Eddic poems—is due to the interference of a later culture more realistic and impressionistic in its mode of experience. We would be greatly in the wrong were we to blame the rhapsodists of a later day for the contradictions in these images. The poetry that lies behind Homer and the *Edda*, that which created these expressions as its form, was not an iota more natural. It is questionable whether the poet of the *Lay of Atli*—who praises the "ring-spreader" for "keeping firm hold of his gold," and calls Hogni "the bold rider" at the moment when he lies bound hand and foot—should be assigned to the epigone host for these lines.

As this poetry speaks, so spoke the people out of whose midst the epic arose. The poetic images in which keen observation and the tendency to association of ideas are peculiarly combined are not a product of style, but the inevitable ex-pression of these distant men's mode of thought, mirroring the people's estimate of its heroes and of itself. Men's outward appearance, their dress, their way of moving, as well as their manner of expressing themselves, are in heroic poetry determined by a certain poetic decorum. A hero who does not utter forth his feel-ings in the traditional style, or a hero who suffers to be named without the title of armed, bold, or long-haired (all attributes that any free man must claim if he have any self-respect)—such a hero may be likened to a king sitting on his throne in his nightshirt. The Germanic prince must be glad-minded, cheerful, and gentle, whatever the actual circumstances. When Grendel harries Heorot, Hrothgar is all the same the glad-minded Hrothgar—the good king, who in all his sorrow had nothing to reproach himself. A man must be *eadig* (steadfast in his luck).

When Hrethel dies of grief over his son's craven deed, the poet cannot divest him of the title of *eadig*, any more than Noah can cease to be the lucky man when he lies besotted with wine and shamed before his son. It lies in the nature of healthy men to be victorious, and no peril can deprive them of their human char-acteristics. When the heroes of Israel are seated on the wall in fear of what to-morrow is to bring, staring out at the threatening camp of the Assyrians, the An-glo-Saxon poet cannot but picture Judith as giving "the victor-folk good greet-ing," and later calling out to them, "Ye heroes of victory, behold the head of Holofernes." The decorum goes far deeper than all poetic or social etiquette. It is related to the massiveness of the persons themselves, which makes it impossible for them to adapt their behavior to what a single situation may demand.

Modern poetry takes as its starting point the fragmentary in human manifestation. Whatever men may be occupied with one toward another—whether discussing the deepest affairs of heart and passion, or carrying on an everyday conversation—whether they are fighting or making love, they show but a small illuminated segment of the soul to each other. The greater part of their soul life lies in darkness, only divined, or lit in occasional glimpses by a fleeting light. But the heroes of old are invariably presented *in* the round. They are like those well-known figures in primitive paintings, standing side-on to the beholder, and yet looking at him with both eyes. They cannot trust us to understand a thing by implication only, because they are incapable of doing so themselves. The consciousness of their whole previous life—the obligations and privileges of their position, even of the whole past of their race—is ever in the foreground of their minds. When their speech with one another touches such disproportionate depths, reaching back to family relationships and family history and going beyond all bounds of the situation that has brought them into converse, this is but one among many expressions of their sense of wholeness.

When the king's retainers lead their lord's bride to the bridal chamber, they feel themselves as shield-bearing, even though their shields of linden wood are hung above their places in the hall. When men lay stone on stone and see the wall gradually rising, they feel nonetheless the grip of the sword hilt in their hands; it is the sword-bearers who are building. When they sit down to eat and drink, they cannot for a moment lay aside their valor and renown, even in this common occupation of all mankind. Even though they take off all their armor and get into bed, it must still be the mail-clad, sword-wielding, horse-taming hero who snuggles down under the blanket. And whenever they strike a blow, the listeners must understand that there lies in that blow all the tradition of a race, the impetuosity of a hero, the untamable thirst for vengeance of a son—or more correctly, this weight in the blow forces the whole of the hero's title, with lather and forefather, into the verse.

It is not the men alone who thrust their entire personality upon the spectators at every step. Homer knows that the queen resting with her husband on the nuptial couch is sweeping-robed. When Judith leaves the Assyrians' camp bearing the head of her enemy, she strides forth in all her queenly dignity, as the wise, the strong in action, the white-checked, as the ring-bedecked. But neither she nor any other Germanic lady of high birth would ever appear otherwise, whatever her aim or errand. Wealhtheow, queen of the Danes, walks gold-bedecked down the hall, greeting the men; the noble dame hands first the cup to the king, at last she comes, the ring-bedecked queen, the strong-souled, to the place where Beowulf sits, and greets the prince of the Geats, wise in words.

And as men and women are, so is the world in and with which they live. The same massiveness is apparent in all that presents itself to thought or sense. The horse champing at its bonds stands there as the swift runner, and the horse that dashes across the plain runs as the fair-maned, single-hoofed as it always is. Coming from afar, one sees not merely the door and front of a house, but at the same time the whole of its appointments, its splendor, and the life within.

The castle that travelers approach is not only high-roofed (so that those seated on the benches need not feel the ceiling close above their heads), it is not only wide (with bench room for a great host), but it is alight with the glitter and reflection of weapons, and filled with gold and treasure. The wanderer espies from the road afar the high-walled borough. He sees—from the road in the distance—halls towering over treasures, sees houses vaulted over the red gold. It is not otherwise, we may take it, with the hills that stand as banks of blue upon the horizon. To one who knows them from having often wandered there, they would be, even when lost in mist, the many-sloped hills, and the hills of shady paths. When thinking of his far-off country, the Northman would probably shape his words much as those of the Homeric hero: "between Troy and Phtia there are both shady mountains and a roaring sea." When a man leaps down to the ground, or falls on his back, the spot his body covers is still the earth of the many roads, the corn-bearing, the many-feeding, or the broad. So speak the Hellenes, and the Northmen say of the serpent that it creeps on its belly around the broad earth.

This fullness and comprehensiveness of the idea does not belong exclusively to poetic speech; it is inherent in the language and leaves its mark on legal phraseology far into the Middle Ages. The lawyer who says turf must add green: murderers, thieves, and such like folk shall be buried on the beach "where the sea meets the green turf," as the Norwegian law book decrees. He cannot name gold without styling it red or shining, nor silver without adding white. In the precise language of law, day is bright day and night is darksome or murky night.

In Homer, there are two strata, easily distinguishable one from the other. On the one hand, that represented by comparisons, the elaborate pictures introduced with a "like to…" For example:

> As East and South in rivalry shake the dense woods in the clefts of the mountain, and beech and ash and slender-barked cornel lash one another in fearsome noise with their projecting branches, while clamor of splintering trunks arises, so stormed the Trojans and Achaeans together, and smote each other. None thought of flight.

The man who speaks thus has his mind full of a situation, a momentary picture: the scene before his inward eye expands to every side, and opens vistas round about to other visions again. The poet welcomes all associations of ideas, and pursues in calm enjoyment the broadest of those roads the situation opens to him. This is the modern spirit of experience. It is otherwise with the images contained in such expressions as "the foot-dragging oxen," "the many-pathed earth," "the blue wave," etc. These are not creatures of the moment, but on the contrary, a product of years of experience. Here, it is not the poet who pursues, but the idea which draws and compels him, being rooted far down in the depth of his soul. The metaphor is more ancient than the simile. It speaks of a time when the soul never lived on individual sense impressions, when it might perhaps, as wakefully as now, accept all that presented itself to the senses, yet without stopping at the isolated impression, rather churning its experiences together into a comprehensive idea. The man of metaphor may be said to remember with all his senses. But all his experiences of any given object exercise a mutual attraction one toward the other, and enter into an indissoluble unity. Each new observation is drawn up by those previously made and forms with them a unit, so that the images that live in the soul, with all their natural truth, their precision and strength, are not individual ideas, but universal ideals—as rich in content, and as weighty and insistent as the heroes of poetry are.

This mode of thinking calls men to account at every moment for their actions and their being, recognizing no distinction between different official and private selves, such as we now enjoy. The figures we meet with in ancient poetry and in ancient history cannot be divided into the public and the private personality, the man of ordinary and the man of special occasion, or into king, husband, man, judge, councilor, or warrior. One cannot say "man" without thinking "armed"; therefore, when we pronounce the latter word, thought builds up the whole. There is thus nothing artificial in the expression of Caedmon:[47] "the armed one and his woman, Eve." It may strike strangely on our ears to hear Jesus called the "ring-giver" and his disciples referred to as the bodyguard, the bold warriors. But to the Germanic mind, it was impossible to avoid these expressions, as long as the ancient circle of thought remained unbroken. There was no actual thought of Jesus as sweeping across the country upon a Viking expedition; the poet does not even say "ring-giver" because it was the custom to rhyme man with generosity. Jesus was the Lord, his disciples the men. Jesus was the man of luck, his disciples those who partook of his luck, and the relation between master and men could not be apprehended in the quality of a fraction. It must take up the idea of entirety, and enlist all words in its service.

The idea of a wolf or of an eagle is made up of all the experiences accumulated at different times concerning the life and character of the creatures named: their habits and appearance, their wills and propensities, etc. And so the animal stands as an inseparable whole, living its life without regard to its place in a

---

[47] The first English poet known by name.

classificatory system, possessing its limbs and its qualities in a far more absolute fashion than nowadays. For thought was so completely dominated by the idea of entirety that it lacks all tendency to take the world in cross-section, analyzing, for instance, the animal kingdom into heads and bodies, legs and tails, or the forest into leaf, branch, trunk and root. The separate parts simply have not in themselves that independent reality needed to produce such word-formulas as "leg" or "head." A head is only conceived as the head of a particular beast; it must be either a dog's head, or a wolf's head, or some other individual variety of head. Even a leap seen ahead on the path will have a particular character; it will be the haste of this or that animal, not a movement in general.

It is thus not the fairy tale alone that lives upon the art of conjuring up an entire organism from a single claw, hair, or thread. The old proverb, "where I see the ears, there I wait the wolf," held good among primitive men in a far more literal sense than with us. At the first glimpse of those two ears, the wolf sprang up and rushed in, bringing with it a whole atmosphere, setting all senses to work so that the eye saw its trot, its stealthy glance behind the dirty yellow of its pelt, so that the nose scented it, and the hand felt a tickling sensation as of bristly hair. And not only does it bring its atmosphere when it comes, but it spreads a whole environment about it. It enters the scene as a character, and radiates its habits, its manner of life out into a little world of its own.

It is but rarely that we find in the popular tongue any mention of such generalities as "tree" or "beast." The earth has its growths of oak, beech, ash, elm, and fir; its inhabitants, wolf, bear, deer, eagle, raven, and serpent. The curse of outlawry, in the Scandinavian, holds good, "as far as *fir* grows." The proverb to the effect that one man's meat is another man's poison runs, in its Northern equivalent thus: "what is scraped off one *oak* is all to the good of another."

"The *fir* that stands alone will rot"; neither bark nor leaf can protect it. It is a good omen when the wolf is heard howling under the branches of the *ash*. The great world-tree is not called the *tree* of Yggdrasil, but the *ash* of Yggdrasil. And poetry retains, here as elsewhere, the old sense of reality. Sigrun sits waiting in vain by Helgi's burial mound:[48] "Now he were come and he had in mind to come; there is no hope now, for the *eagles* sit perched already in the *ash* and sleep is in their eyes." And when its fellows have withered one by one, thus runs Gudrun's plaint: "Lonely am I now as the *aspen* on the bill."

---

[48] The *Poetic Edda* contains two lays of Helgi Hundingsbane. In these lays, Sigrun is described as Helgi's lover. However, she is betrothed by her father to the son of King Granmar. Unwilling to marry him, she assembles an army and invades Frekastein, Granmar's kingdom, and kills everyone of import except her brother, Dagr (the personification of day), on the condition he swear fealty. Sigrun and Helgi then marry. Dagr later seeks Odin's aid in taking vengeance, and slays Helgi with Odin's spear. Helgi is then laid to rest in a burial mound, whereupon Sigrun visits his grave and spends one last night with her deceased lover. She soon dies of grief, and is said to have been resurrected as a valkyrie.

In the language spoken on the steppes, the moorlands, and in the forests, specific and classifying terms play but an insignificant part. The general terms fall completely into the background; they form but the shadow of reality, not the stem of reality itself, as they are with us. The individual manifestations stand so abruptly one against another, rise so independently out of the natural soil that they can have no immediate contact with one another. Thus, the systematical arrangement into animals and plants, into species and classes—which to us is of primary interest—has no footing at all.

Wholeness and independence: these are the two main qualities of images in the simple mode of thought that still shows through in the offshoots of the heroic poetry, and to which we find parallels about us among non-European peoples. Our words are wide and vague, because we see and feel things loosely, and accordingly concern ourselves more with the interaction of phenomena than with actual objects. Our world is built upon generalities and abstractions, and the realities of life recede behind the colorless "facts," as we call them, of cause and effect, laws and forces, and tendencies. The words of ancient and primitive races are narrow and precise, answering to the experience of men who did not run their eyes over nature, but looked closely at every single object and took in its characteristics until every item stood forth before their inner eyes in its fullness, as a thing unique. This definiteness of experience seriously hinders analysis and classification, but this does not mean that the spiritual life is kept down to a simple verification of the actual facts, or that ideas are merely acknowledgements of the impressions. On the contrary, ideas have, for these thinkers, a strength and influence that can at times lead strangers to regard the barbarians as philosophers after all; the truth, however, is that they are distinct from the philosophers by the very force and power and reality of their ideas.

The conceptions that make up the body of our spiritual life, such as color, beauty, horse, man, etc. exist by themselves in the intervals between the things of the world, and our sensations are but the pegs on which they are hung. In the primitive mind, every idea is firmly connected with an object; the thing is seen in its perspective, as it were. Answering to the narrow scope of the word, we find a dizzying depth in its idea, since this in itself includes all that can be thought of the object named. The meaning is not restricted to cover only the body of things, but embraces their soul in the same degree. In the idea of "oak" lies all that one can think of *quercus*, from the oak itself as it rises before the eye, or can be felt with the hands, from its speech, its form, its peculiar manner of moving, its fertility, and the like, to "oakness," the state of being oak, the quality that makes one an oak tree. So comprehensive is the thought, and so intimately wrapped about reality. The full depth of the word is not reached until we arrive at the state of pure being, a being that in respect of spirituality has every claim to admittance among the company of the highest ideas, but that differs nevertheless from our venerable abstracts in having a marked character—a pure being, in which lie pre-destined the qualities of lobed leaves, gnarled branches, broad-crowned growth, and edible shell-fruits.

Endeavoring now to track down these thoughts, it may be that the exertion we feel in the task involuntarily applies itself to our estimate of those old think-ers, and induces us to think of them as profound reasoners. And there is still greater danger that the motion of our thoughts may be transferred to the ideas we are following, so that we imagine primitive ideas as something complex or com-plicated. For us who endeavor to think again the strange thoughts of a stranger, the difficulty lies first and foremost in keeping firm hold of the unity and banning all suspicion of musing and profundity. Primitive idea is not created by a reflec-tion whereby something is abstracted from reality, nor by an analysis losing the separate elements from their connection and rearranging them in logical catego-ries. On the contrary, it depends on a total view, the nature of which is inimical to all analysis.

We call the primitive idea oak—oakness two-sided, but with only condi-tional justification, inasmuch as the ideas of primitive peoples do not contain anything that can properly be called dualistic. It points simultaneously out toward something spiritual and something material, but it has no seam in it where matter and spirit meet. Idea and reality—that which is perceived and that which is felt—are identical. They are, so to speak, two opposite poles of the conception. We can begin with something concrete, like a wolf or a stone, and gradually—through its character and qualities, its evil nature and goodwill, its mobility and weight—arrive at the qualities of wolfness and stoneness, as subtle as any philosopher could spin it, and yet at the same time as strong in its reality as any sense impres-sion. And we can commence with a "force," the force of being a wolf or a stone, and through the effects produced by that force arrive once more at the solid ob-jects before us. We can move forward or backward from pole to pole, without any somersault, without even the least little hop. The connection is unbroken, because the thought never at any point loses hold of the idea of a limitation in character and form.

The things of our world are flat and silhouette-like to such a degree that they shade into one another and merge into such vague entities as "nature" or "world." Primitive facts are all-around objects and shapes that stand out free of the back-ground, and when our comprehensive phrase "the whole world" is translated into Old Norse, it takes this form: "As far as Christian men go to church, heathen men worship, fire bursts forth, earth bears fruit, son calls mother, mother suckles son, men light fire, ship strides, shields flash, sun shines, snow drifts, fir grows, falcon flies the spring-long day when the wind is full beneath its wings, heaven vaults, earth is peopled, wind howls, water flows into sea, men reap corn."

Thus, we are led to see that the primitive way of depicting life is realistic in the truest sense of the word. The epic formulas, as we are apt to call them, paint the world as it is, but their world is very different from the place in which we move and have our being. Primitive men differ from Europeans not in theories about reality, but in the reality itself.

VII. LIFE AND SOUL

It is a melancholy fact that modern researches into primitive thought have led us further and further away from any real understanding of foreign cultures and religions. And the reason is not hard to find. The European is hampered by his naive faith in his own system and his own logic as the measure of all things. The missionary and the ethnologist invariably try to force a ready-made scheme on cultures of radically different patterns, in the same way as linguists formerly arranged all tongues after the scheme of Latin grammar. Just as the introduction of gerund and supine and ablative only served to obscure the structure of Indian or Australian languages, so our rigid dualism cannot but distort primitive psychology. The Scandinavians, the Greeks, the Hindus, the Israelites, as well as the Indians and the Australians have been examined by the catechism: what do you believe about the soul? How do you conceive the interaction between body and soul? What becomes of the soul when it leaves the body? As if the Hellenistic and European dualism as it is embodied in the catechism and the handbooks of psychology were at the root of all experience. By such an examination from outside, facts may no doubt be brought to light, but the facts are often worse than false, because they are wrenched out of their natural coherence. Without an understanding of primitive thought as a consistent whole, our forefathers' talk of life and death, soul and body would be incomprehensible.

All peoples recognize a body and a soul, or rather a material and a spiritual side to everything that exists. The bird has a body that is lifted in the air, and it has a soul that enables it to fly, as well as to strike with its beak. So also the stone is a body, but in this body there is a soul that wills, and enables the stone to do harm, to bite and strike and crush; a soul that gives it its hardness, its rolling movement, its power of prophesying the weather or showing the way.

Thus far—to the extent of establishing soul and body as two halves of existence—we may safely go in our analysis of the ancient mode of thinking. But as soon as we endeavor to give each half its proper share and delimit its scope of influence as against the others, we fall from one difficulty to another. If we begin by seeking the soul in the body, we may split and dissect it lengthwise and across; we can never attain to set our finger on the spot where it is not, nor on the spot where it exclusively resides. And if we proceed to examine the qualities of the thing, one by one, as a test in the hope of getting the thing separated out into an active, initiative side (that of the soul) and a slower, obedient, executive part (that of the body), we end as surely in arbitrary definitions. We shall soon find ourselves obliged to distinguish on our own responsibility, if we are to preserve the system. There is no seam to be found. A reliable indication of what soul is and what body is in stone or bird according to primitive thought is a thing impossible to discover.

It is not difficult, however, to find the soul. Wherever we grasp, be it stone or beast or tree, we lay hold of it. It comes toward us conscious of itself, as a thing that knows and wills, acts and suffers—in other words, as a personality. We may add, as far as the Teutons are concerned, that the body is the seat of a soul. That is to say, that there resides in it a little mannequin, which enlivens and sets in motion, guides and directs, and on occasions, impatient of its clumsy medium, sets out naked into the world and settles things on its own account.

There is undoubtedly something in the idea that keen-sighted folk have seen a little sprite, or a little animal, leave the body, and slip in again when it thought no one was looking—this little sprite was the soul. But on attempting to grasp the soul and draw it into the light so that we can note its form and other peculiarities, we shall soon find that it mocks us by oozing out through the meshes of the web that itself has woven in letting itself appear as a personal being, in human shape or the likeness of a beast. The soul that was but now so firm in qualities and so massive in personality dissolves away into a mist of power, shaping itself to and filling whatever space it may be—nay, without even the limitation of independence, so that it can be assimilated by other souls as a quality. The soul of a man can reside in a stone or a sword; it can enter as a power into a fellow man by a touch or a breath, adding to the receiver's strength or cunning. The soul that was but a moment ago so independent reveals itself as a neutral something that is the polar opposite of personality.

But even now, its tricks are not at an end. Step by step, or by degrees, it slips away between our fingers to more and more spiritual forms of existence. Power, quality, will, influence—there is nowhere it can be stopped. We are always behind, grasping only its transformation. When we have chased it through all existences—from that which stands at the transition from material to spiritual, through the more and more spiritual refinements, out to the limit where we think we can check it on the verge of absolute nothingness—it changes over into a state our language cannot express, but that may be most nearly rendered by our word "energy," or even "principle." It manifests itself suddenly as life. And if we then are bold and crafty enough to grasp at it in order to tear it from its body and hold it fast, lock it away to see what happens to the thing without it, then we find that it was existence itself, the very being that we caught hold of. It was the soul that made the stone hard and the bird fly, but it was also the soul that enabled bird and stone to be at all. Without soul, no being—to take the life from a stone is the same as making it vanish into absolute nothingness.

But this is more than lies in our power. Tear up existence—this we cannot do. But we can hold fast. Despite all its transformations, the soul is not grown too spiritual for human hands to grasp. And if we crush it in our fingers, we shall find sooner or later that it hurts. In a little while, life gives birth to a sharp, hard, edged object between our fingers. If we have courage and wit enough to follow the soul through all its forms and hold it unyieldingly, then it must at some time or other resume its first form and answer with all its personality. Then it must stand forth, not only visible and material, but in the form in which it appears as a part of the world.

Not until then is the transformation complete. Now we have learned the secret of life in primitive experience. The soul is something more than the body, as it is seen and felt in space-filling reality, but it is not anything outside the material.

When we cannot find the boundary between the inner and the outer, there is nothing to be done but give truth the credit, and say that the body is a part of the soul, or even the soul itself. The moment we grasp a stone firmly in the hand, we have grasped the soul of the stone—it is the soul we can feel. It is always possible for the body to be sucked up by the soul and vanish away, to emerge into the light again some other time. The spiritual can leave the material to reveal itself under other forms, but when it does appear and lets itself be seen, heard, and felt, then the manifestation takes place in virtue of that nature the soul possesses. However far away it may go, it still has matter bound up in it. To a certain degree, it is possible to speak of soul and body, but the distinction does not go so deep that it is possible to wrench the one from the other.

A soul cannot be caught in any of our narrow formulas. Language gives us a hint to build our thoughts wide, and at the same time a warning not to bring along too many of those distinctions that are so useful in our world. We must begin with the material, pass through—not around—personality with its will and feelings, from that out into the neutral (what we call life) further again through life into the ideal, existence, being. Only there, in the simple power to be, can we find the limit of the soul.

But when we have reached so far, to the bottom of the single soul, the way stops suddenly just at the point where, to our imagination, all roads meet. When, in our own philosophy, we reach the depth that we call life or existence, we feel ourselves standing at the entrance to the origin of all, the wellspring that opens out into a network of channels from soul to soul. Life is to us a colorless force that is able to inspire any number of disparate forms, and our problem of life lies in explaining how the one and all transforms itself into the manifold shapes of the world. It is otherwise with the practical thinker. For him, all thought ceases at this point. Between the souls, there is set that most impenetrable of all barriers, a gap, a void, nothingness. The separation is absolute, from the very fact that it does not consist in a wall built by thought itself, but in the lack of all conjecture and in the lack of all inducement to speculate, because all the things of the world are complete in themselves. Involuntarily we feel that in the word "life," or "existence" as we should rather say, there lies an invitation to speculate upon the common condition of all that exists. But, in primitive culture, such a question can never arise to demand an answer, because it can find no foothold on the given basis.

Life, existence—so wide is the idea of the soul, but the extent of this sentence is only realized when we turn it about: soul, so narrow is the idea of existence. Life is not a common thing, something connecting, but rather that which makes the greatest distinction in the world: not a universal support, but an individual quality. Life is always determined as to character. It explains, nay rather, it contains all that distinguishes the possessor of life from all other beings. It contains all his qualities and abilities, all his tendencies and needs—it contains him even to the structure of his body.

How deep the distinction is between our thoughts and those others on this point only becomes clear to us, perhaps, when we see that the primitive soul reaches farther than the mere person, so as to embrace also the sphere of life. Not only does it contain the manner of life of an animal, but also its area of life belongs to its soul.

Poetry retains a distinct reflection of this idea of entirety. The raven cannot appear without bringing with it the idea of blackness, of dewy-wingedness, but no less surely does it bring with it a whole atmosphere of carrion. The poet of the Anglo-Saxon Genesis is altogether in the power of the ancient mode of thought in this respect. In his source, it is stated that Noah first sent out a raven from the ark, but it flew backward and forward until the earth grew dry, and this forms of itself the following explanation in his soul:

> Noah thought that if it found no land on its flight, it would at once come flying back over the broad waters, but this hope failed; it seated itself gladly, the dark-feathered one, upon a floating corpse, and sought no further.

Blackness and the lust of carrion, the devouring of corpses (even the corpse itself) form part of the raven's soul. When the raven is called greedy of battle or greedy of slaughter, this means in reality that just as a raven properly belongs to battle, so battle (or rather slaughter) forms part of the raven's life. The wolf, too, is of a carrion nature: it is called the carrion beast, but to this must be added something more, that which is expressed in the name heath-walker or heath-treader. The wilderness is a part of its soul. Or the additional words "in the forest" follow of themselves as soon as the creature is named; the wolf rejoiced in the forest, the wolf howled in the forest, nay, the gray wolf in the forest ran over the heath among the fallen.

The gulf between souls is impassable, reaching down to the very root of the world. All beings rise straight up from the ultimate ground, separate from top to bottom. No bridge is built at any point. There is something misleading to us in the fact that all things—even that which we call lifeless—had a soul, and consequently also a life. It might seem to us as if the distance between the different existences was then rather smaller than now, seeing that all things were united in the possession of will and feeling, nay, even understanding and the power of expression. But this life was not, as we naturally imagine, a common essence, and far from bringing the thousand things nearer to one another, it kept them rigorously apart.

Life is will. All that is, acts because it feels an impulse, feels pleasure in this and displeasure in the other. The soul of the stone, as well as that of the tree and the animal, is filled with desire and purpose and preference, but the stone's will is not the animal's, and neither is that of the human being. Man had soon to discover that every one of his surroundings loves and hates in its own fashion, according to its unassailable principles—after its own kind. It is this discovery that has made man so watchful and sensitive to all manifestations of the souls surrounding him. Woe to him who thought that things had human will and human power! He who is to fight his way forward, and be able to hand over to tomorrow his conquests of today, he needs first and foremost to understand what it is his surroundings will. All education is directed toward giving the novices soul-knowledge, and thus enabling them to take up the battle of the world. There is then in the human being a strong sense of the difference between the passions and the self-control in himself and the spiritual powers that clash with him on every side.

In the variety of his ritual proceedings, primitive man manifests his power of distinguishing between the different wills operating in his world. The ceremonies for obtaining a plentiful downpour of rain are not the same that he employs when he wants to secure the goodwill of the buffalo, and the buffalo rites differ in their turn from his addresses to other animals. We are deluded by our language and our propensity to use all abstract words in the singular, but our singular form "will" is the result of a work of thought that was not carried out at all in those times. That is, when the tree and the animal and the stone were realities, and not, as they are now, mere shadows on the background of nature. We misinterpret what we call natural man's personification of nature, because we view mythology in the light of Hellenistic philosophy. Our poetic language, as well as our scientific terminology, is descended from Alexandrian anthropomorphism, and all European speculations on myths and legends have been dominated by the mentality of the Stoics and Neoplatonists who tried to convert the original Greek thoughts about nature and man into a rationalistic and sentimental system. Primitive words that Europeans translate "soul" take in a large part of the meaning covered by our words "existence" or "being," but on the other hand, all primitive existence is life.

If we would know how despotic life is in Midgard, we should do well to ask, for instance, if the stone is not a dead thing. Judging by all analogies from other peoples, and from the hints contained in Teutonic poetry and customs, our forefathers would have shaken off this paradox with a gesture of displeasure, as a thing not merely idle, but altogether meaningless. Death, in this connection, had no significance for them. They would not oppose the idea, for they would simply fail to understand what lay in the question.

Man's task has been to think his way forward to the conception of lifelessness, and he has found the task a hard one indeed. Again and again he manifests his astonishment at the phenomena that seem to oppose the reality of life. He prefers to wrestle with hypotheses of transformation, metamorphosis, the changing of life into forms acting in other ways. And the roads here are long. It takes centuries before he has explored them so far that he is forced to turn about and face the problem as a merciless enemy. The closer it presses in upon him, the more he places himself in stubborn opposition; he denies death, declares it an impossibility. He will not even admit that the termination of life forms part of the order of things. In face of the hard facts, he falls back upon the explanation that "death" came into the world through a misunderstanding. Now it is a violent assault on the part of something outside the home of men, which has brought about this disturbance in the original state of things. Now it is man's own foolishness that is to blame, in that some race long past made a false step at some critical moment, and by neglect of some rule of life reduced the general vitality. And only very slowly is this "death" that to him is and remains an illusion only, deepened down toward an annihilation; that is to say, he thrusts life over the salient point, and dumps it down into a nothingness, which he again and again conceives as something positive, a nothing in being, a massive hole. Death itself he has never found.

It is thus not by any deduction from himself to others that man sets a foundation of life under existence. When he says life, he does not utter the word as a discovery the extent of which he realizes. Life is a *sine qua non* for everything. Man has no more discovered life than he has discovered light. In modern thought, lifelessness is still only a modification of life reached by gradually shutting out the most prominent qualities of organic being, such as moving and feeling; we try to reduce life into lifelessness, but all we can attain to is a negation. We are never able to establish an existence of another order, and consequently the characteristics of life turn up as soon as we start speculating on matter and death. The great difference between primitive speculation and modern thought does not consist in our saying existence where the myth-makers say life, but in our extending one sort of life to all things, and so making life the basis for a hypothesis of unity.

European philosophy has emancipated thought from experience to such a degree that it becomes possible to picture all nature in the likeness of man. We have discovered—or rather learned from the Greeks and carried the discovery further—that it is human life and human existence that resides in plant and stone. For the last three centuries, the task of philosophy and science has been to deprive life and existence of the most prominent human features and reduce them to vague colorless ideas applicable to all organisms (and in a wider sense to all phenomena), but even if life and existence have changed name and are now called force, or tendency, or law, they have not changed character. In the formulas of the evolutionaries—to name but one instance, in the struggle for existence and the groans of nature—pure anthropomorphism comes to the surface. On the strength of this anthropomorphism we have established an inner relationship between all things of the world. All questions are thus gathered up into one problem: the origin and nature of life, the meaning of the world. Here the difference comes in that makes it so difficult for modern men to understand the thoughts and the problems of primitive culture. Life, existence, being, soul, and body are naturally used by us in the singular form, conveying a generalization of experience that has no counterpart in the myth-makers. To primitive man, life is not one but legion; the souls are not only many, but they are manifold.

In order to understand the thoughts of foreign peoples, we must necessarily convert their self-revelation into our own terms, but our words are apt to carry such a weight of preconceived ideas as to crush the fragile myth or philosophy in the very act of explanation. If we want to open up a real communication with our fellow man, we must take care to revalue our words before clapping them on his experience. As far as possible we must hold back our set formulas until we have walked around the object he is confronted with and looked at it from every side. But analysis will not carry us all the way to intimacy. Culture is not a mass of beliefs and ideas, but a balanced harmony, and our comprehension depends on our ability to place every idea in its proper surroundings and to determine its bearings upon all the other ideas.

Primitive ideas about life and existence are neither congruous with our concepts nor diametrically opposed to our science and psychology. The belief in souls does not include personification of natural objects, but on the other hand it does not exclude the possibility that Sun and Earth may assume a humanlike appearance. In Scandinavia, nature is peopled by powers in human shape. Up from the earth and out from the hills, elf and dwarf peer forth, and a host of giants bellow from the mountains. From the sea answer Ran's daughters, those enticing and hard-hearted wave-maidens, with their cruel mother. At home in the hall of the deep sits venerable Ægir. Over the heavens go Sun and Moon. Some indeed declare that the two drive in chariots with steeds harnessed to their carts; the sun is chased by two wolves eager to swallow its shining body. Of the Sun and the Moon it is said both that they were given and taken in marriage, and that they have left offspring.

In the Old Norse series of small poems called the *Riddles of Heidrek*, the wave-maidens play with the freedom almost of nymphs.

Who are the maidens that come mourning; many men have sorrowed for their coming and thus they manage to live.
Who are the maidens that come trooping many together, they have fair locks wrapped in a white kerchief; no husbands have these women.
Who are the widows that come all together? Rarely are they merciful to voyagers; in the wind they must keep vigil.
Who are the maidens that come in shifts of breakers moving in through the fjord; the white-hooded women find a hard bed, but little they play in a calm.

But these verses express only half the thoughts of the Northmen. The other half lies indicated in the names borne by those fair-haired cruel ones: one was called "Heaving," another "Heaven-Glittering," a third "Plunging," a fourth "Cold," and a fifth "Bloody-Haired." And these two halves must be joined together if we are to get the true value of the ancient descriptions of the sea. Modern readers unconsciously remodel the pictures of the riddles under the influence of contemporary poetry of nature. Our rendering changes the perspective of the scene, because our words are fraught with other associations. When joined together, they create an atmosphere foreign to the old poems. In reading these descriptions of the waves breaking on the shore or of the billows chasing one another in long rows, we enjoy the sight of clear-cut shapes, and we sniff in the salt spray of the breakers.

However, this reconstruction of ours is at once too plastic and too impressionistic, because according to our mode of experience, it is the overwhelming sense of the moment that seeks an outlet in poetic images. The ancient words do not reproduce the impressions of moods of the moment. In order to recapture the depth of the old picture, we must replace the modern allusions and their emotional values with the hints conveyed in the names of the wave-maidens: Plunging or Cold or Bloody-Haired—all of which break the pretty picture of clean-limbed nymphs, and at the same time banish all emotions roused by the momentary beauty of the sea.

"Much hath Ran stolen from me; the sea hath sundered the bonds of my race." Thus, Egil wails when his son has been drowned, and his words may be taken as meaning that he has seen Ran standing as a fearsome woman with hands grasping that which belonged to him. "Ægir's wench!" he cries to her in his challenging defiance. But the poets could, even in late historical times, speak of Ran and Ægir as the sea they were, without veiling their personality. "The horse of the sea hills tears his breast out of white Ran's mouth," says a skald speaking of a ship plowing its way through the sea. Another describes a vessel plunging heavily in these lines: "The wet-cool Ran leads time after time the vessel down into Ægir's jaw." The poet of the *Lay of Helgi* now hears Kolga's (i.e., Cold's) sister and a ship's long keels rushing together with a roar of breakers. The next moment sees Ægir's fearsome daughter endeavoring to capsize the ships, and sees the beasts of the breakers (the ships) wrenching themselves loose from Ægir's hand.

In the same way Earth is at one time a woman—screaming, threatening, or conceiving and giving birth to children—at another time she is capable of fading or of burying men in her womb. One moment a river rises like a man to challenge the wader, the next moment it rushes like a flood at its enemy and drowns him in its rage of waters. In a laudatory poem on Haakon Sigurdsson, Hallfreðr seeks to impress on his hearers that the upstart chief of the North has really conquered Norway, and by his victories has established his right to govern the country, in spite of the hereditary claims of the fallen kingly house. And he is not content until he has twisted the fact about and shown it in four different poses. The main theme is that the earl has won Earth and drawn her into a firm alliance. The warrior was loath to let Aud's fair sister sit alone, and he used the sword's speech of truth upon leafy-haired Earth, the promised bride of Odin.

Thus the marriage was concluded: they entered into a compact that the earl, wise in counsel, won for his bride, the only daughter of Onar, the forest-clad woman. He has enticed the broad-featured daughter of Báleyg with the compelling words of steel. In his eagerness to extol Haakon's might and right, the poet exhausts the metaphors of the language, and he unintentionally gives us a catalog of the family relationships into which Earth entered with other powers. Although Onar, Aud, and Báleyg are little more than names to us now, we need not doubt that these persons and their intercourse with Earth were founded in ancient belief and true myths. Hallfreðr does not force the language when he represents Norway as a kingly bride worthy to be wooed by an ambitious earl like Haakon, but the attributes of the queen are not those of a human woman. Onar's daughter is the "forest-clad," Báleyg's woman is "broad-hewn of feature," Odin's betrothed is "leafy-haired," and in this embellishment Hallfreðr also draws upon the conventionalities of poetic speech.

The same versatility and deftness in juggling with traditional words is shown by a fellow poet, Eyvind, in the mocking songs he sings of Harald Grayskin, the close-fisted king, who, after the manner of small freeholders, hid his treasures in the earth. In the days of good King Haakon, he cries, the rings shone on the arms of his warriors and skalds; the gold is the sun that should shine on the hawk-hills—the arm of the warrior where the hunting falcon perched—but now it lies hidden in the flesh of Thor's mother.

The courtly poetry of Norway is hardly illustrative of ancient Teutonic imagination in general; the metaphors were to poets like Hallfreðr and Eyvind more like parts of speech that could be mixed freely by an ambitious skald to show off his ingenuity. It is not only that art has degenerated into artifice; the poets often manipulate the words to produce novel and startling effects. The contrast between the golden sun on the hills and the dark womb of the earth is a pretty conceit that proves that Eyvind is a modern poet with an imagination touched by Western civilization. But these medieval skalds of Norway cannot cut themselves loose from the traditional language prepared for them by men of the past; they try to work out their individual fancies and conceits in the material that lay to their hands, and thus their verses exhibit the working of ancient imagination as it was embodied in phrases and figures.

When earth is called the wife of Odin, the mother of Thor, when wind is styled the son of Fornjót, and the sea is conceived as Ran (the wife of Ægir), the myths are not anthropomorphism or personification in the modern and Alexandrian sense. Human likeness is joined to the other qualities of natural phenomena or, more truly expressed, human appearance enters as a quality among other qualities into the soul of earth, wind, and sea, but it does not in the least interfere with the impersonal workings of the forces of nature. There is no contradiction between subject and verb in the skald's description of the winter gales: "Fornjót's sons began to whirl." Nor is there really any breach of common sense in a storm scene such as this: "The gusts carded and twined the storm-glad daughters of Ægir."

The moon gives birth, the earth is a mother, stones bring young into the world, and that is to say that these beings beget, conceive, and are delivered, for thus all procreation takes place under the sun. But this does not imply that earth must transform itself into a human being and seek a couch to bring forth its children. The little we know as to our forefathers' practical relations with the world about them indicates, as will soon appear, that they did not appeal to the objects of nature as pseudo-personalities. Like their primitive brethren all over the world, they tried to win the friendship and power of animals, trees, and stones by much surer means. When the poet lets Frigg send messengers about to fire and water, iron and all kinds of ore, to stones, earth, trees, sicknesses, beasts, and birds to get them to swear they will never harm Baldr, he has plainly no idea in his mind of such messengers going out to knock at the doors of nymphs and demons. His hearers must have been familiar with a method of appealing directly to the things themselves, to the souls.

To get the whole idea as it lived in the minds of the Teutons, we must try to fuse elements that are incompatible in our thought, and still more we must discard our habit of looking at nature in the light of the moment. The word "storm-glad" applied to Ægir's daughters, that now calls up to our fancy the playfulness of the waves, had a more intense and far less instantaneous meaning, as we partly understand by comparing it to the war-gladness of heroes in ancient poetry. The modern substitutes can never capture the energy of the Teutonic words; it is not enough to add that the adjective was formerly more powerful or that the joy of battle was more violent. To our feeling, the ecstasy of fighting arises out of the collision between the warriors. In the ancient psychology, joy of battle and the battle itself are a permanent quality in the man or part of his soul. In the same way, storm-gladness is an inherent quality in the soul or nature of the waves.

When the wave is called cold, or Ran is called wet-cool, the adjectives do not mean that the woman is cold as the sea, but that she has the cold of the brine in her. The shivering iciness belongs to her soul just as oldness or long-living belongs to the bear's nature, for which reason he is called in Anglo-Saxon—and still in popular speech—"the old and terrible one."

We can piece together the primitive soul, but we can never succeed in expressing its living unity in our language, because our words are modeled upon totally different ideas, and resist all attempts to switch them off into another plane and joining them into a new pattern. But to understand the ways of primitive man, we must to some degree be able to realize his experience. We must see that the soul or idea of earth is a whole, spanning from being many-pathed to motherhood without a break. The Northern Hel is death, just as neutral as we are able to think death, but Hel is also a realm for the dead, and she is a real person, not a pale personification who acts as death and is putrefaction itself, blue and black of hue. *Hildr* means battle,[49] that is, the clash of arms, the surging mass of fighting men, and it means battle-maiden, too.

---

[49] The Old Norse noun *hildr* means "battle," but there is an extra layer of subtext here. Grønbech could possibly also be referring to the legendary character Hildr. According to the *Prose Edda*, Hogni's daughter Hildr was kidnapped by Prince Hedin, which sparked a battle. After the battle was over, Hildr cast a spell to resurrect the dead soldiers, who would continue to fight endlessly until Ragnarök. This is known as the Hjaðningavíg, or the Battle of the Heodenings. It is possible that Hildr is a personification of battle. However interesting the connection, it is not known if the poets necessarily named the character of Hildr after the word.

Anthropomorphism has its root in primitive experience, because personality lies in the being of every soul from the beginning, but it cannot make its way through until thought is emancipated from experience. Not until man is so firmly established in his place that he does not need to be fixing his surroundings every moment with a dominating glance, not until he begins to look his own nature more consciously in the face and starts speculating on the processes going on in his interior, does the inclination arise to humanize the universe.

Then he becomes a nature-poet. Only when this standpoint is reached can he venture to face his environment as his equal, meting out to it the same treatment that he himself appreciates and bows to. Before this revolution, he knew only too well that in order to exploit the goodwill of nature and guard against its power to harm, it was necessary to know the character of souls.

Anthropomorphism true and proper is born when man ensconces himself in towns or castles, shutting out nature by means of thick walls, and confining himself to social intercourse with his fellow men. The great change takes place at the moment when the personality, from being dependent on the natural qualities, turns to acting from purely human prejudices. When the soul is emancipated so as to stand above its phenomena, then, and only then, is it a human being. When nymphs no longer ripple, when earth can no longer hide its children in itself, when the sun stands up in a chariot, guiding a gleaming pair of steeds, which he can put into stable together with all the qualities of sun, then nature is broken, and personification is born.

It is a difficult matter for us to get such unconditional ideas as life and existence narrowed down to the small circumference they must have in order to be applied to the soul of the past, without letting the depth disappear at the same time. We can perhaps get nearest to the old thoughts by saying that life and existence were in those days a nature—nature understood in the old sense, as something included from birth or from the first origin of a thing, something that goes with it inseparably, and determines not only its appearance but also its essence and characteristic features. A nature can only bring about certain definite results, namely those which lie in itself. For instance, four legs of that particular sort a wolf has, together with such and such a smell, jaws that open and close in such and such a way, or a tendency to thieve and sneak about in wild places. Another nature can only produce something rugged, hard, and heavy, which under certain circumstances will roll down and bite off the toes of a man standing in its way. But then, too, it is inherent in nature that it cannot refrain from producing its effects. Wolfness may indeed exist as soul, but sooner or later it must manifest itself as a biting beast.

Wherever character is different, the besouled are divided by the impassable gulf which separate life denotes. The uncombinability of nature outweighs and overshadows all external, as well as all inner similarity. The nature of the tree, its character, will be judged from its appearance: whether it has rough bark or smooth, leaves round or long, whether it shoots up to a height or spreads broadly around, but also from its ways. One tree has bark that glistens in bad weather, that of another will turn dark and threatening; one tree rustles its leaves, even when the weather is calm, another flings its arms about wildly in a storm, but otherwise hangs dully drooping. There is in this habit of the tree a revelation of its innermost soul, and much luck of wisdom consists in being able to read the soul of a tree from its behavior. It is known that one tree possesses knowledge and a power of divination that the other does not exhibit, or not in that distinct manner.

And finally, the usefulness of a tree is part of its soul. It is in the nature of oak to sail, as in that of ash to form spear shafts. The specific classification of trees and bushes in the ancient languages is based upon their importance to human life. They are divided into trees with hard wood and trees with soft wood, and into the barren and the bearing, such as cast fruits to men and beasts—also perhaps between those good for fire and those which burn slowly. From the Anglo-Saxon runic catalog we gain a picture (weak and fractional though it is) of the souls of trees. The yew is "rough on the outer side, hard, firm in the soil, feeder of fire, deep-rooted," and something more that we do not understand. The birch is "fruitless, yet bearing branches without offspring; it is fair in twigs, gaily decked as to the crown, swelling with leaf, intimately responsive to the air." The oak serves "the children of men to feeding of the flesh, often it voyages across the sea, and the wave puts its firmness of core to the test." The ash is "greatly high, dear to men, firmly it holds its place in the ground, even though many men make onslaught against it." We must also add (or the meaning will be but partial) that it holds its own stoutly, whether it be rooted in rocky ground, or as an ashen spear in the warrior's hand.

Stones, too, have their nature, which gives them their sluggishness and their hardness, as well as their power to move at times, their keenness in biting, and their power to crush—each stone according to its kind. The unfailing sense of locality among these people is due to the fact that they know from their childhood every tree, every stone, and every little rise of the ground. They are accustomed to carry what they have once seen so accurately impressed upon their memory that no slight variation escapes them, and the slightest change is noticed. Then too they know well that stones on open ground have their different character, manifest not only in their shape, but also in their ways perhaps in the power of pointing the road.

The mountains and hills that form the horizon have, as he who has observed them year after year will know, each their own peculiarities. They are all susceptible to what happens in the air, but they do not prophesy the day to come, its weather, and its events in the same way, perhaps not always with the same wisdom. Several of them are entrusted with the task of pointing the time of day; according as the sun is on this or that point of the horizon, so men apportion their daily work and their hours of rest, and their nature is indicated by such names as The Hill of Noon and The Peak of Even.

Our forefathers, it would seem, followed with especial confidence the counsels and warnings declared by running water, and there are indications that they read with keen insight the souls through the form and movements of the mountain streams—perhaps also listened to peculiarities of voice in the falling waters. A poet who felt himself beyond the childish wisdom of the world, the bishop Bjarni Kolbeinsson, defends himself in the *Jómsvíkingadrápa*,[50] expressly against the suspicion of having drawn his wisdom "beneath waterfalls," as if his conscience writhed under all the paganism he must allow to pass his lips when he made poems in the ancient form. What Plutarch tells of the Suebi under the leadership of Ariovistus is perhaps more widely applicable:[51] they prophesied from the eddies of streams, and from the curves and foaming of the waters. At any rate, even if the sentence were born as a whole in Plutarch's brain and not authorized word for word in the thoughts of the barbarians themselves, it may doubtless be taken as expressing the essential element in the mind of a Germanic observer watching attentively beneath a waterfall.

In our minds, animals are cataloged according to their teeth and morphological structure, and we carry our zoological or botanical systems with us when we set out to investigate the world as it is seen by a Hindu or a Buddhist, by an Australian or an Indian. With a charming naivete we break up into fragments the information obtained from other peoples, to make it go into ready-made categories, thus making nonsense or superstition of all the mythologies of the world. What is wanted in all parts of the world is patient study of primitive and non-European experience. The ethnologist must learn how to see and what to see; he must observe every animal with the eyes of the natives without any reference to his own textbook, and thus piece together a new zoology and botany and mineralogy, or rather as many zoologies and botanies as there are different observers. On the prairies of North America, he must discard his popular notion of the radical difference between flying and running creatures, to learn that the crow and the buffalo are related in the same way as the wolf and the heath in the North of Europe, because it is an inherent trait of the crow's character to hover over the herds of buffalos and indicate their presence.

---

[50] A skaldic poem paying tribute to the Jomsvikings, legendary Viking mercenaries. They are mentioned in a number of Icelandic sagas. Bjarni Kolbeinsson's *Jómsvíkingadrápa* is a skaldic poem in *drápa* form paying tribute to fallen Jomsvikings at the Battle of Hjörungavágr. (see: *drápa*, Battle of Hjörungavágr)

[51] A Suebian king and one of Caesar's primary rivals during the Gallic Wars. Most of our knowledge of Ariovistus comes from *Commentarii de Bello Gallico*, Julius Caesar's firsthand account of the Gallic Wars.

Among the Scandinavians he must slowly piece together his view of the moon by learning that it marches, it counts the years, it determines luck and un-luck, and it sends disease. To understand what a Teuton meant by "oak," we must simply learn that seaworthiness belongs to its qualities as well as its gnarled stem and edible fruit. Prophecy is included in the nature of running streams in addition to swiftness and coldness.

There is no other way for outsiders than gathering facts piecemeal and com-bining them into a new totality, taking every hint that falls from the stranger's mouth when he is looking at things, without any magisterial distinction between details according as they fall in with our ideas, or clash with our natural philoso-phy. In the North of Europe, our material is scant and fragmentary, but neverthe-less we are able to piece a likeness together from the remnants of poetic and legal speech. As to the sea, we learn that it is cold, salty, and wide. Furthermore, it is called by the Icelander coal-blue, and by the Anglo-Saxon *fealu*, fallow, in words that suggest other associations than those of mere tints. *Fallow* possibly conveys an indication of the barrenness of the deep, like the Greek epithets. It is cruel, and possibly coal-blue carries some hint of its deadly power. It is the road of the land of gulls, swans, and gannets; the land of seals, whales, and eels; the road of the ship and the seafarer. And to these epithets must be added the picture of Ægir, the man of the sea, and Ran, the woman of the deep. Earth is wide, great, enor-mous, and spacious; it asserts itself as immovably steady. It is called the green—even the evergreen—and the growth-giving, bearing, nourishing. "As wide as the world grows" is a Northern expression for "all over the world."

But it is also part of earth's nature to be arable. In offering tracks and free stepping space to men's feet it wins the name "road" or "roads." And here we can see with our own eyes how deep the words go down into daily thought. In verse Odin can say—referring to his experiences when he crawled through a fis-sure in the mountain to woo Gunnlod, the giant bride—that over and under him stood "the roads of the giants." In everyday speech, Norway is simply the North-Ways, and the East-Ways denotes Russia. "Green Tracks" is in Norwegian a name designating Midgard as contrasted with the barren Utgard; in the com-pound two qualities of the earth join: her fruitfulness and her fertility, the teeming and the wide-pathed. To these indications must be added the hints from practical life. We hear that men called in the power of earth in cases of need, either to ward off the effects of strong drink, or to guard against evil influences. In an Anglo-Saxon formula, direction is given to take earth in the right hand and place earth under the right foot and say, "Earth has power against all manner of beings, against envy and forgetfulness, against the tongue of a mighty man."

The verses are included in some instructions for farmers when their bees have swarmed, but the matter of them appears to suggest their applicability to many other circumstances of life. Possibly the idea of firmness and of the fruitfulness of earth meet in this incantation. Finally, earth is a woman who conceives and gives birth, who hides men and things in her lap or in her body.

In bearness, wolfness, ravenness, and in oakness, beechness, elmness, the soul ends on one side. But when we turn about to look for the limit of the soul on the outward side, toward the light, we soon find that the road is longer than we thought. The two flanks of nature—that which goes down into existence, and that which goes out into manifestation—must be of precisely the same length, as far as nature goes. That is to say, as far as qualities and appearance are the same, life is identical. All wolves, all oaks, and all stones have the same soul.

And not only are all members of a class partakers of a certain kind of soul (shareholders, as it were), in a fund of vital force, but they are identical both in body and soul, so that they suffer one another's sufferings and feel one another's offenses, anger, and goodwill. Primitive thought regards separation in space as an insignificant, accidental circumstance. One might be tempted to express it thus: it feels the solidity of matter, of the body, but is blind to its extent in space, and perhaps that expression is more than a paradoxical image.

In the primitive experience of life, identity has a deeper foundation than mere continuance. We combine our separate sensations and make a whole of them by conjecturing that the world is filled with individual beings and every single individual lives a linear life of its own. When the animal slips out of our view, we fancy that it trails a line of existence somewhere hidden among the thousand things of the earth until it reappears across our path. The universe is crossed by millions and millions of threads, each one spun by an isolated individual.

According to primitive experience, the facts arrange themselves into a different pattern. All bears are the same soul and the same body, and every new appearance of a bear—whether it is no other than that we saw yesterday, or the most distant of all among the kin, as we reckon it—is a new creation from the soul. A bear is a new birth every time it appears anew, for the deep connection in the existence of the soul is a steady power of regeneration. In our observation, animals are either counted or they are lumped together in a collective genus or type. We speak of a wolf, of wolves, and of the wolf, but in primitive language and poetry, the animal is neither this particular wolf nor *the* wolf that crowns a chapter in natural history, but wolf simply. It is this individual and yet all-embracing personality that forms the subject of the Anglo-Saxon gnomic verses such as this description of the bear: the bear shall be old and terrible. Or paraphrased into modern words: old age and terror is his nature or soul.

The popular tales have retained the ancient mode of telling, and under cover of the traditional language still persists a vague reflex of the old idea: the wolf that swallowed Little Red Riding Hood is surely not a particular beast that had taken its station in that part of the woods, but rather is the wolf of the woods.

The sun also is the same from day to day, for there is not more than one sun-soul. But when it is said in legal language regarding something or other agreed upon that it must be carried out before the fifth sun or on the day when five suns have come to an end in the sky, then the words do really mean that there comes one sun today, another tomorrow, and finally a fifth to shine over the completion of the undertaking. And it is no matter for wonder to find oneself suddenly, in a ritual or a story, brought face to face with a whole series of sun-gods. Every day is a fresh birth, but all days are nevertheless Dagr (Delling's son, to speak the language of Northern myth), just as winter is the son of Vindsvalr and summer the son of Svasudr. The myths are simple statements of fact when they create, as they sometimes do, a great being: the chief of all bears, or the father of sun and of moon, who incorporates the life of bearness or sunness and sends his messengers out into the world. But when we approach the mythical idea from the angle of poetic thought, we need no reminding that fatherhood is *toto coelo* different from our begetting, which presupposes individual life as the line on which existence is built up. The "Wind-Cold" who is winter's father and the "Sweet-Breeze" who is summer's father are nothing but the everlasting soul that bursts into appearance at the proper time.

VIII. The Art of Life

No wonder, then, that life in Midgard seems so safe in spite of all its perils and unforeseen happenings. Man stands firmly and self-confidently on his feet, undismayed in face of all those Utgard beings that now and again come roving about the earth; he is fighting on his own ground, and with a host of allies about him.

We saw man stumbling blindly outside the limits of his world. Every step was the guessing at a riddle, riddles of the sort that giants propound when life depends on their solution. Out there, a rarely gifted hero may manage to win safely through a few days and come safely home, but to live there is impossible. If Midgard had been so constituted that men were forced to feel their way thus blindly, then the giants would have ruled over earth to the end of all things.

There is no such stumbling now. Men know the soul of all things and know what there is in every being of will, both good and evil. They know the nature of hate and the nature of love, and they can utilize goodwill and guard against the power to harm. They can turn aside at the proper place, and grasp a thing at the right moment. In virtue of their wisdom they can rule, and where power does not suffice they can lay their crafty plan with certainty, without fear of its missing its aim, as it would so often out in yonder land of demons. They can force the souls of things to serve them, by making them friendly. Plants that house a hostile will, and would infallibly eat up the ignorant from within become, for one who knows their soul, sources of strength and healing—if properly dealt with during growth, or wisely handled after they are plucked. Man has taken the stones into his service, made them into implements wherein all harmful and annihilating will is directed outward, and all goodwill inward toward the user, so that he can confidently wield them and attain his end. He is surrounded by tamed souls.

There is perhaps no soul that can testify more strongly to the wisdom of man than fire. What it has been, and what it still can be, we may learn from the names given it at times. It shares the name *frekr* with the wolf and is thus brought into company with the "shameless, voracious" beast; cruel and greedy, runs another of its characters. And now, what is the best thing in the world? "Fire is best among men's sons, and the sight of the sun, health, and life without blame": in such a series ending with the greatest thing in life, blameless honor, fire can hold its own. "Fire guards, or aids, against disease," runs another ancient saw, and he who knows something of folk-life, and the part there played by fire in the welfare of men and cattle, knows the depth of significance covered by this little sentence. Fire is even the nourisher of life, says the poetic speech. And this transformation of the restless element is due to man himself; men are ever taming the flame anew and anew, consecrating it and devoting it to use in Midgard. The rites of this old consecration have been lost, but from later customs of the people we can at least form an idea of their character. On certain festivals, or when the decline of luck indicated that a renewal was needed, the fire was quenched on every hearth. The inhabitants of the town assembled and called new fire to life by means of the ancient and venerable fire drill that lets wood beget fire out of wood. And from the newborn flame blessing was spread to stall and barn, and new life kindled on the hearth.

But when all is said, the dwellers in Midgard are not dependent upon good-will in the souls. They are not only the crafty ones who know how to exploit the weakness or generosity of another: they can force him to obey their will. The hunter can master the game he pursues, so that it does not escape him, but on the contrary comes in his way of its own free will. It bears him no grudge and does not plan vengeance for his onslaught. It is a far cry from soul to soul; there is a great gulf fixed between man and the things around him, and none can, in virtue of the life that is in him, directly influence another being so as to raise up impulses and tendencies out of its soul. But the easier, then, it is to steal into an alien soul, and set it in motion by its own limbs and of its own strength.

Appearance and qualities are not, as we have seen, accidental results of nature. Therefore, by accepting one of the peculiarities of the soul, one gathers up the soul in its entirety and makes it one's own will. If one can establish connection with the soul on a single point, one has the whole. Life is as fully inherent in a little torn-off fragment of the body as in the leaping, spying, willing organism, and can one assimilate that little section into oneself by eating it or binding it to one's body. Then, one sucks up the whole soul. But the end can be attained as effectively by spiritual means. By mimicking reproduction of the ways and behavior of the body, one acquires the nature, and becomes possessed of the whole great full-bodied soul—or draws it at least halfway into oneself. One can enter into the nature of a beast by pursuing its aims with its gestures, by imitating its stealing out in search of prey, its cry, its leap, its mode of eating, perhaps even its mating. And one can then, from within, bend the beast to one's will.

Indeed, the "idea" itself, as we would say, is really sufficient to gain mastery over the soul, if one can get the idea fixed in a form amenable to treatment. Possibly the name is such a true symbol in which the soul is enclosed that it is a charm to overcome the enemy. Some dangerous being or other places itself in a man's way, opens its jaws to swallow him, and glares at him as if to turn him to stone—but the man flings out, "I know your name!" against the monster. If it is true that he masters its name, the monster sinks down impotently or steals away scowling. But mastery implies that he knows all that the name stands for: the ways of the beast, its ferocity, and its dodging. Mastering implies real knowledge and familiarity. In other words, power.

But he who knows the nature of things and understands how to avoid conflict can also take action himself and exploit the world. Not only can he bind and cow his surroundings for a time, he is also able to establish a lasting feeling of solidarity, so as to build up frith between himself and the beings around him. He can unite himself with a soul outside the circle of mankind, imposing on it certain obligations toward him, with a reciprocal responsibility in no way inferior to the honor of the circle of kinsmen. However, this can only be attained by his mingling mind (as the old phrase runs) with the animal. He engrafts upon himself soul of its soul, so as to bring about between the two kinds of life an identity similar to that which binds all individuals of the beast species together in bodily unity. Such union takes place by transference of soul fragments, and where it occurs must bring about full and complete transference of the alien nature into the foster brother. Man adopts the soul of his new kinsman, acquiring both right and power to use its luck when need arises.

Among the Germanic peoples, we find but a few scattered relics of the time when men united themselves with animals, but right down into historical times we find evidence of a feeling of foster-brotherhood—a very strong one at that. In the neighborhood of Eric the Red's homestead in Greenland, there appeared one winter a great white bear which ravaged around. When Thorgils Leifsson (then a guest at Brattahlid) slew the beast to save his little son's life, he gained the praise of all men. Only Eric was silent, and though he made no objection to the customary disposal of the body for useful ends, it was understood that he was incensed at Thorgils' deed. Some said that Eric had cherished "ancient faith" in the beast. The saga hints that the relationship between the two men was from that day even cooler than before; indeed, Eric sought to lead Thorgils into peril of life.

The wolf was generally considered as an uncanny beast: *unheore*, and belonging to Utgard. But as part of the battle, the beast entered into the soul of the professional warrior. The language had need of two words: *vargr* (Anglo-Saxon *vearg*) and *úlfr* (Anglo-Saxon *vulf*). *Vargr* is the demon beast, and no man could be *vargr* unless he was bereft of frith, given over to trolls and roving beastlike in the woods. Wolf, on the other hand, is a friend of the king, and his name is often borne among men. To be true to the ancient sense, we had perhaps better say that language needed two words, because there were two beings: the animal that enters into league with man, and the wild beast of the trolls. The use of Wolf as a title of honor for warriors and as a man's name—and still more the existence of Ylfing or Vylfing as a family name—implies that men might contract alliance with the beast, overcome the strangeness of the animal, and draw it into a firm alliance. Such wolf-men surely had wolf-nature: the strength of a wolf and part of his habits. It is a fair guess according to the hints of the ancient literature that the Ylfings were real wolf-men.

Possibly some phrases in one of the Eddic poems hark back to a half-forgotten reality. In the *Lay of Helgi*, the young prince who is a "scion of the Ylfings" once, when he went about in disguise, alludes to himself as the gray wolf. Ketil Hallbjarnarson Haeng (the Salmon) belonged to a race of the Lofotens where people to a large extent depended on the bounty of the sea for their living. His name is accounted for by a myth in the family saga, a pretty sure sign that there was some inner relationship between the man and the fish. Perhaps we may also see a legendary reflex of everyday fact in the story of Otr, the fisherman who was able to change himself into an otter to catch fish for his meals. The words with which the *Völsunga saga* describes the nature of this Otr are too discerning to seem wholly dependent on late romancing. Most likely, the author is indebted to popular wisdom, if not to ancient tradition. One such example:

> Otr was a great fisherman, more skillful than other men. He took the shape of an otter and dived in the river and caught fish with his mouth. He had in great measure the habits of the beast, and used to eat in solitude with his eyes shut, lest he should discover how his food dwindled.

In the *Ynglinga* saga,[52] the author has accidentally inserted a queer fragment of a family legend regarding a sparrow man. We learn that King Dag was wise enough to understand the language of birds, and further that he possessed a sparrow that flew far and wide, bringing information back to his master. In one of its rambles, the sparrow settled in a field to peck at the ears of corn, whereupon the peasant picked up a stone and killed it. When Dag found out in what land the bird had lost its life, he set out on an avenging expedition and harassed the country of the slayer cruelly.

---

[52] A Kings' saga about the House of Ynglings (otherwise known as Scylfings in *Beowulf*) written by Snorri Sturluson. It is the first part of the *Heimskringla*, the most well-known of the Kings' sagas.

By virtue of his dominance over nature, man can also combine souls, and engraft the essence of one upon another. Thus, he inspires that which his hands have worked on, and equips his implements with qualities calculated to render them useful in their calling. When he fastens a bunch of feathers to his arrow, he gives its flight the accuracy of a bird, perhaps also something of a bird's force in swooping on its prey, as surely as he gives himself a touch of bird-nature by fastening feathers about his body. Or he may, in the strength of his artistic faculty, content himself with a presentment of nature. He chisels a serpent on his sword, lays "a blood-painted worm along the edge" so that it "winds its tail about the neck of the sword," and then lets the sword "bite." Or he may use another form of art: he can "sing" a certain nature into his weapon. He tempers it in the fire, forges it with art and craft, whets it, ornaments it, and "lays on it the word" that it shall be a serpent to bite, a fire to eat its way. So also he builds his ship with the experience of a shipbuilder, paints it, sets perhaps a beast at the prow, and commands that it shall tread sure-footed as a horse upon the water. Naturally, the mere words are not enough, if there is no luck in them; they take effect only if the speaker can make them whole. How he contrives to accomplish this is a question too deep to enter into here, but as we learn to know him, we may perhaps seize upon one little secret after another.

The poet is a great man of luck. He has more word-luck than other men— this is apparent not only in the ring of his words, but also in their effect upon men and natures. We, in our one-sidedness, are inclined to see only the aesthetic side of his production, as if all his art consisted in describing how the battle serpent smote from the hand of the warrior and bit deep into the brain of his foe, how the war-flame shone as the hero swung it aloft, and bit its man to death at every blow, how the birds of battle flew singing from the bow, how the sea-horses—the wave-gangers—trod the fish-meads. Such images are not to be thus lightly dismissed. "Sea-horse" is not a comparison; the poet does not say the ship is like— no, the ship *is* the thing, he says. The ship does not go over the waves as a horse trots along firm road, but the sea-horse treads the wave with an unfailing step.

The poetic portrayal of the warrior as the tree of battle, which serves as padding in every other line for the sedulous skald, seems to belong to the North. At any rate, there is no certain trace of the figure in the poetry of other Germanic peoples. But whether especially Scandinavian or not, it has the authority of age. Later poets take pleasure in the picture of warriors as trees, standing in the storm of battle and waving their arms wildly while the death-dew pours down the trunk. The paraphrase itself says no more than that the warrior is the thick-stemmed, fast-rooted tree that is able to withstand many a cut of the axe without toppling over. The description of the ash in the runic catalog is perhaps the best commentary here: "firm in the ground, holding its place even though many men make onslaught." These are words that take their light from the double play of thought between the tough ash as a tree and the invincible ashen spear. Undoubtedly, that poet was a great man of luck who first inspired his chieftain with a soul that had for its dominant quality the stubbornly swinging firmness of the ash. The beauty of the poetic figure lay in its truth, for if the metaphor failed to express a reality, it had no poetic justification.

Through innumerable kinships, natures are knit together this way and that, until the world hangs in a web of frith. So man draws souls into his circle. For the present age, the war-cry is: rule, and be master of the earth. Subdue creation is the watchword running through our time, and it looks as if this commandment sympathetically strikes the heart-note of our culture and ever sets the pace—not only for its actions, but also for its speculations. All hypotheses about past ages in the history of our race hinge on the assumption that man has made his way through an everlasting battle, and that civilization is the outcome of man's struggle for existence. But modern civilization, with its cry for mastery and its view of life as a continuous strife, is too narrow a base for hypotheses to make history intelligible. The evolutionary theory of an all-embracing struggle for food and survival is only an etiological myth. As the ethnologists put it, it is a simple contrivance to explain modern European civilization by throwing our history, its competition, and its exclusive interest in material progress back on the screen of the past. When ancient and primitive cultures are presented in the light of modern economic problems, all the proportions and perspectives are disturbed. Some aspects are thrown into relief; other aspects are pushed into the shade without regard to the harmony inherent in the moral and intellectual life of other peoples. And the view as a whole is far more falsified by such capricious playing of searchlights than by any willful distorting of facts.

The keynote of ancient culture is not conflict, neither is it mastery, but conciliation and friendship. Man strives to make peace with the animals, the trees, and the powers that be. Or deeper still, he wants to draw them into himself and make them kin of his kin, until he is unable to draw a fast line between his own life and that of the surrounding nature. Culture is too complex—and we may add too unprofitable—a thing to be explained by man's toil for the exigencies and sweets of life, and the play of his intellect and imagination has never (until recent times perhaps) been dominated by the quest for food or clothing. The struggle for daily bread and for the maintenance of life until tomorrow is generally a very keen one in early society, and it seems that the exertion calls for the exercise of all faculties and powers. But as a creature struggling for food, man is a poor economist. At any rate, he is a bad hand at limiting his expenditure of energy to the needs of the day. There is more than exertion in his work; there is an overshooting force, evidence that the energy that drives him is something more complex than the mere instinct of existence. He is urged on by an irresistible impulse to take up the whole of nature in himself: to make it, by his active sympathy, something human, to make it *heore*.

Primitive man has never been able to limit his needs to what is strictly necessary. His friendships among the souls are not confined to the creatures that are useful to his body or dangerous to his life. When we see how man creates an imaginative counterpart of his surroundings in his poetry, myths, and legends, how he arranges his ceremonial life—at times indeed his whole life, according to the heavens and their movement—how at his festivals he dramatizes the whole creation of his limited world through a long series of ritual scenes, we gain some idea how important it was to him to underpin his spiritual existence. His circle of friends spans from the high lights of heaven to the worm burrowing in the soil; it includes not only the bug that may be good to eat, but also innocuous insects that never entered into his list of delicacies. It comprises not only the venomous snake, but also harmless crawling things that have no claim on his interest save from the fact of their belonging to his country.

The traces handed down from our forefathers of their ritual life are slight and few, but numerous enough to show us that they communed with things high and low. They were able to make friends among the leaping and growing creatures, as we have dimly seen. Their life was both a sun-life and a moon-life. The sun had entered into their soul to such a degree that actions were orientated from east to west. If there is to be luck in an undertaking, it must be done clockwise, from east to west. The Swedish king had to ride his "Eriksgata"—a sort of triumphal progress from town to town throughout the kingdom—clockwise through the land. And it was clockwise, we may presume, that men carried the fire when consecrating a new homestead and drawing the wasteland into their luck.

When Iceland over time had grown more thickly populated, and land was not so plentiful, it was decided that no man should take more land than he could compass with fire in one day. The procedure was to light a fire while the sun was in the east, move on and light another within sight of the first, and so continuing until the last fire flamed with the sun in the west. Even down to matters of everyday life, the law of the sun holds good. Clockwise the drinking horn is to pass from hand to hand around the hall. Under ordinary circumstances, it seemed, men would walk clockwise around the house, to judge from a passage in the saga of Droplaug's sons.[53] Grim and Helgi lost their way in a blizzard and had no idea of their whereabouts when they suddenly came upon a house wall; they walked clockwise around the place and discovered that it was Spakbessi's place of sacrifice. Their walking thus was, according to Bessi's view, the cause of the storm's continuing for a fortnight. If we may believe that the saga writer knew what he

---

[53] The *Droplaugarsona* saga, which tells the story of Droplaug's two sons Grim and Helgi as adults. Grim avenges his brother, who was killed. There is some overlap with the *Fljótsdaela* saga, which also features these two brothers, though some details differ.

was talking about, it must be the actual movement about the temple that gave the weather so powerful a forward thrust that it could hardly stop. On the other hand, by going against the sun, men can throw nature back upon itself in such a manner that it breaks and is put out of joint. We learn that in Iceland, witches were able to cause destructive landslides by walking around the house.

The sorceress Groa, who held a grudge against the powerful sons of Ingimund, prepared a feast of death and sent a gracious invitation to her victims. But as usual, the luck and wisdom of the family proved too strong, and the guests were prevented by portentous dreams from attending. After sunset, Groa walked around her house counter-clockwise, looked up at the mountaintop, and waved a cloth in which her gold was tied. With a sigh, she mutters, "It is hard to stand against the luck of these sons of Ingimund," but then wishes, "May that now come to pass which has been prepared." She closed the door after her, then came a landslide down upon the house, and all perished. The same device was used by Audbjorg to avenge the degradation of her son by Berg Shortshanks.[54] She could not sleep due to her unrest at night. It was calm outside with a clear frost. She went out, walked counter-clockwise around her own homestead, lifted her head, and sniffed at every quarter of the horizon. At once the weather changed, a drift set in, the wind brought a thaw, and an avalanche came down over Berg's dwelling so that twelve men met their deaths.

For one who understood the business, this counter-clockwise movement need not perhaps have unnatural effect; it might even, if wisely directed toward a certain end, do good. At any rate, we read of a man who calmed a storm by walking against the sun around a circle formed by his companions. That he should find it necessary to speak Irish while doing so is probably nothing more than an indication that culture proper was at an end, and the time came for mysticism to replace the simple meaning culture had taken with it to the grave, by its practical or speculative abracadabra. The action in itself might well have its authority in culture.

The close association between man and sun is also indicated by legal custom. Legal acts and bargains were not valid unless they had been accomplished in the light of the sun or in broad daylight. It is unlawful to take an oath by night after the sun has passed below the woods, to cite a Swedish instance. Killing by night was deemed murder, and the reason is not to be sought for in the secrecy of the act. What was done in the dark is altogether different in character from what was performed in league with the sun, or in the spirit and power of the sun. To catch the full weight (we may say the psychological force) of the saying "night killing is murder" we must remember that murder is a dishonorable act, a nithing's deed, and undermines the doer's moral constitution. It discloses some morbid strain in

---

[54] This is referencing the *Gísla* saga, or *The Saga of Gisli the Outlaw*.

his character or, as the ancients would say, some taint in his soul. Consequently, acts done at nighttime lack the sound, honorable initiative that needs the full luck of the doer; in the temporary weakening of this luck, a demonic element may insert itself.

With regard to the moon, Tacitus informs us that it served to regulate the popular assemblies. At a new full moon, men assembled at the law-*thing*, "for in all undertakings they regard this as the best beginning." Caesar's observations also about the Germanic choice of days are evidently very significant: "Ariovistus and his people knew from the prophetic warnings of the womenfolk that they could not hope for victory if they opened the battle before new moon." We might easily add to these casual hints from modern popular superstition with its hundreds of rules for what shall be done at the time of the waxing moon, and what be postponed till the moon is on the wane. With caution, we can draw so much wisdom from this thickly muddied well that the influence of the moon was not restricted to matters of public life, but penetrated the whole of life, even in everyday affairs. Unfortunately, however, the insight into the being of the moon is lost, and its character stands now as a dark riddle. Only this much we know: it was the moon—the year-teller—which determined the passage of time and days, and thus gave day its force by giving it of its soul. The luck of time thus ebbed and flowed with that of the moon.

We cannot be in doubt as to the importance of clockwise-moving thoughts; men accept and fix the sun's nature in themselves. In this respect, they must have gathered enormous powers and great luck, but if they gained good fortune by such friendship, they would necessarily acquire something more: namely, peace of mind. That the ancients felt veneration for the sun, feared it, and sought to enlist its strength; that they wished to use it to their advantage, win its favor and force it in under their own will—all this is true, for it is all one and the same thing. What men strive for, and what they attain, is frith and mutual responsibility. Without kneading natures together, no kinship is possible. Men make nature part of themselves by engrafting of their own life upon the alien element, or—what is the same thing to them—drawing something of that alien life into themselves.

But man has a wider object in sight when he concludes friendship and mingles mind with the souls around him. By weaving a web of community, he introduces peace and order in the world. The Northmen say that there was once a time when the world was *unheore*: the giants ruled as they pleased, spreading themselves as masters throughout all existence. But a race of mighty and wise beings came down upon them, and now the spawn of the ogres sit beyond the frontier, gnawing bones and biting their nails. Thus, land is marked off from unland, *heore* from *unheore*. But even to this day, the frontier is only held by strict watchfulness.

The gods, it is said, instituted the first massacre of the monsters and slew the primeval giant so that hosts of the brood were drowned in his blood, and they swept the rest away out of Midgard. Even now, Thor, the guardian of Midgard, still makes his exterminating raids. There is still danger, even for sun and moon; now one, now another dweller in Utgard has sought to yoke them under his giant will. The present order and beauty of this "fair world" has not instituted itself; it is brought about by the care of some god or hero. And in this view, the Northmen are in accordance with peoples in other parts of the world. The poet of the *Voluspa*—who was a medieval philosopher with ideas of his own,[55] but drew upon ancient myths for his material—has rescued an account of the state of the heavens as it was before the arranging powers had manifested themselves: "The sun knew not where its halls were; the moon knew not what strength [i.e., luck, determination] it had. The stars knew not where their places were."

In the legendary shape that the myths took on when they were reduced to stories by the philosophy of a new religion, it would seem as if the fateful trial of strength took place between gods and giants, while the dwellers on earth were left to look on with bated breath. The poet gives his narrative in the past form as if it were something over and done with. From the form of the words, it might seem as if the listeners enjoyed an enhanced sense of security by calling up the memory of a moment when the fate of the world hung in the balance and then swung over to the proper side. But the literary form that the myths acquired in the hands of the poets during the Viking Age and later obscures the actual meaning that was plain to the listeners when the legends were recited at the feast and illustrated, or rather supplemented, by rites and ceremonial observances. The fight is waged from day to day in the midst of the human world; no one is sure of keeping the light and the warmth, unless he and his fellows by some ceremony or other are ever strengthening the bond between themselves and the high-faring lights. If the alliance fails but for a moment, then the heavenly bodies will lose their way—then sets in the state which the poet of the *Voluspa* still knew and could describe.

And the peril that hangs so threateningly in the sky lies actually in wait for every soul in Midgard. Behind all security, there is this grave fact that natures have potential hostility in them; they can run wild and become *unheore*.

And they do so at times, when men fail to maintain themselves and their luck, and thereby their alliance with their environment. Then the clammy soil grows barren, then cattle lose their power of yielding, and trees become bearers of ill-luck. The fish move in dense shoals out to sea, while the waters fling destruction upon land. If the peace of the world is to be maintained, there must be

---

[55] English: *Prophecy of the Völva*, or *Prophecy of the Seeress*. First book of the Codex Regius, an Icelandic codex making up a large portion of the *Poetic Edda*, a collection of Norse poetry. *Voluspa* tells of a seeress' address to Odin on the creation of the world, its end, and rebirth.

great self-restraint among men, and at the same time great watchfulness and care to do all that is fitting at every festival and ritual beginning.

Without this intimate connection between man and the other natures about him, neither he nor Midgard could exist. If properly read, the myths tell us that man has created a habitable, well-ordered world in the midst of chaos, and that to live and thrive he must forever uphold his communion with every single soul, and so constantly recreate the fixed order of the world. Primitive man never thought of pointing triumphantly to an eternal order of things; he had the sense of security, but only because he knew how the regularity of the world was brought about and thus could say how it should be maintained.

Man is never able to embrace all beings and draw the whole round of creation into his sympathy and understanding. The beings left out cluster on the borders of reality as a threatening and disquieting force. Through all cultures runs a chasm separating the warm, friendly reality from the cold, strange fact—the known from the unknown, or in Old English words, the *heore* from the *unheore*. And deep-rooted in all humanity is the fear of the unknown, a feeling that, while seemingly simple and clear enough, leads down on closer scrutiny to depth upon depth. Uppermost lies the fear of a will that no obligation hinders from harming and molesting; barely hidden under this superficial dread lies the anxiety as to what the alien thing may hit upon, what it may have strength to do, the uneasy restlessness that comes of being without means to estimate the danger. But in reality, this fear of the unknown extends far beyond a sense of danger threatening life and limb: it opens out into a painful anticipation where despair is every moment on the point of breaking out, for where souls are not in some way or another welded together, man must be prepared to find actions striking with the force of a catastrophe. The forces emanating from the alien source are of another kind, and take effect in a different way, so that the sufferer may perhaps not feel the effect until the harm is done, and has at any rate no means of defense calculated to ward off the influence.

The line of demarcation runs through all cultures, but its place shifts from one people to another, and it is never possible to lay down a rule as to which beings will be found on either side of the frontier. Naturally, the desert and the sown, the rough mountains or wild woods and the pleasant ley, with their kinds, are separated by a sharp border. But the reason why one animal is drawn into communion and another is left out as *unheore* must be sought for in the individual experience of each race. In one place, the snake is a sacred animal; in another place, it is an uncanny beast, such as in Northern Europe, where the wriggling, striking reptile was held in execration and placed in demon land. Later mythology makes a family of Fenrir, the Serpent of Midgard,[56] and Hel or Death, and

---

[56] The serpent Jörmungandr

names as their mother Angrboda, an ogress. This construction proceeds from the fact that Fenrir, the chief wolf or father of wolves, and the great serpent, together with death, have their origin and home in the *unheore* world of the ogres.

The chasm extends into the world of human beings. Humanity proper is made up of all the families and tribes with whom our people have intercourse, for companionship means constant mingling of frith, honor, and luck. Outside the pale, the "strangers" crowd, and the strangers are another sort of men, because their minds and ways are unknown. When they are called sorcerers, the word only emphasizes the fact that their doings are like the doings of demons and trolls: dark and capricious, admitting of no sure calculation. The only means of overcoming the wickedness of strangers is by annexing their luck and honor and mingling mind; by mingling minds, the will and feeling in the two parties are adjusted, and henceforth their acts interlock instead of running at cross purposes. Between men, there may be fighting, community may be suspended by enmity, but the struggle is human and carried on by the rules of honor. Against strangers, men have perpetual war, and the warfare must be adjusted to the fiendish ingenuity of the demons. Toward vermin or wild beasts, men cannot feel responsibility or generosity.

That Utgard is full of witchcraft and *unheore* is known to all, and all fear with which man looks out over the limits of human life is, after all, of a different sort from the fear of homebred witchcraft. For when a member of the community separates himself from spiritual intercourse with his brothers, or when the worker of things *unheore* establishes himself within the boundary between land and unland, his presence lies like an incubus on all thought, paralyzing both will and power. His doings, even his very thoughts, are a constant danger to the luck of the inhabitants; they will infallibly cause strife among neighbors, and wither up the fertility of the land. Their presence is a breach in the cosmos, and as destructive of spiritual security as the sun or the earth would be if they broke loose from the friendship of man and ran wild. To uphold the world, man must destroy and annihilate all sorcerers, with their houses and all their goods. The boundary that separates magicians from humankind is so sharp, because it is independent of all petty external estimates of black and white; it can never be effaced, however much the acts and powers of the magician may resemble those of everyday man, and it cannot become sharper through the fact that the magician's arts go far out into the dark.

We see in Northern literature that the practices of the wizard did not differ markedly from the ritual proceedings of common men. When he changes himself or transforms things out of recognition or practices optical delusions, he may know some particular trick caught up perhaps from neighboring peoples (the Lapps for instance), but generally he works along the lines laid down by the experience of his race. He is hated because he practices his tricks in the spirit of darkness and seclusion; he is a stranger who stands outside the pale of frith, and therefore his deeds are in every case full of *unheore*, and when they are further marked by an uncanny cruelty, these qualities are but a necessary manifestation of the nature of his will.

It is a toilsome thing to be a human being, far more so than one would be predisposed, from human needs and human conditions, to believe. The demands of every day in regard to food, housing, fire, clothing, arms wherewith to face an enemy, and implements for necessary purposes can, by their incessant urging, keep men going. However, the struggle for food cannot produce that incitement of the blood in the veins that drives a man beyond himself. It may seem a stern task enough to have to compel the sun and moon to hold on their course, keep the sluices of the rain adequately open, bind the fish to the coast, equip the woods with leaves in spring, and maintain the harmony of the world. But this task nevertheless is altogether overshadowed by another, far more difficult, and even more impossible to thrust aside: to hold thoughts in their courses, and keep the soul together. The god who brings the universe into shape is only a grand mask, and behind the mask is a man who works at the no-less-grand task of creating a clear and coherent unity out of the mass of his experience.

The anxiety that drives man to intertwine nature with his own will and feeling is deeper than all fear for his bodily safety, for it is the dread of inner chaos. We Europeans are born late in the day in the sense that our social and scientific contrivances are removed by several stages from direct experience of the world. Our psychology and our philosophy are built up by scholastic modifications of the thinking done by the primitive Greeks, Israelites, and Teutons whose successors and spiritual legatees we are. Modern man, who deems himself much wiser than his ancestors, derives most of his strength from that very part of his spiritual work that he is most apt to hold in contempt as childish or "superstitious." We awake in an illuminated world, where all we need is to kindle a blaze or turn on a light when the sun is out of the sky and the moon is in the dark season; we find ourselves seated in a well-supplied larder where we have only to fetch the food we want. We have made ourselves independent of the rhythm in nature between richness and dearth, growing and declining; the caprices of nature do not afflict us directly, but come only disguised as economic crises, as storms in the social realm. We look upon the world as a regular, easygoing machine, and all this order of things we take as a matter of course. As we stand here in the common center of innumerable circles—wherein sun and moon and stars, summer and winter, day and night, beasts great and small, birds and fish, move without ceasing, without breaking out—it never occurs to us to enter this regularity among the great deeds of our forefathers. Least of all do we realize that without them there would have been a chaos which had whirled us poor wretches to the bottom.

Man is born into an overwhelming ocean of sounds and sights that hurl themselves at him piecemeal without cohesion or unity, and it is left to him to arrange the welling mass into forms and structures. He must create sun and moon, clouds and rain, animals and trees into coherent personalities and shape a course for all these abrupt momentary apparitions so that they may coalesce into a continuous recognizable form All those peepings out of heads and whiskings of tails, gleamings of eyes, and fleeting movements have to be sifted and sorted into bodies and labeled wolf, fox, or badger. The work of establishing order and harmony calls for selection and elimination as well as addition. We cannot make a sun or an animal that includes the whole body of experience, so we boldly ignore part of the facts or sometimes make two beings that overlap one another, as the Teutons did with the wolf, and as we do now with the flower of beauty and the flower of botany.

But to create a unity, we must also necessarily supply some connecting links that may be called theory, but are to us part of the experience. The dark masses cleaving to mountaintops may be recognized as belonging to the hills as part of their nature or soul—this will often be the primitive view. Or the clouds may be severed from their resting places and combined with the steam rising from a boiling kettle into a separate entity akin to water—thus modern experience that sacrifices one very important point of reality to gain coherence on another point. According to our classification, fire and matter are kept separate, and we boldly disregard the fact that certain stones strike off sparks and certain kinds of wood produce fire when rubbed. Primitive men arrange the facts in another pattern, saying that fire belongs to the nature or soul of tree and stone—the sparks are conceived and begotten by the fire drill. Consequently, there is an innate kinship between stones and trees on the one hand and the fire that comes down from the heavens on the other.

In our conception of men and animals, we fasten on the outward bodily coherence and continuity, thus creating a mass of isolated individuals where primitive man sees manifestations of grand souls or ideas. In our world, the reality of man is determined by the circumscribed and isolated status of his body, and his soul is made up of the thoughts and feelings confined to his isolated brain. The solitariness of the human being is so strong in our culture and so prominent in our experience that we slur over all other facts, such as the spiritual influence of his presence, the power of his words, and the inevitable concatenation of fate between individuals that makes a family—and often a still larger body of men—suffer for the imprudence and guilt of one sinner. To us, the individual is the reality on the basis of which all practical and theoretical questions must be solved, and we look upon all the other facts as secondary, prepared to grapple with them as problems. We go on tackling them, piling one solution upon the top of another, even when they prove insoluble. On the other hand, primitive culture gathers the whole mass of facts into the reality called man, and constructs a "soul" in which the power of words and spiritual emanation—the "suggestive" force and the touch of hands are included as well as form and features—in which the solidarity of the many is recognized as well as the responsibility of the individual.

IX. The Soul of Man

In the midst of the world of souls stands man, and he stands there in virtue of a soul, a life. This soul can bear precisely the same antitheses as the other souls or natures in Midgard. One may quite well begin in the Anglo-Saxon riddle fashion by saying, "I know a strange thing: it is invisible, yet stands forth before the eyes of all men in the hall. It is no more than six feet tall, and yet none can see more than one end of it. It can be felt with hands and without hands, and yet none can grasp and hold it fast. It goes over heath and breaking wave as swiftly as a cloud before the storm, and a dog can overtake it. It flies in the air, and yet lies sleeping in the hall." It is bound to matter, and free to move about in spite of time and space and gravity. It is formless as the heat that passes in a grip of the hand from one arm up into the other and invisible when it spreads as a force from a warrior to his entire host, and inspires them all as one man. And it is obliged sooner or later to take shape.

If we want to know what human life is, we must first of all discard our preconceived notions about soul and body and their antagonism and simply look out for the distinguishing signs of human nature, or in other words, for its modes of manifestation.

We may call it by the name of *megin*: in this word there lies an idea of power, and in this word, all living things meet. The soul of the earth, its *megin*, is often spoken of as a costly essence. A drink with which earth-*megin* has been mixed is stronger than any other liquor; on the other hand, earth-*megin* seems to contain a spiritual strengthening to counteract the overly powerful effect of ale. It is said the *megin* of the weather is the clouds: "the weather, too, has its *megin*." In the earliest days, before the world was fully set in order, moon and sun existed, but they knew not their soul, their *megin*. They did not know their power, their purpose, or their career.

These suggestions will help us to understand man's *megin*. Man's *megin* is his power—and first of all his bodily strength. But there is something beyond muscle in man's *megin*; there is power, action, and victory. And finally, *megin* reaches up into the strength of the soul, so that he who loses his *megin* will fall unconscious, as we should call it.

That which distinguishes the god (or *áss*) from all other beings is naturally the fact that he has *ásmegin* (the soul of an *áss*, or god),[57] with its mighty qualities. "If you grow, Vimur, then my *ásmegin* grows as high as the heavens," cries Thor when he stands midway out in the Utgard river and it swells up until it foams about his shoulders. Thor had, in the course of his perilous wanderings, plenty of occasions to put on his full *ásmegin*, when the giant powers gathered thickly about him. And we understand that his godhead swelled out not only in marvelous strength and wrath, but also in divine greatness of stature.

Again, the soul is called by the name of *fjör*, a word that practically became extinct with the passing of the old world. *Fjör* is life, that which enables a man to walk and speak and have his place in the light. *Fjör* is also the soul, that soul which sets out upon its own ways after death. *Fjör* is the self, that which makes man a man; it is the man himself and can therefore be applied to the body, even after death has touched it. And it is luck hearing its man, giving wings to his wit, giving him thoughts, sustaining him, and equipping his plans with progress. When Haakon Adalsteinfostre came back to his own country as a claimant for the crown,[58] it seemed for a while as if the elements would overpower him. His fleet was scattered, and rumor spread abroad that Haakon was lost with it. King Eric took the message as a welcome certainty, but Gunhild, his queen, shook her head; she was a sagacious woman and knew that Haakon had *fjör*—and as it proved, he did arrive in Norway with his ship safe and sound.

The soul is called *hugr* (Anglo-Saxon *hygi*), thereby indicating it as desire and inclination, as courage and thought. It inspires a man's behavior: his actions and his speech are characterized according to whether they proceed out of whole *hugr*, bold *hugr*, or downcast *hugr*. It resides in him and urges him on. Thus ends Loki when he has said his say among the gods: "Now I have spoken that which my *hugr* urged me to say." Thus also Sigurd when he has slain the serpent: "My *hugr* urged me to it." It sits within, giving counsel or warning: "my *hugr* tells me" is a weighty argument, for when the *hugr* has told a thing, the matter is pretty

---

[57] When referring to the Æsir, the author uses "ase" (singular) and "ases" (plural) for what is now almost always called "áss" (singular) and "Æsir" plural. This has been updated throughout the book, as well as for the Vanir: "vanr" has been used for the original "vane" (singular) and "vanir" for "vanes" (plural).

[58] Haakon Haraldsson, Haakon the Good. He was the youngest son of King Harald Fairhair.

well settled. And thus, Ingolf exhorts his brother to turn away a vagabond who comes to the place: "He seems to me unreliable. You will see he will soon turn the evil side outward. It is against my will that he is with you, for my *hugr* tells me evil about him."

A winter passed, and Ingolf could say that all had fallen out as his *hugr* had warned him. And Atli Hasteinsson, of noble race, confidently gives directions to his household after the fight with Hrafn: "You, my son, will avenge your father, if you take after your kin. My *hugr* tells me you will become a famous man, and your children after you." And when the *hugr* is uneasy, as when one can say with Gudrun, then life is not healthy: "Long I hesitated, long were my *hugrs* divided in me." But when a man has followed the good counsel from within and attained his end, then there rises from his soul a shout of triumph: it is his *hugr* laughing in his breast. Now and again, the soul has its knowledge directly, as we should say. At times, it has acquired it by spying out the land, and then it may chance that the enemy has seen his opponent's *hugr* coming toward him, whether in human form or in the shape of a beast. He dreams of wolves, and is told that it is the *hugrs* of men he has seen.

Finally, we encounter the soul as *mód*, as the Anglo-Saxons put it. A man's *mód* is his mind, the will and strength of him, the long-remembering, that which keeps both injury and friendship alive in the foreground of his consciousness, and the boldness that will not suffer will and memory to consume each other in indecision. *Mód* is quite properly the soul in its fully awakened state. When Thor is altogether himself, he appears in his godly *mód* (*ásmóðr*); the giants put on fiendish *mód* when they assume their full nature. The gods hired a builder to raise a wall around Asgard, and promised him the sun and moon with Freyja brought into the bargain for the work if it were completed before the first day of summer—but they knew not with whom they were dealing. The work went on with terrific haste; the builder's stallion drew whole fragments of rock together in the night, the master himself piling them solidly up during the day. When he had compassed so nearly around that they could begin to take measurements for the gateway, the gods held a council, and it occurred to them then that Loki had been the intermediary when the agreement was made. And Loki was forced to promise he would find a way out of the difficulty. Thus, it came about that the stranger's horse went running, and dashed away in chase of a whinnying in the woods. Its master ran all night but failed to catch it, and the next day he stood looking at the gap. There were only two days now till summer and no hope of finishing the work—then he burst into giant's *mód*. But when the gods became aware that it was a mountain giant who had come, they waived all questions of a pact and called for Thor to settle the account with a blow of his hammer.

To assume the giant's *mód* or bring it into play is understood to imply all such peculiarities—violence and ferocity as well as features—which show him a being of demonic land.

We are led farther and farther toward the holiest center of the soul. Life is recognized by honor. We have learned how intimately connected luck and honor are, or rather, we have seen that they are two sides of the same thing. The ancients were quite certain that the moment they allowed their good repute among men to decline, the moment they neglected the reputation of their forefathers, when they failed to maintain their own fair fame, when they committed any dishonorable act—then their luck would sicken. Their certainty was based upon experience. They had realized the importance of a due regard for honor in its effect upon the health and initiative of the coming generation, its stature, muscles, and courage. They knew, indeed, that dishonor could kill a child in its mother's womb and render women barren. Honor was nothing less than life itself, and if a man kept his soul in a half-stifled state, then his descendants would be hampered in their growth, coming into the world as weaklings, crippled, and without boldness.

On the other hand, if a man had nourished his soul and enriched his life by gaining dominion over others' honor, then heroes would be born in his house—men keen of eyes and mighty of strength, children who reached out after weapons before they were well out of the cradle. Night-old the hero appears in mail; one would be justified in saying of an Ylfing. More in everyday style, perhaps, we may read that the boy sternly pulled his chastiser by the beard, and achieved his first killing at an age when other children hold onto their mothers' apron strings. Or perhaps there would be such strength in the children that they themselves craved life. We read of a boy named Thorstein, son of Asgrim, a prominent man of the Telemark, that he was to have been exposed to perish at birth. In the meantime, while the thrall was preparing to carry out the child and bury it, all present heard the babe sing:

> Let me go into my mother. It is cold here on the floor. What other place is fitting for a boy than his father's hearth? Leave that whetting of steel, leave the turf in peace—I have a future among men.

But even though children may be a sure indicator of the state of the soul, this does not mean that one has to wait for the coming generation to see how dishonor gnaws at the vital root. To the Icelander, the two combinations: "preserve one's honor" and "preserve one's luck" are synonymous. When he says, "I do not think I can maintain my honor if I sit idle in this matter," then his words have a weight that proves that this sentence—for the heart if not for the brain—is equal to avoiding death, maintaining one's existence.

Honor has the reality of life, or soul, and therefore the bitterness of death is removed by a hope of resurrection in fame. The hero rejoiced to think not only that so and so many would utter his name hereafter—his confident faith in the future lay in the certainty that in this naming and this praise, his innermost self spread out, ruling and enjoying, living life. When the Northmen say, "Cows die, kin die, and man too must die. This I know that never dies: dead man's renown," the words, at the time when they were pronounced, perhaps mean nothing more than we approximately read into them when we repeat the lines. But they have their power for that age from a reality extending far beyond what we can imagine in posthumous fame, a reality that we can only appreciate adequately by substituting such a word as rebirth, or resurrection. The same applies for when Beowulf comforts the king in his distress with this:

> Sorrow not, wise man. Better it is to avenge a kinsman than to sorrow much for him; each one of us must see the end of his life in this world; let him who can, win fame before death: this is the greatest joy for a warrior when life is ended.

To live in fame hereafter (and preferably for as long as the world should last) was the greatest ambition of the Northman. The word comes to his lips of itself in the most solemn moments of life. When Hoskuld welcomes his son with a blessing at the son's new homestead, his wishes for welfare shape themselves finally thus: "This I surely believe, that his name will long endure." And throughout the whole of the Germanic region runs this thirst for fame. The cry for posthumous honors, for something that shall last beyond the hero's day, rings out as insistently through the Christian verses of the *Heliand* as ever it did from the lips of any heroic poet:

> It is man's pleasure to stand firm with his lord, willing to die with him. Thus will we all follow him on his going, counting our life of little worth, and die with the king in a strange land. Then at least there will be left us honor and good fame among those who come after us.

Thus, Thomas encourages the other disciples. The Anglo-Saxon Seafarer, who cannot quite get his Christ to command the waves (whether those within or those afar), clings to the same faith in the judgment passed on the dead. For him, the whole world lies mournful and hopeless, as a chaos of toil, hardship, want, broken hopes, and parting where one looked for meeting. He can find nothing lasting. Sickness, age, and battle vie with one another in plundering mankind. There is then nothing else to build upon but the praise of posterity.

His advice is this: make use of time before the end comes, to manly faring against enemies and devils, that the children of men may praise thee, and thy fame live among the angels. Late-born as he is, he regards the manly age of the world as at an end. The time when men lived and had faith in life, gave jewels and thrived in luck because they were strong—that time is forever past and gone, or so runs his plaint. And with the inconsistency of bitterness, he brings his accusation against existence itself, and holds up its unalleviated wretchedness before the eyes of all. But though the cynics of all times are alike, their resignation yet bears the stamp of their age and place. One says, "Well, let us eat and die," and another says, "Let us think and die." The Seafarer says, "Let us die and be remembered."

If we take the word "fame" as meaning something lying solely in the mouths of others, or something dependent upon the goodwill of strange people and their power to appreciate what was great, then it would after all have been too uncertain a value to reconcile the Teuton with death, or even make of death a gain. The joy in a great renown had its indomitable strength and its ideal value from the fact that it was based on a reality. The life of fame after death was a real life.

It is easy enough for us to grasp the enthusiasm in the ancients' pride of death. We are quick to see what is flaming and bright in the words, but we are hardly able now to feel their power of spreading warmth. The modern reader probably thinks he is showing the poet all possible honor in taking the words in as spiritual a sense as can be, but actually, he is merely killing their true life by his ideal admiration. Another expression of the value of the name is found in the ancient exhortation to warriors, as we find it in the Norse *Hirdskraa*, the law of the king's bodyguard: "Have in mind, that he who once dies as a nithing, he shall never another time [i.e., again] become a brave man, but as he dies with that name, so with that fame shall his memory live." Here, the old sense of reality still speaks dearly. If we can bring ourselves—with our minds filled with those praises of fame after death—to take this exhortation literally as it stands, then we shall ourselves feel both the solemnity and the vital seriousness of the ancient longing for great renown.

The name then goes out from him who bears it as a conqueror, lays the world at his feet, and goes forward undeterred by life or death because he has in himself the soul. If the man dies in body, then all life shrivels in his honor, his fame after death, and his name, and lives its life therein undisturbed. It can at any moment fill out a new body and inspire it to a life in honor and luck. When the name is given to a kinsman, the soul emerges into the light again, as if nothing had happened. He is come again, men said.

Another word designating the human soul is Icelandic *aldr* (Anglo-Saxon *ealdor*), which from the point of view of our languages must in some places be rendered as "age" or "lifetime," and in other places simply as "life." The texts speak of losing age, staking age, and taking age from another man. A man can hazard his *aldr* and lose it, and he can take another man's *aldr* from him in battle.

Aldr is the *fjör* residing in the breast, into which the sword can force its way to bite. But this soul, or life, does not exist merely in a pale generality, as a white board on which the world casts its shadow. It has some contents; it is a fate. According to the *Lay of Helgi*, the Norns came to the homestead of the hero on the night of his birth and created, or formed, his age; they bade him become the most famous king, greatest in renown among princes.

A man's age is determined from his birth, say the Norsemen, meaning thereby that one's history, as we should say, or one's fate, as they themselves would put it, is a given thing. Through such and such happenings, he is to be led to his end. One can recognize a hero of the past in one's contemporary by his courage and by the contents and strength of his honor. His career also provides its evidence (and this perhaps is the clearest) as to the connection between past and present. When we know what sort of a soul there is in a man, we can say with immediate certainty what awaits him, and what his end will be. A man's fate is predetermined, and therewith friends and enemies alike, alliance and conflict, tradition and aim; with the characteristics of a race there follows, in rhythmic repetition, the same history. After the fight with Hrafn, Atli Hasteinsson refused a friendly invitation from Onund: he would rather go home, for in all likelihood it would follow from his name that he should die of his wounds, as did his father's father, Earl Atli, whose name and life he bore.

The truest commentary is furnished by this paragraph in the *Prose Edda* (Icelandic *Snorra Edda*): "Good Norns of noble birth create a good *aldr*, but if men fall into unluck, ill Norns were at work." The Norns were at heart nothing but the manifestation of the kin's luck and history.

Our word "fate" is scarcely applicable to the thoughts of the ancients as to life and its course insomuch as we chiefly apprehend fate as a mysterious and incalculable force. The fate of our forefathers was a being with impulses, passions, and peculiarities: a tendency always to choose one particular side of a thing, to choose combat and the decision of arms rather than discussion, or always to look about for possibilities of negotiation. It was the tendency rather to kill one man too many than one too few, or an inclination always to do that which serves one least. We have always to deal with an individual fate, that which belongs to a single man and distinguishes him from all others. This fate may fairly claim to be called nothing less than soul. It can proceed out from him and communicate itself to others, and it can find an individual rebirth.

According to the prose passages of the Helgi Lays in the *Edda*, Helgi Sigmundsson and his love, Sigrun, are supposed to be reincarnations of Helgi Hjorvardsson and Svava, and then to be reborn themselves in the persons of Helgi Haddingjaskati and Kara Halfdan's daughter. We have here three parallel legends, of a hero whose mighty and hasty pace of life is due to a semi-supernatural woman. Helgi Hjorvardsson is awakened to action by the valkyrie Svava, and consecrated to death by his brother's reckless vow to cheat him of his love's right. Helgi Hundingsbane, in the course of his warlike expeditions, wins the love and protection of Sigrun, daughter of Hogni, but for her sake he is driven to slay Hogni and thus prepares his own downfall. The third legend is known only from a dim reminiscence in a mythical saga where Helgi, striking too high, wounds his love and protectress, and thus forfeits luck and life for himself. How the separate parts of this trilogy stand one to another as regards to their origin and contact we do not know. Only this we can see: the reason of their being so threaded together lies in the similarity of the fate that unites the *pair*. Helgi and Svava do not enter into life again, but life has reborn the group, hero and valkyrie maiden— and their love with its tragic result.

Whoever interpolated these prose passages into the poems would hardly himself have arrived by speculation at this hypothesis of rebirth. But whether there were some germ of combination in the legends themselves or not, these lines of prose have their authority in the ancient thought. Life is known by its doings. The soul has a course of life inherent in it, as one of its qualities. Fate, or as we also might say, history, is not, any more than luck, a thing lying outside a man. Nor does it merely hang about him as a necessary result of his character. It is luck itself; it is his nature. It is born out of him in the same way as fruitfulness and victory. It is on this identity between fate and will that the bold fatalism of the Northmen depends.

And so it is not from resignation that an Atli speaks as he does. The Northmen did not let themselves be dragged off by fate. They went willingly, chose themselves that which they knew was their destiny. They chose the inevitable of their own free will, paradoxical as it may sound. Fate was to them a necessity man could not avoid, but they felt it nevertheless as a matter of will. They took up the counsels and plans of their kinsmen as warmly as their own, and in the same way they lived through the fate of their forefathers with eager appetite. They grasped firmly at their destiny with a will that is the will of fate itself— here lies the secret of their sturdy sense of life, the imperturbable contentment with the solidity of existence that keeps them from ever going into the depths to search for treasure. All the while, they never think of dreaming and consoling themselves away from what is and must be.

Name and fate interpenetrate. The name was a mighty charm, because it carried the history not only of the bearer, but of his ancestors and of the whole clan. Deeds lie concealed in its sound, and they may blossom out into an addition so that the name becomes an epic in brief. Such names as Bow-Wielder, Sigurd Fafnirsbane, or Hroerek Ringslinger are the nuclei of family legends.

But there is still a whole side of the soul untouched. Nature needs a body. When the mother had given birth to her child, it was carried to the father, that he might see which of the old kinsmen it was that now appeared in the light again. Possibly his keen eyes could discern the character of the departed in the movements of the child. Some children came into the world with clenched fists; others uttered the cry of a hero at the very commencement of their career. The child looks promising, men say; he will be a hard fellow, but true to his people. First and foremost, the father scanned the newborn child for likeness in features, eyes, and build. The soul did not alter. Powerful limbs, sharp eyes, and waving fair hair were not accidental attributes of the hero-soul any more than the hardness and cold of a stone are accidental qualities of the body that a stone-soul takes for its garment.

It is a standing expression in the sagas that the young chieftain to be is distinguished by his eyes. He has keen eyes, and he whets his eyes after the manner of true princes of war—so we read of Helgi Hundingsbane. So also of the birth of Sigurd Fafnirsbane: "The king was glad when he saw the sharp eyes in his head, and said that none would be his equal." These eyes are in poetry the chieftain's patent of nobility: a glance that could tame or cow both men and beasts. Sigurd's murderer had to go out of the chamber twice without achieving his aim, for the eyes of the Volsung were so keen that not many dared gaze into them. The horses dashed aside and would not tread on Svanhild, as long as her eyes were open.

Saxo's description of Olo Vigetus is a study in the heroic glance: his eyes were so sharp that they smote the enemy harder than other men's weapons; the boldest cringed under his glance. He comes, unknown, to the king's court. The king's daughter was accustomed, in passing around the hall, to observe the guests. From the features of their faces, she could read their quality and standing. But at sight of Olo's countenance, she falls three times swooning to the ground. "Here is a kingly-born hero," she says, and all cry to him to throw aside his hood. When he obeys, all the men present sit staring in admiration at his beauty and his yellow locks, but he kept his eyelids lowered deep, "lest they should see and be afraid."

Saxo, modern as he is, wonders at the girl's perspicuity. At any rate, he thinks it as well, with such a remarkable piece of divination that he put it in inverted commas. "Men believed" that she could read the standing of the guest from his features. But as a matter of fact, it needed no great art to point out a king. It is hopeless for him to disguise himself. Let him put on the kirtle of a slave and a kerchief about his head, and set himself to turn a mill. It will yet be seen that the wench has sharp eyes; this young blood is never come of cottar's stock. He cannot help turning so that the stones fly asunder and the casing is sent flying. Such an appearance, and such strength, belongs once and for all to his luck, his nature. Tall, stately, and handsome—handsome, that is to say, without the laborer's features of the peasant type. He must be handsome to be a chieftain, and could not be otherwise if chieftain he were. When the soul is reborn, it shapes a human form about itself with such limbs, such eyes, and such hair, for it cannot do otherwise. Or let us perhaps rather say that the soul itself is yellow-haired, blue-eyed, and strong of sinew—this after all is the true meaning.

All these individual determinations of the being of a soul fuse in one single word: luck. The soul is luck in the all-embracing sense that opens before us when we follow patiently its activity throughout the full circle. When luck is at an end, then we know life itself is ended—not because it was dependent upon certain external conditions, but because it was existence itself that ceased when luck broke off. To be in luck, to show oneself in luck, means the same as to step forth in light and life.

This vitalizing power of man that thus manifests itself under different aspects is (according to our terminology) appropriately named soul, but we may call it life or existence without changing the point of view. Here the radical difference between the primitive and modern experience makes itself felt. When we set our reflection to explore the premises which lie at the bottom of our talk of the power that moves in us and moves us, it arises with the idea of a clear, transparent stream taking up in its course feelings and moods. Life is something we have in common with all other creatures, and it becomes man's life by taking on or evolving purely human elements. It is otherwise with the life that bore forward the actions of our forefathers; life to them was purely human, and not only a merely human, but a personal thing—as personal as a nickname. Force and effect are to our experience so far apart that we can interpolate the question: let us see what effect comes of this force. To primitive experience, power and its result are one, and grow together.

As soon as we replace our "soul" by the word *hamingja*, the thought is translated from our pale view of life to the full-blooded and muscular view of the past. *Hamingja* is a nature that can only act in its essentially determined manner, and only to the end that lies in itself. *Hamingja* is a character that can only manifest itself as these or those particular persons, but must on the other hand produce its predetermined effect: this particular honor, will, and fate, and it must create these or those personalities, in their peculiar relations within and without. Therefore, it comes now as a man, now as something human, now as a personality, now as a force—and always it is itself, never more and never less. Whether it marches at the head of an army, in bodily manifestation of one sort or another, or it emanates from man into the soil and make the germs sprout through the mold, makes no difference to its nature. Luck constitutes, we know, a close whole, alike throughout and indivisible. Therefore, every single quality of man possesses the whole force of the *hamingja*; fame after death bears in itself a living soul or a living human being.

In this homogeneity of life is implied the necessary condition for such expressions as the following Old English: "The heathen fell frithless on the field of battle," and, "The time came for him to suffer a parting from frith." These passages are not understood when taken one-sidedly as evidence that life on earth was, to the forefathers of the Anglo-Saxons, first and foremost a common life, a frith. Nor can they be taken as instances of poetic use of frith in the sense of soul. The explanation lies deeper: frith was really a form of life, and that, in the Germanic thought, means the soul itself, and thus to lose frith and luck was literally to die.

Here, the contrasts that are of primary importance to us lose their authority. Body/soul, neutral/personal, whole/fraction: these definitions have a place in ancient thought, but they are not fundamental. When we read of a man's *hugr*, that it meets his enemy in the shape of a ravening wolf, then we know that it is a personal soul. If we are told that a man has a bold *hugr*, then we know (or think we know) that it is a quality of character that is spoken of. But in other cases we are tortured, perhaps, by an unpleasant sense of doubt. If a man feels himself impelled by his *hugr*, or warned by his *hugr*, is it then the spirit—(his mind, as we should say) or a spirit (his genius, in other words) that speaks within him? As long as we take it for granted that the two exclude each other, we can only hesitatingly weigh *pro et contra* on reading a verse such as that which Gro sings over her son: "If enemies bar your way, with evil in mind, then let their *hugr* change over, to your service, and their mind be turned to peace." Now all either/or disappears; *hugr* is everywhere as personal as it is impersonal.

The ancient thought does not oscillate over the contrast between soul and body. There is a contrast between the material and the spiritual existence, and the divergence between the two forms of human manifestation is great enough to set thoughts in motion, but not wide enough to range them into two hostile arrays. The tension between existence of the spiritual and sensing of the tangible is not yet grown so strong that the two poles will separately draw experiences to them and hold them fast in two groups so as to make a breach or a problem. For modern men who are under the sway of Hellenistic philosophy and religion, it seems as if primitive men leap backward and forward over a hole from contradiction to contradiction, but there was no gulf and no contradiction in them. The connection has such solidity that it can stand whatever pressure facts may bring to bear upon it. As long as we look at the body, we can dwell as continually and as one-sidedly as we choose upon the corporeal limitations of man. And if we look at man from the spiritual point of view, we need not hedge around our description of the capricious soul with qualifications through fear, lest our former words should rise up and witness against us. Indeed, it is only when we have given each its due,

fully and uncurtailed what it deserves, that we can maintain the equilibrium between them.

No one will dispute the power of the soul to separate itself from the body in
order to live a free, untrammeled existence while the body apparently, and perhaps also in reality, lies idle as a house without a tenant. The soul can go to
whatever place it will, set out on its own errands, spying out, preparing, and also
acting on behalf of the whole person. There is a story to the point about the
Frankish king, Guntram. Once, it is told, while out hunting, he was overtaken by
great weariness, and lay down to sleep beside a stream. When he woke, he could
still remember how he had crossed a river by an iron bridge into a mountain
where lay great treasures of gold. The soul had seen correctly, for when men
went to dig in the place the king had pointed out, they found enormous treasure.
But he who sat with the king's head in his lap had seen that out of the king's
mouth came, while he slept, a little snake that hurried backward and forward
along the water, until he laid a sword across the brook, when it at once disappeared across the bridge and into a little hole in the mountain side, returning
shortly after the same way.

At any rate, we know that the soul now and then can go wherever it will, but
we know also that it carries the body in it. If that royal snake had met anyone
strong enough to do it harm, then the king would have seen the marks on his body
when he woke. At any moment, this soul can burst out into a body, as it were
turning inside out and showing outwardly the matter that in its airy state it bears
within. And then it appears not only as a vision, a picture of the person, but as a
hard and fast, powerful body—a corpus certainly not to be passed through without perceiving it. A man's *fylgia* (as the soul is called in this state by the Icelanders) can both strike with its weapons and crush with its arms so as to take away
a man's breath.[59] It is told of two Icelandic peasants that they met one night in
animal shape between their homesteads and fought out the quarrels of the day,
and when they awoke in the morning, each lay with battered limbs pondering
over the events of the night.

The Northern *fylgia* stories indicate plainly enough that the soul has an advantage over the person as a whole: it can choose what form it will take. When
the body is at rest, the soul sees its chance to take on another shape than its customary clothing, one better suited to the needs of the moment. We hear of men
taking the form of birds, either to travel through the air, or to gain entrance
through openings not to be reached from any highway but "the bees' road." When
the slaughter of Gunther and Hogni was imminent, Kostbera, Hogni's wife, had
warning dreams of Atli's soul coming into the hall. "Methought I saw an eagle
fly in and down to the end of the hall. Bitter is that which waits us now. He was

---

[59] A *fylgia* (alt. *fylgja)* is a guardian spirit bound to a family or clan.

dripping with blood. I saw from his threatening looks that it was Atli's shape," says the verse in the *Atlamál*.[60] The words, poetic as they are, reflect an everyday reality.

Gunhild, the queen of the Norwegian king Eric Bloodaxe, was a wise and indomitable woman whose strong *hugr* so moved the imagination of her contemporaries that she has passed into history as a half-supernatural being. It happened that Egil, who was no friend of the king's, was shipwrecked on the coast and forced to throw himself on the hospitality of the king. Egil had no other way to buy the goodwill of Eric than by composing a laudatory poem, but during the night, when he sat working at his *Hofudlausn*—the poem to save his head—he was pestered by a bird that kept twittering at the window. Late saga writers hold it beyond doubt that the bird was none other than the *hugr* of the implacable queen.

Where strength was needed, the soul would come running up in the shape of a bear, and with a bear's force:

> This Hjoryard and his men see that a great bear goes before King Hrolf and his men, and always nearest the king. He kills more men with his paw than five of the king's champions. Sword and arrow turn aside from him, but whether it be horse or man that comes in his way, he strikes them down and crushes them with his teeth.

The bear was Bodvar Bjarki, whose body sat at home in the hall, asleep.

Without doubt, this power to take on another shape is something peculiar to the soul as distinct from the body. The trance (or temporary dying) of the body is a condition required to give the soul full freedom to exploit that other nature, and utilize all the qualities that lie in the shape adopted: its massive manifestation, its peculiar powers, its swiftness, and its wildness. As soon as Bodvar awoke and drew his heroic body about him, the bear vanished. But we unconsciously introduce our preconceptions in translating these reminiscences of the ancient experience into our modes of thought. The *hugr* could not take on the body of a bear, unless its luck had something of bear-nature in it. The elements of which the soul builds itself a body (*hamr*, as it is called) are not taken from outside; they lie within it and are likewise present in the everyday body. He who really appeared as wolf, as bear, as ox, or as eagle had the character marks of wolf, bear, ox, or eagle in him always. His luck was of such a sort as to imply an essential relationship between him and his beast. He used its strength, its courage, its wildness, its craft, its power of divination, and its power of tracking, also in daylight and in his own body.

---

[60] Also known as *The Greenlandic Lay of Atli*. It tells largely the same story as the *Atlakvida*, or *The Lay of Atli*, but in greater detail.

When the human shape lies bound in sleep, the other peculiarities that are contained in its nature can realize themselves in exterior form. Perhaps we had better say that when the other powers evolve their shape-giving qualities, human form is bound to be in abeyance. And looking more closely at such genuine representatives of soul-force as Bodvar, we can still (despite the fact that the story has been robbed from its living soil) discover the birth marks.

The name of Bjarki is nothing else but bear, and the story of his origin perhaps still holds some shadowy trace of his having belonged to a bear clan which had established a state of frith with the bear, as had the Ylfings with the wolf. They cultivated this frith as their mutual luck, by constantly assimilating something of the animal's nature in themselves. His father's name was Bjorn (bear), his mother was called Bera (which means a she-bear), and his father went about in the shape of a bear at the time the son was begotten. The story of his father's unlucky fate when he was bewitched by a step-mother on account of his virtue is spiced with romance and imagination, but there is a bear in the story from early times. If the form in which it is handed down to us is nothing more than a medieval tale, the story is molded over a type of family legend familiar to our ancestors. It is not at all unlikely that Bodvar may have had his mark somewhere about his body, as the Merovingians had their boar bristles down the back.

In late times, when the ancient reality was weakened into something half-imagination, and literature fell under the influence of medieval poetry, the *hamr* was sometimes described as a pelt into which the shape-shifter slips, and which he leaves behind when he returns into his own body. But this conceit sits loosely on the original idea that comes to light everywhere in the living language. Originally the *hamr* was, as the poet of the *Atlamál* is still half-aware, the very soul itself, the *hugr* or *hamingja*. The man who has suffered scathe in his luck, and thus no longer has his full *megin*, is *hamstoli*, (i.e., robbed of his *hamr*); he cannot remember, understand, or dream. When a man took on his *hamr*, he assumed all his strength and put all his powers into requisition. Not all had this power to "ham" (*hamask*) in the same degree. The strong man—he who had much and powerful luck and could therefore send his will as well as his *hugr* abroad in mighty shapes—was called *hamramr* (i.e., strong of soul).[61]

The common people have, on this point, preserved the ancient faith that strong characters are able to show themselves in several places at the same time. And according to the unmistakable evidence of Viking times, to be *hamramr* meant having the power to take on another shape and appear as an animal. This is the highest degree of the power in question, but surely too it was a quality that made itself apparent while the man was in his normal bodily form—as violence in battle, as invulnerability, insensibility to pain, and increased bodily strength.

---

[61] Hamramr means that one is capable of shapeshifting or entering a berserker rage.

This is the Bodvar nature, acting in the full light of day: "Then they took their swords and bit the edges of the shields, went around the ship, along one bulwark and back along the other, and slew all the men. Afterwards, they went howling up on land." Such grim warriors were called *berserkir* and *ulfhednir*, because they wore bear skins and wolf skins as an outer garb, and this accoutrement no doubt has to do with their strength and ferocity. Of a man called Odd, it is told that he crossed Iceland in a single night from the extreme northern point to the Southland when his sister needed his aid sorely. Whether he trotted along as a bear, whether he flew, or used his legs, we do not know. One thing is enough: it was the fact that he was *hamramr* that gave him the speed.

In Christian times, the word *hamramr* was degraded to serve as a branding adjective, and in its decline it shared the same fate as *fjölkunnigr*, later used of those individuals who kept to the ancient practices and thus became sorcerers. Properly, *fjölkunnigr*, or "much knowing," meant nothing more than being able to use one's luck in manifold ways, as a man would naturally be when possessed of knowledge of things past, and of such insight and sympathy as enabled him to draw strength from the souls about him.

At the time when Olaf Tryggvason scoured the country to carry the light of Christ into all Norwegian homes and hearts, there was a man in the extreme north called Raud, who stoutly defended himself against royal conversion by setting storms to guard the coast. For a whole week, the king's fleet battled against the wind in the mouth of the fjord without making headway, but at last the pagan gusts were overcome by a liberal application of candles and crosses and holy water. The king succeeded in capturing Raud and dispatching him to Hell when he proved too obstinate to change his faith on the spot. The sturdy heathen was derided by the king's followers—or by his pious biographer—as *fjölkunnigr*.

But Olaf, who defied the storm until it obeyed him, who sent forth his luck to aid his friends and took the wisdom out of his enemies' thoughts—or even at times appeared bodily to turn a deadly weapon aside from his servant's head in danger—must have been as *hamramr* and *fjölkunnigr* as any, as is but natural in a man who comes of good kingly stock. And the nickname *fjölkunnigr* is returned with proper justice by the adversaries of the most Christian king, when they were mysteriously overpowered by his "luck and *hamingja*." Both parties were right. In the case of strangers whose powers and ways are of another kind, *fjölkyngi* must really be witchcraft, and it is thus no twisting of words when Christians and heathens accused one another of underhanded practices. When Christian *hamingja* and the Christian God remained in possession of the field, the men of the new faith naturally turned the word wholly against their enemies and made it a byword of reproach for people of the ancient faith.

It is thus clear that there is no contradiction between the neutral life—the spiritual power that a man radiates out to his surroundings—and the personal soul that sets forth on its own legs and grasps at things with its hands. The two are only opposite poles of the same luck. We have seen how a man's *hamingja* can go out and lay itself like a fog upon another's mind, shadow his far-sightedness, stifle his initiative, and suck the strength from his plans. And we have no need at all to imagine the active agent as a man, stifling with hands, sucking with lips, or treading with feet. The king's *hamingja* passes like a warmth from his hand into the warrior whose hand he grasps; his *hamingja* enters as a force into men and fills their bodies, penetrating to the outermost joints, and from these over into their weapons.

Foresight itself is *hamingja* that rises up from the depth of the soul and spreads out in him who prophesies: "I know of my foresight and from our *ættarfylgja* [i.e., the *hamingja* of the clan] that great sorrow will grow for us from this marriage." Thus warns Signy, in the *Völsunga saga*, when the marriage with Siggeir is proposed. But at any moment the *hamingja* can spring up in its full personality—but a slight turn in the mode of observation, and it changes from a something into a someone. In the same way, the Northman's *hugr* often passes from the idea of mind, will, desire, and thought to what we understand by soul (in all its shades of meaning), so that such a manifestation of the man outside himself, as that described in the legend of Guntram, can well be set down in the words: "It is a *hugr* we have met," or, "Those are *hugrs* of men." Thus says a man who has seen his enemies in a dream, and this, in sober words, means that the souls of those enemies steal about him, watching, lying in wait, preparing.

Neither is there any contrast between the *hamr* and the *mód* and *megin*. The giant is instantly recognized when he puts on his full giant's *mód* (the wild, raging soul of the ogres), just as Thor is able to out-tower the mighty swelling of the river when he puts on his god's *megin*. The metaphorical expression that the spirit bears the body bound up in it (if it is indeed metaphorical) is in danger of thrusting upon truth an appearance of profundity. But when we have done everything to remove the temptation of taking the words as a piece of modern wit, they contain just what must be said. And we have undoubtedly the right to use just such a form of speech as this, that the neutral luck bears in it personality as a quality among all its qualities—or better perhaps, that it is impregnated with a personality, just as it is impregnated with victory, fruitfulness, and wisdom.

Life is a homogeneous whole, but it is distributable into parts. The soul can be strewn about in small particles. If one has a great soul, such as made a man a king, then he can share out his soul among his warriors so that one part goes east to quell a revolt, another westward on an expedition at sea, and a third upon some peaceful errand elsewhere. Undoubtedly people would have regarded it as a sorry sign of lacking spiritual force in their prince if one of these souls sent out—whether he had at the time three or seven armies in the field—lacked sight or hearing, wisdom, or the power of action. Every one of his redes—or powerful thoughts and counsels—indeed, must be equipped with eyes and ears. The entire soul-mass is impregnated with humanity in the same way that a stone is with hardness, or the tree with treeness, so that the man is mortally vulnerable in every little part of his honor. It is possible to kill a man bodily by slaying one of his redes. If a chieftain is divided temporarily into four parts, then no doubt his body will be present as a whole with one of these tetrarchs, but this does not imply that the other three must remain incognito or invisible, or that they are in the least degree inferior to the whole man in fullness of qualities.

Each one of them can very well assume the waving hair, keen eyes, fresh complexion, and stately limbs of the chieftain's luck. We can, if we will, credit the man with four souls. But each of these four nevertheless contains at every moment its fellow-souls, and is responsible for them in every point. Indeed, in the deepest foundation of the matter they are not separated at all. Separation in space counts for nothing, or almost nothing.

The words *megin, mód, fjör,* and the others do service by illustrating the ways and conditions of the *hamingja,* but it would be wholly arbitrary to limit the description of the soul to enumerating a string of "animistic" terms. The same comprehensive meaning of "life" as "soul" resides in all words describing processes of mind. Icelandic *heipt* means enmity or hate, and it is hate felt, as well as inimical thoughts and wishes sent out to enter into the foe's mind as an oppressive force, or dispatched to lie in ambush for the hated man. It manifests itself as battle and mighty blows. *Munr* (Anglo-Saxon *myne*) means love and pleasure, but it is love as a manifestation of the soul; when the hero in his barrow mourns (as Helgi in the Eddic poem) that he has lost joy and land (*munar ok landa*), *munr* is not to be understood as the joy of life, but as life that is in itself joyful. And in other places, we cannot catch the weight of the word without rendering it as soul or life. Ydun, who kept the apples of youth, is called by a poet the maiden who increased the *mun* of the gods—who by administering the immortal food preserved the gods from old age and weakness. In reality, not a single word denoting mental processes can be adequately rendered in phrases of modern psychology without being either unduly widened or unduly narrowed.

X. THE SOUL OF MAN IS THE SOUL OF THE CLAN

The ancient view of life necessarily leads thought beyond the individual; one always looks about among the family to find the sources of his will and his fate. That honor that the individual bequeaths to his successor with the prayer to have it raised on high like a banner in the light is, after all, only an individual's share of that honor, which all the kinsmen combine to guard and unite in enjoying. This grandiose manner in aim and fate and will, to be never content with less than a kingdom, ever constrained to know one's fame the greatest within the horizon— this is, indeed, no less than the keen eyes, something appertaining to a whole circle of men. The father's eye is gladdened when he sees himself and his kinsmen again in his sons, when he can "see the luck of the family" in his son, as the saying goes.

They all had one *hugr* in common, shared one mind among them. The walls of the brain formed no boundary for thoughts. What was warmed in the mind of one kinsman did not come to the others with the cold of strangeness. They were one body as far as their frith and honor extended. The kinsmen were identical, as surely as the single deer leaping across the path was identical with all its fellow deer, and bore in itself the whole nature of deer—the whole great deer-soul. And the pain that ran around the fence of kinsmen when one stave in it suffered a blow was something more than a spiritual suffering. Limbs, as well as *hugr*, gave notice when a misfortune had chanced, long before any messenger came running with the news. The same peril of death threatened them all. They had one life together. It may be said of two contemporaries, father and daughter, that they had one life and therefore died on the same day. This community of life is but a stronger form of that which is found among all kinsmen. True, the whole family would not die with the father (not immediately, at any rate), but we know already well enough how fatally the falling away of one affected the future of all members of the family, how careful all had to be in regard to their spiritual health, how eagerly they sought after increase of soul, "restitution." The frith-fellows of a dead man were *fey*,[62] and their life could only be saved by energetically combating the germs of death in the organism of the clan.

In a Welsh story, the king asks an unknown kinsman, "Who are you? For my heart beats toward you, and I know you are of my blood." These words might be the simplest expression of an everyday feeling, and date from a time when every kinsman knew by experience the peculiar beat of frith in his breast. "The *hugr* told him," a Northman might have said, for he felt by the movements in the luck within him that luck of his luck was approaching, as also he would perceive the approach of an enemy by an alien luck "lying upon" his and disabling it. A good woman, Orny, the daughter of the distinguished chieftain Geitir, had been seduced by a guest from Norway, and when the child was born, her brother ordered him to be carried out and left to his fate. But the boy was found by a neighbor and adopted by him, and in his early years he ran about the homesteads, and might also come as a guest to Krossavik, his mother's home. One day, he came running headlong into the room, as a child might do, and fell full length on the floor. Then it chanced that his grandfather burst out laughing, while Orny burst into tears. Little Thorstein Oddnyarson went straight up to Geitir, and wished to know what he was laughing at. But the old man said:

> It was because I saw something you did not see. When you came in, a white bear ran before your feet, and it was that you stumbled over, because it stopped suddenly at sight of me. I should fancy you must be of higher birth than you are taken to be.

This sight of the boy's *fylgia* was enough to awaken the feeling of kinship in Geitir, and when the boy was about to go home in the evening, the old man bade him come again often, and added: "I should think you have kin here."

Kinsmen make one soul together, and yet they were naturally so or so many individuals. The clan is not a whole in the sense that it can be compared to a being with many heads. Nor do the kinsmen stand as shareholders in a fund of life that they agree to administer. The community lies far deeper, so deep that all conflict between the individual and the clan as a whole is out of the question. Nor can we find the truth in a compromise that reduces the claims of one side or the other. The individuals are each a separate reality; each is a person, and both reality and personality are so marked that they can come to stand against each other as will against will. But the personality that makes the one kinsman a character

---

[62] To be touched by death.

is the same that gives his brother and his son their silhouette-like sharpness. The kinsmen own one another. They *are* one another, and every single one of them encloses the whole soul in each of his acts.

The only way to reexperience the peculiarities of this common soul is probably to see how the unity of life affects men's practical doings. In the kinsmen's social state of mutual dependence, as in their individual independence, the thought is vitally and faithfully illustrated. The old community allows the personality no importance whatsoever in itself. A man thinking and acting alone is a modern conception. In former times, the solitary had no possibilities. His ideas, even though amounting to genius, would perish, just as he himself perished, leaving no trace. The fir that stands alone decays; neither bark nor leaf clothe it, says the *Hávamál*. And the words bear this literal meaning: that the tree that stands alone in the field can *only* fade, for it uses all its force to delay the decomposing action of wind and rot a little while. The individual could not exist save as thrall or nithing, in whom only the animal part of human life remained, and barely that. A freedman was the imperfect creature he was, because he had not properly any clan. The man of family is free, because he stands in the fence of kin; he has no weight crushing him from above. It is otherwise with the freedman: he stands alone, and therefore must have a power above him.

And to stand in the fence of kin means forming part of a solid order, which no genius and no strength of mind can change. We have really no word to measure such habits as bending the will of every man the way it would not go, as if it were acting of its own accord. What we want is a word to express a law that works its will not by hindering or repressing the plans of the individual, but by lending itself as a force and an initiative in the thoughts and ambitions of every willful single man who is under the sway of the rule. Frith lays the regard for kinsmen into the plans while they are still in process of conception. And when it happens, as it may very well do, that a member of a clan is inspired with a spirit of opposition against the nearest of kin, his refractory desire comes into the world with the will of his antagonists imbedded in it as its innermost self.

A change in the inherited honor, that which one's forefathers had regarded as right and useful and needful—whether the change were one affecting relations with men, or an alteration of what we call methods of working, or sacred customs—such an alteration was hardly to be affected by one man's will. In a sense, the laws governing our relations to our fellow men are stiffer and less plastic than the social rules of ancient society, but they correspondingly leave a way open to artifice and persuasion. We can get around the law if it is too narrow to have room for conscience, we can render it lip service and without breaking it save our souls, and we can maintain our position in humanity by living an official outward life. Thus, we save ourselves from spiritual isolation, and gain that contact with the neighboring community, which is necessary if a man is quietly to get on with his own work. In those times, a man could not, whether by craft or defiance, break through the constitutional laws of life without getting strangled in the process. A man stood in the fence of kinsmen, and only that which could be attained without breaking the chain was attainable at all.

But on the other hand, it would be rash and contrary to all experience were we to conclude that the clansman is necessarily duller and less of a character than the isolated individuals of modern times, or that he has fewer possibilities of working out what we call his personality. As long as the strength is turned outwards and does not attack the unassailable frith and honor, the clan has no choice, save between defending the unruly members and cutting them off from itself, and a healthy stock will be slow to bleed itself. As long as the undertakings of the individual are inspired by the honor and "fate" that is within him, and his ambition is the prolongation of his ancestors' deeds, he can let himself go and drag his kinsmen along with him. Frith lays the kinsmen at the mercy of the individual—and his initiative. He can screw up honor as far as he pleases, and the others have no choice but to follow. They cannot force him down; they have nothing to trust to against him beyond the power of words to persuade. They may try to talk him over, but if he is not amenable to reason, then they are obliged to enter into his undertakings and make themselves participants, both in the responsibility and in the risk. The fact of his being a part of the soul himself enables him to coerce the whole soul. The man who has a tenfold or hundredfold soul not only possesses an inner strength that is lacking in a man whose life is confined to his own single body, but he also has deeper opportunities of becoming a rich and many-sided character.

Frith was a constitutional law harder than we can easily find nowadays, but then again, it was a power that could be used both for good and evil. A man can force his way into the center of luck and appropriate luck to himself. He can assimilate the souls of others and make them dependent on his own, and then fling men forward toward whatever object he pleases, as long as he is sure of himself and his luck. There is hardly any formal authority that the strong man can take up and inspire with his peculiar gifts, his courage, his initiative, his craft, his wit, and his insolent self-reliance. But he has that which is better: he makes the others parts of his thought and will, and digests them, as it were, into his soul. The strong man uses his fellows as his own limbs.

The authority in such a clannish society is of a peculiar sort: it is here, it is there, it is everywhere, and it never sleeps. But there is no absolutely dominant power. The circle may perhaps have its leader in chief, but he cannot force anyone to his will. In Iceland, this lack of subordination appears in the crudest light. Iceland had men who gladly paid out of their own purse for the extravagances of their restless kinsmen, if only they could maintain peace and prevent futile bloodshed, but their peacemaking was an everlasting patchwork. There was no power over those who did not seek the right. To take firm action against them was a thing even the most resolute of their kin could never do, for it was out of the question for the clan to disown its unruly members and leave them to the mercy of their enemies. When Chrodin, a man of noble stock, was chosen for his cleverness and god-fearing ways to be majordomo in Austria, he declined with these significant words:

> I cannot bring about peace in Austria, chiefly because all the great men in the country are my kinsmen. I cannot overawe them and cannot have any one executed. Nay, because of their very kinship they will rise up and act in defiance.

Primitive soul is generally described by European historians as something exclusively belonging to mythology and religion. But to catch its true character, we must recognize that it is a psychological entity as well. It is so far from being dependent on speculation and belief that it is first and foremost an object of experience, an everyday reality. The thrall has no soul, our ancestors say, and they know because they have seen that it is lacking in him. When a thrall finds himself in a perilous situation, he goes blind, so that he dashes down and kills himself out of pure fear of death. How a soulless man would naturally behave we can learn from the story of the fight at Orlygsstad, where the wise and noble chief Arnkel met his death. When Arnkel unexpectedly found himself attacked by a superior force, he sent home his thrall to bring aid. On the road, the messenger was accosted by a fellow servant—and willingly fell to helping him with a load of hay. Not until the evening, when those at home asked where Arnkel was, did he wake up and remember that his master was fighting with Snorri at Orlygsstad. There is no need of any hypothesis as to soul and life to make clear the fact that the thrall lacked *hugr* and *hamingja*. His soullessness is discernible by the lackluster of his eyes. The only possibility for a thrall to rise into something like a human being is by inspiration of his master's luck and life, and thus faithfulness and devotion are the noblest virtues of a bondman.

An excellent illustration of the way a thrall is able to reflect his master is given in a short story from *Landnáma*. One autumn, a body of men who were shipwrecked on the Icelandic coast sought refuge at an outlying farm belonging to Geirmund, a noble chieftain of royal birth. The bondman steward invited the whole company to pass the winter as the guests of Geirmund, and on being asked by Geirmund how he had dared to fill the house with strangers he answered, "As long as there are men in this country, people will not forget what sort of man you were, since your thrall dared do such a thing without asking your consent."

Absolute unity (i.e., community of life within the clan) must find its justification in absolute unlikeness, essential difference from all other circles. "Our" life is not only peculiar in character, it has its own stem, its own root, and drinks of its own wells. There seems but one inference possible: viz, that our ancestors narrowed humanity down to their own circle and looked upon all persons outside their frith as nonhuman. But this inference that presupposes our pale but extensive category of humanity does not hold well in ancient or primitive culture. The question as to human beings and nonhuman beings, human life and nonhuman life, lay outside the plane where their thoughts moved. The problem could not be set up in the form it involuntarily assumes for us, still less could it be answered.

The ancient world was divided differently from ours. The difference lies not so much in the fact that the boundaries ran otherwise, as in the fact that they were of another sort. On one side, man was separated from nature by a deep sense of strangeness, which he might break through at certain points but could never overcome. On the other hand, when he has bridged the gap between himself and the souls of his surroundings, the strangeness is converted into close friendship. If he has overcome his aversion in regard to this or that animal, he at once goes to the other extreme and calls the beast his brother, and this with an unfigurative earnestness that plainly shows he does not regard human dignity as a class privilege that shuts certain two-legged creatures out as a caste apart and assigns to them a standing over and above all other creatures. He does not feel the distance between himself and the bear as greater than that between bear and wolf. Each of the three is an independent existence, and their relations with one another can thus never be expressed in any fixed constellation as with us, who invariably set man uppermost and never between the two.

The living and non-living things of the world do not form a scale starting out with the inorganic world, and rising through degrees to man as the crown of the creation. Nature is to primitive man a realm filled with free self-existing souls, human and nonhuman, which is all on the same line of existence and can enter into all sorts of combinations through bonds of friendship or kinship. Among primitive people, a worm is no farther and no nearer to man than a tiger—no being is classed beforehand as low in the scale. The thrall does not stand outside humanity in our sense of the word, only he has no life of his own and so does not count as a soul. His existence is so faintly marked that he cannot even do wrong and cannot be summoned to account, whereas animals, on the other hand, are not excluded from the honor of being called upon to defend their actions and suffer judgment.

When we cross the frontier that separates our civilization from primitive culture, we pass into a different world altogether. The world inhabited by souls does not form a wide plane in which creature touches creature edge to edge as in our universe, where things and beings are viewed chiefly from outside as space-filling bodies. Our fathers' horizon was apparently far narrower than ours, thought to have reached earlier to the walls of the world, but the smaller circle held far more than we could crush into a corresponding area. In reality, the capacity of Midgard is unlimited, for this folk-home consists of a number of worlds overlapping one another, and thus not dependent on space for their extent.

In Midgard, the animals do not run in and out, one among the rest, crowding for elbow room. The wolf is called heath-walker because the heath is part of its soul, but this does not necessarily make it akin to the deer, which is called heath-treader. The haunt of the wolf is not necessarily the same as that of the deer, however closely they may coincide geographically. The heath, as heath, was a thing by itself, an independent soul as well as a space. But when we say heath-walker, or heath-treader, we only get to it through the animal that fills out the foreground. When the heath is an attribute of unluck, we get to it now through the gray, carrion-eating, "bold" wolf. And when the heath is instead a soul quality, we get to it through the "antler-crowned," "oak's shelter-seeking," "head backward-curving" deer.

In the sphere that we dismiss summarily with the formula day and night, there was room for a number of souls meeting one another as independent beings, whole to whole instead of limiting one another. First, Day and Night live there.[63] Day is the light—the shining one and the beautiful one—but he has other characteristics, as the Anglo-Saxon language indicates by calling him noisy, the time of bustling, or the time of men being astir. Independently of light and day, the Sun has his going among men,[64] and his individual nature is expressed in the following names: Ever-Shining, Terror of the Giants, Fugitive. The Sun drives his steeds, Arvakr and Alsvinnr, with the same right as Day drives his Skinfaxi—to emphasize their mutual independence in the mythical language.[65] The essence of Night is darkness and blackness, sleep and dream, but her nature also includes anxiety and the uncanny—therefore she is derived from the home of the giants. But her soul goes still further. Dominion over time must have been part of Night's luck, since our fathers reckoned by nights. Moon,[66] too, is a hastener, but it has other powers of its own; it counts the years and wards off evil thoughts. Thus, it is wholly different from the other light.

Next to these great gods must be added a series of smaller divinities, which to us are only names save for some shreds of myths. Ny, the waxing, brightly shining moon, and Nid, the dark moon or the moonless night, both live as "dwarfs" in an antiquarian's catalog of minor mythological beings. We should not wonder at finding the phases of the moon as beings apart from the moon itself, and having their own nature. Their former independence has left its mark

---

[63] Also known as Dagr and Nótt, divine personifications of day and night in both the *Poetic Edda* and the *Prose Edda*.
[64] The divine personification of the sun (Old Norse *Sól*, Old High German *Sunna*).
[65] Skinfaxi and Hrímfaxi are the horses of Dagr and Nótt, respectively.
[66] Also known as *Máni*, divine personification of the moon.

faintly in the verses of the *Voluspa* about the gods who gave Ny and Nid their names, and in the teaching of the *Vafthrudnismál* as to the gods who set up Ny and Nid as a means of counting the years. Of Bil and Hjuki, two beings connected with the moon, we should know nothing if they had not slipped into history, because in literary times men could remember a legend of their past, when they went to the well and were stolen away by the moon. It is possible that Bil represents the relation between the moon and woman's weakness, though this is nothing but a guess suggested by the myths of other peoples.

Under the heavens fare roaring storms, driving snow, and these are not merely servants carrying out the will of a greater, any more than Ny and Nid. They are independent souls whose nature is indicated by such names as Boisterous Traveler or Breaker of Trees, and they have their own origin, being called sons of Fornjót. Nevertheless, heaven itself has as its *megin* both light and wide extent. And it has clouds, storm and hard weather, clearness and drift, and close heat, as we see by the names applied to it in poetry. Possibly, too, the sun formed part of its power. And in the same way, the moon, as the reckoner of time, included the hours of light and day in itself, without encroaching upon their independence as souls. This side of the moon's personality is expressed in a myth that makes Day the son of Night by Dellingr.

For a modern mind approaching the question in the assurance that the parts of existence are dovetailed into one another, it is dangerous to venture out into Midgard. If one cannot change one's being and become as one of the natures in this kingdom, then one is crushed between the soul-colossi that fill that little space. The souls come, growing apace, with an unlimited power of filling new spaces, and overwhelm the inexperienced from every side. So great is the independence of every soul that the recalcitrant souls are not even fused together by having a common origin. If ever anything came into being (if not rather all things simply were from the beginning), then day and sun, moon and night alike arose independently. The *sine qua non* for finding oneself at home in Midgard is to see everything, each thing by itself, as world-forming and world-filling, and not as part of a world. Neither animal nor tree, heaven nor earth is regarded as occupying a greater or smaller portion of space in existence, but as a great or a little world.

In the same way, the souls overlap one another among men. Each clan contained the luck and soul of neighboring clans, and was in turn contained by its friends, without in the least hazarding its independence as a person. Where people meet people or tribe meets tribe, they are not men-filled surfaces cut across by a political or linguistic line; the two circles have an earthly boundary between them, but this line of demarcation is only the upper edge of their mutual contact. Below it stand friendship and enmity, intercourse and feud, with all the shades that the character of honor and luck gives to these relationships. For one who, himself a soul, regards the others as souls, friends are not something outside him—their selves, their honor, their work, and their forefathers enter into him as part of his nature. And the others again possess him and his, not as tributary or subject, but as contents of honor. Each group of people—larger or smaller according to the intensity of intercourse—is the world. Their folk takes up the earth—partly as inhabited land, partly as wasteland—and fills it out to its farthest bounds. Our folk is Midgard, and that which lies beyond is Utgard.

Moreover, the earth itself is not an area in which many tribes are huddled up, but rather, as we have seen, a living being conceiving from the plow and the sower, a woman and yet the broad, green expanse of soil and "roads." And this broad, teeming, immovable earth is part of the soul of each tribe, not a common mother of all. Not as it is seen in the legends and cults when every tribe tells its personal story of the origin of earth without questioning the right of their neighbors to give their account of how the world (or rather, how *their* world) arose. So it is among primitive peoples whose cosmogonies are better known, and so it was among ancient peoples in the North—as the spirit of their myths and the diversity of their traditions bear witness.

The question, of how a human compares to a nonhuman, thus disappears when faced with the simple fact that all that is not our life is another soul, call it what we will.

Foreigners have no legal value. In later times, they were accorded only an illusory recognition in law and judgment; in older times, their life and right was a matter of indifference. One does not kill an animal or cut down a tree out of sheer idleness, not without some reason or other—whether this consists in the harmfulness of the thing while living, or in its use when dead. To understand these strictures, we must remember that primitive men are far more careful about destroying souls than men of civilization who feel no responsibility whatsoever toward the creatures around them, because they recognize only their value as things. In the same way, formerly one would hardly strike down a barbarian for simply existing. But killing a stranger did not differ in character from violating one of the innumerable nonhuman souls in existence.

Within the misty horizon formed by the hordes of the mumbling or speechless men stands a community where the individual has a certain legal value, characterizing him as a being of the same sort as the being who attacks him. The member of a community has the right to possess his own in peace. His life is costly. But within the narrow circle that is held together by a common law-*thing*, common chieftain, and common war and peace, homicide is after all not a crime against life itself, not even to be reckoned as anything unnatural.

On the other hand, from the moment we enter into the clan, the sacredness of life rises up in absolute inviolability, with its judgment upon bloodshed as sacrilege, blindness, or suicide. The reaction comes as suddenly and as unmistakably as when a nerve is touched by a needle. With this slight movement from society over to clan, we have crossed the deepest gulf in existence.

Such is life in primitive experience: not a mere organism, not a collection of parts held together by some unifying principle, but a unique soul apparent in every one of its manifestations. The being is so homogeneous and personal that all its particles, as well as all its qualities and characteristics, involve the whole creature. When a man grasps a handful of earth, he has in his hand its wideness and its firmness and its fruitfulness. We may explain the fact by saying that a grain of the soil contains its soul and essence, or we may say that the fragment is the whole—both expressions are right and both are wrong insofar as the fact is not expressible in our language, but only to be got at by resurrection of an experience foreign to us.

When a man eats an animal or drinks its blood, he assimilates bearness or wolfness. By this act, he not only assumes the ferociousness and courage of the beast, but its habits and form as well. The bodily shape of the animal enters into his constitution and may force itself out in some moments, even perhaps to complete transformation. You cannot mimic the gambols of an animal without an inner adjustment taking place, any more than you can behave like a woman without inducing a mood of feminine feeling, for by the dramatic imitation the dancer evokes the being which expresses itself in those movements, and takes upon himself the responsibility of giving it power to manifest itself.

It is told of an Icelander that he killed a man-eating bear to avenge his father and brother, and to make the revenge complete, he ate the animal. From that time on, he was rather difficult to manage, and his nature underwent a change that was nothing else but the bearness working within him. And similarly, by striking up friendships, men are vitally associated, more or less strongly, with their fellow men, as the brethren of the clan are not only one soul, but one bone and one flesh—in a literal sense that escapes modern brains. So the soul of the clan is really knit with the souls of its neighbors and friends, to quote an expression from the Old Testament, which has now lost the force it originally carried among the Israelites as well as among the Teutons.

XI. BIRTH

In the circle of friends, the soul exhibits its features and its strength, but the *hamingja* of the clan is not restricted to that human fence that now encloses the sacred field. The soul is not a thing born with each generation and renewed with each brood of kinsmen that steps in. It reaches forward. It will, as surely as anything is sure, flow through those sons' sons, which all good kinsmen hope and expect will follow one another. And it reaches back over the known part of the past, embracing all former kin, and extends behind them into the primeval darkness whence their fathers came.

The soul that works restlessly in the present generation is a legacy from the forefathers who made it by always letting it have its own way, never suffering it to hunger, but willingly gathering honor together so that the *hamingja* was forever growing beyond its former bounds.

From where had Harald Fairhair obtained his kingly luck, his kingly soul, with its wide-spreading avidity, its plans for a Norway united into one, and with the power to carry out his will? The question has been put forward in the past, and has also (at least in part) been answered. According to the legend, his soul's foundations were laid with luck of many sorts. He himself was a son of Halfdan the Black, a prince of considerable distinction in a small way, victorious and very lucky in harvests. Halfdan was first married to a daughter of Harald Goldbeard of Sogn, and on the birth of the first son, the mother's father took the boy to his home, gave him his name and his kingdom, and brought him up. This Harald died young, about the same time as his namesake. The name then passed—together with the soul—to his younger brother, despite the fact that the latter was born of a different mother, who was a woman of the powerful race of chieftains from Hadaland. Thus, from several different sources, was gathered together the foundation of Harald's great luck as king. We have every right to say that the first king of Norway was a highly complex character.

The race of Halfdan became the greatest in Norway, because its members had understood how to draw other sources of life into their own and fill themselves with *hamingja* to the point of overflowing.

The old forefathers lived in their posterity, filled them out with their will, and wrought their achievements through them anew. A scornful reference to the departed actually strikes a living soul. For whereas the soul transmigrant merely repeats itself and saves itself by again and again coming into existence when he slips from one body into another, the kinsmen actually are their fathers and their fathers' fathers, and maintain them by their being. Since it is the same soul that animated the ancestors and that now makes bearers of honor and frith out of the living generation, the present does not exclude the past. The identity of *hamingja* that bears the clan includes all the departed.

There is indeed really no question here of past and present in the same uncompromising sense as with us, who always move with faces half-buried in a dark cloud, and with a clammy feeling about the neck. Time lay spread out about those people of old. The past was north to them, and that to come was south; time present was as east and west: all in a way equally near, all in a way equally present. And to the right as to the left, straight ahead and behind, the horizon was bounded by the luck of the circle. Time was penetrated throughout by its flood, as it flowed about men and through men, filling them and space about them— always and everywhere with the force of movement in it, always and everywhere with the fullness of expansion, again and again crystallizing into a human being, who lived his time in the light to fall back again and be kept until another time. For the *hamingja*, present and past are not strata superimposed, but a double existence, through the spirit walls of which man passes to and fro without hindrance.

When a new man came into the family, the Northmen said expressly, "Our kinsman is born again; so and so has come back." And they confirmed their saying by giving the old name to the young one. Thorstein Ingimundson consecrates his son to life with the following words: "This boy shall be called Ingimund, and I look for *hamingja* for him because of the name." The soul and luck of the old grandfather, Ingimund, is now to enter into life again, to new activity in the light. Later in the story, we are told that this younger Ingimund brings about the reincarnation of his uncle Jokul, by uttering these prophetic words over his second son:

This boy looks as one who will be quick to undertaking: keen eyes he has. If he lives, he will surely gain the mastery of many and one, and not be easy to get on with, but true to friends and kin—a great champion, if my eyes can see. Should we not now call to mind our kinsman Jokul, as my father bade me? Surely, he shall be called Jokul.

The firmness of this custom in the matter of names shows that the ancients meant what they said. Names were not spent recklessly; the family had a certain stock of regular appellations that were borne in turn. The children were named after a deceased relative, and took over the vacant name. It is a thing quite conceivable in itself that Olaf Geirstad-Alf was buried at Geirstad and later, about 1020, visited his own grave. Or, as we may also put it, that Olaf the Saint had once been called Olaf Geirstad-Alf and, if he wished, could remember his dwelling at Geirstad. Men asked Olaf once, when he rode past his kinsman's barrow, if it were true that he was buried there. Rumor declared that he had there uttered the words: "Here I have been, and here I went in." This is the same unecclesiastical mode of thought obtained in Iceland. "Kolbein is come again," we hear folk say, with an intense delight of recognition, when they saw the prowess of Kolbein's nephew, Thorgils Skardi. Here they had the whole of that much-admired man before them: his friendliness, his generosity, his delight in feasting—his chieftainly character altogether.

While the Northmen in naming new kinsmen after the old lay stress on the individuality of the reborn, the remaining Germanic peoples follow a different custom, the scion of a race not being called directly after his predecessor, but given a name that assimilates portions of the kinsmen's name material. And from all appearances, the Nordic method is due to a restriction of the underlying principle. The clan had two or more appellatives in which it saw expressed its will and honor. The kinsmen bore one or another of these family signs, extended to form a name by the addition of a word such as strong (*bold*), mighty (*ric*), lucky (*red* and others) or *berht* (i.e., radiant, to be recognized from afar). The princes of Kent were called Eormenric, Eormenred, Eorconberht, Eorcongote, and Æthelberht, Æthelred. Their women were called Eormenbeorh, Eormenhild, and Eormengyth. *Eormen* and *eorcon* are both words indicating something great or imposing in the luck of the Kentish stock. The proud and ancient race that held the throne of Essex called themselves after the *sax* (or short sword), after *sige* (victory), and *sæ* (which is probably nothing other than sea). There were Saebeorht, Saeweard, Seaxred, Seaxheald, Sigebeorht, Sigeheard, and Sigebeald. Among the West Saxons, we find *coen*, *cuth*, and *ceol* predominating, indicative of progress, renown, and seafaring. *Ceol* is probably keel or ship, such as in Cuthwulf, Cuthgisl, Cuthred, Cuthwine, Ceolric, Ceolwulf, and Ceolweald. The Northumbrian kings proclaimed their gods—*os*—and their holy places or things *ealh*. This can be seen in their names: the men were called Oslaf, Oswulf, Oslac, Osweald, Ealhred, and Ealhric, and the women Ealhfrith or Ealhfled.

In *Beowulf*, the memory of the ancient Scyldings is preserved: Heorogar with his brothers Hrothgar and Helgi, and the later generation of Heoroweard, Hrethrek, Hrothmund, and Hrothulf. These had for their name-mark the sword (*heoru*) and renown (*hroth*, *hreth*). The Frankish house of the Merovingians was proud of its *chlod* and its child, renown and battle.

The mark of the Ostrogoths was, as far as can be seen, first and foremost the ancient sacred *amal*. But in addition to this, there was the kingly sign of *theod*—not only meaning people, but also in a wider sense indicating greatness, that which surpassed ordinary measure: Theodomer, Theodoric, Amalaric, and women such as Amalafred and Amalaberg. From the first century—the very dawn of Northern European history—we find through the medium of Southern annals a couple of names handed down among those born by the royal family of the Cherusci:[67] Segestes, Segimundus, and Segimerus are the names of three kinsmen in their Roman form. We may perhaps in these names discern the word for victory.

The difference between the ancient pan-Germanic method of naming and that of the Northmen indicates perhaps a breach in the mode of thought—a revolution, whereby the individual was brought forward and given a free hand to make the most of himself over the course of time. But in all spiritual changes, the new is contained altogether in the old, and the old unimpaired in the new—the difference at the outset lies in a slight shifting of the accent. The contrast between the two systems certainly means nothing more than a dissimilarity in the emphasis laid on personal and general. The period that fostered the new system of nomenclature would hardly have been preceded by a time when the deceased ancestor was not recognized in the newborn child at all. Then, as well as later, men believed in man's living on after death. But in the rebirth of the family, the thought dwelled more on the idea of its reincarnation than that of *his* coming again. The dead continued their life until they were forgotten—or, so to speak, dissolved in the luck. Meanwhile, the regeneration of the inexhaustible went on.

On the birth of a child, the luck of the kinsmen breaks out again in a new individual. Possibly, the event may have an external occasion in that a portion of luck has fallen vacant, but death and birth, to the deeper insight, do not stand in any so straightforward relation to one another. The living cannot by simply plunging into the reservoir of soul make its waters ooze forth in a successor.

When one is born, it is the wellspring of luck overflowing, and if a dead man is to bring about such overflow, it must be in virtue of all that honor he has in himself, or that the avenging of his death brings with it. When the race increases its honor, then kinsmen rise up and make the fence wider. The will is not shared

---

[67] A Germanic tribe from modern-day northwestern Germany, closely associated with the Suebi and Chatti. The Cherusci are also the tribe of which Arminius, the general who led the Germans in the Battle of the Teutoburg Forest, was prince before being taken in by the Romans.

out among a greater number of individuals, but grows so that there is more will and need of more implements for carrying out its work.

When the men of a race are rich in honor and luck, their womenfolk bear children. The luck must pass through the mother to gain strength for life, but the fact that the woman brings forth her child is not enough to inspire it with life and give it a share of luck. In the North, the child was at once brought to the master of the house, and accepted by him with a name. For instance, we read: "This boy shall be called Ingimund, after his mother's father, and I look for luck in him because of the name." Or "This boy shall be called Thorstein, and I wish that luck may go with the name." The meaning of this "look for" or "wish" lies midway between an "I know," and an "I decree, I will, I give him hereby such and such a definite portion of luck, I hereby give him birth." The father can say this, because he has with the name the soul itself in his mouth, and breathes it to the child. He inspires him with that luck, that character and will, that strength and that appearance that lie in the soul that hangs over him. With the name, luck and life—and thus also frith and the dignity of a kinsman—entered into the child.

Not until then had it a living soul. Here and there in the laws we find indications of a time when the life of a child was reckoned from the day it was given a name. In England, even after the law had advanced so far as to place the little child equal to the grown man, it was necessary to invalidate expressly all earlier distinctions, by adding whether it has a name or not. Among the Franks, the child not yet named was still kept in a category by itself, with a smaller fine for its killing than for real human beings.

It would be regarded as a vital injury if another, acting on his own responsibility, gave a name to the child and thereby stamped its mind, body, and fate. In the Germanic consciousness of law and right, there is a firmly rooted hatred of him who dares to give a man a nickname and thereby plant new soul qualities in him. On the other hand, it may be said that a cognomen brings luck, in that it increases the honorable distinction of the receiver. The depth of this pride is still discernible in the "superstition" of late times that a man with two names lived longer than a man with one.

A boy who started his career with a rich and powerful name—one that his father, grandfather, or another kinsman had filled with honor and progress—had a great advantage to begin with. Sincere Christians such as King Magnus and his true man Thorstein Siduhallson have not lost an iota of their confidence in the blessings of a good name. Thorstein comes on his homeward way from a pilgrimage to his king, when the latter lies at the point of death and has already set his house in order and given gifts to his men. Nothing is left for the latecomer, but Thorstein himself cares not for goods: "But this I would, that you should give me your name."

The king answers:

You have in many ways deserved of me that which is best, and I give you gladly this name for your son. Even though I have not been a very great king, it is still no little thing for a simple yeoman to name his children after me, but since I see that it means something to you, I will grant your prayer. My *hugr* tells me that there will be sorrow and honor in the name.

The child receives with the name a fragment of the king's luck, but this he must know: that the king's luck is strong, so strong that an ordinary mortal would hardly have power to carry it safely through.

The act of the father is clearly just as much an act of birth as is the mother's delivery. The little empty possibility had in itself no part in the race, and had no claim to be called kinsman. And if he showed evil tendencies and appeared likely to become a nithing—as might be discerned from such sure signs as deformity, or physical qualities alien to the stock—then he would simply not be allowed to enter into the luck, but was placed outside life until the trifle of mobility in him also disappeared. He was carried out to perish. The Germanic father would have looked askance at so unreasonable an accusation as that he had carried out a living being. And if the matter were touched upon at a moment when he chanced to be inclined to discuss it, he would undoubtedly have set the phrasemaker's errant wits to rights with a blow of his axe. He knew well enough what life was worth. If the child had had the least share in frith, then its separation must have caused a breach that demanded careful and precise attention.

So effective a part is that of the father in making a human being of the newly born, that one might be tempted to regard the consecration as itself the real birth. What can be the value of simply being born, when the child, until adopted by the father or male kin, is after all but a thing one does not even need to kill, but can merely thrust out as not belonging to humanity at all? It may be difficult enough for us to harmonize the father's absolute veto with the ancients' praise of noble origin, and their frowning suspicion of men who had to cry aloud their father's name that their mother should not be mentioned.

For the Northmen, high birth was the only qualification for honor and respect, or in a deeper sense, the sole condition that enabled a man to possess the skill and self-assurance that honor and respect presupposed. No false pretender could remain long undiscovered. The changeling could not hide the fact that he lacked a soul, as we witness in Queen Hagny's vain attempt to exchange her two ugly, black sons for a fair slave child. The two spurious slave children lay one day playing in the straw upon the floor, while Leif, the changeling, sat in the high seat playing with a finger ring. Then said one of the brothers: "Let us go and take the ring away from him." The other black mite was ready enough to try, but Leif only cried. In this little scene, Bragi the Skald finds sufficient indication of the real state of things. He tells the queen, "Two are in here. They please me,

Hamund and Geirmund, King Hjor's sons, but that boy Leif is the slave woman's son, not yours, woman—a wretch beyond most."

In this story, we find that which was the silent foundation for the Northmen's judgment of men—emphasized with polemic force. In everyday life, it is apparent in the scorn of the lowborn, wonder at the ability of an upstart, and most of all, in the unconditional respect paid by free men to one with tradition behind him. This much is certain: no man could be brave and skillful unless he came from a brave and skillful stock. He who was born of a great luck had a guarantee for his life that one who saw the light in poorer circumstances never could have; he could grasp with fuller hands, without fear of letting fall. He was sure to have such and such qualities of luck—those that pertained to the *hamingja* of his race, and he would always choose with unfailing certainty the one decision that was the only right and only possible one in any matter.

Glum, the old man of luck, once had an experience that taught him that a fault of birth, even though well hidden, can always break out at the critical moment and upset one's thoughts. In the Thvera clan—which traced its descent right back to Viking Kari (one of the great commencements in the genealogy of Norway) and was connected on the distaff side with Norway's kings[68]—there had come a strain of slave blood. A man whom Glum had given his freedom—and who had somehow or other managed to raise himself to a position of wealth—had married a kinswoman (her name is not stated) of the man who had freed him. Their son, Ogmund, was a promising young man, whom Glum took into his house and regarded as the equal of his own sons. When the time came, Ogmund also went abroad on board his own ship, as fitted the cadet of a great house. In fitting manner also, he announced his arrival in the Norwegian fjords by ramming a longship and sending it to the bottom.

The ship belonged to Haakon Sigurdsson, who was naturally incensed at the news, and did not exhort the survivors from the wreck to deal gently with the offender. Ogmund received a blow that kept him in his bed the greater part of the winter. And now it seemed as if he had suddenly lost all his nobility. He saw his kinsman Vigfus Glumson as one of Haakon's retainers, and knew the earl would take vengeance on him if anything happened to one of the Norsemen. And he could hardly reconcile it with his duty to Glum to bring misfortune upon Vigfus. So he argued, and left the blow unavenged. Vigfus, however, thought otherwise. His retort shears through Ogmund's justification right down to the diseased spot: "Neither I nor my father care to have you looking after me if I do not do so myself. It is other things that teach you to be so cautious. As might be expected, you take after the thrall stock rather than after the men of Thvera."

---

[68] The distaff is the female branch of the family.

And Glum's bitter outburst against Ogmund after his return is a stronger antistrophe to this: "What call have you to guard him if he did not guard himself? Rather had I seen you both dead, and you avenged." And he calls to mind the old truth that unfree race is ever short of manhood. It was the mark of birth of the thrall's descendant that he saw the lesser thing first, and it grew in his eyes, whereas men of the true Thvera stock saw only the thing that mattered.

The Northmen had a keen eye for psychological signs of mixed race; a saying often on their lips was, "Who is it that you take after?" And we have no grounds for supposing that it was only the one side that counted. Thorolf's opponents, the aforementioned sons of Hilderid, never got over the disability in their birth: that their mother was of an inferior stock to their father's. It was a fault plainly seen in every word they spoke, when they stole into the hall from behind as soon as Thorolf had strode out of the front, and explained and interpreted the action of their enemy, while Thorolf let his act carry its own interpretation. The sagas also have an argument to the effect that a man's rascality is due to the mother's blood.

Among the other Germanic peoples, it may be difficult perhaps to find any testimony directly showing the judgment of the day in regard to the half-breed. Even in King Guntram's day, however, a bishop named Sagittarius, whose eyes had been opened by adversity and loss of office, can realize that the disregard of birth was a factor in the moral decline of the people: "How should a king's sons ever come to rule when their mother came straight from the thralls' bench, into the king's bed?" This was his everlasting theme when the talk turned on matter of serious import. The experiences of poor Sagittarius were just of the very sort that generally gives the sufferer the most unprejudiced view of his adversary. He had been deprived of his office without having any righteousness of his own to set up against unrighteousness.

Gregory, on the other hand, who has found a place for his eccentric brother-prelate in his panorama of Frankish society, looks more historically at the matter: "Sagittarius did not reflect that nowadays all who can call the king father are reckoned king's sons, whatever their mother's birth." But even if we had not the opportunity to hear judgment passed in definite words, we can read it in the practical behavior of men. It does not take long to perceive the importance of birth, even outside Scandinavia.

This refinement of feeling would naturally appear in its strongest form as public ill will against marriage with inferiors. And we are indeed told of the Saxons that they made equality of birth a legally indispensable condition between parties entering into matrimony. No marriage was suffered to bridge the gulf between noble and free, any more than between freeborn and freedman, or freedman and thrall. Our authority here is a clerical biography from the ninth century, compiled by a monk whose ethnographical knowledge is restricted to a good page of excerpts. It is one of those sources whose sentences are not to be estimated word by word, but taken *en bloc* at discretion; whether the words refer to a written or an unwritten law, whether they apply to many of the Saxons or only a little clique at some given time, must be left open. At all events, such pedantry of class is not a general Teuton characteristic, but the Saxon caste feeling may probably point indirectly to a marked regard in our forefathers for the importance of blood. And the Saxons elsewhere show themselves as finicky formalists who would doubtless be the first to make a sound dogma out of refinement.

There are two things in which all good Germanic stock is agreed: that a free woman surrendering herself to a slave becomes a prey to the unreality of slave existence and loses her soul, and that an unfree woman gives her children spirit of her slave spirit. In Sweden, the Church—with its hate of adultery and its disapproval of slavery—had entered protest against the prevailing view. Then the law may run that true marriage always ensures freedom of the child. But on all sides of the paragraph extends the old conception of the man as the one who is borne by and has his validity from a clan and the honor of a clan. The words happen to stand in the same chapter with an old sentence in which an earlier age expressed its condemnation of the woman: the woman who enters into matrimony with a slave shall go backward, or rather back foremost, out of her clan. The word "backward" indicates an unlucky mode of exit involving disgrace and loss of human status.

A free man has, of course, the right to use his slave woman as he pleases, but children begotten in the slaves' corner will be unfree—without right to walk, sit, or inherit with the children of a free woman. That child sits in the corner and eats from its bowl among the thralls, as is said in the law of Norway. The same thing may be expressed as in Denmark: if a man has begotten a child with his woman thrall, and the child not freed, then the father shall not pay more in fine for his deeds than for those of any other thrall. It is the woman who stamps her child. We find this also in the words wherewith the Lombards have rendered the idea of a man's right to marry his own female slave: he must first give her her freedom, and raise her to the standing of a rightful wife; then her children will be legitimate and free to inherit. The word used by the laws to indicate her new standing, whether it be *virdibora* (noble born) or *viderbora* (reborn), plainly embodies the thought of her moving from one existence into another, into one that is really life.

In all Germanic law, as far as we have any evidence, distinction is made between children born in wedlock and the illegitimate, even though the latter are both freeborn and recognized by the father. Among the Lombards, as among the Northmen (Danes, Swedes, and Norwegians), the rule for the illegitimate child runs: not as the others, not entitled to equal share of inheritance, or more strongly: let him have a gift from his father, and go content with that to his own. Whatever may have been the position of the freeborn illegitimate in the clan among different peoples, there is a deeply rooted feeling that he lacks something that the others have, or a fear lest he be not so strong as his kinsmen, not the rock that unconditional faith can build on without fear, or that an inheritance would not be safe in his hands. Possibly, such feeling of difference was not always or everywhere suffered to make the decisive factor in the social arrangement of a bastard's position, but it has everywhere contributed to the judgment passed upon him, if not as fear, then at least as caution.

There is in an Icelandic saga an everyday scene and a passage of words that point out the essential weakness in an illegitimate daughter: viz, that she may possibly not be able to pass on to her husband the full frith and honor of her father. In the last battle between the two Helgis, Helgi Droplaugson and Helgi Asbjornson, the latter was faithfully supported by his son-in-law, Hjarrandi. The other Helgi tauntingly shouted to his young and lusty adversary: "Hey, how you would have laid about you, if it had been a freeborn daughter of Helgi Asbjornson you had taken to wife." The words surely had their sting, for they goaded Hjarrandi so that he fell to still more violently. Though the speech is altogether Icelandic in its form and not to be drawn upon too indiscriminately, it plays upon an uncertainty that is present beneath the legal provisions that set the place of the bastard at the extreme limit of the line of kin. On this point, the Church, in its endeavors to lower the status of the bastard in order to strengthen monogamy, had an ally in the old thoughts—and this moreover, a strong ally acting from strong, half-felt instincts, and thus capable of affecting great and rapid changes.

Surely enough, a man is born to be what he is. Between marriage and the looser relations, between children whose parents were of equal rank and those whose mother was not a wife proper, between birth and half-birth is drawn one of the sharpest lines in Germanic thought, a limit never veiled. Whatever Tacitus may have imagined out of his own head as to the solemnity with which a barbarian woman took her bridegroom's hand and mentally reviewed the perils she was determined to share with him, his description of the marriage contract is at least in agreement with all later authorities in emphasizing the marriage ceremony as a principal act in the life of our forefathers. The contract was an event, the social and legal influence of which was emphasized by detailed ceremonial. It was concluded with the same thoughtful care as a treaty of peace, where the foundation was securely laid by welding together two whole clans and their luck; it was prepared with caution by a series of solemn acts, the formality of which was in proportion to the legal importance of the proceeding.

We cannot gain a real understanding by harmonizing and squaring the facts. Again and again, it will be found that our words are too narrow, or that the ideas that the words call up in our minds are incongruous with the thoughts that bore the ancient institutions. We give the act of bringing forth an absolute validity that the moment did not possess in the old times, because our conception of life as something purely physical is totally different from the primitive idea of a human being. The modern word "birth" must be stretched to its utmost possibilities so as to embrace the whole weighty conception of race, breeding, and family. Birth is not solely parturition and not solely the ceremony of naming, but something more extensive—it is the past breaking forth anew.

The child's social state depends on the complete process of its coming into the world, and into the world of its kin: a process that begins with the mother's birth pangs and ends with the father's solemn recognition of the infant as admitted into the clan. It is impossible to conclude directly from the cry of a woman that a child is being born. However, the distinction is not between delivery and giving soul, but between the double act of giving birth and naming whereby a human being is born, and the insignificant bringing forth which is no birth at all. The only place where one can see what takes place is in the clan itself, and standing there, as a kinsman among kin, we have, in the one case, the happiness of seeing a kinsman come into the world. In the other, we are merely spectators of a happening of no importance, whereby an individual passes before our eyes out into nothingness, into the unreality of thralldom, or perhaps into a reality with which we have no concern.

The son inherits birth and luck from his mother, but his maternal birthright is not derived from that little moment when the mother acts and the father waits—it depends fully as much upon the life that his father names into him. Going back through history to find the moment whence the act of birth derives its weight and its power, we pause first at the evening when the pair solemnly commence their life together. The fact of their openly going to rest together is more than a merely legal sign that their connection is to have all the effects of a marriage. But then, too, we shall find that the intercourse before the leading to the couch (the "ale") is emphasized as a sure sign of the depth and genuineness of the alliance. From the ale, we are led further to the bargain made beforehand—the legally binding contract sealed with gifts—and given to understand that this buying is the sign that the two are married in truth.

The high social state of the mother depends on the fact that she is honorably bought with the bridal gift. But even here we are not at the end of the matter; the nobility of a truly wedded woman shines out on the morning after the bridal night when the husband honors his spouse by giving her the portion of a true wife. Very rightly, the "morning gift" is reckoned in the Lombardic law as the concluding blessing that releases a bondwoman from her state of thralldom and makes her a "born" wife. Each of these ceremonies can by itself be taken as the fundamental and the decisive one, without in the least detracting from the importance of the rest, for all of them stand as proofs of the fact that a change has been affected in the minds and the souls of the parties concerned. Before the alliance was made, the two family circles were strangers; now, they are united by a fusion of luck and will. On both sides, there has been an assimilation by each of the other's soul, so that the *hamingja* of both is strengthened by the bargain.

At the moment the father takes to himself luck of another's luck and unites it with his own, the foundation of a legitimate son's life is laid. And so, indeed, the boy can be called a string—a close-twisted string. But he is not twined of two strands lying loosely beside each other. His luck is one throughout: that of the father and that of the mother in one. In reality, the *hamingja* that now inspires the son is fully active in the father. The father with his clan already resembles the mother's kin and takes after them, and he must do so, as surely as he has so much of his kin-in-law's honor in himself that he can suffer with them and stand with them under one shield. The principle of birth and naming in the North is thus fully explained in the simple scene where the father (or whoever names the child) decides upon either one of his former kinsmen or one of the wife's circle, and fixes the child's position in the clan by uttering the blessing: "Let the boy take his name and luck!"

But to understand fully the effect of lawful marriage, it is necessary to bear in mind that the right and power of calling a child after the brothers-in-law is not and cannot be restricted to the man who has actually married a woman of the other clan. The fusion of soul, luck, and history that is affected by one of the friends mating must go through the whole race and work a change in all the members who have one soul together. In other words, the child is not named after his mother's father or brother, but in him the whole clan regenerates the *hamingja* of their brothers-in-law.

Hence it comes naturally that the genealogies of the ancient families were in themselves a history or an epos, and at the same time a portrait of a character. And though the registers are to us but catalogs emptied of the rich memories that clung to the names for the original bearers, we can still in the crossing and clustering of names old and new catch glimpses of life and growth, and even re-experience something of that earnestness that for the race itself made the reckoning up at once a serious business and an edification.

History knows little about King Penda of Mercia, and still less of his father, King Pybba. We must content ourselves with a few facts from ecclesiastical history, just such as might go to a verse in the Book of Chronicles, of a king who did that which was evil in the sight of the Lord. Only a single trait of human expression is preserved in this mask. Heathen as he was, he used no weapon against the Christians but scorn when they did not act according to their faith, we are told. And in this scornful grimace, we seem to recognize one of the marked characters who might rightly find a place beside a Harald, a Haakon Sigurdsson, a Clovis I. But even though Penda was the founder of a kingdom, and one who, like Harald, elevated a chieftainship to kingly rank, he perished with his fathers. Culture threw him down, with its unwavering judgment, as one of those who was not borne on by the tide, but left high and dry by the current of civilization.

In England, the new age and the new spirit were not, as in Norway, built into the old; every stake there hammered in to support the new served at the same time to keep the old from walking. With the last of the heathens fell the kingdom itself, and if it rose again, it was with the first Christian king of Mercia. But if the kingdom of Mercia stood fast after the fall of its king and his culture, if it passed unscathed through the crisis that follows upon a period of creation, when maintenance must take the place of the natural equilibrium of progress, and if, after the crisis, it asserted itself as a great power, then it was because these ruthless warriors, Penda and his kinsmen, had also been men wise in counsel. These men laid the foundations of their kingly luck sound and deep.

This race had, like that of Halfdan the Black in Norway and that of the Merovingians in the Frankish realm, the wit to lead the great luck of the surrounding world into their own souls, and give birth to their *hamingja* again and again— not only stronger, but also richer, by impregnating their house with the war-luck and the ruling-luck of new regions. One sure sign of the power these princes of Mercia possessed to support their spiritual growth by acquiring luck from outside is seen in the alliance with the royal house of the West Saxons. When the two families first intermarried is not known; only this is certain: that Penda's sister was married to King Coenwealh of Wessex. And now we see that one of Penda's brothers was already named after his brother-in-law; he is called Coenwealh, and despite the fact that the peace was soon broken between them when the West Saxon cast off his wife, Coenwealh's branch of the family still continued to use only West Saxon names.

Furthermore, the new *hamingja* was transmitted to two of Penda's grandsons, Wulfhere's son Coenred, and Æthelred's son Ceolred, despite the fact that one's mother was from Kent, and the other's a Northumbrian.

Northward, also, we can follow the aspirations of the clan. Penda's fierce conflicts with the pious kings of Northumberland, Oswald and Oswiu, are in some way connected with the fact that two of his sons had married daughters of King Oswiu. And even in the same generation there appear in the Mercian genealogy those peculiar Northumbrian names that tell of a family that was proud of its gods; Penda's brother Eowa calls his sons Alwih and Osmod.

The *æthel*, too, which appears in the name of one of Penda's own sons, Æthelred, is of old standing in Northumbria, but owing to its general character it is not a distinct family mark.

Another ambitious race whose list of names still bears witness to the enriching power of luck is that of the Merovingians. Its first historical name is Childeric. This king comes nearest to ranking as the Harald Fairhair of the Franks, and like the Norse founder of a kingdom, had part of his luck from a neighboring realm. It is related in story form that he stayed for some time in the East, in "Thuringia" at the court of King "Bisinus," and that the queen of the East, won by admiration of his gallantry, followed him to France and became the mother of the next great man in the race, Clovis I. What this myth may mean, translated into modern historical proportions, we do not know, but that it has some significance is indicated by the names of Childeric's daughters Audefleda and Albofleda, since we find elsewhere an *alb* and an *aud* pointing back to the same mystical Thuringia with its even more mystical King Bisinus.

Later, Childeric allied himself with Theodoric the Great, and gave him one of his daughters in marriage. Clovis I, as one historian expressly states, looked for great things from this alliance, and hastened therefore to incorporate the luck in his family by naming his son after the great king of the Goths. The following generations are distinguished by the alliance with the Burgundian royal house: names with *gunn* (as Guntram) and *chrote* (as Chrotesind) are the symbol of the union. What the remaining name combinations (such as Ingomar, Chramn, or Charibert) signify in the history of the race we are unable to explain; one might say at a guess that they appear in the annals of the family partly as a memorial to the rival Frankish clans that were gradually swallowed up by the conqueror's line. All these adopted names indicate firstly alliance, but thereafter the usurpation of luck and will. With so much Burgundian soul in them as had the Merovingians, men could safely seat themselves in the alien places without fear of luck failing them in the strange land.

In face of these old realists who absorbed alien luck and alien right into their own flesh and blood, our faint conceptions of acquisition by marriage and inheritance prove inadequate. Our words and thoughts permit us only by a very roundabout way to reach the sort of soul history that lies in these family registers. But when once we have allowed ourselves to be led so far, genealogy does leap forth as the expression telling all, and telling all in the right manner. That is to say, as the authentic illustration of birth, which cannot be fully replaced by any other, for the very reason that the succession of names is a series of landmarks left by the very flow of life. And the symbol it calls up before our eyes is not a father who from his place in the order of the race casts a searching glance along the two roads that meet in him, in the hope of its finding someone that can furnish a name for his child; we see a man sitting, inspired by a luck that is truly his, whether he himself or another have brought the latest addition to it, taking this *hamingja* and determining the "age," or fate, of his son.

"I wish this boy luck of the name": this is a saying potent to affect just what lies in it according to the old mode of speech. He who utters it knows that he can make his words "whole," or real. The ancient idea had no respect for half or conditional results. If the father could not give his child real life, and life unimpaired, then he had affected nothing. He might indeed also take something of himself and of his soul to give birth to a human being after it had grown old. When the Icelanders relate the story with a purpose that tells how Harald Fairhair forced Athelstan to adopt one of his sons by letting the messenger set the child on the knee of the English king, these words rise of themselves to the lips of the narrator: "The child is now taken on your knee, and you must fear and honor him as you fear and honor your son." Whatever the author and his circle may have meant by these words, the force of them goes back to the experience that an act such as that which the Norseman tricked Athelstan into doing really twined a thread between the man sitting there and the child seated on his knee. This ceremony might affect a change in the parties concerned, not only creating new responsibilities, but also giving rise to entirely new feelings of frith and kinship.

Undoubtedly, the soul could be renewed in a man so that he was born into another clan than that to which he originally belonged. By such adoption, the new member acquired a new luck, new plans, and new aims ahead of him; he had memories and forefathers in common with his new kinsmen, received their frith into his mind, their will to vengeance, and their honor. Even through the pompous Latin of Cassiodorus, we can hear an echo of the Germanic reliance on one so adopted. This quill-driver of Theodoric's touches casually on the memory of Gensemund:

[Gensemund was] a man whose praises the whole world should sing, a man only made son by adoption in arms to the king, yet who exhibited such fidelity to the Amals that he transferred it even to their heirs, although he was himself sought for to be crowned. Therefore will his fame live forever, so long as the Gothic name endures.

Obviously then, the man must have been reborn completely, and received an entirely new soul. A change must have taken place in him: a birth that not only affected his mode of thought, but also what we should call his character.

The half-born was then not excluded from the chance of being fully born; he could be renewed, nay, born, so thoroughly that there was in reality nothing left either of the old body or of the former soul. Such rebirth lay in the act of adoption, the seating on the knee, or as the Swedes called it: seating in the lap. When the Uppland Law in one paragraph admits legitimate children to full honor on the subsequent marriage of the parents, but in the heading of that paragraph calls them "lap-children," we have here again one of those characteristic instances of contradiction between the old-time words and the thoughts of the Middle Ages.

In the Norwegian laws, we find adoption described in its full dramatic content: a three-year-old ox was slaughtered, and a shoe was made from the skin of its right foot. At a solemn feast, the shoe was placed in the principal part of the room, and one by one the members of the family set foot in it—first, the father adopting, then the adopted son, and after him the remaining kinsmen. From that moment, the son had in himself the full life of the family, as may be plainly seen from the legal consequences ascribed to the act. He inherits, avenges, brings lawsuits, and is one of their own. The formula whereby the father confirmed this kinsman's dignity contains, in old words, that unity of soul that we expressed by luck, honor, and frith: "I lead this man to the goods I give him, to gift and repayment, to chair and seat, to fine and rings, and to full man's right—as if his mother had been bought with bridal gift."

The same thing may be expressed in Swedish by saying, "until a man is adopted, he may not stand among jurors, may not close a bargain, and all that is done to him is done as to a slave," but when he has been duly adopted, when the kinsmen have uttered their solemn: "we take him into clan with us," then he may both attack and defend himself at law, and may take his place among the compurgators when his family bears witness in a process between men. And when the adoption has been completed in due form, then the adopted one is born as fully as one who has lain naked and kicking between the knees of a highborn woman. Whatever he may have been, slave or free man, no one can distinguish between him and others of the race. He does not differ from his brothers in being born of a father without a mother, for in the case of a complete adoption, the luck of the wife and her kinsmen was included in the soul that the father named into him. The adopted member has received a whole soul and a past.

In Norway, it was required that all kinsmen should be present at the adoption ceremony and step into the shoe, in order that they might one by one hand over to the new man right to life and a share in the rights of life. Infants not yet of an age to take part in the ceremony by themselves confirmed the adoption of their brother by sitting on their father's arm when he stepped into the shoe. The same condition for the validity of adoption was probably required by other Germanic peoples, though we cannot conclude from this that it always restricted the right of the father in the same way as in Norway. The main object of the ceremony is not to announce the change in the new man's state, but to make the change itself real, so that it could face the world as a fact that all must feel. The child did not sit on his father's arm to figure as an announcement; he radiated luck into his new brother, and he would, when he came to man's estate, feel the kinship that he had unknowingly established. Consequently, the public announcement at the law-*thing*—required by Danish and Swedish law—was not in itself more effective than the act a father undertook himself, when he had great luck concentrated in himself.

Beside true kinsmen there appears to be a class of men who have life, who act in luck, whose honor is guarded by the clan, but who yet lack something.

When the slave woman sent for the father at the time of her delivery, and he consented to come in order to receive the child and name it (as did Hoskuld with his son Olaf the Peacock), then the boy was free, and might rise to fame as Olaf did. But he was, after all, forced to stand aside in the division of inheritance, with nothing but his gift, that which his father had given him out of the whole. And so the laws actually describe the condition of the illegitimate son, both in South and North. The father might, if he chose, set up his son in life, but after his death, the bastard had no claim on the property of the family. From the Germanic stand-point, there is apparently something unnatural about this class of kinsmen who do not inherit, but can yet receive a portion of the inheritance as a gift: kinsmen who have honor enough to take oath, who take part in the pursuit of a cause, and have a share in fines as well as in the giving in marriage of their kinswomen, but always at last, by themselves, with a portion inferior to that of the rest. Kinsmen who may indeed be entrusted with the responsibility of maintaining the family honor, but only when no better man is left alive. Their position is a compromise against the spirit of the age.

We must, however, pause at the fact that such a halfway position was possi-ble in societies based on the ancient culture, and living on the ancient honor as the foundation of all humanity. We can perhaps read the fate of these half-born and the cause of their weakness in the old words used in Norway with reference to an adopted son when he undergoes the full process of adoption: "That man shall be led to the laps of men and women." If the meaning is that he is thereby fully established on the mother's as well as the father's side, then the sentence indicates surely enough the psychological disability that distinguished the una-dopted from his brothers. In the legal terms of the Lombards, the legitimate son is distinguished as *fulborn*, from the illegitimate but recognized son. Since the word plainly dates from a time when the difference was a reality and not a jurid-ical distinction, we cannot get away from the literal meaning: fully born, in con-tradistinction to incompletely born. The words "led to the laps of men and women" did not, perhaps, carry the meaning that the ceremony included the bod-ily assistance of the wife, but they imply that the adopters have asked the consent of their brothers-in-law to introduce the new kinsman into the full right that the matrimonial alliance seemed to themselves.

Because birth means an infusion of *hamingja*, there are several degrees of birth or adoption possible. The Scandinavian child-fostering was in its innermost essence an act of adoption, though the act was not carried through so far that it severed the link that connected the child with the race of his father and brothers. The foster son felt frith toward his foster father, so that he would feel an injury to the latter as an injury to himself, and maintained his right whatever others might think of the character of that right. Vigfus Glumson's piety toward Hall-vard, whose character can at best be described as doubtful, is no exaggerated example of the intensity of this feeling. Hallvard was regarded as having a grasping nature, and it was whispered that he had few scruples as to the means he employed. There was much to suggest that half a score of sheep and a fat hog had found their way to his homestead, and it is certain that they never found their way thence again. His end was a wretched one. When the son of the offended owner came to him on an errand of the law, he saw at the first glance that the thief's head was loose on his shoulders, and wisely spared himself the trouble of summoning him. Glum let him lie on the bed he had made, without an honest fine to ease his pillow, but Vigfus (who had been abroad while the matter was decided) could not rest until he had met the slayer of Hallvard, and given his foster father vengeance in his grave.

Where frith has been drawn in, *hugr* and mind must surely follow after. The assurance (or rather the experience) of this soul change is petrified in the proverb that says a man takes after his foster father to a fourth of himself.

Adoption full and complete involves a radical change in the son, so that all his thoughts are given a new direction, and the fate (or *aldr*) that was implanted in him at his first birth is exchanged for that of his new friends. His former past, even to his ancestors, is wiped out, and a new descent is infused into him through the *hamingja* that now envelops him. But the weaker forms of adoption only imply an addition of past and present to the *hamingja* that has come down to him through normal inheritance. Haakon Adalsteinfostre did not renounce his right to the luck of the Norwegian kings, and probably the adoption of Gensemund into the family of the Amals was more nearly related to the Scandinavian child-fostering than to the Swedish setting in the lap or the Norwegian leading into the shoe.

We must without hesitation accept the thought that a human being could be born several times. And we may safely grasp the consequence that our thoughts teasingly put forward: that an individual would then have two or even more fathers. The words do not burn. The foster son felt that the man in whose house he had grown up was his father, and he felt that he had also a father in the home where his brothers were. But he did not regard the relationship in the same way that we do. He did not say what we say, because it did not occur to him to take the two together and say "one-two." And if we would know how his thought ran, we have only to listen with understanding when the son calls his father and the father his son by the name of *freond* (kinsman).

This name was the fundamental note in all closer family designations, in the same way as we on the other hand now have father, mother, son, brother, according to circumstances, as the fundamental note in the word "relative." Kinship consists in having a share of the *hamingja*, not in having been born, and therefore the fatherhood was overshadowed by frith, and derived its strength from the bond uniting all members of the clan. The begetter did beget in virtue of his kinship, and thus it comes that "kinsman" has a ring of intimacy and is the word best suited to express the feeling of trust and pride in the begetter toward his begotten. An Icelandic or Norwegian father will introduce his warning, encouragement, or praise with the intimate "kinsman." For example, when Jokul dashes out of the house with anything but gentle intentions, Ingimund says to his eldest son, "Thorstein, kinsman, go with your brothers, you were always one to know where gentle ways were best."

From all outside appearances, the life of Haakon Adalsteinfostre is a forcible illustration of the power of form. It is told Harald Fairhair had begotten him with Thora Mostrstong. When the mother felt that her hour was at hand, she hastened northward by sea from Mostr to Sæheim, where the King then was. The child was to be born in King Harald's house and into his hands. But she did not reach so far, for on the way, when the ship put in to stay the night on shore (as was customary with coasting voyages), she gave birth to her child on a stone by the landing stage. In place of Harald, it was the king's close friend and brother-in-law, Earl Sigurd, who planted the name in the child; he called him after his own father, the old earl of Halogaland. The child was thus born straight into the mother's side of the Harald family, and never, perhaps, became properly related to Thora's kin. Later, Harald undoubtedly recognized the boy as his, and accepted him with full validity as his kinsman, since he let him be brought up at the royal courts with his mother. When Haakon, a youth of fifteen, professing Christianity, came home from the mysterious sojourn with his foster father Athelstan to claim his right of inheritance, his first thought was to go straight to Earl Sigurd. And throughout the whole of his troublesome reign, the earl of Lade was everything to him that a kinsman could be. Sigurd's solidarity is unconditional; it is independent of moods, unassailable by anything that could come between, even at the moment when Haakon's new faith stands in sharp opposition to the old mode of thought in the earl and his circle. The earl's assistance is not limited by any possibility of his adopting a different position, and when he remonstrates with the young king for alienating the proud yeomen of Norway by his excessive zeal for Christ, his words are never edged with any suggestion that he himself might pass over to the king's opponents. When Earl Sigurd's eldest son was born, Haakon baptized him and gave him his own name, and the boy grew up to become that Haakon Sigurdsson who for a time succeeded in filling the throne of Harald Fairhair.

XII. Death and Immortality

In the unity between the individual and his kin, all thoughts of death likewise meet. For the Northman, a name and a reputation were enough to take away the bitterness of death, because fame after death was a real life—a life in the continued luck and honor of kinsmen.

There has entered a touch of something modern into the Northmen's cry for life; we feel a new time through it. The word "fame" has acquired a spiritual ring in the Viking Age, and it cannot be denied that fame after death has bought its delicate sheen at the cost of inner, substantial life; it is risen so high as almost to rend the roots that gave it earthly nourishment. And as always happens when a culture begins to purge its values to super-spiritualism, the ideals ended in something overstrained and vacillating; the cry for fame becomes more and more strenuous, as if the crier were trying to outcry himself. In place of the old-time heroes of honor, we have now athletes in the field of honor, who rush about the country seeking renown, and groan in weariness of life when they can find none with whom to measure their strength. The strained tone in the cry for fame during the centuries verging on the Middle Ages suggests that the roving warriors had partly lost touch with the realities of life. And yet they were not so modern as to grasp the idea that the true and only immortality consisted in people's speaking of one after death. The fame and honor that was to console a man in death must have a compelling force, not only to beget songs, but also to beget a successor in whom the honor shone out anew.

Another trait of the Viking Ages is the budding anxiety for individual rebirth. In the opening of the *Vatsdoela* saga, we are told how the famous family of Ingimund was founded by the welding of a Norwegian clan with the luck of a royal race of Gautland farther east. The union is dated from a fight between the

Norwegian youth Thorstein and a scion of the Gautland kings named Jokul. Before dying, Jokul requests his slayer to marry his sister and revive the name in the offspring of this alliance, adding, "and I look for blessing to myself from this." Thus it comes that the name Jokul runs in the Vatsdoela family. The same theme occurs in another saga, the *Svarfdoela*, where Thorolf, a brave youth from Naumudal, who on his very first Viking expedition receives a mortal wound, in his dying moments asks his brother Thorstein to transmit his name to posterity:

> My name has lived but a little hour, and thus I should be forgotten as soon as you are gone, but I see that you will increase the family and become a great man of luck. I wish you would let a son be called Thorolf, and all the lucky qualities [heillir] which I have had, those will I give him. Then I think my name shall live as long as men dwell in the world.

And Thorstein answers: "This I will gladly promise you, for I see that it shall be to our honor, and good luck shall go with your name as long as it is in the clan." He keeps his promise, and the new Thorolf becomes like his kinsman.

These tales are conventional romanticism, and as far as the *Vatsdoela* is concerned, the story is nothing but an afterthought to explain the actual alliance between a Norwegian and a Gautland house. But this romanticism reflects some tendencies of the saga age. There is undoubtedly in Thorolf's and Jokul's longing to have their name and fame restored to the light an egoistic passion, something approaching the anxious hunger for a future and a hope, which we know from other times and places. But their greed of life is satisfied in the assurance that their honor and luck will not be suffered to wither away. They are fully content to relive their life in another man, and the question of their own identity simply cannot penetrate through the mass of the old premises. In Thorolf's words: "To him [his namesake that is to be] I will give all the luck I have had, then I think my name shall live as long as men dwell in the world," we have in a way two different modes of thought laid one above the other. The old ideas of luck and soul form the pattern into which new thoughts about the hero's personal immortality involuntarily fit when they come to demand expression.

Immortality, accordingly, consists in remaining in luck and honor and knowing it safe. Let the thought of one's own well-being arise as potently as it will; it cannot take this form: what is to become of *me*? As long as life is inseparably bound up with a whole—so that the individual cannot exist at all as individual—the sting that should set the thought of one's own incarnation in motion is lacking. The dead as well as the living kinsman lives in his kin; he thinks their thoughts and their honor, he wills their will, he feels their feelings, he is their body. He is warmed through by the heart-refreshing honor founded by himself;

he is fed with luck, and he acts with them, thinks, and counsels. And thus the dilemma: to be or not to be, is disposed of beforehand.

When a man has received the assurance that his luck and honor are in safe keeping, and he closes his eyes, he sets off to the place where his kinsmen dwell—"sets forth to visit his kinsmen," as Egil says of his son—and arrives there in his whole, full person, with body and soul and entire equipment. Not as a spirit that has laid its case aside and comes with chattering teeth stealing down the road to Hel, but as a human being with human nature. The whole man simply continues his life, under somewhat different conditions, but always in luck— probably somewhat less than before, perhaps also in certain respects a little stronger. He rides his horse and carries his sword, which he flashes at the armed council where the dead assemble, and for his restless goings about he has need of solid equipment: a well forged weapon nicely balanced to the hand, such as he is used to. He is a solid person that one can feel and fight with. We should not, it is true, characterize him altogether from the comically dreadful ghosts that go haunting about in several of the Icelandic sagas: fellows who twist people's necks, or perhaps even run about with their own head in their hands, using it for banging at people's doors. Indirectly, however, these ghosts do reveal something of the nature of the dead. This Glam, who rides on the roof of a house until all the beams creak, and comes near to breaking Grettir's arms and legs; this Thorolf Boegifot, who runs after the herdsmen and beats them black and blue, have little reality about them, but they have a reality behind them. They are descended from tangible departed ones, who were quite capable of coming to grips with living men, and perhaps would not give in until their backs were broken or their heads cut off.

On a single occasion—in the story of Hermod—we read that the dead tread far more lightly on the bridge of Hel than do the living. When Hermod is dispatched to fetch the god Baldr from the dead, his firm steps on the bridge leading into the valley of death fill the bridge-keeper with wonder. "Yesterday," she says, "four hosts of dead men rode over the bridge, but they made less noise than your single horse's step. Nor is your face like a dead man's face."

But this observation is probably only relatively valid. Judging from the experiences of the living who have ventured into the underworld, both roads and bridges were fine and solid, evidently built with a view to good sound footsteps, as against the true spirit-worlds, where everything is aquiver. The poet of the *Lay of Eric* attains his introductory effect by perfectly legitimate means,[69] when he lets Odin start up from sleep at the resounding steps of Eric Bloodaxe and his men:

---

[69] Also known as *Eiriksmál*, a skaldic poem specifically commissioned by Queen Gunnhild in honor of her slain husband Eric Bloodaxe. Only the opening stanzas of the poem have survived.

What dreams are these? Methought it was in the dawn, when I made room in Valhalla for those dead in arms. I woke the einherjar,[70] bade them arise, spread straw on the benches and rinse out the ale mugs. The valkyries should carry wine around, as if it were a king that had come.

The dream was not an illusion—this he knows from the way it warmed his heart. He cries out, "What is this heavy sound, Bragi, as if a host of a thousand or more came moving forward?"

"The walls groan from gable to gable," comes the answer, "as if it were Baldr returning to the halls of Odin."

In the verses where dead Helgi is visited in his burial mound by Sigrun, the idea of the Viking Age as to the reality of the dead has found its ideal expression.

Sigrun's slave woman went one evening past the barrow and saw Helgi riding to the mound with a host of men. She told Sigrun what she had seen. Sigrun went into the mound to Helgi:

"Lifeless king, a kiss first, ere you cast bloodstained mail. Your hair is thick with rime, Helgi. You are soaked through with the dew of blood. Your hands are clammy and cold. Tell me what I must do."

"Now we will taste the cup, though I am driven from lust and land, and none to sing a plaint, though the wounds gleam red on my breast. Now is the woman come—and closed the door behind her—into the burial mound to me who am dead."

"Here I have spread a good couch, Helgi, sorrowless. I will sleep in your arms as gladly as were you alive."

This Helgi and this Sigrun personify, in poetic transfiguration, the thoughts of Viking times as to the relation between death and life. Men thought of the dead as like Helgi, and like Sigrun men maintained a practical footing toward them, even though of course it would be only the exceptions who felt any call to go to bed with them. All that these two say to one another is marked throughout by the romantic—anything but Germanic love tenderness that brings them together. One might say it is a new feeling that gives color to the words, but that which gives them life—and which renders the meeting of the pair so natural and straightforward—is the poet's unreflecting ideas of the dead. There is nothing in these verses to suggest that he is outwardly repeating a literary lesson.

A man remained the man he was in regard to form and shape—somewhat reduced, perhaps, but not changed. And in the same way, of course, he would retain his freshness of soul as surely as he was an honest dead man. He remained like himself, with the same full honor, the same prejudices, the same family pride,

---

[70] Those who have died in battle and are brought to Valhalla.

and the same family restrictions, as well as the same respect for the realities of life. Here lies the weakness of the comical Icelandic ghosts—they differ from their forefathers in having lost something, and this something is nothing else but humanity. The honor and luck that shut up the activity of the dead in the circle where surviving kinsmen move, and attune the doings of the dead to the aspirations of the living, have faded in them.

The author of the *Eyrbyggja* saga is on surer ground.[71] He tells how a body of men that had been drowned out in the fjord, incommoded the living by coming nightly to sit by the fire. At last, a wise man hit upon the device of using the force of law against the intruders. The dead men quietly heard out the son of the house while he brought the summons for unrightful entering of the house, but as soon as judgment had been passed upon them, one by one they rose from the warm seat by the fire and walked out into the cold. The dead man retained his loyalty to the home and his interest in all that went about the homestead. Quite naturally then, he would choose himself a good dwelling place with a wide, free outlook over the neighborhood and his home. Or he might wish to be as near as possible to the house, so as to be able to constantly attend to his customary work. Thorkel Farserk was a very powerful man, both in spirit and in body; he had voyaged with Eric the Red to Greenland, and once, when Eric came to visit him at his house and no seaworthy boat was in at the time, he swam out to an island in the fjord to fetch a sheep for food. No wonder that he went peaceably about his homestead after death, and made himself useful.

A good illustration of the dead man's unity with his past is found in the one-sided but clear light of the humoresque, when we read *Grettir's saga* of Kar the Old's activity after death.[72] He dwelt in a solid barrow strengthened with baulks of timber, and from here led the little war with the peasants of the district, so that, in company with his living son, Thorfin, he extended the family property from a single homestead until it covered the entire island of Haramarsey, near South Moeri. Naturally, none of the peasants who enjoyed Thorfin's protection suffered any loss. Kar was pursuing an exclusive family policy, only with the higher means now at his disposal.

And that which was the free man's mark of nobility—his "gladness"—went with his luck into the higher existence. One might hear the dead man singing from his barrow or his ship about his wealth and his renown, in verses such as that known to have been sung by the barrow-dweller Asmund of Langaholt. This distinguished man had been buried in his ship, and the family had with thoughtful care given him a faithful thrall to share the grave, but this company proving by

---

[71] English: *Saga of the People of Eyri*. A saga about two feuding chieftains in Iceland.

[72] *Grettir's saga* (*The Saga of Grettir the Strong, or Grettis saga Asmundarsonar*) details the life of the Icelandic outlaw Grettir. Grettir at one point fights and defeats Kar the Old, a draugr who was guarding the treasures in his burial mound.

no means to his taste, he begged to have the curmudgeon taken out. And then he was heard to sing with the proud boastfulness of life: "Now I alone man the ship! Room better suits the battle-wont than crowding of base company. I steer my ship, and this will be long in the minds of men."

What life really is, we only rightly learn by seeing its dissolution. It is the nature of health to be coldly unapproachable, and it is thus of necessity and not from inclination that the psychologist goes to the sick mind in order to learn what is moving in the sound. If we did not know the ideas of different peoples with regard to death, we should in most cases probably be unable to ascertain their views of life. Dissolution shows us not only what life is worth to them, but also in what this life consists.

We do not find among our forefathers any fear of the ending of life. They passed with a laugh of defiance through the inevitable, we are told. Or they faced the thought of an earthly ending with a convinced indifference, plainly showing that they did not attach great importance to that event. Life was so strong in its reality that death simply could not count against it, and could not in any way exert the slightest pressure upon its demands. Defiance was part of honor and of what was demanded of a man, and we are thus constrained to seek the roots of this contempt for death deep down in the soul. And the Northern appreciation of life is fully and entirely shown in the picture given by Tacitus of the young men:

> If their fatherland grows idle in long peace and inaction, then most of the highborn youths seek their way to such peoples as are at war, because these men are not by nature given to peace and quiet, and because it is easier to win renown where perils play one against another.[73]

This is undoubtedly one of the least romantic of Tacitus' psychological descriptions, and most genuine as to its contents. These "highborn youths," then, would hardly have lived in an environment where death was regarded as an object of dread, a thing that stole up behind men and breathed coldly down their necks.

When a man had received his final wound and realized that his time was come, he strode with firm steps to the barrow and settled himself there for the future, well content with the equipment his kinsmen had given him there. But does he not after all become a man of less moment than he was in the flesh? Naturally, he would need to have his luck unimpaired in order to continue his life within the portals of the grave, but this does not imply that he took it all with him. Does he after all become weaker in bodily strength? Will his wisdom, his foresight, sink? Will there be less activity in him? The answers to our questions are perplexingly contradictory.

---

[73] Tacitus, *Germania*, Chapter 14.

We find indications that death could give a man deeper wisdom and higher insight in the future. Why should Odin go out and question the dead sibyl[74]—as he does in the Eddic poem *Vegtamskvida*[75]—if it were not that the dead at times stood at the highest stage of insight? And Odin's voyage to the kingdom of the dead was undoubtedly modeled on real life. Old Kar seems to have increased his vitality after settling in his grave, but at other times it is clear that a strong man shows a rather marked falling off after his decease. Sometimes life in the transit fell to a decidedly lower measure of happiness. When Helgi meets Sigrun in the barrow,[76] he speaks as if this meeting with all its joy were something he stole from life; he will have happiness, even though he is driven from lust and land. But on the other hand, the pictures of Valhalla suggest a tendency to reverse life and death, and regard the afterlife as an enhancement of the sense of life. On the fields of death there grows an inexhaustible crop of honor; this must be the meaning of the daily battle outside the gates of Valhalla,[77] and thus we have the clear and strong expression of the conviction that existence does not decline in quality. In the halls of death, the joyful intercourse is continued—life in honor and frith with gladness. Everything we have found that life depended on, in the eminent sense, the hero takes with him through the doorway of the grave.

Valhalla belongs to a particular sphere of culture. The active, boisterous life of the einherjar is hardly imaginable without the exalted and overly hasty pace of life in Viking days, where such ideals as honor and fame after death were forced up to such a degree that the root could no longer support them, and they flowered to death. But Valhalla could not be built up loosely above the earth; it must have its foundation deeply laid in popular feelings. Prior to the poetic consecration of a heaven of battle, there must be a direct faith in the future—not a faith vaguely in the clouds, but a sure conviction that man finds himself again in the burial mound. From the story in the *Eyrbyggja* about the end of Thorstein Cod-Bite, we can form an idea as to how the einherjar's dogma appeared as a family myth. It is told that the same evening Thorstein was drowned, a shepherd saw Helgafell open:[78] in the interior of the hill burned great fires (as in the hall, of course), and there came a sound of merriment and the rattle of drinking horns;

---

[74] A woman with the ability to tell the future. Also known as a seeress, prophetess, or as one is often called in Eddic poems, a *völva*.

[75] An alternative title for *Baldrs Draumar*, or *Baldr's Dreams*, a short Eddic poem in which Baldr's nightmares prompt Odin to ride to Hel and resurrect a seeress, who tells of Baldr's fate.

[76] For background information, see footnote 48 on page 156.

[77] The *Poetic Edda* attests that the einherjar in Valhalla would engage in daily battle and be resurrected in order to train for Ragnarök, the end-of-the-world scenario in Norse mythology in which Odin and his einherjar would fight against giants, trolls, and other monsters. Many gods, including Odin, would die during Ragnarök.

[78] There are several mountains called Helgafell ("holy mountain") in Iceland. The *Eyrbyggja* (in English, *The Saga of the People of Eyri*) describes the one on the Snaefellsnes peninsula first settled by Thorolf Mostrarskegg, who built a shrine to Thor there. Today, a Christian church stands there.

listening carefully, the man could distinguish voices bidding Thorstein and his companions welcome, and inviting him to be seated in the high seat opposite his father. This herdsman brings us a message from an everyday world and an everyday habit of mind, which but for him would have been lost without a trace. He gives us at the same time the means of understanding what it is that makes the einherjar such powerful figures, and the stories of their life with Odin myths instead of poetry. But on the other hand, it is easy to see why the belief in Valhalla came to be something entirely different from its premises. The confident faith has become conscious of itself. Before the joy of the warriors in fighting and drinking in the hall of death—*mandream*—could become an enhanced enjoyment of life, there had to come a reflection whereby the value of life was loosed from life itself, and regarded independently. The undismayed attitude toward death has undergone the same process as honor and posthumous fame; from being realities, they became ideal values, and ended as qualities of a virtuoso.

And now on the other hand, Helgi's touching lament for what he has lost! The scene belongs rather to Germanic Middle Ages than Nordic antiquity, we may fairly say. The hero's sentiment, his wistful dwelling on his loss and longing is medieval in its tone. But the wistfulness is nevertheless warranted in the thought of the old regime. The modern element lies in the fact that the contrast between past and present breaks out into a lyrical mood. The contrast does not come in with the *Helgi* poet, but it takes on a new aspect, because men become conscious of themselves and their feelings. We cannot dispose of the contrast altogether by arranging the stories into historical perspectives. In reality, the brighter and the darker view of the state after death are not so wide apart that they can face each other in hostility; they supplement each other, they take it in turns to overlap each other.

The difficulty that we feel does not lie in the answers, but in the question. It is natural to us to put the problem generally: is death a boon or a calamity? Will death improve the condition of a man or not? And we transfer our problem into the discussion of primitive and ancient peoples and their "view of death." The Teutons had no permanent, ever-valid solution, because they had no everlasting problem. Death is to them only a variety of life dependent upon the forces that act in the light of the sun. The dead man lives in his kinsmen, in every sense of the word: his luck is incorporated in those who survive him, and the life he leads in the grave and in the neighborhood of the grave has now as formerly its source in kinsmen's luck. It means a difference, certainly, if a man loses "land and lust," so to speak, without compensation, and merely glides over into the shadow. Or on the other hand, if he fills himself with honor, luck, and life in the very moment of death, falling in a circle of down-stricken enemies with whose warm blood he has sprinkled himself, and whose honor he has used as food for his own. But when all is said and done, the hero who takes a host of enemies with him into the grave cannot himself determine whether he is to enjoy his wealth. His power of utilizing the abundance gained depends on how far the surviving kinsmen can assimilate the surplus and save it from rotting in stagnation.

A man then died as his power of life enabled him. The great man of luck slid with a little bump across the reef, and sailed on. Inferiors, poor folk, might find themselves stranded, to sink and disappear. He who had a great store of soul could, according to human calculations, live forever. The poor in soul stood in sore peril of using up his stock in this world.

The faith in the luck running in the clan can lead to a class organization, as soon as external circumstances direct the human tendency to draw conclusions toward a social system. The proud men of luck find unity in a common feeling of kinship in life. The lower types join (or are thrown together) in a spiritual middle class, and midway between the two there may perhaps arise a buffer state of intermediate nobility aiming upward, but moving inevitably downward. And with this class organization follows a fair distribution of life here and life here-after for both high and low, in close agreement with the qualifications of birth. Along this road, it is possible to arrive at a system firm and clear as that which obtained among certain of the South Sea Islanders,[79] before European democracy stepped in and ruined it.

Among the Tonga Islanders, immortality ceased midway between the first and third orders of rank. That is to say, the first class—the chieftains' families—would be fully entitled to life in the underworld. The second class of life hereafter would depend upon a sort of personal nobility in the case of the male head of a family in actual service at court, with succession vesting in the eldest son after the father's death—almost in the English fashion. Our authority states, it is true, that among the excluded there were some who preferred the uncertainty of trust-ing in themselves to the safe and ordered exclusion. The old system, then, was not altogether overcome.

The Northmen never attained to a system of immortality arranged on such beautiful lines. We find here and there an incipient class formation, as for in-stance when certain laws set a sliding scale of fines for manslaughter according to the social position of the slain. The chieftains could perhaps be called men of godly descent, but the great would yet hardly anywhere have reached so far as to occupy their position in virtue of belonging to a category. And the process of development had certainly nowhere advanced to the stage of establishing state control and regulation of the life to come, when that development itself abruptly ended. The arrangement current in Viking times of kingly halls for men slain under arms—for drowned men, for honest tillers of the soil—has its roots in the

---

[79] In Australia, descendants of Pacific Islanders brought to work the sugarcane and cotton fields in Queensland in the late nineteenth and early twentieth centuries.

popular belief. It was taken for granted that men in the life hereafter would find one another, drink, and pass judgment with one another, and had not lost the need of definite forms and recognized custom that had regulated the gatherings at the law-*thing*. But the idea of a realm for the dead never went beyond the imagination of poets fired by contact with the Christian eschatology. Each had to arrange for his own future, and would receive hereafter according to his means and power while here. He had still to depend on the luck of the clan. The king lived a kingly life in his barrow; the day-laborer's slender luck would probably but just avail to win him some little span of shadowy existence in the grave. From all we can learn of the thoughts of everyday life in the North, each clan had its own private Hades. And if a clan were not powerful enough to procure a suitable dwelling place for its departed, there were certainly no public halls open to admit homeless souls.

The king sits as a king in his burial mound, and rules in all probability as king from there, just as in life he sat in his hall and by virtue of his kinsmen ruled from there, at the same time letting his clan-luck act upon the neighbors about him. He is king in death by virtue of what he is, not of what he was. And what he is depends entirely on the activity of his kinsmen.

XIII. The Nithing

Death was not dangerous—for those who had something to live on.

Death held more possibilities than it ever can embrace with us. It opened up prospects of broad well-being, as well as every possible degree of bodily and spiritual poverty. It opened the vista of power as of total extinction. In face of so arbitrary a master, one might think there would be room for many kinds of feeling, for the boldest confidence as for the most miserable wailing. But all the evidence goes to show that the fluctuations were not great, and we have full authority to speak of serenity in the face of death as a mark of Germanic culture. There is nothing to suggest that the feeling ever sank below the dispassionate taking things as they come. In all the monuments preserved, there is, as far as I know, no trace of any dread at the change, still less any shriek of horror. From the equanimity of the Germanic attitude—where life and death weigh so nearly equal that a transposition can hardly bring about any violent concussion of the soul—there is, then, a far cry to dread. Or rather, ill will toward the great change which stands out so crudely among many other peoples, an unwillingness toward death as something unnatural, a thing only to be explained as arising out of malice on the part of other human or spiritual beings. On closer scrutiny, however, there is after all a nearer relationship between the two modes of regarding death than would appear at first glance. They can, after all, be traced back to the same soul stratum. The gladdest of the bold admit to the wretches who run about trembling for their lives, that the actual transition from one state to the other involves a certain risk.

The ancient language has a special word for the man who has the germ of death already in him, one whom death has already touched: he is called *fey* (Anglo-Saxon *fæge*, Icelandic *feigr*). A *fey* man does not make a good comrade; there is no luck in him. Such a man is known, indeed, by the fact that his counsels turn awry, his wit fails him; he cannot even make use of the wisdom of others. When the enemies of Njál rode up in sight of his house, the old man ordered his sons and his followers indoors. Skarphedin,[80] who did not like being shut up in an inflammable building instead of fighting in the open, shakes his head at his father's demand: "Our father is marked for death now," it seems to him, and he adds resignedly: "still, I may well humor my father in this by being indoors with him, for I am not afraid of my death." To this may come even one so wise in counsel, so far-sighted, one whose resourcefulness never failed before. The approaching death so dims his eyes that he cannot foresee the house being fired over his head. In a former chapter, it has been told how the proud woman Thurid, the Great Widow, brought about an unlikely revenge on the slayers of a kinsman of her husband's. Her deep schemes were hurried on by the colossal blindness of her adversary, Sigurd; he would have his brother Thord marry her in spite of all scruples, and he would visit her in spite of all urgent representations. "You must be *fey*, to rush on like that," says Thord resignedly. The uncanny character of *feydom* is also plainly evident in the close relationship it bears to outlawry that the two words are often classed together. Thus, *fey* naturally comes to mean unhappy, useless, and craven—in fact, luckless.

Death is earnest—this the Northmen give us plainly to understand. And even the merriment at the arval,[81] or feast of succession, is in itself evidence of danger near. The time of death amounts to a crisis, which may lead to the worst results, unless due precautions be taken. All those who were joined in frith with the departed stand poised on the verge of misfortune. Contempt of death is based solely and entirely upon the fact of having all measures for surety in one's power. The scorner of death is at one with him who fears it in regarding death itself as an irruption into luck, an offense against life that must be repaired as soon as possible. And when there is none who can be called to account, it may happen that fear takes the form of fury, even to the point of rushing headlong against the invisible. The dirge of Egil contains a soul-stirring confession that terror stands just beyond the gate and can at any moment make itself felt as the superior.

In normal cases, death means a stranding of life. If the individual (as well as his kinsmen) stricken by the change shall get afloat again and sail on without harm, there must be reparation of some sort or another, to remove the germs of unluck. If it were a death that called for vengeance and vengeance were not taken, then the future loomed dark for the departed.

The terrible menace lurking in death is made manifest in the story of Hjorleif, who was murdered by his own thralls shortly after having settled in

---

[80] In *Njal's saga*, Skarphedin Njalsson is a hearty warrior, but known for his sharp tongue and ill temper. His insults wind up isolating his family from their allies during their decades-long blood feud, which gets them all killed.

[81] A Norse funerary wake in which bread and ale were served.

Iceland.[82] The Norwegian youth who landed in Iceland, together with his foster brother Ingolf, might claim to be reckoned among the great men of luck. He was descended from a family of high standing, and had himself increased his inheritance of honor by yearly expeditions throughout his youth. Immediately after landing in the new home, he built himself a house and remained there quietly through the winter. But at the commencement of spring, he began to cultivate the land, and having only one ox, he set his Irish thralls to pull the plow. They wearied of the work, and killed the ox in order to lure their master away in chase of the bear supposedly prowling about the place. While he was alone in the forest, they fell upon him and killed him, and his body was left lying in the open, until Ingolf came and made a grave for him in spring. "Wretched fate for a brave man that slaves should be his bane!"—this lament of Ingolf's tells us that a great misfortune has happened, but if the saga writer had left the matter here, our farthest-reaching guess would hardly have reached the full extent of the grief that weighed on Ingolf. The land was desolate when Ingolf found it, the thralls having fled after committing the misdeed, and desolate it remained for a very long time, for Hjorleif became an evil sprite haunting the neighborhood and making it unsafe— *unheore*—so that none could dwell there.

It may be, then, that in our asking after death, we have not touched the true goal, in using the word "death" in our own sense, as implying the stillness of the heart. We have only reached the possibility of death, not death itself. To exist in a clan meant to have a share in an individual life, with its sum of enjoyment and activity. And the common possession of life was thus not broken by the conclusion of one's existence in this light, if the dead man left kinsmen behind him to keep up his honor and maintain connection with all his fellows, both those here and those elsewhere. But the fellowship could be sundered. The isolation of the nithing was a thing that rent the vital artery in twain and uprooted every hope. Looking now, we can discern enough of the fear of death among our forefathers, enough of that barren terror of death that stifles all there is of nobility in man and leaves only the panic cry of the beast in him, or perhaps brutalizes him beyond the beast.

The nithing is he who rightly should bear the name of dead, for he is the exact opposite of the living human being. In his life, the human *hamingja* turns its wrong side out. His weapons have no bite. His ship can never find a wind. The current of power that gave success to the tilling of the soil stops: his fields burn dry; his cattle drop dead.

---

[82] The *Landnáma*, or *Book of Settlements*, describes the Norse settlement of Iceland. Brothers Hjorleif and Ingolf are two such settlers. Hjorleif captured slaves during a raid in Ireland and brought them to Iceland.

In the curses upon those who have sinned against life, we find the picture of the nithing clearly translated. Thus Sigrun says to her brother Dag, when he has slain his brother-in-law:

> Let the ship never stride that strides under you, even though the wished-for wind blows from behind. May the horse not run that runs under you, even though you are fleeing leap on leap before your foes. May the sword you draw never bite, save when it swoops down on your own head.

A corresponding dedication to the "life" of a nithing is found disguised in the first book of Saxo, where the curse is invoked upon Hadingus by a woman after he "with many strokes had slain a beast of unknown sort":

> Whether you stride on foot over the land or hoist sail at sea, the hate of the gods shall follow you, and everywhere you shall see the elements oppose your aim. On land your foot shall stumble, at sea you shall be tumbled about; an everlasting storm shall howl about you where you go, and never shall the ice thaw from your sails. No roof shall give you shelter—if you creep under one, it shall fall before the gale. Your herd shall perish of frost-bite. All things shall fade and moan that your breath has touched them. You shall be shunned as one stricken with the plague. No sick man shall be fouler than you.

The story as it stands here is not clear to us. Possibly, the fact was that Hadingus and the beast (or more likely, society and the beast) had mutual obligations. Hadingus' "unluck" would then consist in his having, willingly or unwillingly, broken in upon something inviolable, upon which life and welfare in that land depended. At all events, the description of the effects of the deed give as good a characterization of the external curse of villainy as could be given: luck in battle, luck in industry, luck of the wind—all are gone. All that the man touches falls to pieces, for in place of life, death goes out from him.

The nithing's plans are futile. Even though they appear sound and wise enough and seemingly laid with all cunning, all the tension is gone out of them. It will prove in the event that in despite of all human calculation, they (like his weapons) strike back upon his own face instead of forward. This reality of spiritual death barbs the point of such a curse as that the old crone calls down upon Grettir in his outlawry:[83] "Here I declare over you that you shall be forsaken of luck, of fortune and blessing, and all guardian strength and wit, the more for all your length of life." When Grettir starts up at the words as if stung by a serpent, it is not so much because he knows that one may expect all sorts of arts from

---

[83] Referencing *The Saga of Grettir the Strong*.

such a witch-wife, but rather because she, with devilish insight, strikes with her mighty words at his vulnerable point, and with one poisonous sting paralyzes his resistance against all witchcraft.

She begins by summing up quite soberly his present state: "These men [Grettir and his brother] might yet be luckless in their boldness. Here good terms are offered them, but they thrust them aside, and nothing leads more surely to evil than being unable to accept good." Roughly translated into modern speech: "You can see what the matter with him is: he is out of his wits; he is branded." Here she hits the outlaw, the man society has declared a nithing, and all she needs now to do is to leave the words fixed in the wound and let them act of themselves. When in a young saga we read that a certain outlaw saw everything in advance, but could do nothing for it, this is but a new proof of how instinctively sure an understanding men had in Iceland of what was handed down: the sentence contains the negative to the proud luck of the sons of Ingimund.

To the eyes of the nithing, all things are wrapped in a mist. He does not know what will come of his doings. His acts are not charged with the lucky power of will that guides them to their goal. The mark of the nithing is that boldness and luck, power and success no longer go together with him. When a man loses his footing and is on the point of slipping from human life, his moral habitus is aptly expressed in the words: "He was brave enough, but no man of luck."

But the cleft in the nithing goes deeper still: it cleaves the soul, so that will and *hugr* cannot reach each other. We read in an Icelandic saga of an outlaw who himself could say: "It goes against my will to share in plunderings and harm with these ill-doers," and yet he stayed with them. The source of luck is dried up altogether. The nithing has no hold on himself. He has no honor, and so all moral judgment is void. He becomes a coward, and he grows malicious. All that an honest man eschews will be habit and custom to a nithing: to break oaths and promises, to slay women and the unarmed, to murder in gloom and dark, to betray those who trust him, to violate frith. He has no frith. All are his enemies. His friendship is like that of the wolves who run in bands together, but rend one another in time of need. The Anglo-Saxon gnomic verses describe his state,[84] putting with a peculiar yet natural lack of distinction between outlawed man and outlawed beast, the position thus:

Friendless, unlucky man takes wolves for his fellows, the treacherous beasts; often his comrade rends him asunder. It buries dead men in itself and howls with hunger. It sends up no complaint, no wailing of woe over death, the gray wolf. Nay, ever it wishes more.

---

[84] Maxims put into verse in order to aid memory.

Or, as we find in the Old Icelandic with even more marked emphasis of the lack of frith feeling: "Are we to bear ourselves as wolves, quarrelling one with another, as the dogs of the Norns, the gluttons, begotten of the wide waste?"

The nithing hacks about him in a blind fury of destruction. Old Swedish records of judgments show him still in all his horror as the ethos-forsaken beast he is, when he flings his spittle full in the face of the living god, swears as if he had all the devils at his call, and challenges all without respect of person. There was one such on a time who forced a priest to give him ale, and rode off to the churchyard with the mug to drink to all the devils he could name, and offer to fight them. It is related of another that when captured, he freely admitted all his misdeeds, and was only plagued by the thought of all the evil uncommitted that he was now prevented from accomplishing. If he could only have managed to gain his freedom for a single week, to arrange matters so that he had something to die with, he would have been content. Such a madness of evil is the state of the old outlaw, and though its symptoms among the peasantry of Småland in the seventeenth and eighteenth centuries may be regulated by somewhat other conditions—Christian, if we like to call them so—the nature of the madness yet remains unchanged.

Compared with the frozen despair of this *unheore* nithing horror, the Icelandic outlaws appear almost too pale. As is but natural, a saga is not written about a specimen of human refuse; no pathos is to be extracted from vileness and bestial cunning. The pathos of life itself is, as the records of judgments distinctly say, too hard for any idealization to work in it. The Icelandic robber stories originate in feelings of kinship and friendship—depicting (or glorifying) the human element in the outcast, and approaching more and more the modern type of bandit legends, in which the exception claims a certain romance purely and solely by virtue of his exceptional position.

The greater, then, is the effect upon the reader of the discovery that the narrators *cannot* clear their heroes from the brand of Cain! So deeply rooted is the feeling that the transition to the state of outlawry is an alteration of character that the Icelanders, even in the romantic days of epigone art, cannot hold a character unchanged through its passage beyond the boundary. No healthy Norseman behaves as Gunnar of Hlidarendi when he went about Iceland as an outlaw who had broken his own promises:[85] he accepts Olaf the Peacock's invitation to seek safety at his homestead, and when the time comes, he remains at home simply because he lacks the will to go. Or, expressed in terms of literary history, no storyteller would think of ascribing to a man of luck the instability that was characteristic of the nithing. And an admired popular hero like Grettir loses ethically

---

[85] Gunnar Hámundarson was an Icelandic chieftain who plays a major role in the first part of *Njal's saga*, before he dies in battle.

(in the old sense of the word, of course) in the course of his outlawry. In the light of beautifying sympathy, the tragic element only appears more bitter when a man enters upon base robbery and villainy with mingled feelings in which the two components, self-scorn and recognition of the futility of resistance, accentuate each other.

Self-assertion is only found where luck is, where there is an honor to fight for, and where the fight leads to an increase of honor. With the nithing, who lives but a fiction of human life, battle and defense are but a blind biting and snapping and snarling as of a beast—or rather, as of certain beasts: the nithing beasts. The more he toils, the greater the dishonor he brings upon himself. Not even the last resource open to any living man, of gaining honor in defiance by his death, is here available. There is not sufficient honor in him to make him worthy of vengeance. To slay him is merely putting him out of mischief.

Without frith and without joy—here we have the end of the nithing's saga. These two "withouts" fix the gulf between kinship and nithing-hood. Without the life that consists in the feeling of kinship, in the tacit recollection of kin-luck's history in oneself and one's kin, in the family pride's faith in the future, none can have the signs of life: the well-being of converse when stretched on the bench, and the half-scornful, half-rejoicing boisterous laughter, produced, apparently, by the mere movement when a man "proud of his strength" breaks out into a run. A man cannot fill his lungs for a burst of laughter when the arteries close their valves. In the nithing, the vital artery is sundered, and therefore, all power of joy rapidly ebbs away.

Death, rightly considered, means a state without luck. We must remember that the word is to be taken absolutely, so that there is no room for intermediate states and the thought of a transitional form cannot find a way in. The poor men of low degree had but a very slender luck—so slender that seen from above it might perhaps be invisible altogether. But none could be called a man of unluck as long as he owned house and home and kin, and still felt himself as the defender of an honor. *How* poor a man might be without falling out of humanity I do not know; the boundary lay probably now higher, now lower, according to the state of things in society. But even the very poorest must, as surely as they were alive, possessed a luck on which they lived, and which they cultivated with religious intensity. Not even thralls can be taken as a sort of transition form, for they are wholly and completely outside all forms of luck. They have no life in themselves, but are inspired by the power of their owner, and remain in equilibrium as long as it is suffered to act through them. There is no other intermediate state but that in which young men found themselves in the time intervening between the slaying of their father and the taking of vengeance: a period when they went about as shadows, in all the ghastliness of a shadow life, making wide circles to avoid any meeting of men. The transition, which with the sureness and inevitability of time completes itself merely by being left to itself, is the only intermediate state between luck and unluck.

In the modern languages, misfortune has something positive about it. Our civilization has imbued calamity with a sort of nobility, or at least clothed it with a sentimental pathos. But in ancient times, unluck—or lucklessness, as the Icelanders call it—was altogether evil, a denudation, and a negative where all ideality sank through without finding foothold. The fearfulness of death consists in its annihilating humanity and setting something else in its place. The nithing is not a mere nothing that one can pass through unscathed, as one cleaves a spirit. To the Germanic mind, he was abhorrent, the most contemptible of all beings, but he was even more feared than abhorred.

Mighty powers are let loose in him. He could not tame them if he would, but he will not. He who is bereft of honor has no will in the human sense, but then there is another sort of will, or rather an impulse, that holds him and rules him. Our forefathers found the opposite of will not in slackness and lack of willpower, but in something which must rather be called witchcraft: the meaningless, mad wickedness that is accompanied by mysterious powers of mischief. We know from the sagas what an atmosphere of dread environed these real wizards and witches, and we know that the devilish element in them lay not in such simple arts as that of acting at a distance, sending their will through the air, and changing their shape and traveling through time as well as space. Whether their actions and movements are externally more or less akin to those of human beings is immaterial, because they invariably take place in other dimensions than the human, and are inspired by other and alien motives. The characteristic feature of the wizard is the evil aimlessness that marks his whole mode of action, in contrast to the man who is conscious of his aim in all he does, whether for good or ill.

A man's weapons may indeed have the peculiarity that no wound from them can heal, but it is luck that gives the power, and luck may be gained from the blood of the owner, when he is slain in revenge. A wizard, on the other hand, has poison of the soul both in his hand and in his weapons, and his blood is a pestilence that one should beware of touching with one's hands or one's clothes. This is why his eyes are so evil that a glance from them is enough to scorch away the fertility of a region, and it is this perverse nature of his soul that makes his mere presence give rise to optical delusions in all bystanders. He can be exterminated, but poisonous as he is, his destruction must be prepared and carried out with the greatest care, so that one can go home afterwards with the assurance than none of his venom has been left in one's garments, and that he is altogether effaced from off the earth. Men try to burn him to dust, to pile a mound of stones upon him, transfix him with a stake to the ground, or drown him far out from land— no precautionary measure is too great.

The fear of the wizard, the nature of the hatred, the eagerness to have him exterminated—all these are applicable to the nithing. The peasants have still retained their fear of the uncanny vagabonds in the human world, whose mere presence brings misfortune. When a thief, a murderer, a whore, a witch—which is to say, in the old tongue, nithings—looks at the naked breast of an infant, the child will fall into a decline. Or, still nearer the old mode of thought, if a whore strikes a man, he will never be able to defend himself against an enemy afterward; all that is in him is poisoned by the pest. The curse of Hadingus lies not only in the fact that wherever he goes he carries with him misfortune that falls upon others by mistake—he simply exhales pestilence. The infectiousness of the nithing is the reality of life behind the law's anathema of the outlaw. None *may* have intercourse with him, sit or sleep in the same house with him, and this prohibition arises out of the deeper fact that people will not allow his company to poison their bread and sleeping place.

The distinguishing mark of the nithing is that one never knows what he will do. In him appears the same unreliability that stamps the demonic character of the giant. Nothing in him and nothing about him is what it seems, but always something else. Outlaw, or breaker of peace, and *unheore* are words that suggest one another when people talk. When the Anglo-Saxon poet comes to describe the fate of Ishmael, who was the opponent of his own kin, he calls him *unheore* and battle-wild. The man of unluck is regarded with the same mixture of hate, contempt, and horror as the real giants of Utgard, for no other reason than that he belongs to the host of the monsters. An essential change has taken place in him: the healthy blood has dried up, and dangerous fluids have taken its place. Venom flows in his veins instead of blood, as with the giants.

It is related of a strong man called Thorstein Oxfoot that he had a nasty tussle with a giantess, and after that time he was a little strange, with a touch of something uncanny about him. The narrator leaves it an open question whether his misfortune arose from his having swallowed some of her spittle during the fight, or if it was a sickness dating from his earliest days when he was carried out to perish as a child. It is of interest to note that the state of a child who has not been regularly born into a clan is placed on a line with the powers that are abroad in the world of the night.

Utgard, then, is not only a power standing externally and pressing upon human life; it thrusts itself into house and home if men are not careful. No wonder that the fight against a thing so horrible should be waged with the greatest force. If the evil one is a king, then so much the greater peril for his surroundings that he should lie at the very center of luck like a venomous worm brooding over the treasure of kings. It is a matter affecting all when his luck is dissolved, and—as we read in Bósi's curse over King Hring[86]—"mountains stagger, the world is disturbed, the weather turns ill, and those things happen that should not." To avoid being stifled in the breath that goes out from him, and seeing all possessions withered in frost and rime and barrenness, there is no other way but to efface him from the earth. And he was indeed torn up by the roots.

---

[86] This is referencing *The Saga of Bósi and Herraud*. In it, Herraud and his father Hring break out in civil war with each other. Herraud and his friend Bósi are captured by Hring and are about to be executed, but Busla, Bósi's foster mother and practitioner of witchcraft, arrives in Hring's chambers at night and curses him until he does her bidding. Herraud and Bósi are then exiled and sent on a quest instead of executed.

XIV. The Realm of the Unhappy Dead

In the army of the dead, we find all in whom life is found wanting. There are those who are luckless by nature (such as cripples, cowards, and fools), for the first essential of luck was a sound body and sane wits. Even in modern times, the peasants of the North have been inclined to place the deformed in the same ill-omened class as thieves and honorless murderers. And when in olden times care was taken as far as possible to avoid the entry of such wretched beings into existence at all, it was because any lack of the full external human character was regarded as a crime, and not as a misfortune in the modern sense. Others, again, were born lucky, and then one fine day before they were aware, came the giant thrusting his head up in the midst of their luck. Death could leap out all of a sudden, so that the man without warning felt his soul sundered. A defeat was peril enough.

If the strong man met a stronger, who drove him suddenly out from land and luck, then he sank down surely and beyond help into the base state of a nithing, gradually losing both will and power to assert himself. Among the defeated and captured, all nobility was forced out by servile fear and inactivity. There is a force of reality in Fafnir's words when he reminds Sigurd that his father fell unavenged, and that his mother had been taken as a slave: "Had you grown up in the circle of kinsmen, one might see you in mighty strokes. Now you are a thrall and a captive, and men know that one in bonds is ever trembling."

When the Norwegian poet, filled with the Christian conviction of the uncertainty of earthly things, seeks an instance from life showing the falseness of riches, he says, "Unnar and Saevaldi did not believe that luck could fail them, but they became naked and bereft of all."[87] And the thought of its own speed tears him headlong into the concluding line "and they ran as wolves to the forest."

We can hardly wonder, then, at the restless eagerness with which Haakon Sigurdsson thrusts aside the thought of lucklessness when Olaf Tryggvason spiritually follows up his victory over him by saying: "It is no lie that you kinsmen are handsome men, but there is an end of your luck [*hamingja*]." Haakon answers:

> Nay, nay, this is no unluck [*unhamingja*] that is come upon us; it has long been so that chieftains have taken victory by turns. I am as yet hardly grown beyond child's years, and we were not prepared to have to stand on the defense. We did not look for strife, and it may yet come about that we prove more fortunate another time.

The feverish breathlessness of these words betrays a lurking fear, which the experiences of the past have stamped down into the soul. And on the other hand, if the wreck of life were not so unmistakable a fact, there would have been no room for the paradox that men at times lost their freedom and yet seemed to retain something of their luck. "She was the queen's washing maid—or slave woman— and yet not altogether luckless," says a Norse version referring to Alfhild, Olaf II's mistress and mother of Magnus the Good.

Or the fall might come stealthily, as when powers and fortune in some inexplicable fashion withered away, and a man felt his leap and his blow fall ever wide of their mark. In *Beowulf*'s description of King Heremod, we feel the growing uneasiness of the bodyguard as they watch the nithing grimace day by day showing through the features of the prince:

> He did not grow up for the joy of the Scyldings, but for slaughter and bitter death to the Danes. Swollen with ire, he caused the undoing of his board fellows, his shoulder companions, till he passed, the proud king, lonely from this joyful world. And yet the mighty God had raised him high above all men and strengthened him with power and blissful command, but in his breast grew blood-fierce thoughts. He gave no rings to his Danes, as was due. Joyless, he bided the time when he gathered the harvest of his deeds: long-lasting war in the land.

When he, as it is actually stated, "fell among giants," the rabble of Utgard, and ended his life as a nithing.

From Iceland, we have in *The Saga of Grettir the Strong* the story of a man in whom barrenness grew from early times. Grettir was strong and quick-witted

---

[87] Characters from the *Voluspa*.

enough to all appearance, fearless and active, but his counsels and his actions always went apart, so that the results recoiled upon himself. It would seem as if his great struggle with the monster Glam formed the commencement of his un-luck.[88] This is also a good old thought, which naturally finds expression in the curse of the dying creature, when he declares that his conqueror's every plan shall from thenceforward turn to misfortune and dishonor. But even before this fateful event, the marks were visible in Grettir. There is a record of the words his uncle spoke before the combat with the monster: "It is truly said that luck is one thing, quickness another." And again: "There are men who see a little way ahead, but cannot guard against what they see." And far earlier even yet, wise men such as Thorarin the Wise had seen enough to beware of the wild fellow with his iron strength. When his foster son Bardi has engaged Grettir's help for his great ex-pedition of vengeance, Thorarin earnestly protests: "True enough, Grettir is a man far beyond others, and weapons will be slow to bite on him if his luck holds, but I have no faith in that luck. And it was well for you not to have only men of ill luck in your following." And it was settled as Thorarin advised.

As Glam had prophesied, so it came about. When Grettir once, at a critical moment, saved the life and health of his companions by swimming across to the mainland of Norway and bringing back fire to the outlying rocks where they were near to perishing, he brought about, against his will, a misfortune that gained him many bitter enemies in Iceland. When he came rushing into the house covered with ice, the people thought him a monster and laid about with sticks and brands from the hearth. He barely managed to escape with the glowing embers he had taken, but the sparks had caught the straw on the floor ablaze. In the morning, nothing remained of the place but a heap of ashes.

And among those burned to death were two sons of Thorir Skeggjason of Adaldal, a powerful Icelandic yeoman. Grettir obtains permission from King Olaf II to clear himself of suspicion by the ordeal of fire, but in the carrying out of the test, his "unluck" runs away with him; he strikes a boy who jeers at him, knocking him down—in God's house, no less. Again, the melancholy word is spoken of him: "You are a man of sore ill luck, Grettir, and it will not be easy to amend it." And now he drifts irresistibly into endless outlawry, farther and farther into nithing-hood, till he ends as the miserable victim of witchcraft.

This showing of the growth of nithing-hood in Grettir is one of the greatest and most poignant pieces of evidence as to the power of mortal fear upon men's minds. One might go so far as to admire the freebooter, but one could not wrest

---

[88] Glam, or Glámr, was a shepherd from Sweden who was tasked with caring for the sheep on a haunted farmstead in Iceland. Glam mysteriously died one night, his corpse found out in the snow. He soon rose as a ghost himself, haunting the area until Grettir defeated him. Glam, in his dying moments, cursed Grettir with ill fortune and unluck.

the thoughts and words in which admiration must be clothed up out of the deep soil of uncanny gloom in which they were rooted.

Typical, too, of Northern modes of thought is the disinclination to stop at a certain deed as the starting point of nithing-hood; men felt constrained to hark back and find the symptoms in earlier acts. Thus, when Sigurd Slembe—the Norwegian pretender of the twelfth century—came to claim the crown to which he considered himself sole heir after the killing of his brother, his unlucky deed at once sets folk thinking of his birth: "If you are really a son of Magnus [III] and Thora [Saxesdatter], then your birth was unlucky, and so also it has fallen out if you have slain your brother." True enough, the single act, or refraining from action—a murder, cowardly behavior, breach of oath, unavenged killing, stealing—form an absolute beginning, giving birth to nithing-hood in the life of the person concerned. It is the source of his unluck, as men say in Norway.

The Northman would thoroughly understand and heartily agree with the utterance of the Anglo-Saxon about those retainers of the king's, who by their base flight brought shame upon their race. When he says, "No more shall any of their clan now grasp joyously at the gold," this "now" would strike the Northman's ear with all its fateful weight. But the "source" sets thoughts on the lookout for earlier symptoms. It was the man's misfortune that he failed to take vengeance, but why was no vengeance taken? Well, there is not time to ask for an answer, for all remember at once something that happened long ago. The nithing's whole past is raised up to witness against him, because nithing-hood, when all is said and done, is but the outcome of an inner flaw in luck. He would never have committed this first villainy of his, if he had not been inwardly marked by his constitution. What the Northmen mean by source is really this: at this moment the villainy that lay hidden in him came to light in this act, and from this act his whole life was infected.

Moreover, death can just as easily strike from behind upon the doer of quite harmless acts. If the clan has not strength to carry through their kinsman's cause by force of arms (or at worst by a fine) and therefore buys peace by sacrificing the culprit, then he becomes a hopeless nithing and a wolf-man for such honorable acts of aggression as homicide or open violent attack upon his neighbor's goods. And the peril lies in wait for a man beyond the grave as well as here. A hero who prefers death to a life in shame, and buries himself under his honor and his luck, has not by any means ensured his existence forever. If he is given up by his kinsmen—or falls as the last of his "people," so that none is left to take up the inheritance—then there is every danger of his turning evil, and haunting men and beasts as a demon the more terrible in proportion to his might in the days of his life. It is not only the thoughts of the living that are bewildered by pain when the clan is obliged to leave one of its members unavenged—when they must let him lie unholy, as the Northmen said, with a word intimating that the unavenged is deprived of his dignity and worth.

The dead man sickens and pines away with the living. The future before him when life stops is so horrible that the fear of the family's dying out can throughout many centuries compete with all the terrors of hell and deprive them of their power over men's souls. And the danger will at all times be equally great, however many happy years the dead man may have behind him. There are nithings yonder, out in the world of night, who were once honest dead. They have not found reincarnation, because the clan declined and became extinct. They have not been kept alive by clever and careful kinsmen, and then comes the time when men learn who it was that lived on the place in former days.

There is no terror in the dweller of a barrow when he can be proved to be a kinsman. In the saga, Hervor goes out confidently to her father Angantyr's barrow and greets him as one of her own, and the dead warrior has not forgotten his frith and his honor.[89] He gives friendly warnings and hands out his wonderful sword as a free gift.[90] If on the other hand, there lay strangers in the barrow whom none living could reckon as kin, then the place was simply unsafe and *unheore*. In the dragon stories, we find, under the somewhat foreign dress, homely experiences of the fact that every lonely or forgotten hero takes on habits of ferocity. The cruel dragon that proved the death of Beowulf lay brooding on the remains of an extinct clan. The last man of the tribe hid his treasure in the cave with a lament for the noble heroes whom death in battle had carried off to the last man but one. There he ended his life, and the old enemy, the walker in the twilight, lay down upon the gold guarding the treasure that was of no use to himself. We can safely conclude that at first, the hider of the treasure himself (or those nearest to him), once so noble and bold, filled the place of the monster. The Northmen are quite familiar with the idea of a dead man turning into a troll over his goods, and jealously guarding the gold with his nithing's venom.

The simple separation from family and land is enough to imperil life itself; no man could live more than a certain time upon the store of soul in himself. "It is ill to live in unland," said the men of the North, and the word carries with it more than an indication of the character of unease. The ancients had no doubt their homesickness, but such a popular word is not calculated to give any idea as to what it was that rose and fell in the mind of an exile when he sat, like Hengest in *Beowulf*—far from his ancestral seat "and thought of home."

The Icelanders said that *landmunr* was at play in the guest, and with this word, the longing for home is at once drawn in upon a definite cultural background; for this *munr* (Anglo-Saxon *myn*) contains in itself not only the meanings

---

[89] This is referencing *The Saga of Hervor and Heidrek*.
[90] The magic sword called Tyrfing.

of love and will; it denotes a whole that these qualities fit: soul, life. And we are brought still nearer to the reality by the Anglo-Saxon use of *feasceaft* of an exile. The joylessness that lies in this word is not of the gentle melancholy type that inspires poets, it is a sickness of the *hugr*, which makes loneliness a thing simply ugly and nothing else. *Feasceaft* is a word that fits equally well applied to the outlaw, and to the monster Grendel himself, the dweller in Utgard.

Banishment was an amputation, only the worse in that it was not a limb, but the whole man that was amputated. A man from one of the Germanic tribes taken by force from the circle of his kin and set down in some civilized inland town as the guest of the Roman people—as the Sicambrian chiefs were by Augustus[91]— might well arrive at the point of preferring death. Or did he perhaps take his own life for fear of death, because he saw no other way of slipping back into life again than by letting his soul return to its proper environment? The Southern peoples understood but little of the feelings of a couple of native chiefs, and did not care to understand more. They knew that the barbarians could not endure the state and killed themselves "from disgust of life," as Cassius Dio says.[92] But their sufferings become more acute when we have the sentence translated into the language of those cast out.

Outlawry, then, is a terrible weapon in the hands of society against criminals who will not do right. The weapon hits so hard because it strikes the very nerve of life itself. The outlaw is thrust out not from society, but from life. But then again, the effect of the sentence depends entirely upon the condemned man's kin, whether they will execute the curse by severing his vital artery. For though the whole known world may excommunicate a man and declare him given over to all the evil spirits, it has not the slightest effect upon his spiritual welfare as long as his kinsmen maintain him and suffer him to drink of their source of life— always provided the kinsmen themselves have a luck strong enough to ward off the mighty force of words that pours in upon them.

Among our forefathers, we may find lofty examples of submission to the general will, side by side with astounding contempt for law and order. Their social conscience was more active, and therefore more elastic than it can ever be among people who seat a judge upon a codex and place a regular policeman behind the offender, ready to deal with him according to instructions. Nowadays, the ideas of right are more or less uniform throughout the whole of a population; the fear of justice hardly attains to anything that could properly be called veneration, and defiance dwindles for the most part to an uncertain taking advantage of circumstances and searching for loopholes in legal paragraphs. In the

---

[91] The Sicambri were a Germanic people during the time of the Roman Empire who lived just east of the Rhine and on the border of what is now the Netherlands.

[92] A Roman senator and historian who published approximately eighty volumes on Roman history.

Germanic society, the means of law were legal adaptations of everyday forms and drew their force from the inner experience of the parties at law.

Consequently, the feelings of men face to face with legal condemnation were of a wider and more plastic character than nowadays. Men could feel themselves enslaved by a word, and they could with sovereign contempt disregard the most solemn anathema. One would be stricken numb by a sentence of outlawry, while his neighbor regards it as a mere insult, possibly even of too slight a character to awaken his interest. If the means of law take root, then they hold with a terrific strength, but where they fail to grasp honor they drift empty away.

Obedience to law and defiance of law—words only applicable in the looser sense are alike in power, because they come from the same stratum of the soul. They do not annul each other, but can exist side by side, even in one and the same person, without any sense of schism.

We know that far into modern times, the common people have preserved their old estimate of outlawry. The kings were generally progressive men in league with the ideas of law and royal rights that were propagated by Western civilization and the Roman Church. The peasants stuck to the old law that lived in the hearts and not in books. No wonder that the king's conviction that right is right and *must* be right comes fiercely into collision with the peasants' failure to get beyond the fundamental morality that right must be *felt* to be right, or it does not exist. The slayer sits at home under shelter of old-fashioned kinship, and the king sits in his court in the light of modern culture, ransacking the language for words strong enough to use for these obstinate fellows who let a decree of outlawry pass over their heads without moving from the spot. "It is insufferable that they should prosper in their unrighteousness," says Haakon Magnusson in 1315.[93] And in 1315, the king is right; the peasants are in the process of becoming defiers of the law, not because their feeling and sense of right have altered, but because the law has changed: it has at last been liberated from the tutelage of experience, and placed under the mighty protection of logical conclusions. But yet, the peasant had no feeling of being wrong, because the experience of the ancestors was still strong within him. A man is no outlaw as long as there is a body of kinsmen willing and able to keep him. Not until he has been severed from life does he become a dangerous being, driven out and shunned.

But when the curse has been uttered, and the clan has renounced the condemned man by taking part in the oath whereby the law-*thing* "swears him out," or the *thing*-men by clash of arms have assumed obligations among themselves against him, the outlaw is dead. He is flung out from the life of men, and may be hunted "as far as men hunt wolves," because he is a wolf (*vargr*, "void of luck and pleasure"). As an outlaw and a nithing, he bears the "wolf's head"; that is to

---

[93] Also known as Haakon VI of Norway.

say, originally, he is transformed into a wolf, running wild on the heath and rend-
ing carrion. And yet he can, by one step across a threshold, enter into life again,
if only he can find a circle willing to receive him into its own life and regenerate
him into a brother. The moment he is greeted in a house and offered a seat, the
bestial nature falls from him, and he is once more a man.

The words uttered by Gudrun in the Greenlandic *Atlamál* as to her own and
her brothers' achievements in their youth might indeed be spoken with the literal
earnestness of prose: "We freed from the forest he whom we wished to save. We
gave him luck that nothing owned."

If life and death were the two schematic magnitudes they are sometimes
reckoned in a practical sense, they would fill out all existence without leaving
space for a thought to lie concealed, and they would then be the safest words to
translate from and into any speech. As it is, they are not quantities, but qualities,
and the task of interpreting them from one language to another may prove the
occasion of years of study. We have inherited the verb "to die" from our forefathers, and we use it of the same process as they did, but in reality, its meaning
has undergone so great a change that linguistic continuity hardly suffices to unite
the two ideas into one personality.

In the Old Scandinavian, it is possible to frame such an expression as this
concerning the underworld: men die into that world, and without commenting on
the genuineness of this form of speech, we may take the word as a useful hint,
indicating that death then was a more complex idea than it is now. Or it seems to
be, for our words are complex in their way, and when we say that a thing is
simple, the words mean nothing but that we ourselves are placed at the focus of
the thoughts concerning it. There was always, in a way, the need for a more precise definition of what men died into. The terms of life and death, which now
appear so unconditionally opposite, were rather two groups of states and their
reverses, linked into each other. Now, the process means cessation of life,
whereas in those days, it was a transition from life to life; now, to die means the
great cut into existence, but to the ancients the transition from one state to another
that left the life of luck untouched could never rank as a catastrophe. If then we
would not relinquish the essential part of our word, its bitterness, its reference to
the end and altering of plans, its regard to the thinning of ranks, its absolute
"halt!" then no etymology can help us find equivalents in the ancient tongue. We
must give up hope of finding an exact counterpart in that culture, but in the transition from luck to unluck we come nearest to the irreparable conversion, which
we denote with that stern word.

This death could befall a man in living life, and he could just as well meet it
in the kingdom of death, or at the transition between the two. In this possibility,
that to expire might mean the passing of the soul, lay the seriousness and the peril
that made the change a crisis—not only for the departed, but also for those nearest

to him. Those left behind took all precautions, we may imagine, though we do not know very much about the ceremonies attending death. In the Icelandic literature, we do not find any other precautionary measure directly described beyond the *nábjargir*—the saving of the corpse, which appears to have consisted chiefly in pressing the nostrils together. But we may doubtless take it that earlier times had a more comprehensive ritual. There was no doubt something of ill omen about a corpse not yet so treated, not least when the catastrophe had been caused by violence, so as to leave vengeance due.

Presumably, a kind of inquest was held in order to arrive at the cause of death; when the wounds had been counted, one of the assembled kinsmen would solemnly assume responsibility for setting matters right, and place himself at the head of the undertaking by carrying out the *nábjargir*. In other cases also, where anything unusual in the manner of death might seem to suggest that unluck had fallen upon the house, there might be reason for care in dealing with the body of the departed. When Gudmund the Mighty, the chieftain at Modruveffir, froze to death from within on hearing a man relate a strange dream, the mistress of the house forbade any to touch the corpse until his brother Einar had inspected it. The latter's wisdom at once discerned the cause: it was the power of the dream that had turned his vitals to ice, and thereupon he attended to the body. People who had been slain by monsters were more than others apt to "walk" in an uncanny sense, and the same took place where a pestilential sickness raged. Balance and security were not restored until the funeral feast had been solemnized with due rites and ceremonies, and the dead man had been "shown" to his place— "shown to Valhalla," as the phrase runs in later language, by a modernizing of an ancient formula. Nevertheless, we must not lay emphasis solely on the uncanny side. For with people who were firmly set in their luck, this interregnum was after all only a brief pause, wherein life was brought to a standstill for a while; there were sure means of re-establishing safety both for the dead and the living. In doubtful cases, on the other hand, where vengeance was uncertain, where luck stood but indifferently on its feet, there was death in the house.

The idea of annihilation has shown itself a hard one to grasp, and thought still fumbles without being able to discover pure nothing or sheer cessation. Our forefathers had practical reasons for trying to affect an absolute death. To live in a district with demon souls was not to be thought of; they were too uncanny and too massive. Somehow or other it was necessary to conjure them over into the wilderness of demons, where they had their kinsfolk and acquaintance. But after all, Utgard lay very near to the world of men, and one ever knew when these ill-boding creatures would be at one's doors again. None could be sure but that he might find himself set upon one evening late. It was better perhaps to bind the spook bodily, by heaping stones on him or driving a stake through him, or moving him over to some outlying reef where the excess of moisture would reduce his mobility. But it happened often enough that all precautions proved vain, however thoroughly they might be carried out. Then destruction was heaped upon destruction, the head, perhaps, first chopped off, then the whole body burned and the ashes strewn in the sea in the hope of thus reducing the soul to atoms so small as to be practically non-existent. But the cessation of existence itself, as the last and decisive opposite of life, was never reached.

Thought and hand thrust their object out to a boundary and dumped it down into a mist, but this mist was after all nothing but forgetting. Renown contains, as we have seen, in a literal sense the highest form of soul and the strongest pressure of life, and thus it is also literally true to the ancient sense that the opposite pole of life is a deep forgetfulness where none knows one's name or one's place.

XV. THE STRUCTURE OF THE CLAN

Against this background, the old poet-chief of Borg, Egil Skallagrímsson, stands out in his true tragic grandeur when he keens for his drowned son and defies the wench of the sea, as he sees her erect on the headland or fiercely rocking the dear corpse in the deep. In a world where all is *hamingja*, his words find their true violence and their true sadness. Not for nothing does the word "titanic" rise to our lips in regard to his challenge of the heavenly powers, for titanic defiance is our highest expression of human helplessness. A titan, in our world, is he who has renounced the task of moving the world, and purposely crushes himself in order to demonstrate that our heads are only made to be broken against that which is stronger. But the contrast between our world and that in which Egil moves is brought out sharply when we compare the modern titan, who is set outside the world as a unit, against the dumb and blind powers of the universe— with Egil standing as representative of a world in which man is the core and ties nature to himself by strong bonds of soul.

It is not titanic obstinacy, not defiance, not megalomania that inspires the old chief, but the simple reality that man's *hamingja* is large enough to include the sun and the moon and the whole world, and can challenge gods on equal ground without any titanic hint of magnificent absurdity. Perhaps there is a modern touch in his despair; Egil belongs to an age in which contact with Western Christianity called forth strange revolutions in the minds of men, but at the very moment when the spiritual community seems to link up between him and us, the character of his melancholy severs all intimacy. He is helpless because the luck and *hamingja* of his family has failed. Egil has few behind him, so runs his plaint, and that means that there is a paucity and lack of strength within him. It is not because his foes are gods and he but a man that he despairs; if he were but enough, he would stand by his word and take up the combat with the powers who have stolen his son.[94]

It would seem that even if all other ideas that issue from human brains will always bear the restricting stamp of time and place, the sphere of numbers should be a common ground where folk of all races and tongues could meet. And yet even here we do not escape the Babel of culture. To have many kinsmen and many children was a necessity of life under the old regime; a numerously populated clan was a sign of great luck. This seems easy enough in alien words, but the thing no alien speech can express is the intensity of this need of kin. Tacitus can say of the Germanic type that the more kinsmen he has on his father's and mother's side, the happier an old age he can look forward to. But for the Roman, the many were stronger than the few, whereas the Germanic idea held one of many as stronger in himself than one of few. We add the numbers up one by one to a total; our primitive cousins see the number as something that puts force into any member of the numerous clan.

But after all has been heard, and the question of what the family is has been answered, we come to the next question: where is it? We have described the contents of the soul, but the problem remains: how far does it go, which people belong to it, and which stand outside of it?

Several investigators have wrestled with this problem in one form or another, when they moved in regions where the population marched up against them in tribes, clans, and families. And they have perhaps often enough given up the task, contenting themselves with a definition that at best covered the bulk of the facts and left the remainder to find a place for themselves. They have perhaps had to deal with a tribe, a clan, or whatever it may properly be called, which was united by the bond of blood and by vengeance to an indissoluble whole in the face of all the rest of the world. And the savants have seen with dismay that this indissoluble whole suddenly fell asunder in two parties that bravely enough by internecine strife helped one another to keep manhood and the feeling of blood alive, when peace became too oppressive about them.

Facts will continue to contradict one another, and the problem will remain unaffected by all solutions, as long as we (like the Neo-Europeans we are) start by supposing that a solid whole must be expressible in a definite figure, and take it for granted that the family must be transposable into a reckoning up of generations.

The secret of primitive society is to be sought not in outer forms, but in the energy of the clan feeling. The one and unchangeable reality is frith and solidarity, and this reality is so strong that it makes one body and one soul of the kinsmen, but the extent of the soul is determined by the needs of the moment. At one

---

[94] Egil's son Bodvar drowned during a storm.

time a body of men will act as a homogeneous clan; next time they will split up into a couple of conflicting groups. The secret of the force contained in the principle of frith is not that it demands a fixed number of men to be effective, but that its power of tension acts unswervingly on the circle so far as the occasion gives it scope to act.

It is then not the construction of the soul that makes the difference between them and us. The life of modern man too has many axes and rotates in different circles. One day he is a family man, next day a citizen of his country. One hour he acts as a member of a corporation, another moment as his very own self—as an individual, and his thoughts and feelings vary in force and content according to the task allotted to them. The difference between modern individuals and primitive clansmen lies in the character of the circles and in the intensity of feeling. In our lives, the single self of the isolated individual is the strongest and most vivid of all selves, and all the other modes of life draw their power of thought and their warmth of feeling from the experience of the soul when it is alone and concerned with its own private happiness. The true religious man is he who cares immensely for his own salvation, and thus learns to take an interest in other people's souls. In primitive culture, the current works the opposite way. The circle can never be narrowed down to a single soul, and the most potent motives in the individual arise from the life he has in common with his brothers. Sympathy in us may be strong and comforting, but it is too vague to need definite forms, and it is too inarticulate to be able to create social institutions; in primitive man, sympathy is so overwhelming and so fundamental that it will determine all the forms of society without exceptions, and life within the different circles is so intense that it will realize itself in outward forms and laws.

The problem of primitive society cannot be solved by our hunting for a typical nucleus of society—either family or clan or tribe or horde—and explaining the manifold forms in existence as variations or evolutions of a fundamental system. The question before us assumes this form: how far will the inner force work in an actual culture? How small can the circle be, and what is its extreme possibility? What can the clan include and what is excluded beforehand?

If we watch the recurrence of names throughout the clans, we can gather an idea of the possible extent of kinship, because a family could not appropriate a name without the right involved by spiritual alliance. In the customs of name-giving as they shaped themselves in Scandinavia, we find some indications of the plasticity of the soul. The habit of naming after former kinsmen shows that to the soul belonged, first and foremost, to blood-kin in the direct ascending line. Often grandfather and great-grandfather are resurrected in the infant, when their demise occurred prior to his coming into the world. With the same frequency, grandfather's and father's brothers are called into life once more as soon as they have gone away.

Furthermore, the luck of the brothers-in-law is eagerly drawn into the clan, the child being named after its mother's father, mother's brother, or more distant kin on the distaff side, but the naming is not restricted to direct regeneration through the person of the mother. All the *hamingja* that belongs to the allied family lies open to the clan. Very often, younger brothers and sisters of the bridegroom or the bride will appear as living witnesses to the bridal pact between the two families; their father will freely remember his newly acquired brothers-in-law in children born after the marriage of his son or daughter. And even more prominent is the tendency to name children after people whom we might call secondary relatives-in-law, perhaps even in the third or fourth degree. After the alliance, the clan drew as a whole upon the brothers-in-law as a homogeneous whole.

In several of these respects the Vatsdoela family provides a comprehensive illustration, filled out as it is by family traditions that (whether historical in our narrower sense of the word or not) show what men thought of their own names.[95] The first man of the family standing forth in the full light of history is Thorstein, a Norwegian who, according to family tradition, won a bride from the kingly house of Gautland. When a son was born to Thorstein, he wished to nail the luck of the Gautland nobles to his family at once, and called the boy Ingimund after his wife's father. The fundamental truth of the family legend is vouched for by this name, which is decidedly not Norwegian but has a Gautland ring. Ingimund continued the two strands in his children. First, he remembered his own late father Thorstein, then in his second son he raised Jokul, the brother of his mother, and when a daughter was born to him he called her Thordis after his own mother, the Gautland princess. With his son Thorir, he sealed his own relationship with the renowned earls of Moeri in the west of Norway. Ingimund was married to a daughter of Earl Thorir the Silent.

With his other children, he reached out far into distant circles of kinship. Through an Icelandic branch of the Moeri family, he became related to a prominent chieftain, Thord Illugi. When an illegitimate son was born to Ingimund, he called him Smidr after Thord's son, Eyvind Smidr. Now Thord Illugi belonged directly through his father to the widely spreading family that was proud of tracing its descent back to Bjorn Buna, a petty king in Norway, and when another daughter was born to Ingimund, he remembered a Jorun of that ilk. Finally, his son Hogni is witness to the fact that Ingimund felt all the relations of the Bjorn Buna descendants as his kin, for one branch of that house intermarried with the descendants of a famous house of Norwegian kings in Hordaland, rich in legends that find an echo in *Hálfs saga*. And in this clan, Hogni the White was a

---

[95] This refers to the family described in *Vatsdoela Saga* (or *Vatnsdæla saga*), which is a five generations-long family chronicle following them through their residence in Norway to their settlement in Vatnsdal, a valley in northern Iceland.

prominent figure immediately before the time when Iceland was colonized. Thus, the Vatsdoela family gathered up luck and *hamingja* through a multitude of channels.

But the circle is not completed with mother's and father's side. The step-father's family may contain a fund of luck to which one would gladly have access. Such a custom accounts for the fact that Erling Skjalgson, who married a daughter of Astrid and Tryggvi and thus became brother-in-law of King Olaf Tryggvason, names one of his sons after Astrid's subsequent husband, Lodin. Erling's daughter was named Geirthrud, and there is a strong probability that this name, which is unprecedented in Norway, is derived from a queen Geira whom Olaf Tryggvason is said to have married in Vendland during his exile from Norway. So also former marriages may have laid the foundations of honor, which it was desirable to preserve for oneself and one's kin. When the poet Hallfreðr took unto himself a Swedish wife, he named their son after her former husband, and thus kept up the luck of the deceased Swede. The unruly Icelander Glum had a daughter, Thorlaug, who was married several times; in her last marriage, she gave birth to a son, and she renewed in him the curious name of her former husband, who was named Eldjarn.

Name-giving would undoubtedly reveal still further possibilities for the healthy greed of the soul, if our material were more extensive. At any rate, in several respects it allowed us to link up a connection between the dry registers of names and the history of the bearers. We may regard it as certain that both adoption and fostering have left their traces in the family archives, but indisputable instances can hardly be cited.

As far as these possibilities go, kinship has weight, and the moment frith is appealed to, men enter into a compact body in which no account is taken of far and near, but all are simply kinsmen to one another. Before a court of law, the individual's oath was valid only insofar as it carried with it the will of a whole family. Therefore, it had to be regularly supported by a circle of compurgators who confirmed with their conviction the assertion of the one who swore as principal. Here, the law can safely be content with demanding so and so many men of his kin, trusting that life in each individual case has beforehand determined who shall be included under that heading, and that the name of kinsman always covers a man who can take his place in the chain of oath.

The action of these kinsmen inwardly shows very soon that they are not a loosely assembled troop, held together by a vague feeling of opposition to all others. The unity they form has sufficient practical firmness to carry out the functions of a social organism. When it is a question of arranging life for a minor or giving away a kinswoman in marriage, then one of the clan stands forward as bearing the responsibility (viz, the natural guardian), or, if he should fall away, then the nearest of kin—son after father, then brother, and so on to the more distant kin, as the rules may run. But behind the individual, we discern for the most part a definite circle of men. We constantly find in the indications of the laws the kinsmen stepping forth out of the gloom, revealing themselves, not merely as interested parties in all important undertakings, but also claiming respect for their participation. When it is hinted that wards can seek protection among their kin against unwarrantable interference on the part of the guardian, or that the clan can step in where a guardian is found to be plundering instead of guarding, this precautionary right is only a pale survival from a time when the clan exercised the guardianship and the individual. Even the father himself only acted as the representative and executor of the kinsmen. The Anglo-Saxons express the full reality when they bring forward as negotiating parties the kinsmen of bride and bridegroom, respectively, at the ceremony of betrothal. They promise with one mouth everything that is to be promised, at the same time singling out one person, called the director of the bargain, to act on behalf of his party.

In the matter that most of all moved the soul of the clan—the matter of loss of life and revenge—the whole is molded into one as far as frith has yet any hold upon men's minds. In the everyday pictures of Icelandic life, the living sense is still effective before our eyes. The individual feels called upon to grasp a favorable moment as it comes, without thought of wasting time in reckoning out degrees of kinship near or far. Here and there, we find mention of family councils, where a leader of vengeance is invested with the full combined will of the clan as a proxy to take the responsibility for bringing the matter to a satisfactory conclusion. Whether such custom in early times was general throughout, or merely a form among others, it arises directly out of the clan feeling. On the other hand, under normal conditions the choice always fell upon the one who was nearest by birth to the right and duty in question: he who stood to the slain man via the relation of son to father, father to son, or brother to brother. The responsibility of the kinsmen increases in weight the nearer they stand to that center where the slain man lies. However difficult it may be to combine a common, unconditional obligation with foremost rank in responsibility for a single individual or a small group, when considering the world from the point of individualism or from the circle of community, the two facts coincide well enough for a man who lives his life in a *hamingja* and under social conditions shaped under its power.

In matters of such personal moments to the clan as marrying, guardianship, or revenge, a fixed definition was needed to exclude all but those concerned. This definition is everywhere among the Teutons contained in one single word: kinsmen, nothing more and nothing less. No other words, howsoever precisely circumscribed, could express more concisely which persons were concerned or which persons felt the responsibility, because the qualification depended on an inner solidarity, and not on a reckoning up of degrees. Life itself would in any actual case point out the men who were kinsmen of the deceased or of the orphan.

When we pass on to discuss the structure of the clan in particular, we probably cannot do better than to take the rules for payment and recaption of the weregild for our guide.[96] In Norway, the fine for homicide consisted chiefly of three "rings." The first ring was paid by the slayer to the nearest of kin of the slain: son and father. The second was called the brother's ring, and with this the slain man's brother was indemnified; the procuring of it was also a matter for a brother in the attacking circle. In the third ring, the two cousin-circles—father's brothers' sons—paid each other. The terms still suggest a time when rings were the usual forms of valuables. Lack of representative for one or another group did not affect the fine. The right to receive and the obligation to pay would in such case vest in one of the others, so that, to put an extreme case, the slayer himself paid all three rings, and the heir received the entire fine.

Payment of the three rings, however, was not sufficient to acquit the slayer and his nearest of kin from their obligation. Before them were still three further classes of kinsmen, each of which demanded a fine for the slain kinsman: from the degrees above, cousins, and below, brothers—uncles and nephews on the male side. They thinned out through mother's brother and sisters' sons to distant relatives on both sides. And when all these have taken the greater or smaller fines due to them from the ring men, they have still to reckon with some gifts from the corresponding circles in the clan of the slayer. Not until the whole of this network of fines has been drawn through the clans is frith declared from one side to the other.

In Denmark, the slayer and the slain man's son stand face to face, with their paternal and maternal kinsmen as a compact host on right and left. The fine is divided into three equal parts. Of these, the slayer pays (or his nearest of kin pays for him) one part; the two others pass from and to the two sides of the clan, and at the assembly of kinsmen, the obligations are divided into smaller and smaller claims, accordingly as the kinship ebbs farther and farther out. The two sides each answer for themselves. As long as a single man is left on the paternal side, the maternal kinsmen have no duty to pay more than their own share of the blood money. But if the branch is altogether withered, then the others must bear the double burden. So says Erik's Law in sure, old-fashioned speech that if it so happens that no kin are to be found on the mother's side, and he who was begotten of the slain should be slave-borne or out of the country so that none knows his kin, and if the father's kin have taken one part and another thereto, then their kinsman shall not be unpaid if he were a free man. In full he shall be paid—and the kinsmen on the father's side take all the fines. At the final peace meeting, where the slayer paid down the total amount of the fine in the presence of his

---

[96] A legal monetary amount assigned to a person's life to be paid if injury or death befalls that person at the hands of another.

kinsmen and of the slain man's family, the head man with twelve of his family promised him full frith and security.

The corresponding system obtaining among the Franks is unfortunately not clearly expressed in the laws. What was done when all went off as it should was known well enough, and it was not found worthwhile to enter such common places in the law book. But what was to be done in the case of a poor fellow who had not the wherewithal to pay was a matter that called for writing down—and this is consequently all we learn. Our position, then, is that of accidental spectators of an action reserved for extreme cases of necessity, forming their own conclusions as to the ordinary course of life by observing what people consider most urgent to do when matters have been brought to a dangerous pass.

The paragraph of the law introduces us into the midst of a scene, where the slayer has thrown all he owns into the scale without being able to make up the amount of the fine. He then solemnly, in the presence of his kinsmen, enters his house, takes there a handful of earth, and throws it upon his nearest of kin, thereby casting the responsibility from himself upon one who can bear it, before he himself takes his staff in hand and leaps the fence so all may see how denuded he is. If his father and brothers have already contributed all they could (and the law appears to take for granted that they would), then the handful of earth falls upon the nearest of kin outside their circle, and can thus pass down the ranks. Three kinsmen on the father's side and three on the mother's—each, of course, representing one branch of the family. If all have been obliged to let it lie, then the slayer shall be brought forward at the law-*thing*, to the end that any man feeling obligation toward him can step in, and not until he has been three times so received at the law-*thing* in silence has he forfeited his life as one who failed to produce his fine.

There we are left, wondering. Seeing that the ancient Franks did not play out their parts for our benefit, but were acting for their own poor selves, they have naturally left much in the dark, without so much as a single informative aside to the spectator. Whether the law here presumes that the slayer paid the whole of the fine or if it is his own ring, he could not manage to procure and had to leave to his kin. As to this, the spectators can, if so inclined, find matter for discussion for the remainder of their lives. But we are told in plain words in one passage that the fine is divided into two equal parts: one going to the son, the other to the kinsmen—further that these kinsmen are represented by three on either side, father's and mother's, and that the three divided their share with decreasing parts according to the nearness of relationship. And a kinsman has no rights save as he has corresponding obligations—or once had such.

There is more than a difference of circumstance between the Northman sitting with his kinsmen reckoning out sums in fractions of rings and fractions of kinship, and the Frank who makes his last leap over the threshold out of house and home stripped to his shirt. But the national peculiarities cannot hide profound unity in essentials. And perhaps the first thing that strikes the spectator is the common responsibility. The Northmen's geometry in the matter of fines may denote sharp heads—it certainly does mean also a pronounced need to see and feel whole family against whole family. In every imaginable way, the degrees are intercrossed in fine and counter-fine, class against class, and man against man.

The kinsmen are divided into groups, and the obligation falls according to class, but above all division stands the common responsibility. The fine must be procured, and if one side fails, then the others must step in to fill the gap. If one link is lacking in the chain of kinship, then the burden falls upon the next. The entire weight can roll over upon the kinsmen if the culprit himself is unable to pay, and it can fall back from a vacant place among the kinsmen upon the principal himself. And as a single side may often have to make additional sacrifices, so also as receivers they take any part unclaimed, for the principal point is that the fallen man shall be fully and duly paid for: "for their kinsman shall not be unpaid for. If he were a free man, in full he shall be paid for," to quote once more the weighty Old-World phrase of the Danish law book.

A remarkable indication of the honor due to a slain man from the slayer's kin is furnished by the law of Gotland. In this island, men had in Christian times set aside three churches as asylums, and "when it so happens that the Devil is at work and a man kills another, the slayer shall flee with father, son, and brother, and take refuge in the sanctuary. But if they are not alive, their places must be filled by other kinsmen." All must bear revenge as long as any portion of what is due remains unpaid: this is the fundamental principle among all Teutons, a principle that reveals its strength by forcing kings and prelates to contradict it in decrees and anathemas without end.

Only against the background of this elastic unity can the legal limitations that here and there occur be properly seen. There was often a need in later times, at any rate, for some rule as to where kinship might be held to cease, as also for a limit within which responsible men could always be found. When then three kinsmen on the father's and three on the mother's side were appointed as a permanent staff, or when "third degree" or seventh man were fixed as the extreme limit, the decision was naturally arrived at in the way life set it to be. The point chosen was where kinship generally ebbed out, or where it glided over into a wider personality, only to be felt by heavier pressure from outside. An interesting hint is given in a Danish law book: the share of the fine to be paid by each kinsman is continually halved for each degree the payer is removed from the slayer, but the share cannot fall to a lower amount than one *ortug* (one third of an ounce).

Thus, the question of the bounds of kinship is solved automatically by an ingenious device. A mere outline of the actual facts: this is all the law can be.

And much that in reality left a more than superficial mark upon the life of the community finds but an imperfect utterance in the schematic average of the laws. By chance, the Lombard edict includes foster brothers among those entitled to make oath. Likely, the solidarity of friendship was brought forward into a prominent place to supplement the clan ties that were loosening among the Lombards, but if the decree is inspired by the anxiety of the lawgivers to uphold the ancient legal system that required compurgators, it will be no less weighty as evidence of the intimate union of sworn brothers with the clan in earlier times. In Iceland, we know that the aid of foster brothers was invoked in matters of vengeance, and it is thus in accordance with the old spirit that certain Norse systems assign to them a right of receiving fines. In Christian times, when baptism created an intimate relationship between sponsor and godson, the spiritual affinity entered upon the rights and duty of the ancient institution. In England at least, the sponsor was entitled to blood money for his godchild. In reality, the limit was far too individually variable for any legal edict to deal with it without itself suffering dissolution.

But in the midst of the great circle, we soon become aware of a smaller group of men who are always found to be more restless than their surroundings. On the one side is the slayer and his house; on the other, the heirs. Even though, of course, the nearest of kin outside must step into the place of the culprit, and "take up his axe" if he himself, his father, and his brothers should be lacking, the obligation of the proxy cannot efface the picture of a minor *hamingja*. This the kinsman first and foremost feels as his soul, in which he ordinarily lives and moves and has his being. Included in this soul-kernel are those whom we should call the nearest of kin, but even this inner circle was not always or everywhere the same.

On this point, the rules for payment of fines cannot give more than a rough idea, and the only way of using the laws psychologically is to lay chief stress upon the discrepancies. In Denmark as well as in the Southern countries, as far as we can judge from the scanty indications, it is a sort of family group—father, son, and brother—which occupies the central position. On Norse ground it seems rather as if the soul extended crosswise through the clan, the strongest light falling upon son, brother, and cousins. The lawmen of the Frostathing even include father's brother and brother's son together with cousin and cousin's son in the narrowest community, thus reaching out a hand toward the Anglo-Saxons, who at any rate regarded the father's brother as a mainstay of the family. Or again, it may happen that father and son overshadow the brother to a certain degree, while elsewhere the brother stands out as a particularly near kinsman, responsible for the important second ring.

Within this narrow circle, there seems some trace discernible of daily intercourse in the steam from the common fleshpot and the smoke of the common hearth. It would then give a pretty theory if the great family represented the group of houses that stood back-to-back the better to resist storms and hard weather. But we do not find anywhere in Germanic society a pattern of so broad and simple a design. The partners found one another in the battle and arranged themselves in order of clan and kinship, it is said. And who would not believe it? And that the kinsmen kept more or less together locally, in those restless times, as well, when the people rather washed to and fro about the land than stayed firmly seated with each group on its own plot, is also more than reasonable. Caesar indeed says of the Suebi that they changed their fields from year to year, and their headmen portioned out annual holdings to the tribes and clans according to their superior wisdom. However, no one who can put himself in Caesar's place, as he stood looking at these human hordes, will think of taking the words as sentences based on results he had arrived at by an investigation of family relationship within the separate groups, or venture to conclude from such general statements that the local lines anywhere exactly coincided with the family figures.

Naturally, the structure of the soul had its counterpart in the social order. There is no doubt that clan feeling normally presupposed neighborly sympathy as a corroborating force, and certainly intercourse in the house during adolescence was also one cooperating factor (and a very strong one at that), but habitual companionship does not suffice to explain the soul unity that existed between kinsmen, nor is the force of frith dependent for its strength on acting in daily communion. When men entered a friendship of absolute solidarity, they might seal their covenant by promising "to act and avenge as were it son or brother." This old and significant formula must be supplemented by another old-fashioned phrase about two friends who have shared all things bitter and sweet together, "as if they were born two brothers." These words vibrate with an experience that does not necessarily coincide with the feeling of having been brought up together. But the innermost community of life was not restricted to descent from a common father.

The rules for paying blood money show abundantly that some of the mother's kinsmen—especially perhaps her brothers, but also her father and her brothers' and sisters' sons—formed a ring near the center of the clan, and any supposition that the maternal kinsmen owed their place to later changes in the family runs counter to the collective evidence of life and laws. Everybody who is fairly well-read in the history and literature of the Teutons will know how directly the invocation in case of need went out to the mother's kindred, and how readily her friends came forward to assist their kinsman. The solidarity is confirmed by one legend after another. When for instance the hero is sent to his mother's brother for good counsel, or when his taking vengeance for his mother's father is made the principal task of his life, the deed shall set him up as a man of honor. It is indicated also in proverbs such as that to the effect that a man takes after his mother's brothers most. Tacitus himself understood as much, since he finds himself constrained to interpolate the observation that a particularly warm affection exists between uncles and sister's sons.

The clan is not an amplified family, but on the other hand, any theory that would square the facts by reducing the group of father and sons to insignificance is doomed from the start.

XVI. Genealogy

The most thoroughgoing attempt to enter the kinsmen into a comprehensive system was made in Norway. In its rules for the payment of weregild, the Gulathing's Law arranges the participants into three groups of men, each of whom has to pay or receive one of the principal rings, but to these "ring men" are added three classes of other kinsmen who are called receivers, or *uppnámamenn*—because they can lay claim to certain additional fees.

In the first group of receivers are those such as father's brother, brother's son, mother's father, and daughter's son. The second group is composed of brother's daughter's son, mother's brother, sister's son, and cousin through father's sister and mother's brother. In the third group, we finally meet mother's sister's son, cousin's son, father's cousin, maternal grandmother's brother, and sister's daughter's son. Apart from these receivers, there are some additional parties to the cause called *sakaukar* (i.e., additional receivers). Counted among them are the son and brother whose mother was slave-born, and half-brothers having the same mother. But the enumeration is not yet complete. The law still adds a new group consisting of men attached to the clan by marriage: the man who has a man's daughter, he who has his sister, further, stepfather and stepson, sworn brother, and foster brother.

These tables are complicated enough to produce something of a roundabout feeling in a modern head, unaccustomed to following family mathematics beyond sums with two or three factors. What a relief, then, to be able to settle down among the Norsemen's less ingenious brothers, with the reflection that artificial systems must have their root in artificial forms. But simplicity—which is to say, something convenient to the pattern *our* brains are built on—is unfortunately, after all, no infallible criterion of age. Complications also arise when a complex feeling, which in practice always goes surely, has to reckon out all its instinctive movements in figures, and struggles with itself until it stands agape before its own inscrutability.

Before accusing the Norwegian lawyers of modern tendencies or of innovations, we must first make sure that their ingenuity has affected a system running counter to ancient clan feeling and affirming a modern family conscience, but the rules for distributing the fines are particularly designed to place all these people in categories running athwart all calculations in lines and degrees. They are herded together—father's brother, brother's son, daughter's son, mother's father by themselves, mother's brother, brother's daughter's son, sister's son by themselves—in groups that certainly cannot have been invented for the purpose of schematizing nearness of kin according to our genealogical principles. And it ought to give us pause that the lawyer in another place, after having struggled to gather the rules of inheritance into a regular system, ends with a resigned appeal to individual judgment of actual cases; for the rest each must manage to make it out for himself: "so manifold are the ways of kinship between men that none can make rules for all inheritance, a cause arising must be judged as is deemed best according to its nature." The group arrangement is undoubtedly based on a principle having broad premises in the Teutons' mode of thought.

It is obvious that here is a man who struggles to force refractory ideas into a system that was not made for him. And this is the difficulty more or less of all Teutonic laws: they are put to the attempt of transposing clan feeling into a reckoning of kindred in degrees and generations that was foreign to indigenous ideas. Latin civilization made history grow like branches or twigs on family trees, and in men's relations with one another, it recognized only this formula: father begot son, and son begot son's son. The Icelanders learned the art of making chronological history and genealogical trees, and even rose to be masters of the profession. Their wits were considerably sharpened by the revolution in all family matters that was the consequence of their emigrating with kith and kin into a new country, and their minds were enlightened by intimate intercourse with people of the western isles.

Thus, it comes that the family history after the colonization of Iceland is a system of clear genealogical lines, while all history before that event is conceived in another spirit and expressed in myths, as we call a form with which we are unfamiliar. On the emigrants' island, the simplest peasant knew every detail of his status by descent and by marriage from the first settlement in the country; among the first settlers, very few knew more than their grandfather, and all the prominent figures of history are introduced with a father and, at most, a grandfather.

Even in the royal family itself, Harald Fairhair's father represents the end of history. Harald's contemporary, the powerful earl of Moeri, can hardly be said to have more than a grandfather. The same applies to Haakon Sigurdsson of Lade, while his most dangerous opponent, Earl Atli of Gaular, is registered in history as his father's son. The noblest born of all the original settlers in Iceland, Geirmund, whose forefathers were kings by full right, had to pass down into history as merely the son of Hjor. All that lies behind these two or three prehistoric generations is myth. And while the Icelandic peasants, with their pride of race, made themselves leaders of Europe in scientific accuracy of reckoning, we find in Norway no great change in men's genealogical sense. As late as the eleventh and twelfth centuries, we find prominent families entering into history in a strangely abrupt fashion:

> A man was called Finnvid the Found. He was discovered in an eagle's nest, swathed in silken garments. From him descends the family called the Arnunga race. His son was Thorarin Bulliback, his son Arnvid, who was the father of Earl Arnmod. He is the ancestor of the Arnmodlings.

This is the simple genealogy of Norwegian grandees of the eleventh century. Generally, the pedigrees lead through a couple of links to a barrow—for instance Bardi, the princeling who was buried in Bardistad, or Ketil, who lies in Vinreid. Exactly the same peculiarity is met with in the Anglo-Saxon traditions about the ancestors of the kingly races in Great Britain.

New organs did not grow forth suddenly in the brains of Englishmen or Icelanders. They had learned at home to keep faith with the past, and steadfastly to keep it alive; they only reshaped the old tradition on a new basis. Earlier, too, men had cherished their family history, handing it down from generation to generation, but in a form that fitted with a view of time as a plane, and the soul as a thing ever present.

Luckily, we are not left to speculate vaguely how the Northmen reckoned their kin before becoming acquainted with the genealogies of the South. Among the literary remains of Scandinavia are found a couple of poems that introduce us to the circle in the hall of the chief, listening when his mighty *hamingja* is praised and his ancestors enumerated. The Eddic poem of *Hyndluljód* is certainly not as it stands a pure family piece; it has been retouched by a poet versed in the poetic fashions of the Viking Age, and by him embellished with some additions from the mythological stock-in-trade. But the additions only affect the framework of the poem: the core is a Norwegian family pedigree as it used to be cited in the ancestral hall. The center of the poem is a young atheling called Ottar, evidently belonging to a noble race of Western Norway, and the words, slightly abbreviated, run thus:

Ottar was born of Innstein, and Innstein of Alf the Old, Alf of Ulf, Ulf of Saefari, Saefari of Svan the Red.

Your mother's name was Hiedis, a woman in noble rings and necklaces she was whom your father took for his honored wife. Her father was Frodi, and her mother Friaut. All that race were reckoned among the great.

Formerly lived Ali richest of men, and earlier still Halfdan, highest among Scyldings. All can tell of the great battles that the bold hero held.

He joined with Eymund, high in worth among men, and slew Sigtrygg with cool sword edge. He brought home Almveig, high in worth among women; eighteen sons were born to that pair.

Thence came the Scyldings, thence the Scilfings, thence Audlings and Ynglings; from them proud franklins, from them chieftains—all these are your race.

Hildigunn was her mother, daughter of Svava and Saekonung—all are your kin. Mark well, it means much that you know this. And now hear yet more.

Dag married Thora, mother of heroes; in that race were born champions before all others: Fradmar and Gyrd and the two Freki, Am, Josurmar, and Alf the Old. Mark well, it means much that you know this.

Their friend was called Ketil, Klyp's heir; he was mother's father to your mother. There was Frodi and before him Kari and earlier yet was born Alf.

Then Nanna, Nokkvi's daughter—her son was kin by marriage to your father. It is an old kinship, and yet more I can count, both Broddi and Horfi—these are all your kin.

Isolf and Asolf, Olmod's sons, with their mother Skurhild, daughter of Skekkil. To many men you may count yourself akin. All are your race, Ottar.

In Bolm in the East were born the sons of Arngrim and Eyfura, the berserks who rushed destroying over land and sea as fire leaps.

I know both Broddi and Horfi: they served among the king's men of Hrolf the Old.

All born from Ermanaric, kinsman by marriage to Sigurd who slew the dragon.

This king was descended from Volsung, and Hjordis [Sigurd's mother] was of Hraudung's kin, but Eylimi [her father] was descended from the Audlings—all are your kin.

Gunther and Hogni, heirs of Gjúki, and Gudrun their sister . . . all are your kin.

Harald Wartooth born of Hroerek, son he was of Aud, Ivar's daughter, but Radbard was Randver's father. These men were consecrated to the gods—strong, holy kings—all are your kin.

The poet then passes on to the enumeration of the gods of the clan.

The reckoning up of Ottar's ancestors is not based on conceiving and begetting. The poem enumerates a number of *hamingjas* that belonged to Ottar and his kinsmen. In the middle stand, as the main stem of the clan, Ottar, his father and mother with their nearest of kin, and about them are ranged a multitude of circles overlapping one another. Some are based on begetting, others on marriage, and others again perhaps on fostering. Among these *hamingjas* are pure Norwegian clans such as that Horda-Kari clan indicated by Klyp and Olmod, a famous race that attained renown in Iceland with the lawgiver Ulfljot, and wrote itself into Norway's history as Erling Skjalgson of Soli. There are families from the East, such as that who is introduced by Angantyr of Bolm in Sweden. There are Danish stocks such as the Scyldings. And the connections of Ottar even reach beyond the frontiers of Scandinavia and draw the luck of Volsungs and Burgundians into his soul.

Within these circles there may occur some indications of fatherhood and sonhood placing the men in relation to one another, but parallel to these indications run phrases that merely affirm how this or that hero "was" or "lived" in former times, or state that "this is an old kinship."

Another poem recording the pride of a Norwegian family is the *Ynglingatal*. This monumental poem is composed by one of the greatest skalds of the ninth century, Thjodolf, in honor of a petty king called Ragnvald Heidumhære. In this poem, the kinsmen of Ragnvald are reckoned up in a direct line to the divine kings of Uppsala, and though there are no indications in the verses that one king begot the next, the commentators are perhaps not so very far from the mark when they suppose it to have been Thjodolf's intention to connect the ancestors into a genealogical line. The *Ynglingatal* is probably a compromise between the old system and the more fashionable form of pedigrees that was coming in. This way of translating ancient facts into modern style can be illustrated by the Anglo-Saxon pedigrees in which the groups of ancestors are piled one on another into a ladder. The original arrangement sometimes shows through the fact that a founder of a race or a god is automatically put into the middle of the list and made the son of mortal men. Thus also Thjodolf's *Ynglingatal* shows traces of the process of adaptation: the old circle system peeps through the lines.

The verses of Thjodolf are compressed and often obscure—to us—because the poet, as already indicated, was not compiling a historical narrative, but hinting at facts well-known in the hall of his employer. Snorri has added a commentary that is partly drawn out of the verses by an ingenious reader, and that partly no doubt rests on additional data that he has evidently elicited by interrogating persons acquainted with the family.

After the poet has, in the first verses, proved divine descent from Freyr through Sveigdir and Fjolnir,[97] he begins with Vanlandi the series of the earthly kings,[98] and loosely paraphrased the poem as follows:

> Vanlandi met his death through witchcraft. The troll-born woman crushed him with her feet, and the king's pyre flamed in the banks of the river Skuta.[99]
>
> Visbur was swallowed by the fire, when the sons urged the mischievous destroyer of the forest against their father, so that he bit the great prince to death in the hall.[100]
>
> In former days, it came about that sword-men reddened the earth with their own lord's blood, when the Swedes, in hope of good harvest, bore bloody weapons against Domaldi, hater of the Jutes.[101]
>
> Domar was placed on the pyre at Fyrir, when deathly illness had bitten that atheling of Fjolnir's race.
>
> Came the time when Hel should choose a kingly hero, and Dyggvi, ruler of the Yngvifolk, fell before her grip.
>
> Thirsting for fame, Dag followed the bidding of death, when he set out for Vorvi to avenge his sparrow.
>
> Surely the deed of Skjalf did not please the warrior host when she, the queen, hoisted Agni, their rightful king, up in his own necklace and let him ride the cool horse of the gallows.[102]
>
> Alaric fell what time he and Eric, the brothers, bore arms one against the other. Those two kinsmen of Dag struck each other with bits. Freyr's children have never before been known to use horse gear in battle.
>
> Yngvi fell. He was left lying when Alf, the guardian of the altar, envious, reddened his sword. It was Bera who made two brothers each the other's bane.[103]
>
> Jorund was robbed of his life long ago in the Limfjord. The rope's horse carried high the king who had formerly taken Gudlaug's life.[104]

---

[97] Frey: A Norse god of fertility, crops, and prosperity (alternatively spelled Frey); Fjolnir: A legendary Norse king said to be son of Freyr. He is most well-known for drunkenly falling into a vat of mead and drowning.

[98] A mythological Yngling king at Uppsala.

[99] Vanlandi was crushed by a nightmare. He had married a Finnish princess and had left his bride, never to return. His wife hired a sorceress to draw him to Finland by charms, or else to kill him. (Author's note)

[100] Visbur deserted his first queen, and her sons avenged her. (Author's note)

[101] Starvation reigned in the land, and when all other means to stop the misfortune failed, the Swedes sacrificed their king. (Author's note)

[102] Agni warred on Finland and led a princess captive. On the bridal night, when the king was in his cups, she tied a rope to his costly necklace and flung it over a bough overhead. (Author's note)

[103] Bera, Alf's queen, preferred his brother Yngvi. (Author's note)

[104] Jorund was killed by the Norwegian king Gylaug in revenge of his father Gudlaug. (Author's note)

Aun longed for life, till he drank horn for milk as a child; with his sons' lives he bought life for himself.[105]

Egil, Tyr's atheling, great of fame, fled the land, and the end of that atheling of the Scilfings' race was the ox that drove its head-sword into his heart.[106]

Ottar fell beneath the claws of the eagles at Vendil before Frodi's Danes. The Swedes could tell of the island-kingdom's earls, who slew him when he offered battle.[107]

Adils, Freyr's atheling, fell from his horse, and there died, Ali's foe, when his brains were mingled with the dust at Uppsala.[108]

The hall flamed to ruin about Eystein at Lofund; men of Jutland burned him in the house.

The word went out that Ynguar had fallen before the folk-host of Estonia; the Eastern Sea delights the Swedish king with its songs.

Onund, enemy of the Ests, fell before the hate of the mistress' son. Hard stones covered the slayer of Hogni.[109]

Fire, the roaring house thief, trod through Ingjald with hot feet at Raening. His death was famous among the Swedes because the atheling of the gods living kindled his own pyre.[110]

The glowing fire loosened the war dress of the Swedish king Olof; this scion of the Lofdungs disappeared from Uppsala long ago.

Halfdan was sadly missed by the peacemakers when he died on Thoten, and Skaereid in Skiringssal droops over the remains of the king.

Eystein went to Hel struck by the boom onboard the ship; the Gautland king rests under stones where Vadla's chilly stream meets the sea.

Halfdan, who had his seat at Holtar, was buried by victorious men at Borro.

Godrod, who lived long ago, was foully slain by Asa's thrall on the shore of Stiflusund.[111]

In ancient days, Olaf ruled over Upsi and Vestmar and the kingdom of Grenland,[112] a godlike prince. Stricken by disease, the brave leader of hosts lies in his barrow at Geirstad.

---

[105] Aun sacrificed one of his sons every tenth year to prolong his own life. (Author's note)

[106] Egil, who had several times been driven from his land by a rebel, was at last killed when out hunting, by a savage bull. (Author's note)

[107] Ottar had dealings with Frodi, the king of Denmark. (Author's note)

[108] Adils is known by Snorri as the antagonist of King Ali of Norway and King Hrolf of Zealand. (Author's note)

[109] The commentary does not say why Onund had killed Hogni, or who the mistress' son who avenged him was. (Author's note)

[110] Ingjald had dealings with the kings of Scania, and when he was taken unaware by Ivar the Wide-grasping, he buried himself and all his warriors under the blazing beams of his own hall. (Author's note)

[111] Godrod had killed Asa's father and married her against her will. (Author's note)

[112] Grenland is a district in the county of Vestfold og Telemark in Norway.

> The best name of mark borne by king under the blue of heaven is Rag-
> nvald's who is called Heidumhære.

The center of the picture is occupied by Ragnvald with the proud title of Heidumhære, the meaning of which is unfortunately lost to us. He ruled at Geirstad
in the south of Norway about 900. His father, Olaf Geirstad-Alf, is well-known
from other fragments of the mythical lore of the clan. No doubt he is a historical
king, but his humanity is half-merged into divinity—as shown by his surname,
Geirstad-Alf, which means the god or patron of Geirstad. In other words, Olaf is
the hero and father of the house. One line—the direct one upwards—of Ragnvald
comes to an end with him.

Above him, there is a clearly marked circle in the line from Godrod to Olaf
and Halfdan. This list of names that may or may not represent a direct succession
of fathers and sons forms an important branch of Ragnvald's *hamingja*, namely
the branch by which the petty king of Geirstad was connected with the family
that conquered Norway, through the person of Harald Fairhair. The unity of this
circle is attested by the fact that the names Olaf, Halfdan, and Godrod are per-
petuated in Harald Fairhair's dynasty. The field of activity of this clan lies in the
boundary lands between Norway, Sweden, and Denmark.

Taken together with the fragments of family legends, which the author of
the *Ynglinga* saga has happily unearthed, these verses give a picture of Westfold
kings. These kings fought and befriended small princelings from the south of
Norway, but also had dealings with the kings of adjacent east (i.e., Gautland),
which formed a region of its own in those days, half-independent, between Norway and the ancient kingdom of Uppsala. This connection is sealed by Ingjald,
who by his name and through his queen Gauthild, is intimately bound up with
Gautland. Ingjald's place in the world is indicated by the tradition that he succumbs before Ivar the Widegrasping (Vidfadmi), a conqueror king of Scania in
the south of modern Sweden.

Above this fundamental stock, we can discern various groups, though it is
not always possible to point out the exact spot where they join. Through Adils
and his father Ottar, we are introduced to a world viewed from another angle in
Beowulf. According to Snorri and the Northern sources, which are dependent
mainly on the family legends of Norwegian princes, Adils fought with Hrolf
Kraki of Zealand without gaining much honor, and won glory by defeating Ali
from the Upplands (or, in other versions, from Norway).

In the Anglo-Saxon poem—descended from another family legend—a vista
is opened into a little world where four princely clans meet in battle and carouse.
Foremost in fame are the Scyldings or Spear-Danes of Leire in Zealand,
Heorogar and Hrothgar, and in the younger generation, Hrothulf. And rivalling
these mighty spear-men, the Heathobards come into prominence: Froda and his

son Ingeld, who was unhappily married to a Scylding princess, the daughter of Hrothgar. On one side stand the Geats or Gautland-men (Hygelac foremost), and on the other side, the "Swedes": Ohthere and Eadgils and their kinsman Onela (Ali), who usurps the kingdom and is slain by his nephew Eadgils. It is a story of feuds and friendships between district kings in South Scandinavia before the time when the North had crystallized into three ethnographical and political groups: Sweden, Norway, and Denmark. To the same circle as Adils belongs undoubtedly Aun the Old. Though perhaps not identical with the Eanmund known to *Beowulf* as Eadgils' brother, he bears witness in his name to kinship with the Swedes, for the family mark Ead is contained in Aun, though obscured by phonetical changes.

An entirely different circle is represented by Yngvar and Onund. They turn their faces to the East, to the Swedish Viking lands of Estonia, where Yngvar fell before the folk of the continent, and Onund, the foe of the Ests, avenged him.

Within the upper portion of the family register we can discern at least two clan circles.

One has for its center the unlucky brothers Eric and Alaric, who slew each other while out hunting, and the sons Alf and Yngvi, who quarreled over a woman.

They are connected by a family fate, and their history is foreshadowed in Vanlandi, Visbur, and Agni. This family is marked by all its men being vanquished by woman's counsel. We have here a race of kings whose *aldr* or *hamingja* had a peculiar taint, giving them into the hands of their women. Now these kings belong to another part of the world, as is proved by the fact that their expeditions are confined to Finland—there they harried, there they procured their wives, thence came the troll-born nightmare who trampled Vanlandi to death. In these men we are confronted with the renowned family of Ynglings whose seat was at Uppsala.

Finally, in this group is interpolated another series: Domaldi, Domar, Dyggvi, and Dag. Where they belong it is hard to say. Domar is called an Yngling, and is burned at Fyrir in Uppland. Dyggvi is also referred to the Yngvi clan, whereas Domaldi is hinted at as the enemy of the Jutes. But this much is certain: with Dag, we are suddenly back in Norway once more, or at least in regions comparatively near. Not only does he recur again and again in the family registers of the Norwegian kings, but his name crops up among the children of Harald Fairhair. Without doubt, he is the mythical ancestor of a chiefly clan, the Daglings, in the southern parts of Norway or Sweden, and it is possibly through this family that Ragnvald is connected with the Ynglings. There are also some hints in other pedigrees that Dyggvi and his mother Drot were recognized by the descendants of Harald Fairhair as belonging to their ancestors, and in their genealogical tables they are brought in as descending from Dag. This does not at all prove that Dyggvi is really descended from Dag, but merely that the Daglings possessed the *hamingja* of Dyggvi and transmitted it through some alliance to the kingly race of Norway.

In the *Ynglingatal*, we catch a glimpse of a family tradition working on the same lines with the *Hyndluljód*. All this shows abundantly that to understand the clan feeling and clan system of ancient times, we must revise our ideas of kinship altogether, and replace our genealogical tree with other images. Kinship was viewed from the standpoint of an individual family, the center of a number of non-concentric rings, and thus the reckoning of relationship in one clan did not hold well for other families as to persons who were common kinsmen to both. The circles were foreshortened in different ways, as we may express the fact in our mathematical language. We cannot get history in our sense by comparing related genealogies and synchronizing their data into our chronological system.

Ragnvald Heidumhære and Harald Fairhair had a paternal grandfather in common, and would, according to our reckoning, be actual cousins. But the *Ynglingatal* was not Harald's pedigree, neither could it be made to tally with his clan feeling, as we very well know through the genealogical lists of the royal family. Harald shares Godrod and Halfdan with his cousin Ragnvald, but these ancestors do not in Harald's case lead up to the Ynglings, but to Norwegian origin. He touches the *hamingja* of his cousin through Dag and through Ingjald and Frodi, all of whom reappear in the ancestry of the king, but these kinships do not extend eastward and connect him with the Swedes. To be sure, when Harald in his past has the sequence of Eric to Alaric, we are fully justified in recognizing something of the fateful family will that rings so loudly through the *Ynglingatal*. This *hamingja* entered into the luck of Harald, but it was far less extensive. And at all other points, the two families run each their own course, and that course is determined by a different tendency in the family luck. The Harald family shows its ambition by incorporating in its *hamingja* the luck of the Danish Viking chieftains and conquerors, as is proved by the presence of Ivar the Widegrasping and the Ragnar athelings in its registers. And through these rising clans of the unruly times in the dawn of Northern history, this Norwegian family reaches farther outward to the Scyldings and the Volsungs of the Franks.

Among Harald's ancestors were Sigurd the dragon slayer and the Nibelungs famous in Northern song. Consequently, in Harald's family, the divine places are not occupied by Freyr and Yngvi, but by Odin and Scyld, the hero ancestor of the Scyldings.

It is always necessary to keep firm hold of the end personage in the list: the man from whom the race is viewed. If he is lost, and the table thus lose its family mark, we can never reconstruct its value. And where links drop out, they can never be set right again by comparison with another pedigree, not even by that of a cousin by blood.

The circles drawn into the community of life, either by marriage or in any other way, are not washed out of their former connections before entering the pale of friendship and kinship. Each family carried along with it the honor, luck, and fate that constituted its soul, and by becoming kin by marriage, Ottar or Ragnvald acquired the ancestors of his new brothers-in-law.

To modern readers, there is a difference not of degree, but of quality between such matter-of-fact persons as Klyp or Olmod, and a dragon slayer like Sigurd Fafnirsbane—who belongs to poetry, as we would say. But the difficulty is all on our side. In ancient times, Sigurd was a kinsman just as real as any historical person. A good many Norwegian and Icelandic families felt affinity with the famous slayer of the dragon and his Burgundian brothers-in-law.

All these clans had lawfully and rightfully acquired the Frankish and Burgundian *hamingja* by marrying or otherwise concluding vital alliance with circles possessing the deeds of the Southern heroes. We are still able to point out the links which connected the families of the North with the mighty clans on the Rhine. How Harald Fairhair acquired the right to enter Burgundian, Frankish, and Gothic kings among his ancestors is clearly shown through his pedigree. His family is connected with Danish kings who claimed kinship with the Ragnar house, and these kings had ancestors who were allied to princes in Russia or on the southern shores of the Baltic. Some Icelandic families evidently concluded the alliance that brought Sigurd into their *hamingja* during their expeditions to the western isles, where they settled temporarily and were brought into contact with descendants of Danish Viking clans, first and foremost that of the sons of Ragnar Lodbrok.

In the case of Ottar, we are not without some hints as to how he came into possession of such a far-off *hamingja* as that working in Sigurd and the Burgundian kings who ruled in Worms.[113] It has already been pointed out that some persons in the *Hyndluljóð* indicate a relationship between the hero of the poem and the family whose most powerful member was Erling Skjalgson, the "king" of the Rugians. Erling married Astrid Tryggvi's daughter, a great-grandchild of Harald Fairhair, and thus became brother-in-law of the Norwegian king Olaf Tryggvason. It is not unlikely that Erling and the *Hyndluljóð* are nearly contemporary, and in Erling's marriage we have possibly an explanation as to how Danish and Southern *hamingja* had filtered into leading families of Western Norway.

These facts suggest another view of ancient poetry and saga than the purely literary theory current now, which rests on the rather naive acceptance of modern literary conditions as applying to all times and cultures. Poems and novels are to us substantial wares brought to market by poets and handed in books over the counter to customers tendering a fixed price. But the sagas and poems of ancient

---

[113] The capital of the First Kingdom of Burgundy, located along the Upper Rhine.

times were property belonging to individual persons, the self-revelations of particular clans. The sagas do not rest on an author, but on an owner—one who acknowledges the past as it is here set forth, maintains it as his own, is proud of it, and depends on it. The true saga, that which in its inmost essence is inspired by repetition by word of mouth, has in reality never worked its way loose from the personal mandate. Even the Icelandic sagas, which in artistic form are strongly influenced by European literature, still bear the birthmark of being told from the point of view of a clan, and expressing the clan's private past.

The *Völsunga saga* is the prelude to Ragnar Lodbrok's, and it ends with Hofdithord, the chieftain of Skagafjord and fifth man from the famous Viking chief, according to the reckoning of the *Landnáma*. *The Saga of Hervor and Heidrek*—the saga of the sword Tyrfing—bears its stamp of proprietorship in the genealogies at the end, referring to a Norwegian and Icelandic family—the Angantyr clan—which prided itself on its connections with the kingly house of Sweden. *Beowulf* has become regular literature in the hand of the late poet, but on a closer scrutiny of the West Saxon pedigrees with their Beow and Scyld, we may get an inkling of the circle in which the interest for the legends was fostered.

In accordance with our notions of the ways of poets who borrow their themes from neighboring literatures and imitate their predecessors in the craft, we talk of the ancient legends as wandering from land to land, and we build up ingenious speculations as to how the Sigurd saga passed from the Franks on the Rhine to the skalds of the North. But in reality, the songs or legends were not handed about loosely: they lived their way through the world from one circle of people to another. These are indeed not legends at all, not poetic treasures, but experiences that are kept living and creative in human souls. They have been passed on from place to place by tingeing soul, in the sense that mind was drawn into mind and made to participate in the honor it held. They went with the maiden when, rich in noble ornaments, she entered into her husband's home and brought with her an honor strong in mind and compelling to action. They spread when a man mingled himself with his foster brother and became a part of him, received his forefathers, received his deeds, received his thoughts, and was bound by his *hamingja*. The predominance of the Volsung deeds and fate in Scandinavian poetry testifies to the fact that the honor of the Volsungs was a treasured heirloom in some of the leading, most influential families of the Viking period.

Going back to the *Hyndluljód* as the truest picture of an ancient clan, we see now that the circles enumerated belong to Ottar and his kinsmen as wholes. All that the allied families had and were flowed into the man's luck. And this spiritual amalgamation is of greater depth than we at first imagine, because Ottar's kindred were not principally a number of persons, but a mass of deeds—luck, honor, and "fate." The names of the pedigree are clothed with epithets and short descriptive phrases indicating the life that had throbbed in the old heroes and pulsated from them into their descendants, the happenings and achievements in which their honor had manifested itself. We cannot understand the poem as it was understood by the Old-World listeners, because to them every epithet and every line called up a host of memories. Our compositions tell a story to an audience wishing to know how it all happened, how it began and how it ended. The ancient poems were only reminders or hints by which deeds that lived in men's minds were called forth and made vivid before their eyes.

The family is primarily a *hamingja*, and as a soul it is incorporated into new kinsmen. The persons are only representatives of the *hamingja*, and their power consists in their having been able to regenerate the life rich in distinctive features that flowed through their ancestors. The *hamingja* is always something present, and the past is only real insofar as its fate has been renewed again and again in a sequence of transient generations. These old heroes have never been outside reality. A Sigurd, a Hrolf, a Ragnar have come to life again and again, have been born forward from clan to clan. They have been ancestors whose deeds were revived in fresh human lives.

The *hamingja* is a present thing, and it is a living whole, not a complex being split up into a number of persons. We see from the example of a Harald or from that of an Ottar how a world met within the individual human being. In the king of Norway they crowd together: Norwegian village kings and chieftains who fought, married, and added to their *hamingja*, Danish throne kings with a mass of deeds welling forth from the nothingness of earliest time, together with heroic clans who lived and battled on the Rhine or in the plains of Russia. It is a whole world, not only countries wide but centuries deep. All differences of time perish in the living renewal that is contained in a couple of generations.

The ancestors, then, are not figures seated in state on a lofty pile of years reached by laborious climbing through degrees and generations. The modern and the ancient ideas as to the founder of a race are far apart. When we lack the number of rings required to make a decent ladder, we must hide our heads among the ephemeral crowd of those who may indeed confess to being, but cannot pretend to have been. The old progenitor simply resided within his children if he existed at all, and his heir grasped him directly by thrusting a hand into his own breast. Thus, the brother-in-law or the friend immediately draws the old hero into his *hamingja* by touching his kinsmen, and after having mingled blood and mind with his new brothers, he feels the ancestor's power in his own limbs.

This suggests a history of another structure than ours, not a chronological series of occurrences hanging on the pegs of dates, but living events coming to light again and again throughout subsequent generations—in slightly different shapes, perhaps, but substantially the same. History to us is something past and done with, a crystallization of completed incidents that can neither be obliterated nor in the least affected by later developments. Primitive history, on the other hand, is living and changing. Not only do later phases rearrange the events into new patterns, but if history does not propagate itself, it disappears, and the events sink into the same nothingness that covers events that never came to be. Primitive history lacks certain time proportions that to us are the foundation of all historical truth, and consequently it cannot wield the blocks of the centuries and build them up to towering pyramids. But primitive and ancient historians can do one thing that we cannot or have not yet been able to do: they can give the past as a whole explaining the present, whereas our history can be nothing but disconnected figures.

The secret of the incompatibility of the two systems lies in the fact that, whereas our history forms a general self-existing organism outside the experience of all individual men, primitive and ancient history is the belonging of clans and peoples. The latter form is incomprehensible to modern men whose lives are arranged in years, and moreover, never merge into one another, but run on each in its own particular grove. Consequently, ancient traditions are naively set down by us as caprice or fanciful legend-mongering. In fact, the chasm is so great between the systems (historical though they both may be) that facts cannot by any key be translated from one mode into the other. It is labor lost to analyze "myths" in legendary and historical elements in order to elicit a "kernel of truth."

Thus, the problem of the structure of the Teutonic clan solves itself. It is a waste of labor to seek a rigid system behind the laws, and it is more useless still to search for a universal Germanic system of which the later schemata are variations. The problem is primarily psychological rather than social; the form of the clan depends more on an inner structure than on an outer organization. All who had the same thoughts and traditions, the same past, and the same ambitions possessed one soul and were of one clan. This inner structure must necessarily develop itself into a strong external organism, but the force worked in living bodies of men that were eminently amenable to the plastic touch of circumstances and might take different patterns among different peoples. There is no earthly reason to suppose that the Norwegians and the Danes, or the Lombards and the Anglo-Saxons ever had exactly the same social and legal customs.

The clan was a living whole, now wider, now narrower, varying in accordance with the strength of the *hamingja*, and adapting itself to the moment. It had as its core a body of friends that could never split up into fragments. This nucleus was never identical with the family or the father's house. Not only did it comprise the brothers-in-law, but it extended literally in the breadth as is indicated by the juxtaposition of sons and brothers' sons in the same category. Under the stress of the moment, and under actual political conditions, it might swell out into the dimensions of a tribe or even a people. Normally, the state was not a *hamingja*; the clans were held together by allegiance to a chief, and by membership in a legal order centered in the law-*thing* or moot place where people met several times a year. This legal community did not prevent the clans from asserting their rights severally and from carrying on feuds among themselves; the law-*thing* meant only that differences among the members could be brought before the community and settled either by sentence or mediation according to compelling forms. But when the people acted unanimously—in war, in expeditions, in any common enterprise whatsoever—all the individual *hamingjas* melted into one, and one frith reigned supreme with one honor through the entire corporation. At such times, killing was murder and villainy.

There is no make-believe in primitive and ancient society. The comrades are really one *hamingja*, and consequently one body. When the fellowship loosened and everyday forms regained their sway, the *hamingja* of the whole slept or was temporarily suspended, as we would say, but it did not cease to exist.

Among the Teutons, this larger *hamingja* was generally (though not necessarily) that of the king or chieftain. In wartime, his luck absorbed the lucks of his followers, and thus his gods and ancestors became the gods and ancestors of the whole people. In history, it is not possible to distinguish between the king's clan and the people he led, simply because the two were identical in their relations with foreign bodies.

"Without rebirth, no eternity": to gauge the fullness of this sentence is a necessary condition for understanding what it means to have life, and to die so that none knows one's name.

GLOSSARY

*Note that due to the naming conventions of the Teutons, names are sorted
alphabetically by first name, not last name. Lifespans are given for definite
historical figures (as opposed to legendary figures) if known.*

Ægir, Aegir: Jötunn and personification of the sea within Norse mythology.

Æsir (sing. áss): Principle pantheon of Norse gods, including Odin, Thor, Loki, Heimdall, etc.

Alaric and Eric, Alrekr and Erikr: Two kings who shared rule of Sweden. According to the
Ynglinga saga, it is said that their bodies were found in a field in such a manner as to suggest
the two men dueled with each other and both died.

Alfhild: Mother of Magnus the Good and concubine of Olaf II of Norway.

Althing, Al-thing: Supreme parliament of Iceland, founded in 930. It is one of the longest-running
parliamentary bodies in the world.

Ango-Saxons: Cultural/racial group that inhabited England in the Early Middle Ages.

Ariovistus (b. 1st century BC): Suebian king and one of Caesar's primary rivals during the Gallic
Wars. Most of our knowledge of Ariovistus comes from *Commentarii de Bello Gallico*, Julius
Caesar's firsthand account of the Gallic Wars.

Arminius (18/17 BC–21 AD): Cherusci prince who was adopted by the Romans and served under
Publius Quinctilius Varus. He secretly plotted with his Germanic brethren against the Romans
and defeated three Roman legions in the Battle of the Teutoburg Forest, one of Rome's
deadliest defeats.

Arnkel Godi: Rival chieftain of Snorri Godi in the *Eyrbyggja saga*; killed by Snorri while working
on his own farm.

arval: Norse funerary wake in which bread and ale was served.

Asgard: Fortified region inhabited by the Norse gods.

ásmegin: The soul of an áss, or god.

atheling: An Anglo-Saxon prince or nobleman.

Atlamál, The Greenlandic Lay of Atli: Greenlandic version of the *Atlakvida*, or *The Lay of Atli*,
which tells largely the same story but in a different style.

Attila the Hun (c. 406–453): Ruler of the Huns and one of the most feared opponents of the
Roman Empire. Worth noting for his inspiring the Hun king Atli in *The Lay of Alti*.

Aud: Wife of Gisli.

Audbjorg, Audbjorga: Mother of Thorstein in the *Saga of Gisli the Outlaw*.

Augustus, Octavian (63 BC–AD 14): First emperor of the Roman Empire.

Baldr, Balder: Son of Odin and Frigg. He is explored thoroughly in the *Voluspa, Lokasenna*, and *Balder's Dreams*.

***Baldrs draumar / Vegtamskvida*, Balder's Dreams, Baldr's Dreams:** Short Eddic poem in which Balder's nightmares prompt Odin to ride to Hel and resurrects a völva (or seeress), who tells of Balder's fate.

***Beowulf*:** Most well-known Old English poem in which the hero Beowulf of the Geats aids Hrothgar, king of the Danes, in slaying the monster Grendel and his mother.

berserker: Warriors said to have fought in a trance-like state, often wearing the pelts of animals, usually bears or wolves.

Bifrost, Bifröst, Bilrost: Rainbow bridge between Midgard and Asgard.

***Bjarkamál*:** Old Norse poem in which two of Hrolf Kraki's twelve berserkers, Bodvar Bjarki (from whom the poem derives its name) and Hjalte, describe Kraki's downfall in Zealand. Saxo Grammaticus' Latin translation is our only reliable source on this poem now, as the Icelandic original has not survived outside of a few lines. We may never know how closely Saxo's version follows the original poem.

***Björn, Champion of the Hitardal People, The Saga of*; *Bjarnar saga Hítdœlakappa*:** One of the sagas of the Icelanders, in which Bjorn (a relative of Egil) and Tord feud.

Bodvar Bjarki, Bödvar Bjarki: Hero of *The Saga of King Hrolf Kraki*. He is a shapeshifter capable of transforming into a bear.

Bolli and Kjartan: Male characters in the love triangle of the *Laxdoela saga*, who feud over Gudrun's attention and love.

***Bósi and Herraud, Saga of*:** Legendary saga recounting the adventures of Herraud and his best friend Bósi. Herraud and his father King Hring of Östergötland go into a civil war against each other.

Bugge, Sophus (1833–1907): Mid-nineteenth-century Norwegian philologist and linguist at Christiania University, now the University of Oslo. He is most well-known for his critical work on the Eddas, in which he posits that the Eddic poems are largely founded on Christian and Latin traditions imported to Scandinavia through England.

byrsæll: To always have the wind in one's favor.

Caedmon, Cædmon (c. 657–684): First English poet known by name, an inspirational Christian poet, and a zealous monk who became a saint.

Cassius Dio, Lucius; Dio Cassius (c. AD 165–c. 235): Roman senator and historian who published approximately eighty volumes on Roman history.

Chatti: Germanic tribe primarily centered around modern-day Hesse and Lower Saxony. They were one of Germania's biggest tribes, rivaled only by the Cherusci.

Clovis I (c. 466–511): First king of the Franks to unite all the Frankish tribes and founder of the Merovingian dynasty. His fours sons were, in birth order, Theuderic I, Chlodomer, Childebert I, and Clothar I.

Codex Regius, *Konungsbók*: Icelandic codex in which many of the poems of the Poetic Edda are preserved.

compurgation: Someone who vouches for the character of an accused person. The practice of compurgation is largely obsolete today, but was commonplace in medieval England, Scandinavia, and France. It even found place in pre-Islamic Arabia, and into early Islamic jurisprudence.

Dagr, Day: Personification of day.

distaff: Female branch of the family.

Domaldi, Domalde: Yngling king and third son of Visbur, first son borne from his second wife. Cursed with bad luck by his stepmother.

drápa: Long form of skaldic poetry with a series stanzas separating by a refrain.

draugr: Undead creature from Norse folklore, often guarding treasures or residing in a burial mound.

***Droplaugarsona saga*:** Tells the story of Droplaug's two sons Grim and Helgi as adults. Grim avenges his brother, who was killed. There is some overlap with the *Fljótsdaela saga*, which also features these two brothers, though some details differ.

earl, jarl: A man of noble birth or rank, a chieftain ruling over a territory. Earl tends to be used more in the British Isles, jarl more in Scandinavia.

***Edda, Poetic*:** Collection of anonymous Norse poems, mostly based on the Codex Regius, which forms the backbone of modern knowledge of Norse mythology and legend. It is distinct from the *Prose Edda*, which is primarily authored by Snorri Sturluson.

***Edda, Prose; Younger Edda*; *Snorra's Edda* (Icelandic: *Snorra Edda*):** Old Norse textbook thought to be primarily penned and compiled by Snorri Sturluson, which forms the backbone of modern knowledge for Norse mythology and North Germanic folklore. It is divided into four sections: the prologue, *Gylfaginning*, *Skáldskaparmál*, and *Háttatal*.

Egil Skallagrímsson: Main character of *Egil's saga*. He was a warrior poet who was a real person, but whose legend has likely been embellished by the Norse legends.

***Egil's saga*:** Icelandic family saga chronicling one hundred fifty years of the clan of Egil Skallagrímsson.

einherjar: Those who have died in battle and are brought to Valhalla.

Eric Bloodaxe, Eric Brother-Slayer, Eric Haraldsson (fl. c. 930–954): Son of Harald Fairhair who later became king of Norway and Northumbria. Married Gunnhild. The sagas portray him as quite savage and barbarous.

Erik's Law: Set of Danish medieval provincial laws, passed as a supplement to another set of laws, Valdemar's Law.

Ermanaric, Jörmunrekkr: King of the Goths and husband of Svanhild. He had Svanhild trampled to death by horses after accusing her of infidelity.

Eyjafjörður, "Island Fjord": One of the biggest fjords in Iceland, situated in the central northern coast.

***Eyrbyggja saga, The Saga of the People of Eyri*:** Icelanders' saga primarily centered on the feud between Snorri Godi and Arnkel Godi, two chieftains.

feasceaft: He who has no part or lot with others, an outlaw with no kin.

Fenrir, Vánargandr: Legendary wolf in Norse mythology and son of Loki, along with Hel (the female deity who watches over the region of the same name) and Jormungand. He is destined to kill Odin during Ragnarök.

fey: To be touched by death.

Fjolnir Yngvifreyson: Legendary Norse king said to be son of Freyr. He is most well-known for drunkenly falling into a vat of mead and drowning.

fjord, fiord: Long, narrow inlet with steep cliffs, often the result of previous glaciation. Fjords are found all over the world, but are particularly common in Scandinavia.

***Fljótsdæla saga*:** Icelandic saga similar to the *Droplaugarsona saga* in that it tells of Grim and Helgi, the sons of Droplaug.

Fredegunde: Wife of Chilperic I.

freondspéd: To have a wealth of friends.

Freyr, Frey: Norse god of fertility, crops, and prosperity.

Frisia: Cultural region encompassing northern Netherlands and northwestern Germany inhabited by Frisians, a West Germanic ethnic group.

frith: A state of peace, or unbreakable bond between friends and kinsmen.

Frodi's mill: Expression for gold originating from the legend of King Frodi's magic gold-grinding mill in the Eddic poem *Grottasöngr*, or *The Mill's Song* or *The Song of Grótti*. In this poem,

King Frodi orders two slave women to exhaust themselves grinding gold at this mill, to the point where the machine breaks. This is a literary warning against excess greed.

Frostathing, Frosta-thing, Frostating: One of the four major things in Norway, and now shares its namesake with the modern Frostating Court of Appeals.

fylgia, fylgja: Guardian spirit bound to a family or clan, capable of taking many forms. They are particularly prominent in *Njál's saga*.

gæfuleysi: Lack of luck.

Geats: Germanic tribe who inhabited modern southern Sweden from antiquity to the Middle Ages. Beowulf is a Geat.

Gepids, Gepidæ: East Germanic tribe who lived in modern-day Romania, Hungary, and Serbia.

giptuvænligr: One luck is to be expected of.

Gísla saga, Saga of Gisli the Outlaw: A saga of the Icelanders in which Gisli must avenge his brother-in-law by killing another of his brothers-in-law.

Gjúki, Gibica: Late fourth century king of the Burgundians and father of Gunther.

Glam, Glámr: In *The Saga of Grettir the Strong*, Glam is a shepherd who is killed on a haunted farm. He dies, and his ghost haunts the farmstead. Grettir slays him, but Glam curses him in his dying moments with unluck.

Glum, Glúmr Eyjólfsson: Main character of *Víga-Glúms saga*. Viga is his nickname, which denotes his murderous tendencies.

gnomic poetry: Maxims put into verse in order to aid memory.

Gotland: Sweden's largest island.

Grágás, Gray Goose Laws: Laws from the Icelandic Commonwealth period (930–1262).

Gregory of Tours (c. 538–594): Gallo-Roman historian, Bishop of Tours, and saint who had personal relationships with multiple Frankish kings, including Chilperic I.

Grendel: The first of three monstrous antagonists slain by Beowulf.

Grettir the Strong, The Saga of; Grettir's saga; Grettis saga: Icelandic saga detailing the life of the outlaw Grettir. He initially leads a successful life of crime but is cursed with unluck by the ghost of Glam. Grettir is eventually exiled and hunted.

Gudmund the Mighty, Guðmundr, Godmund: Character found in both *The Saga of Grettir the Strong* and *The Saga of Burnt Njál*.

Gudrun, Kreimhild: Major figure in Germanic mythology. Wife of Sigurd, sister of Burgundian king Gunther, and mother of Svanhild. When Sigurd is later murdered, she marries Atli, the Norse legend version of Attila the Hun.

Gudrun Osvifrsdottir, Guðrún Ósvífrsdóttir: Icelandic woman renowned for her beauty and a main protagonist in the *Laxdoela saga*. Not to be confused with the more well-known Gudrun, wife of Sigurd.

Gulathing, Gula-thing, Gulating: One of the first Norwegian things, or law assemblies, and is still a court of law in western Norway.

Gunnar Hámundarson: Tenth-century Icelandic chieftain and close friend of Njál in *Njál's saga*.

Gunnhild, Mother of Kings, Gunnhildr Gormsdóttir (c. 910–c. 980): Wife of Eric Bloodaxe.

Gunther, Gunnar (d. 437): King of Burgundy who married Brunhild after having Sigurd ride through the flames around Brunhild's tower in his stead.

Guntram, Saint Gontrand (c. 532–592): King of Orléans from 561 to 592, son of Chlothar I.

Gylfaginning, The Beguiling of Gylfi, The Deluding of Gylfi: First major part of the *Prose Edda*, not including the prologue.

Hadingus, Hadding, Hading: One of the earliest legendary Danish kings, according to the *Gesta Danorum*.

Haakon Magnusson, Haakon VI of Norway (c. 1340–1380): King of Norway from 1343 until his death in 1380, and King of Sweden from 1362 to 1364, son of Magnus Eriksson, great-grandson of Magnus V.

Haakon Sigurdsson, Earl Haakon, Haakon the Powerful, Haakon the Bad (c. 937–995): *De facto* ruler of Norway from 975 to 995, son of Sigurd Haakonsson, and defeated by Olaf Tryggvason.

Haakon the Good, Haakon Haraldsson, Haakon Adalsteinfostre (c. 920–961): Youngest son of Harald Fairhair, king of Norway from 934 to 961.

Haakon the Old, Haakon IV Haakonsson (c. 1204–1263): King of Norway from 1217 to 1263. His rule put an end to an era of civil wars in Norway and brought about a golden age.

Halfdan the Black: Ninth-century Yngling king in Vestfold, a region in southeast Norway, and the father of Harald Fairhair.

Hallfreðr Óttarsson, Hallfred the Wayward Skald (c. 965–c. 1007): First poet of Haakon Sigurdsson and protagonist of the *Hallfreðar saga*.

hamingja: Happiness, luck, fortune.

hamramr: Capable of shapeshifting or entering a berserker rage.

Harald Fairhair (c. 850–c. 932): First king of Norway, father of Eric Bloodaxe and Haakon the Good.

Harald Hardrada, Harald III of Norway, Harald Sigurdsson (c. 1015–1066): King of Norway from 1046 to 1066. Historians consider his death in 1066 to mark the end of the Viking Age.

Harald Wartooth: Semi-legendary Danish king said to have ruled over Jutland and Zealand in the eighth century.

Heathobards: Germanic tribe inhabiting northern Germany and probable branch of the Langobards; they are primarily known for their role in Beowulf as an antagonist to the Danes.

Heimskringla: Best known of the kings' sagas.

Hel: Afterlife location in Norse mythology, presided over by the female being of the same name.

Helgafell: Several mountains in Iceland are called Helgafell, or "holy mountain," but usually this one refers to the one in the *Eyrbyggja saga* that stands on the Snaefellsnes peninsula first settled by Thoralf Mostrarskegg, who built a shrine to Thor there. Today, a Christian church stands there.

Helgi Hundingsbane: Hero who appears in the *Volsunga saga* and in his own lays of Helgi Hundingsbane. He is the lover of Sigrun, and is killed by Dagr because Sigrun kills everyone around him in order to marry Helgi instead of honoring her royal arranged marriage.

Heliand: Largest known work written in Old Saxon, an epic poem detailing the life of Jesus.

Hellas: Antiquated name for Greece.

heore, unheore: That which is mild, gentle, pleasant, or safe; the opposite, harsh, unpleasant, or ill-boding.

Heorot: Mead hall in *Beowulf*.

Herules, Heruli: An early Germanic people who harried the Romans in the Balkans and Aegean Sea, and were described by Roman authors as one of the tribes of the Scythians. They were later absorbed into the Hunnic confederation under Attila. They also participated in conquest of the Italian peninsula alongside Theodoric the Great of the Ostrogoths and Justinian of the Byzantines. The Herules were largely destroyed by the Lombards in the early sixth century, and its scattered population were later absorbed into the Eastern Roman Empire and ceased to be a distinct group.

Hervor and Heidrek, The Saga of; Hervarar saga ok Heiðreks: Saga about the characters Hervor and Heidrek and several generations of their family, including Hervor's quest to retrieve her father's sword Tyrfing. The saga tells of the wars between the Goths and Huns and of Swedish medieval history. There are three separate manuscripts, known as the H, R, and U versions, from the fourteenth, fifteenth, and seventeenth centuries, respectively, with varying levels of completeness.

Hildr: Valkyrie daughter of Hedin and Hogni, who would revive the dead over and over to keep the battle going perpetually between Hedin and Hogni

Hjorleif and Ingolf: Brothers Hjorleif and Ingolf settled Iceland after hearing rumors of its potential. Ingolf had the resources he needed, but Hjorleif did not, and so set upon a raiding expedition in which he captured slaves from Ireland and brought them to Iceland. Eventually, they killed Hjorleif and his men, escaped with his women and possessions. Ingolf later tracked down these slaves and killed them, avenging his brother.

Hjörungavágr, Battle of (c. 986): Semi-legendary naval battle between the Norwegian Earls of Lade and the Danes, spearheaded by Jomsvikings. This battle was pivotal in securing Haakon Sigurdsson of Norway.

Hogni, Högni, Hagen, Hagena: Burgundian warrior and brother of Gunther.

Hoskuld Dala-Kollsson (c. 910–965): Early Icelandic chieftain and a main character in the *Laxdoela saga*. He is also the father of Olaf the Peacock.

Hraesvelgr, Hræsvelgr: Eagle-shaped jötunn responsible for the wind.

Hrafnista: Term often used to refer to the family members of Ketil Trout, named after Hrafnista, which is modern Ramsa, Norway.

Hreidmar: Sorcerer and father of Regin, Fafnir, and Ottar, who received Andvaranautr after Ottar was accidentally killed by Loki. Hreidmar ignored Loki's warnings about the ring and was later killed by his own sons Regin and Fafnir for it.

Hrethel: Previous king of Geats in Beowulf. Father to Hygelac, Herebeald, Haethcyn, and foster father of Beowulf.

Hrímfaxi, Hrimfaxi: Horse of Nótt.

Hróa þáttr heimska, Tale of Roi the Fool: Icelandic short story in which Roi, an unlucky merchant who routinely lost his wealth at sea, struck a deal with King Sweyn, convincing the king that the king's good luck would overpower Roi's own bad luck. It works, and Roi becomes wealthy.

Hroerek Ringslinger: Legendary seventh-century king of Zealand and grandfather of Prince Amleth.

Hrolf Kraki (d. 500s): Danish king who appears throughout multiple Scandinavian and Anglo-Saxon sagas, including *Beowulf, Song of Grótti*, the *Ynglinga saga*, and more. He also has his own saga named after him, *The Saga of King Hrolf Kraki*.

Hrothgar (d. 500s): Semi-legendary Danish Scylding king notable for his appearance in Beowulf as the king who pleads with Beowulf to kill Grendel.

Hrut Herjolfsson: Icelandic chieftain in *Njál's saga* who visited Norway and had an affair with Gunnhild, who then cursed him with priapism (disorder in which the penis remains erect for long periods) and ruined his marriage to Unn.

hugr, hygi (Anglo-Saxon): Norse word for the soul.

Hygelac (d. c. 516/521): King of the Geats and Beowulf's uncle.

Ingeld: *Beowulf* character, son of Froda and engaged to Hrothgar's daughter.

Ingimund: Nephew of Jokul and Thorstein in the *Vatsdoela saga*.

Jokul and Thorstein: Bickering brothers in the *Vatsdoela saga*, uncles of Ingimund.

Jómsvíkingadrápa: Tribute in drápa form to the Jomsvikings composed in the thirteenth century.

Jomsvikings: Tenth- and eleventh-century legendary Viking mercenaries who partook in many pivotal battles in Scandinavian history. They are said to have been devoted pagans, but would fight for anyone, including Christians, if paid enough.

Jörmungandr, Serpent of Midgard, World Serpent: Massive serpent that dwells in Midgard, encircling the entire world and eating its own tail (i.e., an ouroboros). Thor and Jörmungandr will fight to the death during Ragnarök.

Jötunheim: Homeland of the giants in Norse mythology.

jötunn: Race of giants in Norse mythology.

Kar the Old: Undead who was frightening the locals in *The Saga of Grettir the Strong*. Grettir fights and slays him in his burial mound.

Ketil "Haeng" Thorkelsson, Ketil Trout, Ketil Salmon: Norwegian Hersir who settled Iceland around AD 900. Makes appearances in *Egil's saga* and the *Landnámabók*.

Ketil Raum: Norwegian Viking leader in the ninth century. Among his descendants are Ketil "Flatnose" Björnsson, who ruled over the Isle of Man and the Scottish isle of Hebrides in the mid-800s.

Krossavik: Location in eastern Iceland in the Vopnafjord.

kynsæll: Lucky in kinship.

Lade, Hlaðir: Today part of the larger city of Trondheim, Norway. In Viking times, it was the seat of power for the Earls of Lade, a regional power near the Trondheim Fjord.

landmunr, munr: Love as a manifestation of the soul.

***Landnámabók, Landnáma* (shortened), *Book of Settlements*:** Icelandic work divided into a hundred chapters detailing the colonization of Iceland in the ninth and tenth centuries.

***Laxdoela saga, Laxdæla saga, The Saga of the People of Laxárdalr*:** Icelandic saga primarily detailing the love triangle of Bolli, Kjartan, and Gudrun. Bolli and Kjartan grew up as friends but grow to enmity due to their shared love of Gudrun.

***Lay of Atli, Atlakvida, Atlakviða*:** Eddic poem in which Atli, king of the Huns based on Attila the Hun, invites the Burgundian king Gunther to his court. Upon arrival, the Huns attack him and his brother. Gunther refuses to disclose the location of his gold, and is thus thrown into a pit of serpents, where he dies playing the harp.

***Lay of Eric, Eiriksmál*:** Skaldic poem specifically commissioned by Queen Gunnhild in honor of her slain husband Eric Bloodaxe. Only the opening stanzas of the poem have survived.

Liutprand (c. 680–744): Lombard king from 714 until his death in 744, not to be confused with Liutprand of Cremona, a prominent Lombard bishop centuries later

Lombards: Germanic people who ruled most of the Italian peninsula 568 to 764. They are thought to be from southern Scandinavia and possibly Suebian and migrated south.

Magnus I the Good, Magnus Olafsson (c. 1024–1047): Illegitimate son of King Olaf II Haroldsson. Was king of Norway from 1035 and of Denmark from 1042, until his death in 1047.

Magnus II Haraldsson (c. 1048–1069): Son of Harald Hardrada. King of Norway from 1066 to 1069, jointly with his brother Olaf Kyrre from 1067.

Magnus III Olafsson, Magnus Barefoot (1073–1103): King of Norway from 1093 until his death in 1103. His reign was marked by aggressive military campaigns and conquest, particularly in the Norse-dominated parts of the British Isles, where he extended his rule to the Kingdom of the Isles and Dublin. He is the only son of King Olaf Kyrre.

mannheill: Man-luck, the luck to have friendship and affection of others.

Marcomanni: One of the tribal subgroups of the Suebi, primarily situated in the north of the Danube.

megin: Power or might.

Merovingians: Ruling family of the Franks in from the fifth century to the mid-eighth century.

Midgard: Norse/Germanic term for Earth, the plane of existence inhabited by humans.

Mjolnir: Thor's hammer.

nábjargir: Saving of the corpse, which appears to have consisted chiefly in pressing the nostrils together.

Nibelung: Clan name usually used to denote the Burgundian clan destroyed by Atli.

nithing, niðingr, niding: A person without honor; a scoundrel, coward, or wretch.

Njál Thorgeirsson: Titular character of *Njál's saga*.

Njál's saga, Njáls saga, The Saga of Burnt Njál: Longest and arguably most celebrated of the sagas of the Icelanders. Written in the thirteenth century, it details a series of blood feuds in Iceland between 960 and 1020, and how honor culture spirals these feuds out of control. At the end, the titular character Njál Thorgeirsson is burnt alive in his home with his family (hence the saga also being called *The Saga of Burnt Njál*).

Nótt, Night: Personification of night.

Olaf I of Norway, Tryggvason (c. 960s–1000): King of Norway from 995 to 1000, son of Tryggvi Olafsson, king of Viken (Vingulmork, and Rånrike), and the great-grandson of Harald Fairhair, first King of Norway. He built the first Christian church in Norway and founded Trondheim.

Olaf II of Norway, Haraldsson, the Saint (c. 995–1030): King of Norway from 1015 to 1028, son of Harald Grenske, a petty king in Vestfold, Norway. He was posthumously given the title *Rex Perpetuus Norvegiae* (English: Eternal/Perpetual King of Norway) and canonized at Nidaros (Trondheim) by Bishop Grimketel, one year after his death in the Battle of Stiklestad. Olaf was believed to be a reincarnation of Olaf Geirstad-Alf and worked to unify Norway.

Olaf the Peacock (c. 938–1006): One of the wealthiest landowners and merchants in the early Icelandic Commonwealth, mentioned frequently in Norse sagas, particularly the *Laxdoela saga*. He got the nickname "the Peacock" from his lavish dress.

Olof Skötkonung, Olaf the Swede (c. 980–1022): King of Sweden from 995 to 1022, son of Eric the Victorious and Sigrid the Haughty. His reign is considered to be the transition from the Viking age to the Middle Ages, because he was the first Christian king of the Swedes, who were the last to adopt Christianity in Scandinavia.

orðheill: Luck of fame.

Paulus Diaconus, Paul the Deacon (c. 720s–c. 790s): Benedictine monk who authored historical works on the Lombards.

Penda of Mercia (c. 606–655): Pagan king of Mercia from circa 626 until his death in 655. He appears prominently in the *Anglo-Saxon Chronicle* and Bede's *Ecclesiastical History of the English People*.

Plutarch (c. AD 46–after AD 119): Famous Greek philosopher, notable here for imparting some knowledge of the Suebi.

Procopius (c. 500–565): Greek historian of late antiquity, chief historian of the sixth century.

Ragnarök: Series of Norse mythological events in which include natural disasters, moral chaos, and a great battle ending in the deaths of the Norse gods. The world will be submerged in water, but will then be made anew and fertile and repopulated by humans.

rede: Having wise counsel and successful plans.

Ragnvald Heidumhære (fl. 800s): Chief or king at Vestfold in southeast Norway, most famous for commissioning Thodolf of Hvnir to write the *Ynglingatal*.

Saemund, Sæmund: *Vatsdoela* character, foster brother of Ingimund and uncle of Hrollief.

sakaukar: Additional receivers of weregild payments outside of direct kin.

Saxo Grammaticus (c. 1150–c. 1220): Preeminent Danish historian and author of the *Gesta Danorum*, the first historical work on the history of Denmark.

Scania: Southernmost province of Sweden.

Scylding: Members of Danish royal family of Skjöldr.

séls and unséls: Good and evil.

Sicambri: Germanic people during Roman times who lived just east of the Rhine and on the border of modern-day Netherlands.

Sigrun, Sigrún: A valkyrie in the Poetic Edda and lover of Helgi Hundingsbane, who wants to marry Sigrun instead of her following through on her arranged marriage to King Granmar's son. Helgi invades and kills nearly everyone there, then Dagr has Sigrun slain in vengeance.

Sigurd, Siegfried: Legendary Germanic hero who slayed the dragon Fafnir. He dies as a result of his tricking Brunhild into marrying Gunther despite being in love with Sigurd.

Sigurd Slembe, Sigurd Slembi (c. 1100–1139): Claimed to be the illegitimate son of King Magnus III. During the civil war era in Norway (approximately 1130–1240), Sigurd was one of many who laid claim to the throne. He raised an army to try to take the throne alongside his nephew, but was captured and tortured to death.

skald: Composer of named Old Norse poetry, (i.e., skaldic poetry, as opposed to Eddic poetry, which is anonymous).

Skarphedin Njálsson, Skarphéðinn Njálsson: Eldest son of Njál in *Njál's saga*.

Skinfaxi: Horse of Dagr.

Snorri Godi, Snorri Thorgrimsson (963–1031): Notable Western Icelandic chieftain mentioned in many sagas, notably *The Saga of the People of Eyri, Njál's saga*, and the *Laxdoela saga*.

Snorri Sturluson (1179–1241): One of the most important historians and poets in Scandinavian history, and is thought to have authored and compiled large swaths of the *Poetic Edda*. Much of what we know of Norse mythology comes from him. He was twice elected as speaker at the Althing before being assassinated in 1241.

South Sea Islanders: In Australia, descendants of Pacific Islanders brought to work the sugarcane and cotton fields in Queensland in the late-nineteenth and early-twentieth centuries.

Stiklestad, Battle of (July 29th, 1030): One of the most famous battles in the history of Norway, in which the peasant army won and King Olaf II of Norway was killed.

Suebi, Suevi: Primarily a Roman classification of a large conglomeration of Germanic peoples originally from the Elbe River.

Svarfdoela: One of the sagas of the Icelanders, in which disputes in a valley in central-north Iceland are described.

Tacitus, Publius Cornelius Tacitus (c. AD 56–c. 120): One of the most influential Roman historians, whose works form a huge basis for the modern knowledge of the Germanic tribes against which Rome fought.

Teutoburg Forest, Battle of the: Battle in AD 9 in which a confederation of Germanic tribes under Arminius of the Cherusci defeated three Roman legions under Publius Quinctilius Varus and ended Roman expansion into Germania. Historians consider it one of the most important battles in the history of Europe, as it and the subsequent Roman retaliations solidified the border between Rome and Germanic provinces.

Teuton: An ancient northern Germanic tribe, but is largely today used as a catch-all term for Germanic peoples generally.

Theodoric the Great (454–526): King of the Ostrogoths from 475 to 526.

Thiazi: Jötunn most famous for kidnapping the goddess Ydun.

thing, law-thing: Early legislative assembly in Germanic society, ruled over by a lawspeaker and composed of free people of the community.

Thorgils Leifsson (b. c. 1000): First son of Leif Erikson, the legendary Norse explorer who stepped first onto the North American continent.

Thorgils Skardi, Skarthi: Tenth-century Viking leader and poet who founded Scarborough, England in 966. He is described in *Kormak's saga*, which is primarily about his brother Kormak.

Thorlaug: Daughter of Glum.

Thorstein Egilsson: Character of *Egil's saga*, youngest son of Egil Skallagrímsson.

Thorstein, Viking's Son, The Saga of; Þorsteins saga Víkingssonar: Seventh-century saga about the adventures of a man named Viking and his sons, the oldest being Thorstein.

Trondheim: City in a deep inlet in the Trondheim Fjord in central Norway, founded in 997 by Olaf Tryggvason and served as a major port city, pilgrimage site, and trade center for hundreds of years.

tuddorspéd: Luck in offspring and power of cohesion.

Tyrfing: Magic sword in *The Saga of Hervor and Heidrek.*

úgiptubragð: The mark of unluck.

Unn: Wife of Hrut.

Uppland: Province on the east coast of Sweden, north of Stockholm.

uppnámamenn: Kinsmen who are receivers of fees in Gulathing law.

Utgard, Útgarðar: Keep and region in Jötunheim, home of Utgard-Loki.

Vafthrudnismál: The third poem in the *Poetic Edda,* primarily describing the battle of wits between Odin and the jötunn Vafthundir.

Valhalla, Valhal, Valhol: Odin's hall in Asgard in which fallen warriors go after death.

valkyrie: Female spirits who guide the souls of fallen warriors to Valhalla.

Vanir: Pantheon of Norse gods associated primarily with fertility, prescience, and wisdom, most notably including Freyr, Freyja, Njord, Kvasir, Nerthus, etc.

Vanlandi: Father of Visbur and legendary Swedish king at Uppsala in the House of Ynglings. Vanlandi married a Finnish woman, but abandoned her later. In retaliation, she cursed him with sleep paralysis to the point where he died.

Vatsdoela saga, Vatnsdæla saga, Vatnsdale saga: Saga of the Icelanders principally about Ingimund Thorsteinsson, a warrior who fought for Harald Fairhair and eventually settled in northern Iceland. The saga follows his family for several generations until the arrival of Christianity.

Vends: Balto-Finnic people residing in modern-day north-central Latvia.

Volsunga saga, Völsunga saga, Saga of the Volsungs: One of the most famous Norse sagas, details the story of the Völsung clan. Notable stories contained within it include Sigurd slaying Fafnir to obtain Andvaranaut, Sigurd saving Signe from Siggeir, Gudrun's marriage to Atli, etc.

völva: A woman believed to be able to tell the future and perform sorceries, a seeress.

weregild, wergild, wergeld, man price: Legal monetary amount assigned to a person's life to be paid if injury or death befalls that person at the hands of another

Worms: Capital of the First Kingdom of Burgundy.

Ydun: Norse goddess associated with wealth, eternal youth, and apples; wife of Bragi.

Ynglinga saga: King's saga written by Snorri Sturluson, first part of the *Heimskringla.*

Ynglingatal, Enumeration of the Ynglingar: Skaldic poem about Yngling dynasty of kings written by Thorolf of Hvnir, a poet for Harald Fairhair. Snorri Sturluson cites in the in the first part of the *Ynglinga saga.*

Ynglings, Scylfings (in *Beowulf*): Dynasty of kings in Sweden and Norway primarily mentioned in the *Ynglingatal,* mentioned as the Scylfings in *Beowulf.*

Zealand: Largest island in Denmark, located in the eastern part of the country. Copenhagen is located here.

INDEX